DAY BY DAY
BABY CARE

DAY BY DAY
BABY CARE

Dr. Miriam Stoppard

VILLARD BOOKS NEW YORK

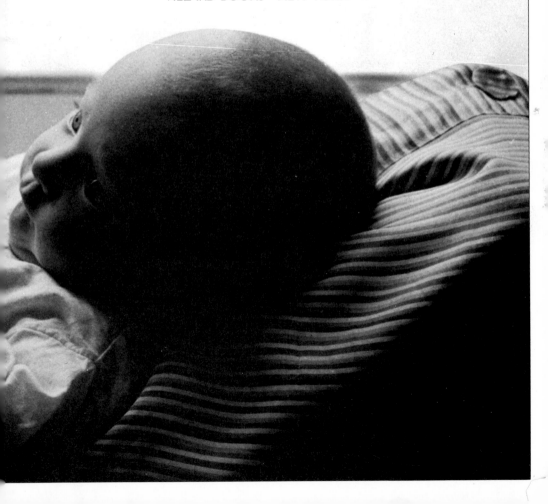

For Oliver, Barnaby, William, Edmund
Oona and Slater

All rights reserved under International and Pan-American
Copyright Conventions. Published in the United States by
Ballantine Books, a division of Random House, Inc., New York,
and simultaneously in Canada by Random House of Canada
Limited, Toronto. Originally published in the United Kingdom
under the title *The Baby Care Book*.

Library of Congress Catalog Card Number: 84-90824

ISBN 0-345-30101-3

Originally published in hardcover by Villard Books, New York

Manufactured in the United States of America

First Ballantine Books Trade Edition: February 1985

10 9 8

Preface

You may wonder, with so many baby books around, how there could be room for another. But there is a real need for a book which takes account of the changing shape of the family and which gives parents proper consideration.

In addition to covering the development, health and happiness of a baby and all the techniques necessary for his or her care, this book pays quite a lot of attention to the parents' points of view. It's a modern book with a modern outlook. One of its basic concepts is that you don't necessarily have to fit around your baby; your baby can and will fit in with family routines and not be one iota less healthy or less happy. This book takes into account the fact that sterotyping of maternal and paternal roles is being rejected by many couples and that greater flexibility brings excellent solutions. Active involvement of fathers is taken for granted so that parenting is as it should be, a responsibility shared by mother and father.

Having read so many baby books which emphasize looking after the baby's needs, I still feel guilty if I occasionally put my own wishes on par with those of my children. I hope no parent reading this book will suffer any such shame. I believe that caring for babies should be fun. Happy parents mean happy babies. If, by taking a few short cuts and putting yourself a little higher on your list of priorities, life with your baby is more fun and you are happier, go ahead and do so.

To achieve a fair balance between the sexes I've alternated "she" and "he" in successive chapters. Whichever pronoun has been used, the text refers to both sexes. Where a topic applies specifically to a boy or girl I have used the appropriate gender.

Contents

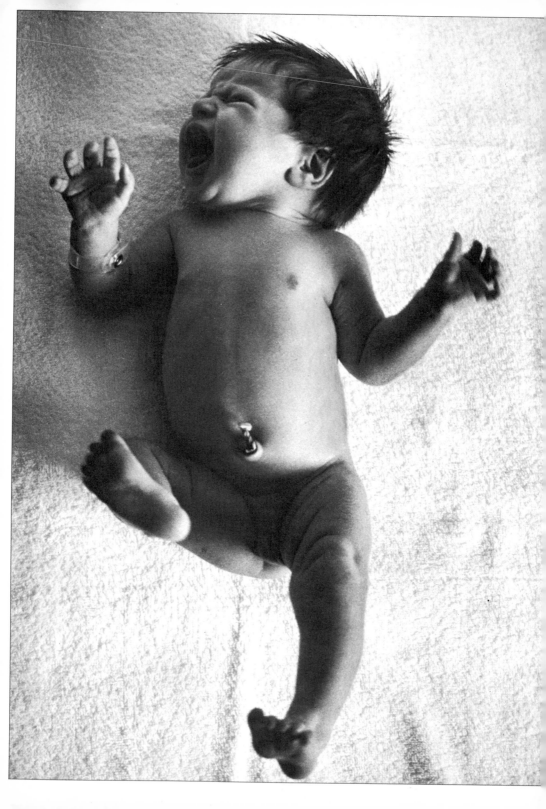

1 Immediate impressions

Your baby may look quite different from what you imagined. He is probably smaller and redder than you thought he would be; his head may seem far too large for his body. If you watch him closely you may notice that he does several unexpected things: he may shiver quite suddenly for no reason; he may make such sniffling noises that you wonder if his nose and air passages are blocked; he may even stop breathing all together for several seconds. None of these is abnormal.

If you concentrate on your baby and observe him carefully over the first two or three days of life you will become familiar with normal infant behaviour and will get accustomed to your baby's idiosyncracies. It is essential that you interpret your baby's signals to you, and the only way to do this is to stay with him as much as possible, to watch him, nurse him, play with and look after him. Your baby will revel in all the attention, so don't worry – you can't give him too much.

PHYSICAL IMPRESSIONS

General proportions

Your baby will almost certainly seem to be oddly proportioned. His abdomen will seem rounded, even distended, and his head will be large in comparison with the rest of his body. In contrast to this his arms and legs may appear stick-like, but these proportions are normal.

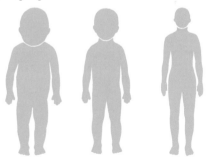

At birth, the head is a quarter the size of the trunk. At two years it's a fifth and by the eighteenth year it's only an eighth.

The head

Shape
Your baby's head is unlikely to be perfectly rounded after birth, but no matter how bumpy or swollen it looks your baby's brain will not have been damaged. This is because the bones in the head are specially designed to move over each other during birth so that the head, which is the largest part of the baby's body, can pass down the birth canal easily.

Sometimes the baby has a large, firm swelling on one or both sides of the head which doesn't go down immediately. Called a cephalhaematoma, this is again caused by the natural pressure exerted by the uterine muscle during labor. It's really a large bruise of the scalp and it's outside the skull. The swelling puts no pressure on the baby's brain and subsides, without treatment, within a few weeks.

Bruising is quite common after a forceps delivery, as are shallow indentations on either side of the head. They are both rectified naturally within a couple of days.

9

The fontanelle

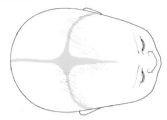

The fontanelle – the soft spot on top of your baby's head – is the space where the skull bones have not yet joined. The bones don't fuse until your baby is about two years old. The baby's scalp that covers this space is really quite tough, but you should make sure that the fontanelle is never pressed very hard. (The purpose of the fontanelle is to allow the soft skull bones to "mould" [this means to ride over one another] without damage to the baby's brain as it passes through the birth canal.) You need take no special care of the skin and hair which cover the fontanelle; however, you should contact your doctor immediately if you ever notice that the skin over the area is taut, if there's a bulge, or if the area's abnormally shrunken.

The eyes

Condition
Most babies are born with rather puffy eyes as a result of the natural pressure during birth. The swelling usually goes down within a couple of days.

Never accept a discharge from your baby's eyes as normal. In all probability it's a common, mild infection called "sticky eye," but it should always be treated by a doctor, not by yourself. Never use eye drops or ointments.

Color
All babies are born with blue eyes. This is because melanin, the body's natural pigment, is not present in the skin or eyes at birth. If a baby is going to have brown eyes or a dark brown skin, the color will gradually develop over a period of weeks or months. The eyes and skin may not reach their permanent color until the baby is six months old.

Eye function
You may find it difficult to get your baby to open his eyes at first, but never try to force them open. One of the easiest ways to get a baby to open his eyes is to hold him above your head. His eyes will usually open then.

You might notice that when your baby does open his eyes, he appears to squint. Don't worry about this. He hasn't yet learned to use his eyes or to focus on things. The squinting will gradually disappear as he learns to focus – at the age of one or two months. Consult your doctor if your baby is still squinting after three months.

Tears
Babies don't shed tears, as you'll discover when your baby cries. It usually takes about four or five months for a baby to produce them.

The mouth

Lip blisters
Such blisters, usually in the center of the mouth, are caused by the baby's sucking. They cause no harm and will go away of their own accord.

Tongue-tie
Your baby's tongue may appear to be almost fully attached to the bottom of his mouth. This should not be a cause of worry. The baby's tongue grows mainly from the tip throughout the first year.

The skin

The vernix
The skin of your newborn will probably be covered with a white, greasy substance called vernix. Some babies have vernix all over their face and body, while others have it only on isolated parts, like their face and hands. Hospital practices in relation to the vernix vary. Some hospitals leave it on because it provides a natural barrier against minor skin infections, others meticulously clean it off after birth. This is generally considered unnecessary nowadays, not only because of the vernix's protective qualities, but also because it is naturally absorbed into the skin within

two or three days. Large accumulations of the vernix in the skin folds can cause irritation, however, and may be wiped away.

Texture
Your baby may be born with a dry peeling skin (most noticeable on the palms of the hands and soles of the feet). This is not eczema, nor does it mean that your baby will be permanently dry-skinned. In most cases the dryness disappears within a few days.

Color
The top half of your baby's body may be pale while the lower half is red. This is due to the baby's immature circulation which causes the blood to pool in the lower limbs. The problem is rectified by changing your baby's position.

You may notice that your baby's hands or feet have turned rather blue, especially if he's been lying down. Once again, this is due to the baby's relatively inefficient circulation. The color will change if you pick up or move the baby. Try to keep the baby's room at an equable temperature, around 70°C (21°F). Blue marks (also called Mongolian blue spots), which look like bruises, often occur on the lower backs of babies with dark skin tones (nearly all African and Asian babies have them). They are completely harmless and fade away naturally.

Birthmarks
Quite commonly there are small red marks on a baby's skin, particularly on the eyelids and on the forehead. You may find them, if you lift up the hair at the back of the neck too, just under the hairline. These are due to the enlargement of tiny blood vessels near the surface of the skin and are traditionally called stork beak marks. Both of my sons had them and they disappeared, as they do in most children, by the time they were six months old. Some babies, however, do not lose them for 18 months.

Another common birthmark is the so-called strawberry mark. This appears after a few days but gradually fades over the years (it should disappear by the time he's three years old). If you're at all worried by your baby's birthmark ask your doctor for advice and reassurance.

Spots
It is not unusual for a baby to have small white spots over the bridge of the nose, called milia. These spots are not abnormal so *never*, ever squeeze them. They are caused by the temporary blockage of the sweat glands and sebaceous glands which secrete sebum to lubricate the skin. They nearly always disappear after a few days.

Weals and rashes
Many babies develop a skin condition which looks rather like nettle rash, called *urticaria neonatorum*. The baby's skin becomes red and blotchy, with small white spots which appear and disappear quite rapidly. The whole rash lasts only a few days and will disappear without treatment. If in doubt, consult your doctor.

Body hair
Babies are born with varying amounts of hair, called lanugo hair, on their bodies. Some babies have only a soft down on their heads, others are covered in quite coarse hair over their shoulders and down their spines. Both are quite normal, and the hair usually rubs off quite soon after birth.

The umbilicus

The umbilical cord is painlessly cut about three or four inches from the baby's stomach. Pressure is exerted on it by an elastic band or clasp and the stump shrivels and drops off within ten days or so. Some babies develop umbilical hernias (small swellings near the navel), but these nearly always clear up on their own within a year. If your baby has one that expands or does not go away, consult your doctor.

11

The breasts

Both male and female babies can have swollen breasts at birth; they may even have a slight discharge of milk. This is caused by the presence of maternal hormones in the baby's body and it resolves itself naturally. *Never* try to squeeze any of the milk out. The swelling will subside within a few days.

The genitals

The genitals of both boys and girls are proportionately larger at birth than later on in life. The scrotum or vulva may even look rather red and inflamed. This is a natural occurrence caused by the mother's hormones. These hormones may also cause a clear, white discharge in female babies, and even a small amount of vaginal bleeding. Once again, this is perfectly normal and will clear up naturally after a few days. If you're at all worried, however, contact your doctor for reassurance.

Sounds

Breathing
An infant's lungs are small and his breathing may seem thin or weak compared to yours. You may not even be able to tell that he is breathing. Don't be frightened – his breath will get stronger each day.

All newborn babies make strange sounds when they breathe. At times the breathing will be fast and noisy, at other times it may be irregular. Your baby may sniffle so loudly with each breath that you think he has a cold. This is not necessarily so. The bridge of a baby's nose is quite low, and the sniffling noise is caused by the air trying to get through the very narrow nasal passages. As your baby grows, the bridge of the nose will get higher, and the sniffling sound will gradually stop over a period of weeks. If, however, the sniffling interferes with your baby's freedom to suck, then consult your doctor. He may need nose drops before feeding (see p. 93). Nose drops should be used only under medical supervision.

You should, however, be concerned about your baby's breathing if it ever becomes labored – especially if his chest is sharply drawn in with each breath and the breathing rate rises to 60 or more breaths per minute. Any of these signs warrants immediate medical attention (see p. 307).
Sneezing
Babies are very sensitive to bright lights and sometimes sneeze whenever they open their eyes for the first few days. This happens because light stimulates the nerves to the nose as well as to the eyes. (You can try this out for yourself the next time you feel a sneeze coming on: look into a bright light and you'll find that you're able to make yourself sneeze.) Even if your baby is sneezing quite a lot, he doesn't necessarily have a cold. The lining of a baby's nose is sensitive, and sneezing is essential to clear out the nasal passages and prevent dust from getting down into the lungs.
Hiccups
Newborn babies hiccup quite often. This is normal, too, and shouldn't bother you. Hiccups are caused by sudden, irregular contractions of the diaphragm and are a sign that the muscles involved in respiration – those between the ribs, the diaphragm and the abdomen – are getting stronger and trying to work in harmony.

Stools

A baby's first stools are usually dark green and sticky and have very little smell. This is because they are mainly meconium, which is digested mucus from the mucus glands in the bowels. It is the only kind of stool your baby will pass for the first two or three days. Gradually over the next three or four days the stools will change color. The appearance and consistency will depend on whether your baby is having breast or formula milk (see p. 131 and p. 132).

Reflexes and movements

All newborn babies have reflexes or instinctive movements which are designed to protect them. These last until your baby learns to make voluntary movements, at about three months. Two of the easiest reflexes to trigger are those that protect the eyes and maintain breathing. Your baby will close his eyes if you touch his eyelids, and he will make struggling movements with his hands if you gently hold his nose between your thumb and forefinger.

The rooting reflex

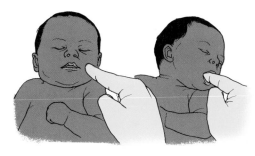

If you gently stroke your baby's cheek, he will turn his head in the direction of your finger and open his mouth. He makes this rooting movement because he is searching for your breast to start feeding (see p. 87).

The sucking reflex

Every baby is born with the reflex to suck. Yours will begin to do so whenever you put something in his mouth or press on his upper palate just behind the gums. Sucking movements are extremely strong and last quite a long time after the stimulation to suck – whether on a finger or a nipple – has been removed. If you want to breast-feed, it's important to put the baby to your breast as soon after delivery as possible. Your baby has to get used to the actual technique of breast-feeding, just as you do, so it helps if he has the powerful desire to suck as a stimulus.

The swallowing reflex

All babies can swallow the instant they are born. This means that they can swallow colostrum or milk immediately after birth.

The "walking" reflex

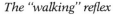

A newborn baby will move his legs in a walking or stepping motion if you hold him upright underneath the arms and let his feet touch a firm surface. This is not the reflex that encourages a baby to stand upright and walk (see p. 184). If you hold your baby upright and let the front of his legs gently touch the edge of a solid object, he'll automatically bring his foot up in a kind of stepping movement.

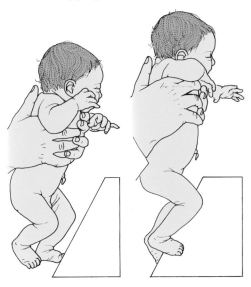

The "crawling" reflex

When placed on his stomach, your new-born baby will assume what appears to be a crawling position. This is because his legs are still curled up toward his body as they were in the womb. When he kicks his legs he may well be able to shuffle in a vague crawling manner and actually move up his cot slightly. This "reflex" will disappear as soon as his legs uncurl and he lies flat.

The grasp reflex

The startle or Moro reflex

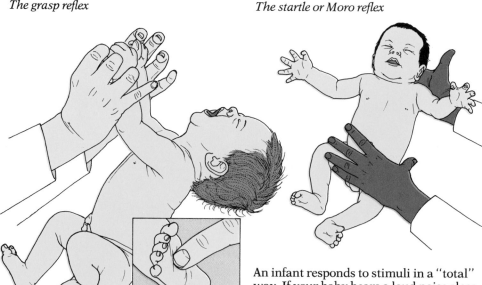

A newborn baby automatically tightens his fingers around anything which is pressed into the palm of his hand. He can grasp very tightly! So strong and powerful is this reflex, that, immediately after his birth, he can support his whole weight by grasping on to your fingers. This reflex is usually lost after about three months. If you touch the soles of your baby's feet, his toes will curl downward as if to grip something.

An infant responds to stimuli in a "total" way. If your baby hears a loud noise close to him, or if he's roughly handled, he will throw up his arms and legs with fingers outstretched in an attempt to catch on to something. He'll let his limbs fall back slowly towards his body and then bend his knees and clench his fists. When he sees you, he will greet you with his whole body. Only when he's eight or nine months old will he simply smile and reach out his arms to you in a more restricted and mature form of greeting.

BONDING

A newborn baby sleeps most of the day, so you should spend all of his waking time with him. Research has shown that physical contact with you – the sound of your voice and the smell of your body – are very important during the first few days of life. During this time your baby forms a bond with you which, if encouraged to form, is unique and unbreakable.

Some key research performed with monkeys has given us insights into what happens during these first few days of life, when bonds are made with parents. The development of two groups of monkeys was followed, each with a different early-mothering experience. One group of monkeys was allowed free contact with mothers while the other was deprived of all maternal contact. The first group matured and developed quite normally, but the second showed two disturbing changes. Baby monkeys deprived of maternal contact for a short time grew up to be somewhat introspective loners. Deprivation of maternal contact over a long period had a much more serious effect, and the animals grew up to be aggressive, quarrelsome, pugnacious and generally troublesome. Similar problems can arise with human babies.

Eye contact is essential

All research points to the fact that physical contact between mother and baby should start as soon after birth as possible. Furthermore, eye contact should follow immediately after birth wherever possible. Most child development experts used to say that babies could not see properly until their eyes could focus, but babies *can* interpret shapes and outlines. The shape and outline of your face will be recognized by your baby within 36 hours. Research has shown that it is your eyes that your baby searches for and concentrates on – and that he can find them within a few hours after his birth. (When my second son was born and I lifted him on to my stomach and called his name he opened his eyes instantly on hearing my voice and flicked them around the room until they came to rest on my face.)

It has been shown that mothers who make early eye contact with their babies and continue to do so, particularly during feeding times when they face their babies and look deeply into their eyes, are much more likely to be sympathetic, understanding mothers who tend to solve problems calmly and logically, rarely resorting to physical punishment.

Early physical contact

After the first few days you should continue to keep your baby in contact with you as much as possible. By contact I mean *on* your body – for instance, in a sling. It has been known for decades that Indian, Eskimo and African children who are carried on their mother's backs rarely cry. The newborn infant finds the close physical presence of the mother very reassuring. She is soft and warm, her smell is familiar. When the baby lays his head against the mother's body, he hears the familiar heartbeat that he has been hearing for nine months in the womb. The baby feels secure and at home in his surroundings. It is more natural for your baby to be jogged about on his mother's body, reliving memories of the womb, than to lie still in a cot.

The importance of smell

We know that one of the first associations your baby makes with you is through your smell. Your particular smell is one to which your baby is very sensitive and to which he responds biologically. Whenever you go into your sleeping baby's room, he wakes. When other people, even your partner, go in, he stays asleep. This is because the baby's very sensitive sense of smell picks up your chemicals, called pheromones, and he recognizes you as his main source of comfort, pleasure and food.

Sounds and their effects

Newborn babies do not like loud noises. While your baby is getting used to your voice, speak or sing in a soft, gentle, soothing voice. Research work at Oxford has shown that babies respond better to the high-pitched female voice than to the lower-pitched male voice. You should chat, sing or hum to your baby whenever you are with him. It's surprising how even young babies enjoy nursery rhymes and simple songs, particularly if they have a pronounced rhythm and rhyme. Some child development research suggests that children who are sung to early in their lives rapidly develop a feeling for, and a facility with, words. They tend to speak and read slightly earlier than other children.

Mother love

Most mothers are exhilarated, although exhausted, after the delivery of a baby and feel great love for the child. Other mothers, however, find that they feel nothing toward their babies.

We now know that mother love, put very simply, is a response to hormones. There are certain hormones produced in the brain almost immediately after delivery, namely oxytocin or prolactin, which trigger lactation and are also responsible for maternal feelings. Different women have different emotional responses to these hormones and may find that their love for their babies takes more time to develop.

A mother's feelings for her baby can also be affected by two other factors: the actual delivery, and her own expectations for the birth and the baby. It's not uncommon for the baby's arrival to be something of an anti-climax after the strain of labor – even if there are no complications. If labor is very hard and long, and if drugs are used, the mother may be too tired and numbed to feel great love for her child. Also, she may have unrealistic expectations of her response to her newborn baby. She may, for instance, expect to recognize him instantly as her own flesh and blood, and to look physically similar to herself and her partner. This very rarely happens.

Most women find that their love grows gradually during the first two or three days after their baby's birth, until on the third day they feel a palpable love for him. But don't be surprised if it takes two weeks – it's not unusual.

Spend time with your baby

A mother's response to her baby can be affected by the amount of time she spends with him during the first few days of life. In a recent study, one group of mothers was permitted nothing more than routine contact with their babies on a hospital ward; another group of mothers in the same ward was allowed to have contact with their babies for an extra 15 hours during their three days in hospital. Interviews with the two groups, both one month after delivery and a year later, revealed a number of surprising differences. The mothers who had been given extended contact were found to be more reluctant to leave their babies, to be more responsive to their crying, to engage in more eye-to-eye contact during feeding, and to be generally more attentive to their babies. What is remarkable is that these differences are accounted for by just 15 hours of additional contact during the first three days of life!

While it's undoubtedly true that early physical contact helps bonding, it's not the only factor involved in the development of maternal or paternal feelings. In a study of premature babies, where the most extreme form of early separation arises because the baby has to stay in an incubator for an extended period, mothers were divided into two groups. The first group, following standard hospital procedure, was permitted only to look at their babies during the several weeks they remained in the incubator. The second group of mothers was permitted to handle their babies in the incubator from the second day on. The mothers were questioned after one week, again after one month, and again after discharge from the hospital. It was impossible to find any consistent differences between the two groups. This important piece of research suggests that a mother's attachment to her baby may not be seriously affected by a temporary separation immediately after her baby's birth. That's just as well, otherwise there would be little hope for adopted children. Mothering is much more complex than a simple dependency on the hormonal changes that occur at childbirth. A woman's mothering and maternal instincts are influenced in part by her own childhood experiences. The capacity for love develops early in life from the experience of being loved by parents. It is the parents who give the child the capacity to love others later in life. In other words, being loved makes one fit for love; a child deprived of affection may be unable to show it for others. This is why it's so important for your child to have your loving attention, care and concern.

2 Equipment

It's advisable to do your shopping during the last few months before your baby is born, while you're still unfettered and reasonably energetic. You'll be faced with a seemingly endless choice of equipment, all of which will be labelled "essential" by the manufacturers. Don't be swayed by clever advertising. Ask friends and relatives which equipment they found useful and, equally important, which they bought and never used.

Shop around and find out what's available before you make your final decision, and always think of the equipment in relation to your lifestyle. For example, if you feel perfectly relaxed about washing your baby in a sink, don't bother buying a baby bath just because most people do. If you really like the idea of a large baby carriage and can afford one, go ahead and buy it. (Make certain, of course, that your hallway is wide enough to accommodate it, and that you can negotiate steps and other obstructions en route to the market or park.) Those people who think it unlucky to buy too much before giving birth should buy what they need, but arrange to pick it up later.

It isn't essential to buy new equipment. Babies grow so quickly that some items, which are essential at one stage (like baby seats for the car), are useless within a couple of months. Many families are quite happy to lend or sell such items, so keep an eye open for garage sales and for announcements in supermarkets and newspapers. Make certain, when buying secondhand, to check for general wear and tear. Be sure the surfaces are smooth and rust-free and that the merchandise complies with the latest safety regulations.

Delay buying clothes until the last moment. Relatives love buying for a baby and you'll probably find that many items are duplicated.

ESSENTIAL EQUIPMENT

Sleeping
Portable crib or cot
Mattress
1 waterproof cover
3 fitted flannel sheets
Blanket or comforter
Blanket or comforter
  covers
2 "receiving blankets"
Protective crib liner or
  "bumper"

Transport
Sling
Buggy, stroller or port-
  able pram

Bathing and changing
Baby bath
Cotton wool
Baby oil
Baby lotion
Large soft towel
Washcloth or sponge
Baby brush
Blunt-ended scissors
Changing mat
Diaper liners
4 packs disposable
  diapers
or
24 terry diapers
Pins
Plastic pants
2 diaper buckets

Clothing
4 suits
4 undershirts
2 nightdresses
2 sweaters

Feeding
If breast-feeding:
Breast pads
2 bottles with nipples
Sterilizing tablets
1 tin formula
If bottle-feeding:
Bottle-feeding kit
1 month's supply of
  formula
Infant seat
High chair

Changing and bathing

If you like the idea of having a special changing area, but don't want to build one or to convert a piece of furniture like a chest of drawers, then a changing unit is probably right for you. Make sure the one you buy is stable and has storage space.

Unless you decide to do without a baby bath – preferring instead to use the sink or a household basin – you'll have to buy a specially-designed one. The specially-moulded, rigid-plastic tubs usually come with stands. There is also another practical model which straddles the bath so you don't have to carry it across the room from the faucet to the stand.

CHANGING EQUIPMENT

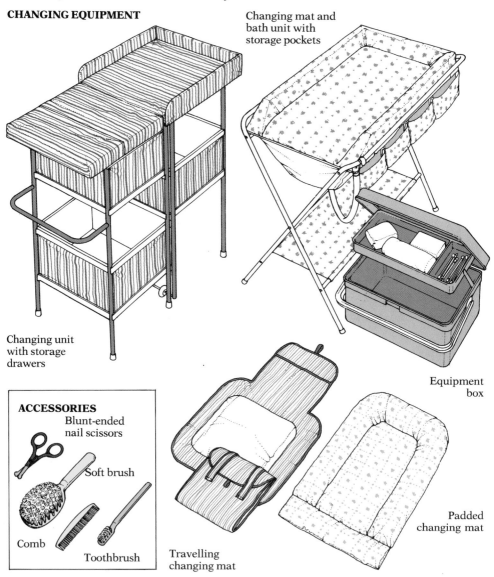

Changing mat and bath unit with storage pockets

Changing unit with storage drawers

Equipment box

ACCESSORIES

Blunt-ended nail scissors

Soft brush

Comb

Toothbrush

Travelling changing mat

Padded changing mat

BATHING AND HYGIENE

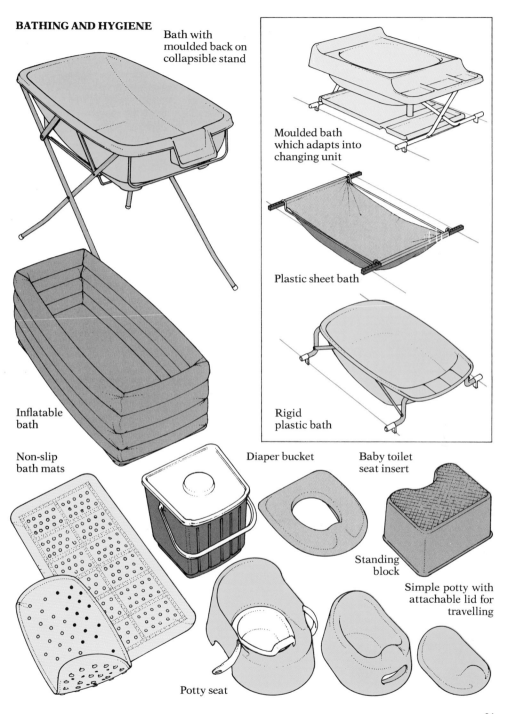

Bath with moulded back on collapsible stand

Moulded bath which adapts into changing unit

Plastic sheet bath

Inflatable bath

Rigid plastic bath

Non-slip bath mats

Diaper bucket

Baby toilet seat insert

Standing block

Simple potty with attachable lid for travelling

Potty seat

21

Feeding

If you're breast-feeding, you'll need the minimum of equipment – a couple of bottles just in case you want to express some milk, or in case you become ill. Bottle-feeding mothers will have to buy a complete feeding kit (see p. 93).

When your baby starts on solids, you'll need equipment which will mash the food into a smooth purée. You'll also need an unbreakable dish to serve it in. Special dishes which keep the food hot are avail-able, although not essential. Bibs, how-ever, are. Probably the most efficient style is the plastic bib with a "catch all" lip which catches all drips or pieces of food and can be easily washed off.

You'll also need some form of high chair. There is a wide variety to choose from, many of which can be converted into swings or tables. Make sure the chair is stable, that it has washable surfaces, a tray with a rim to catch spilled liquids, and safety harness hooks.

NIPPLES AND PACIFIERS

The variety of nipples and pacifiers available can be seen, above. Some are moulded to the shape of the baby's mouth, others are designed to move in and out like a human nipple when sucked.

BOTTLES AND STERILIZING UNITS

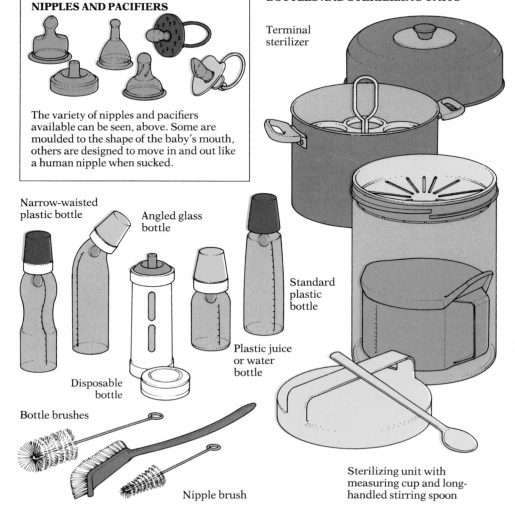

Terminal sterilizer

Narrow-waisted plastic bottle

Angled glass bottle

Standard plastic bottle

Plastic juice or water bottle

Disposable bottle

Bottle brushes

Nipple brush

Sterilizing unit with measuring cup and long-handled stirring spoon

BIBS

Short-sleeved bib

Long-sleeved bib

Fabric bib

Plastic bib with "catch all" lip

WEANING EQUIPMENT

Hand blender

Grater

Electric blender

Strainer

Hand grinder

Steamer

EATING UTENSILS

Plastic bowl with handle and suction pad

Double-handled, easy-grip cup

Cup with drinking spout

Warmer bowl with suction pad

Shaped cup with handles for easy drinking

Easily-held baby utensils

HIGH CHAIRS

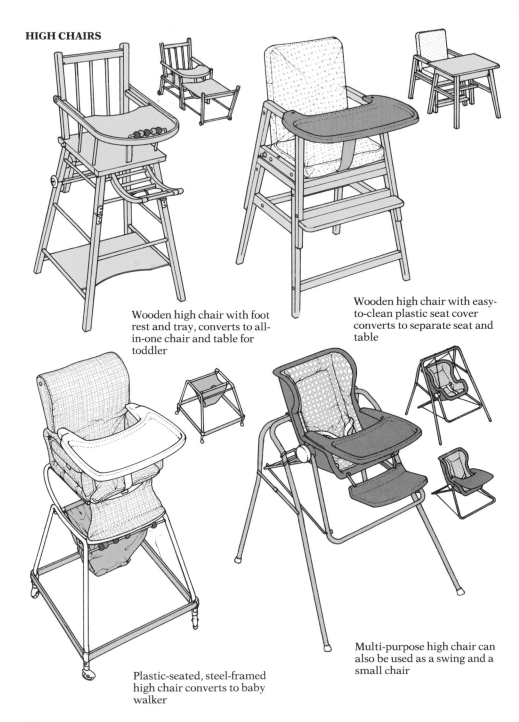

Wooden high chair with foot rest and tray, converts to all-in-one chair and table for toddler

Wooden high chair with easy-to-clean plastic seat cover converts to separate seat and table

Plastic-seated, steel-framed high chair converts to baby walker

Multi-purpose high chair can also be used as a swing and a small chair

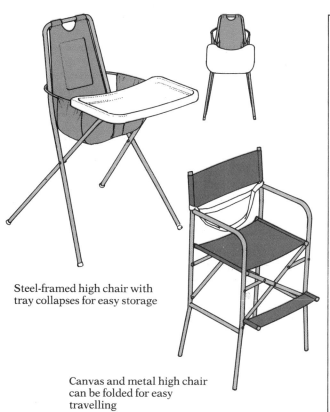

Steel-framed high chair with tray collapses for easy storage

Canvas and metal high chair can be folded for easy travelling

ACCESSORIES

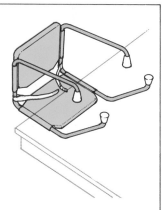

Solid, washable high chair seat

Padded, washable high chair seat

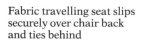

Protective plastic sheet for underneath the high chair

PORTABLE HIGH CHAIRS

Light, moulded plastic seat raises child up to table height

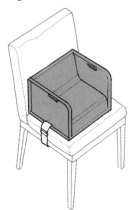

Fabric travelling seat slips securely over chair back and ties behind

Portable baby chair with arms and legs which grip on to the table edge when the child sits in the seat

Sleeping

Bassinet cribs are very attractive to look at, but if your budget is tight I suggest that you don't buy one: your baby could easily outgrow it within 12 or 13 weeks. Instead, use a relatively cheap Moses basket or carry-cot which can also be used as a stroller when he's older. When he outgrows these, he'll need a cot. The mattress you buy should fit snugly, allowing no more than one finger to slide between the mattress and the cot side. Make sure that any side rails are set closely together, so your baby's head can't get stuck, and buy the cot with sides which drop down – it's much easier to get at the baby this way. Fabric-sided travel cots, which collapse and roll up into easily-manageable units, are ideal for going out with the baby, either on holidays or for the evening. Once the baby can clamber out, you'll need to buy a bed – some are actually designed to convert from cots.

CRIBS AND COTS

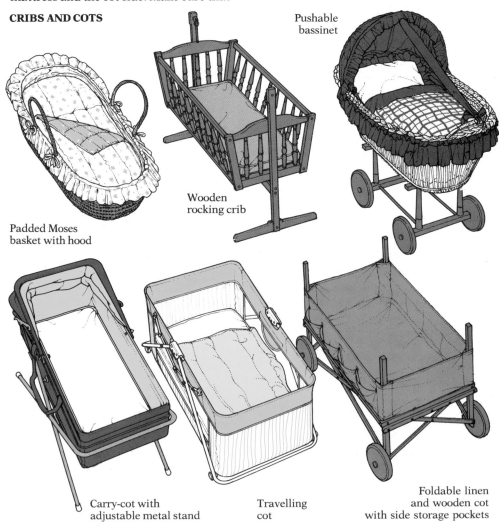

Padded Moses basket with hood

Wooden rocking crib

Pushable bassinet

Carry-cot with adjustable metal stand

Travelling cot

Foldable linen and wooden cot with side storage pockets

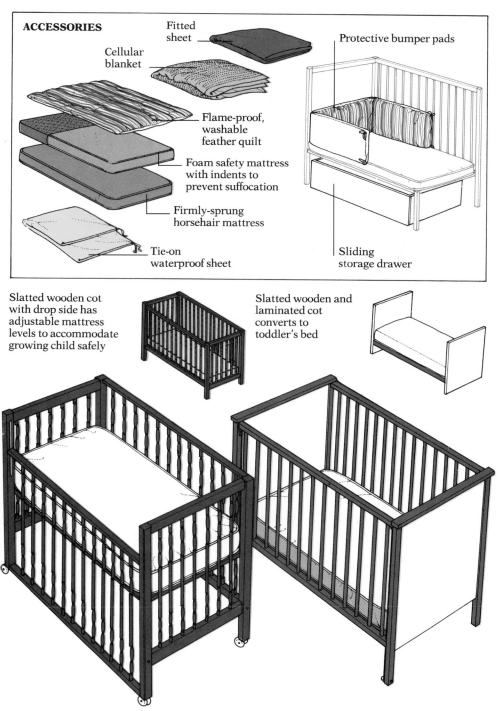

ACCESSORIES

Fitted sheet

Cellular blanket

Protective bumper pads

Flame-proof, washable feather quilt

Foam safety mattress with indents to prevent suffocation

Firmly-sprung horsehair mattress

Tie-on waterproof sheet

Sliding storage drawer

Slatted wooden cot with drop side has adjustable mattress levels to accommodate growing child safely

Slatted wooden and laminated cot converts to toddler's bed

27

Outings and travel

One of the simplest ways of carrying your baby around is in a sling, which you can use until he grows too heavy for it. It should be used with a neck attachment until he can support his own head. You'll also need some form of baby carriage. The one you choose will depend on both your budget and your lifestyle. If you live in a small apartment, three flights up, a fold-able lightweight stroller or a pram with a removable carry-cot will be much more

suitable than a large carriage. Whatever you buy should be easy to push, and have good brakes. It should also have rings for a safety harness, and rings to prevent the handle from collapsing.

Whenever you take your child in a car you must comply with safety regulations and secure him either in a car seat or in his carry-cot with straps. If you ride on a bike you'll have to use a specially-designed seat.

BACKPACKS AND SLINGS

Front-carrying fabric sling with neck support for newborns

Adjustable carrier allows newborn to be completely enclosed and older baby to have his legs out

Mesh sling which can be used for all ages, on the hip or across the breast

Steel-framed fabric backpack with adjustable neck support and sunshade

Lightweight fabric backpack with adjustable inside seat for both babies and toddlers

STROLLERS

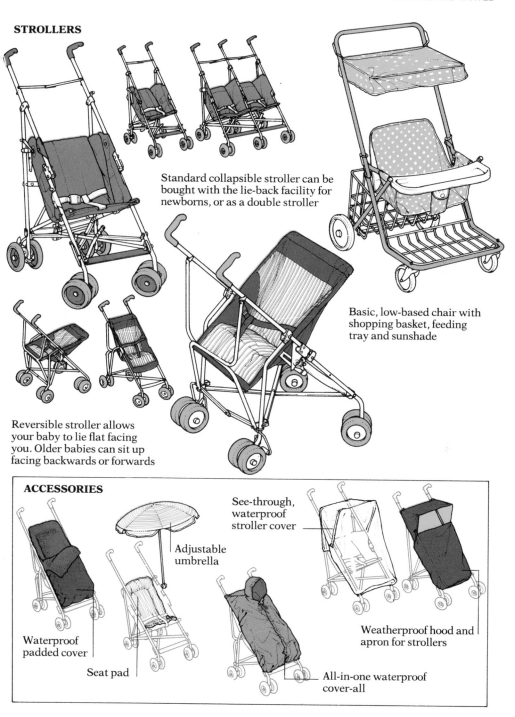

Standard collapsible stroller can be bought with the lie-back facility for newborns, or as a double stroller

Basic, low-based chair with shopping basket, feeding tray and sunshade

Reversible stroller allows your baby to lie flat facing you. Older babies can sit up facing backwards or forwards

ACCESSORIES

Adjustable umbrella

See-through, waterproof stroller cover

Waterproof padded cover

Seat pad

All-in-one waterproof cover-all

Weatherproof hood and apron for strollers

29

PRAMS

Carriage pram with solid body
and collapsible fabric hood

Pram with removable
carry-cot

Carry-cot on pram base
converts for use as a stroller

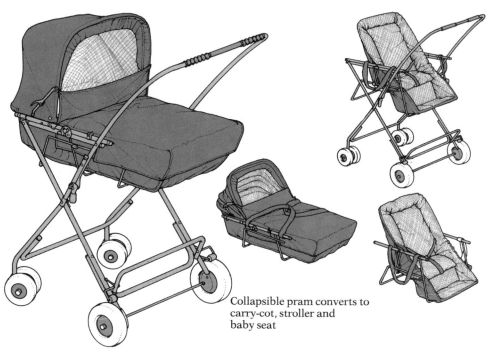

Collapsible pram converts to
carry-cot, stroller and
baby seat

ACCESSORIES

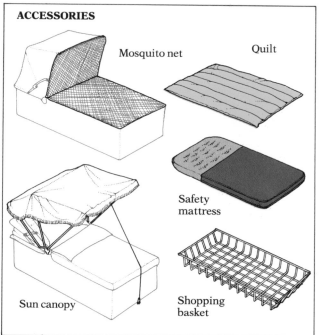

Mosquito net

Quilt

Safety
mattress

Sun canopy

Shopping
basket

HARNESSES

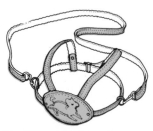

Traditional leather reins

Washable webbing harness for
use as reins or a safety harness

CAR SAFETY

Standard side-fitting pram carry cot

Steel-framed, front-fitting fabric cot

Moulded plastic seat can be adjusted horizontally to hold the baby safely

Padded plastic seat with front shield can also be used in the backward facing position for a baby

Protective shield with side-buckling belt

Moulded plastic seat with fabric interior and foot rest

Brushed nylon seat for use as soon as the baby can sit unsupported

Additional equipment

Baby chairs are more solid than pillows and allow young babies to see what's going on around them. The fabric chairs bounce up and down when the baby kicks his legs; the plastic ones are rigid but the angle of the back can be altered. Your baby will need to be occupied when he's awake, so consider placing him in a baby bouncer hung from a door frame. If possible, let him try it out before you buy it — he may not like the sensation it gives him. Many parents find play pens invaluable. If you buy one, your choice will be between a wooden and a steel and net one.

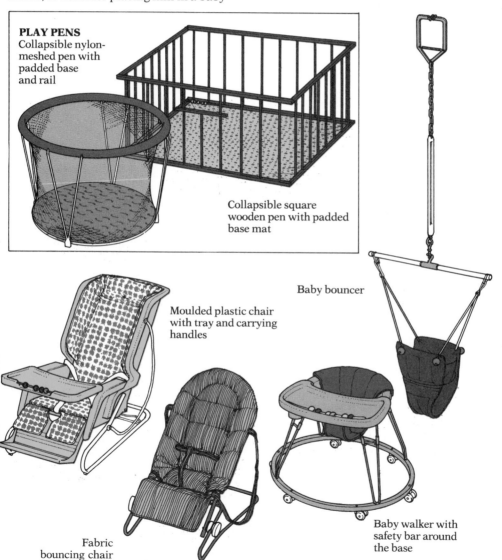

PLAY PENS
Collapsible nylon-meshed pen with padded base and rail

Collapsible square wooden pen with padded base mat

Baby bouncer

Moulded plastic chair with tray and carrying handles

Fabric bouncing chair

Baby walker with safety bar around the base

Arranging a nursery

It is worth planning the lay-out of your nursery well in advance of delivery; afterwards, you'll probably be too busy and too tired to think of anything apart from feeding and changing the baby. Whichever room you choose – even if it's your own – make sure that it's as hygienic as possible, with easy-to-wipe surfaces. All furniture that the baby will come in contact with should have smooth, rounded edges and should be painted with non-toxic, lead-free paint. There should be plenty of storage space, especially above or to the side of the changing area. If you plan to build your own area, you'll want a wide, flat surface on which to place the changing mat. Wide-topped bureaus make ideal changing tables because they have a large surface area and plenty of storage space. You may want to build some shelves overhead. Cover the changing area with a washable covering and a padded changing mat. The floor covering should be warm but hard-wearing; cork tiles and flat weave carpets are ideal.

The baby's room has to be kept at a constant temperature of 75°F (24°C). If you don't want to run the entire house at this level, especially during the day, buy a thermostatically-controlled heater for this purpose.

The lighting should ideally be controlled by a dimmer switch so that you can gently bring up the lights without frightening the baby, and so that you can leave it on low and avoid having to buy a night light.

Always try to decorate your baby's room in light, cheerful colors. The colors of nature – yellow, blue and bright green – have been shown to be good colors for children. Splashes of primary color also help to brighten and enliven the room.

Make sure you put interesting pictures on the walls and hang several mobiles above your baby's cot and the changing area. Buy fabrics and wallcoverings with lively designs so the baby is visually (and therefore mentally) stimulated.

Easily-accessible si[n]
for cleaning ba[t]

Blind with lined
curtains

Easy-to-clean walls

Cupboard with
shelves and hanging
space

Portable bath and
stand

Washable cotton rug
with non-slip backing

Changing area with
storage shelves above
for diapers and below
for heavier boxes and
bottles

Dimmer switch

Baby intercom

Kitchen towel for
spills and wipes

Mobile to occupy
baby while changing

Washable flooring
(vinyl, cork,
flat weave carpet)

Low chair
for feeding

Wall tidy for baby
lotion and cleaning
equipment

Cot with mobile for
stimulation

Table for feeding
equipment

TIPS

Sun-shaped lampshade

Night light

Safety mirror for
your baby's cot

Fluorescent stars
and moon for the ceiling

Music box

Adapting the nursery for a toddler

Your baby's room is going to have to change to accommodate his needs as he becomes more mobile. As he begins to crawl and then walk, you'll have to increase the amount of floor space. Be sure there's as little furniture lying in his way as is possible. Any furniture that's left in his room must be completely stable so that there's no risk of his pulling it down on top of himself. Be extra aware of the safety risks involved with a small, inquisitive toddler and follow all of the recommendations given on p. 294.

As soon as he shows signs of being able to clamber out of his cot, you'll have to buy a bed. Beds with drawers underneath are invaluable if storage space is limited. Position the bed in the corner or flush against the wall so that you leave as large a space as possible in the center of the room. Families who find that space is at a premium should use double-decker beds rather than take up valuable floor space with two single beds. If you're planning to have more children, think about buying a bed that can be converted into a double decker, or buy a trundle bed. You should even consider buying a bed which folds down from the wall.

Your toddler will accumulate more toys, clothes and shoes over the next few years and you'll have to provide plenty of storage for them. Regular shelves and drawers aren't your only alternative. Try painting some sanded wooden boxes and hanging them on strong chains or rope, low enough for your child to reach.

Your toddler will enjoy sitting at his own table, so if you didn't buy the kind of high chair that converts to a table and chair, you'll have to provide one. A blackboard or a special wall area where your toddler knows that he can scribble will also be welcome.

Safety-step for toddler to reach basin

Bulletin board for special pictures

Towel ring for toddler's own towel

Blackboard

Safety rail

Changing area converted to bookshelves and toy storage

Easy-to-reach hooks for coats and scarves

Height chart

Cupboards added for extra storage

Low table and chair for drawing and playing

Table moved nearer bed for night light, books and drinks

itable single bed th comforter and ety pillow

STORAGE TIPS

Plastic crate for shoe storage

Painted baskets for toys and play clothes

Plastic toy box on castors for easy pushing

See-through shoe rack for small toys

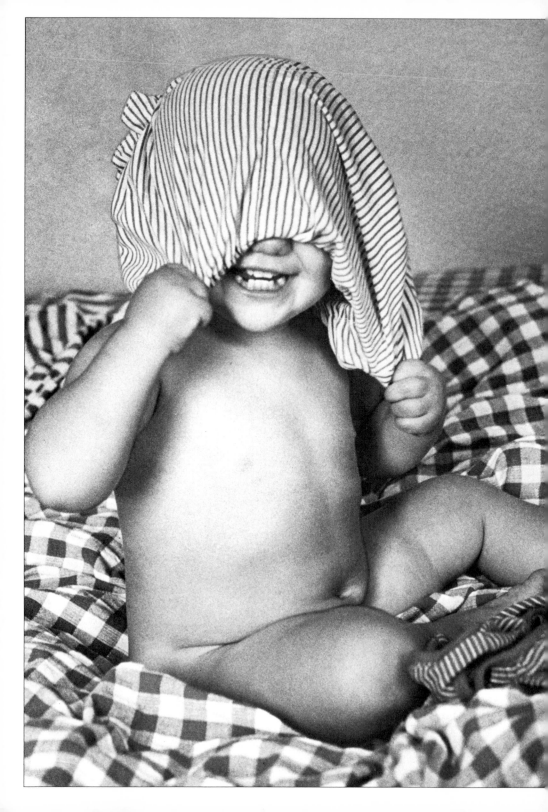

3 Clothing

All parents take great pride in their new baby's appearance and there's a great temptation to rush out and buy lots of clothes for her. So long as you realize that your child is going to grow rapidly during these early years, and that the clothes will have a relatively short life, the styles you choose and the amount you spend are up to you. However, no matter what the age of your child, clothing must be comfortable to wear, easy to put on and, above all, washable.

CHOOSING CLOTHES   0–1

Buying an outfit

Choosing baby clothes is an occupation most parents enjoy. While you might like to buy some dress-up clothes for special occasions, there's absolutely no need to spend a lot of money.

Your newborn baby won't be very active, but that does not mean she's going to stay scrupulously clean. Dribbles, leaks from diapers (despite plastic pants), and other accidents will require fairly frequent changes of clothing. Make sure you have enough clothes to keep up with your baby's needs.

For a summer baby buy:

4 summer-weight one-piece stretch suits

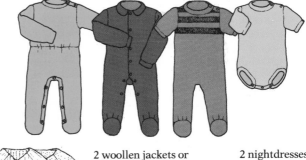

4 wide-necked cotton T-shirts or undershirts

1 summer hat with a brim

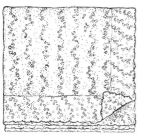

2 woollen jackets or cardigans

2 nightdresses

1 shawl or receiving blanket to wrap your baby in

2 pairs cotton socks

For a winter baby buy:

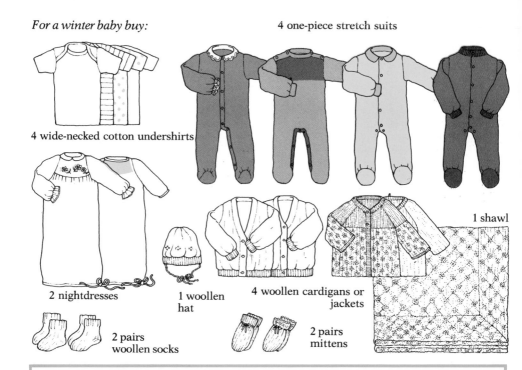

4 one-piece stretch suits

4 wide-necked cotton undershirts

1 shawl

2 nightdresses

1 woollen hat

4 woollen cardigans or jackets

2 pairs woollen socks

2 pairs mittens

CLOTHING TIPS

● Whatever size notations the manufacturer uses, make sure you buy sizes that last until your baby is at least two months old. Clothing that's slightly too big won't bother her and will be more practical than the newborn size which she'll quickly grow out of.
● Buy only machine-washable, color-fast clothing.
● Clothing should permit easy access to the diaper, to keep undressing time to a minimum. Buy stretch towelling suits with snaps in the crotch or down the front and leg.
● In the early weeks you may find it easy to use nightdresses which can simply be lifted up to get at the diaper.
● Babies hate having their faces covered, so buy clothes which open down the front or have wide, envelope necks.
● Clothes which do up the front eliminate the need to turn the baby over when you're dressing her.
● Material should be soft and comfortable with no hard seams or rough stitching; check the neck and waistband before buying. Buy towelling, cotton or pure wool clothes; if you buy clothes made of man-made fibres, check that they feel soft and comfortable.
● Buy non-flammable clothing.
● Avoid lacy shawls or cardigans – your baby's tiny fingers can easily get caught in the holes.
● Avoid white – it gets dirty quickly and needs more care when washing. Bright colors are just as appropriate for children as pastels.
● If you buy a hat, either buy one with a chin strap, or sew some ribbons on. Many babies hate wearing hats and pull them off unless they're tied under their chins.
● Clothes with snaps at the neck quite often last longer. Babies often outgrow clothes because their heads can no longer go through the neck opening; snaps can be left undone to accommodate the head.

Buying additional clothing

The kinds of clothes you buy will be determined basically by finance and personal taste. There is no one essential piece of clothing for your baby; but there are some items which are more practical than others. In the summer, for example, cotton T-shirts and shorts or cotton dresses are the most suitable because they're cool and leave the baby's limbs free; in the winter dungarees are practical alternatives to one-piece stretch suits. Once your baby is mobile, she'll need clothing which gives adequate knee protection. As mentioned before, stick to clothes which give you easy access to the baby's diaper; by the time she's crawling she's not going to want to lie still for very long. All clothes that you buy should be machine washable.

Check clothes in stores for the correct tightness in the legs, neck and wrists and then buy whatever is one size larger. You'll probably learn how to gauge your baby's size quite accurately, but if you're at all worried always go by the height and weight charts, not by age. Not all countries and manufacturers use the same size notations, so if you're in doubt, ask the sales assistant's advice. If your child isn't with you, make sure that clothing can be exchanged.

TOP CLOTHES

Pull-on track suit

Neck-buttoned jumper with crotch-opening dungarees

Matching dress and pants set

Pull-on play suit

Wool boots with non-slip soles

NIGHTCLOTHES AND UNDERWEAR

Initially, there is no need to make a distinction between day- and nightwear. By far the most suitable nightclothes are stretch suits. As your baby gets older, sleep suits make a cosy alternative. On very cold nights, sleeping bags solve the problem of kicked-off blankets.

If you buy undershirts make sure to buy wide-necked ones so that they go on easily. Buy brightly patterned sets that can be used as T-shirts.

Undershirt and pants set

Sleep suit

Sleeping bag

One-piece undershirt

CHOOSING CLOTHES 1–3

As your baby grows, your main concern when buying clothes will be that they're comfortable and that they allow easy movement. As your baby spends less time sleeping, and more time moving about, she's going to need more clothes. Like an adult's, they'll have to be suitable for various weather conditions (rain, cold, sun), and they'll also have to be tough enough to withstand the wear and tear of active use. Once she can crawl she'll need sturdy protection for the knees; once she can walk, she'll need shoes to protect her feet.

Buy clothing in a material that moves with your child so that however active she is there's no risk of discomfort, or of the material tearing. Towelling, cottons and corduroys are ideal. When she's being "toilet trained," the clothing must be easy to pull down or up. When she's learning how to dress or undress, avoid clothes with zippers or fancy fastenings. Use elasticized waists as long as possible.

BUYING TIPS

● Always keep your child's measurements jotted down in a notebook. While she's growing so quickly, make sure that you take new measurements frequently.
● Buy unisex clothes whenever you can. There is no reason why a girl shouldn't wear boys' clothes – they are usually sturdier anyway.
● Get outdoor clothes on the large side so that extra layers can be worn underneath. These clothes are often more expensive, so buy sizes large enough for a child to grow into. With clothes that are worn every day, buy the best quality you can afford; they will last longer and may even be passed on to other children.
● Brightly-colored clothes are useful if your toddler wanders off – she'll be easier to spot.
● T-shirts can double-up as pajama tops.
● Buy patterned undershirts so that they can double up as T-shirts.

● Put extra buttons on dungaree straps so that they can be gradually lengthened as your child gets taller.
● Small boys find short zippers difficult to manipulate, so buy trousers with elasticized waists as long as possible.
● Buy tube socks without shaped heels so that they "grow" with the child. Buy all socks in the same brand and the same color so that you don't have trouble matching them. For articles of clothing like pajamas, try to stick to one brand, one color, and one design. You can then match up trousers and tops from various pairs when your child's size and proportions change.
● Buy clothes with elasticized waistbands and trousers or skirts with shoulder straps so that they can be let down.
● Avoid "fitted" clothes – your toddler will grow out of them more quickly than loose-fitting clothes.
● Avoid man-made fabrics – they don't "breathe" like natural fibers and can make your child uncomfortably hot, especially in summer.
● A loose coat, like a duffel coat, will last two winters: one as a coat with the sleeves rolled back, and the second as a jacket with the sleeves at their usual length.

● Some sleepsuits have plastic soles on the feet. So that your child's feet don't sweat, cut a small hole in the middle to let the air circulate.

OUTDOOR CLOTHES

Splash suits, which fit over outdoor and indoor clothes, protect your child from puddles and dirt. Two-piece pram suits keep your child warm in cold weather and are essential when she's being carried in a sling with her legs out. The trousers can be pulled down quickly when you need to change her diaper. Thick winter coats should be bought large enough to grow into.

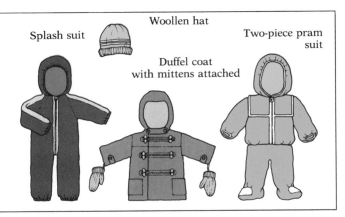

Splash suit   Woollen hat   Two-piece pram suit   Duffel coat with mittens attached

Making clothes last

☐ When sleepsuits get too short for comfort, cut off the feet for an extra month's wear.

☐ Reinforce the knees on the inside of new jeans with the extra fabric you trim from the bottoms of the legs, or use iron-on patches.

☐ Add another tier to a tiered skirt using identical or contrasting fabric.

☐ Make summer pajamas from winter pajamas by cutting down the legs and cutting off the sleeves.

☐ Make summer shorts from long winter trousers that are too small or worn at the knees.

☐ When your child outgrows an expensive jacket, cut off the sleeves and let her wear it as a vest.

☐ Run a dark blue crayon, indelible pencil or a fountain pen filled with blue/black ink over the white line when jeans have been let down.

☐ To allow for growth, choose one-piece garments with raglan or dolman sleeves and undefined waistlines.

Choosing shoes

There's absolutely no need to put your baby into shoes until she's walking. The bones in your baby's feet are soft and pliable – so pliable that even the pressure of tightly-fitting socks can misshape the toes if your baby wears them regularly. When it's very cold, or when she starts to crawl, you can put on socks or woollen bootees, but make sure that there's plenty of room for the foot to move about.

When the time comes to buy your child shoes, go to a reputable shoe store and make sure that you deal with an assistant who's been trained to measure and fit children's shoes. He should always measure the foot for width and length before bringing any shoes for your child to try on. Once the shoes are on, he should press the joints of the foot to check that the foot's not restricted in any way. He should also check that the buckle or laces hold the foot firmly in place, without slipping about.

Your child should stand up and move about in the shoes to check that the toe doesn't turn up and hurt when he's walking. Double-check that the foot doesn't move about inside the shoe.

The type of shoe you buy will be determined by when and where it's to be worn. Buy a sturdy, well-made pair of leather shoes for general outdoor wear, especially once the child is running about and playing. When it's raining, however, it's only sensible to put your child in rubber boots. Leather sandals in summer are as solid and sensible as they look, but there is nothing wrong with canvas shoes or sneakers so long as they fit properly. What you should never do is buy second-hand shoes. No matter how expensive children's shoes are, they are an essential means of ensuring that your child has good feet in adult life.

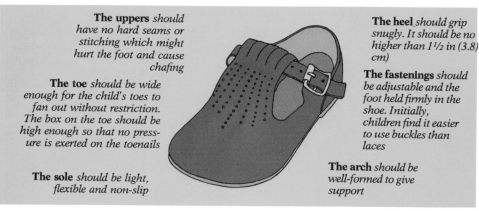

The uppers *should have no hard seams or stitching which might hurt the foot and cause chafing*

The toe *should be wide enough for the child's toes to fan out without restriction. The box on the toe should be high enough so that no pressure is exerted on the toenails*

The sole *should be light, flexible and non-slip*

The heel *should grip snugly. It should be no higher than 1½ in (3.8 cm)*

The fastenings *should be adjustable and the foot held firmly in the shoe. Initially, children find it easier to use buckles than laces*

The arch *should be well-formed to give support*

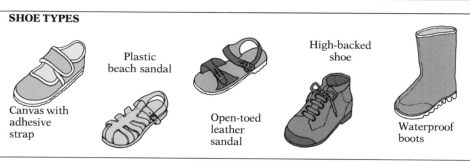

SHOE TYPES

Canvas with adhesive strap

Plastic beach sandal

Open-toed leather sandal

High-backed shoe

Waterproof boots

Washing

Once your baby starts eating solids she's bound to get messy, even when she's wearing a bib. Once she starts walking her clothes will get dirtier, too. Make sure all the clothing you buy is color-fast so that it can go into the family wash. Obviously, the more changes of clothing you have, the less often you'll have to do the washing.

To minimize your wash load, put some kind of protective overall on your child whenever she plays messy games; you could even use a cut-down shirt of your own.

WASHING TIPS
- Spray the cuffs, collars and knees of garments with a fabric protector. Most spills will run into beads and can be wiped off with a damp cloth.
- Keep sneakers looking new by spraying them with starch before the first wearing – this will keep the dirt from becoming embedded.
- Rub white shoes with a raw potato, a liquid non-abrasive cleaner or alcohol before cleaning. Keep them white by spraying with hair spray to prevent the polish from coming off.
- Don't add soiled clothing to the diaper sterilizing solution. The color will be bleached out.
- Get grimy socks clean by soaking them in a solution of washing soda and water before laundering. If they are white and made of cotton, boil them in water with a slice of lemon.
- With nylon, rayon, and all fine fabrics, you can safely add a tablespoon of dishwasher powder as a substitute for bleach.
- If you have no bleach substitute, add a cup-and-a-half of vinegar to a gallon of water.
- Clean sneakers or other fabric shoes with a soap-filled scouring pad.

DEALING WITH STAINS

Egg
If there's an egg stain, soak clothing in cold water for an hour before laundering in the usual way.

Grass
Remove grass stains with alcohol if they are resistant to laundering.

Fruit and Chocolate
Douse tough stains such as chocolate or grape juice with soda water. Rub until the discoloration has gone and then wash as usual.

Blood
Soak blood stains in cold water for 30 minutes; if they don't come out, use an enzyme-containing washing powder. If this fails, try a few drops of ammonia on the stain.

Tar
Tar stains from the beach can be removed by rubbing eucalyptus oil gently on the stain.

Milk
Remove milk stains by rinsing the clothing thoroughly in cold water and then using an enzyme-containing washing powder.

Chewing gum
Soften the gum with carbon tetrachloride or methylated spirits before gently pulling the gum away from the fabric.

Lipstick
Gently rub vaseline or glycerine into the stain before washing it in warm, soapy water. Once it's dry, sponge it clean with carbon tetrachloride.

Vomit
Use an enzyme-containing washing powder after you've rinsed the garment.

DRESSING AND UNDRESSING   0–1

Babies need changing quite frequently during the first months and, initially, you may not be fully confident about supporting your rather fragile child and dealing with the clothes at the same time. Don't worry: it's perfectly normal to feel awkward at first, and any fears you have are easily overcome with a little bit of practice, patience and gentleness.

Always dress and undress a new baby on a flat surface: a changing mat, a bed or the floor are all ideal because they allow you to keep both hands free. Keep the amount of time that she's undressed to a minimum and don't get flustered when she cries as you take off her clothes. Young babies hate being undressed; they're scared of the air on their naked bodies, and the removal of the comforting fabric makes them feel very insecure. Your baby's discomfort is going to make her cry – very loudly. It's not because of you, so don't think that you're a bad parent! Keep calm and get on with the task in hand, using something, like a mobile (see p. 145), to attract your baby's attention.

DRESSING A NEWBORN

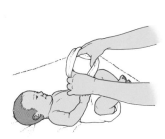

1 *Lay your baby on a flat surface. Make sure that the diaper is clean; change it if necessary. If you're putting on an undershirt, bunch up the material and stretch the opening around the neck with your thumbs.*

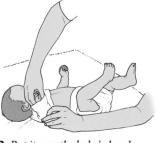

2 *Put it over the baby's head, raising her head slightly as you do so. Widen the right armhole and gently guide your baby's arm through it; repeat with the other side.*

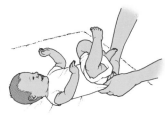

3 *Pull the shirt down and then undo the zippers of the one-piece stretch suit, keeping an eye on your baby as you do so.*

4 *Lay the suit out flat so that it's ready to put on. Pick up your baby and place her on top of it.*

5 *Bunch up the right sleeve and put it over your baby's fist. Guide the arm through, pulling the sleeve up the arm as you do so. Repeat with the other side.*

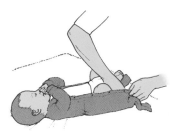

6 *Guide your baby's right leg in to the foot of the suit; repeat with the other leg. Do up the suit.*

Using your lap

When your baby has more muscle control and you yourself are feeling more confident, you can sit the baby on your lap to take off her clothes. If you sit with your legs crossed, she can sit neatly in the hollow of your legs, cradled in your arm. Alternatively, you could begin by using a flat surface, and then transfer her to your lap to put on the top layer of clothes. You'll probably need to distract your baby in some way, so have some toys for her to hold.

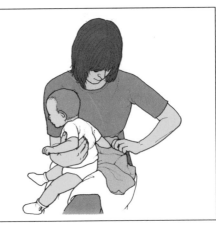

UNDRESSING A NEWBORN

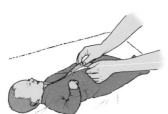

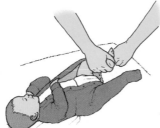

1 *Lay your baby on a flat surface and undo the suit down the front.*

2 *Because you'll probably have to change the diaper, gently pull both legs out first. Change the diaper if necessary.*

3 *Lift the baby's legs up and slide the suit up the baby's back to her shoulders.*

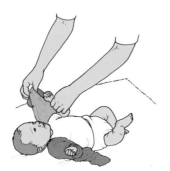

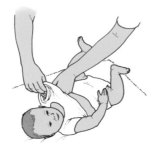

4 *Slide the baby's left hand out gently. Repeat with the right hand.*

5 *If your baby's wearing an undershirt, roll it up towards the neck. Hold the baby's elbow, bunch the fabric and gently pull it off the arm.*

6 *Stretch out the neck and lift the shirt carefully over your baby's head so that you don't scrape her face.*

47

Dressing the older baby

Once your baby can crawl she won't want to stay still for long and you may have to dress her "on the move." However, towards the end of the first year she will also gain the ability to help as you put on the clothes. If, for example, you ask your 11-month-old baby to make a fist, or to stretch out an arm, she'll probably do so and you'll be able to slide the sweater or jacket on without having to draw her hand through yourself.

Always name the clothes as you put them on or take them off, and make a game out of the whole procedure. Play hide-and-seek, for example, or peek-a-boo: "Where's your arm gone, then? . . . Oh, look, here it comes now."

Here are some other tips which will make changing your baby easier:

□ Pull up trousers, tights or even trainer pants while your baby stands immobilized between your legs.

□ Put your baby's shoes on while she's sitting in her high chair and can't squirm away.

□ Put on boots or overshoes when your child's sitting on a box or on the bottom step of the stairs. You can make a game out of her stepping down into her shoes.

□ Always try to undress your baby when she's occupied with something else like doing a puzzle or listening to a song.

□ If your baby has a favorite song, sing it and while dressing or undressing her, and encourage her to sing along.

DRESSING AND UNDRESSING   1–3

It will take a while for your child to develop the coordination required to dress successfully, but by the time she's 18 months she'll be attempting it with various items of clothing, even if it's just pulling off skirts or pants, or wriggling into sweaters. Any attempts at dressing or undressing should be encouraged. They're a sign of growing independence and maturity, not to mention coordination.

Try laying out the clothes in such a way that your child can go up to them and maneuver them on easily. Even if she seems to be fumbling, don't step in until it's really necessary. You will, however, have to deal with most of the fastenings until your child has the skill to cope with them.

DRESSING TIPS

● Stop your toddler's overall straps from slipping down by pinning them together where they cross over at the back with a large safety pin.

● When teaching your child to handle buttons, show her how to button from the bottom upwards.

● Use Velcro, wherever appropriate, but not near the neck, as it may rub and cause sore patches.

● Tiny hands find zippers difficult to manage, so put a key ring through the zip flap for easy handling.

● When your child is learning to use a zipper, teach her to pull it away from both skin and clothes to prevent it from catching.

● Until your child is toilet-trained buy trousers with elasticized waists.

● Put a badge or clear marking on the front of a garment so that your child can tell front from back.

● Mark the hole in a belt that your child should use with a stick-on gold star or a piece of tape.

● Until your child learns to hold a sweater when she is putting on a coat, sew elastic loops inside the cuffs so that she can hang onto them and stop the sleeves from being dragged up as the coat is put on.

● If the zipper is sticking, run a soft lead pencil or a bar of soap over the zipper to make it run smoothly.

● If your child is unwilling to make a fist when you're putting on a sweater, put a small treat such as a raisin or a potato chip into her hand. She will grasp it and make a fist, allowing you to push the sleeve on.

● Attach gloves or mittens to a long piece of tape and thread it through the arms of the coat.

● Wet shoe laces before tying – the bows won't slip and they will stay tied.

● When you first put on your baby's shoes cover the slippery soles with a piece of adhesive tape so that she won't slide on a slippery

floor; alternatively, score the soles with scissors so that they grip.

● If the ends of shoe laces become frayed, coat the ends with clear nail polish or wrap some sticky tape around them.

● Always buy boots large enough to accommodate an extra pair of socks. Rubbers aren't very warm so put a pair of thick socks over your child's usual socks to keep her feet warm.

● When your child first starts to use buttons, dew large ones on to her clothes so that she can handle them easily. If possible, sew them on with elastic thread.

4 Holding and handling

In the first few weeks of life your baby will seem very vulnerable and desperately in need of your protection. Many parents, and especially fathers, are rather scared of picking up their newborns, fearful that they may somehow damage their child. Babies, however, are quite robust creatures and once they have enough muscle control to support their heads, there's no need to take special care.

HANDLING YOUR BABY 0–1

It's an instinctive reaction to hold your baby close to you, to talk soothingly and lovingly as you look into her face and eyes. Many experiments have shown that children do in fact need and benefit from this physical contact. Premature babies gain more weight, for example, when they're laid on soft, downy sheets simply because the fluffy sheets give them the impression of being touched. Your newborn baby will be comforted by any kind of holding, cuddling or caressing, and skin-to-skin contact, with both of you lying naked in bed, is probably the best of all. In this way she can smell your skin, feel its touch and warmth and hear your heart beat clearly.

Make sure you hold your baby firmly, especially in the early weeks when the sensation of being tightly enclosed (whether by your arms, by clothing or by a receiving blanket), gives a great sense of security. When it comes time to move your baby, do it as slowly, gently and quietly as you can.

Picking up your newborn baby

Don't worry about picking your baby up; she's much tougher than you think. The only thing you really have to take care of is her lolling head. Until she's about four weeks old she'll have no control over it at all, so whenever you pick her up do it in a way that supports her head.

PICKING UP YOUR BABY
Slide one hand under your baby's neck to support the head. Slide the other underneath her back and bottom to support her lower half securely. Held in this way, the baby can easily be transferred to any of the carrying positions. Make sure you pick the baby up gently and smoothly.

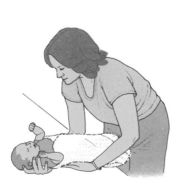

51

Putting down your newborn baby

When you lay your baby down you must make sure that her head is supported. Unless you do, her head will flop back, which may give her the sensation that she is going to fall causing her startled body to jerk and her arms to stretch out in fear (see p. 14). Either put your baby down in the same way that you picked her up – so that your whole arm supports her spine, neck and head – or alternatively, wrap her fairly tightly in a blanket (far right) so that her head is supported until she is down in the cot. You can then gently unwrap the blanket.

Babies can lie in any one of four positions: on their back, on their front or on either side. It really doesn't matter which you choose. Some mothers, however, feel that lying on the stomach, with the face to one side, is the safest, since if the baby spits up, the liquid will run out of her mouth and she won't choke on it. I would suggest that you let your baby lie in whatever position she seems to find most comfortable.

Whichever position the baby's put down to sleep in, her head must always be carefully supported. Young babies can be propped on their sides with a rolled blanket.

Carrying your newborn baby

In your arms

There are two main positions for carrying your baby in your arms. The first is in the crook of either arm, with the baby's head slightly higher than the rest of the body. The baby rests on the upper part of your arm and is encircled by the forearm and the hand which support the back and bottom. This is a good position because it allows eye-to-eye contact – you can talk and smile at your baby, and she, in turn, can watch all your expressions and see you talking.

The second way is to hold your baby against the upper part of your chest, using your forearm, with her head resting on your shoulder supported by your hand. This leaves one hand free, which is essential if you're alone and need to pick up something. If you feel wary of doing this, you should support the baby's bottom.

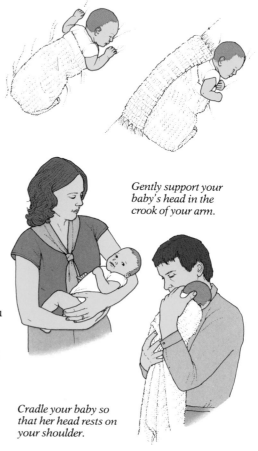

Gently support your baby's head in the crook of your arm.

Cradle your baby so that her head rests on your shoulder.

In a sling
There is no reason why your newborn shouldn't be carried in a sling, so long as it provides adequate support for the baby's neck and head (see p. 28), and comfortably envelops her body so that she can't slip out of either side. The best kinds of slings are the very soft, pouch-like ones which allow the baby to lie curled up. Most parents feel happiest with the sling worn on their chest because they can see and cuddle the baby easily, and generally protect her more efficiently than if she were on their back.

Using shawls

Wrapping a baby tightly in a receiving blanket (see p. 142) has been shown to comfort a child not only because it simulates a caress, but also because the tightness of the blanket makes the baby feel secure. Because most babies go to sleep when they're wrapped up, it's a useful way of calming them when distressed. You can either put the baby down to sleep in the blanket or use it as a kind of sling.

PROPPING

Instead of leaving your baby staring up at the ceiling, prop him up with pillows so that he can see what's going on; you can do this as early as six weeks (see p. 180). Wherever you prop the baby, make sure that he can't topple forward or sideways.

USING A BLANKET AS A SLING

1 *Drape the blanket around your shoulders, with a slightly shorter length on the side where you'll hold the baby. Pick up the baby in the crook of your arm.*

2 *Fold the shorter edge over her body, leaving the feet free. Wrap fabric securely around the baby.*

3 *Bring the other length of fabric over and under the baby, then pull the fabric up between your chest and the baby.*

4 *Tuck the remaining fabric neatly inside the "pocket" you've just folded. The blanket will leave you with both hands free if you want.*

Picking up your older baby

Once your baby has control of her head, there's no need to take the kind of care you did when she was newborn. At this stage, the best way to pick her up is to put your hands under her armpits and lift her toward you. Once she's been picked up you can carry her in the crook of your arm or against your shoulder. As her back, neck and head muscles become stronger, she can be placed astride one hip with your arm going diagonally across her back and holding on to a thigh.

Once your baby can support her head she can be lifted up under the armpits. As she gets heavier, take the strain on your legs, not on your back.

Carrying your older baby

By the time a baby is four or five months old, most parents carry her on one of their hips; which one is determined by whether the parent is right- or left-handed. You'll inevitably develop your own methods of carrying your baby which may well vary according to her mood. For longer journeys you can also carry your baby in a front sling or in a back pack.

Putting down your older baby

You don't have to be as careful putting down an older baby as a newborn one. She can be put down in exactly the same way that she was picked up. Alternatively, you can support the upper part of the baby's body with one hand curved diagonally across her back and with the other hand supporting her bottom. If you're putting your child into a high chair, support her under the armpits and let both legs dangle so that she can place them easily between tray and seat.

CARRYING THE OLDER BABY

Sitting astride your hip, your baby has the advantage of being able to look in three directions, but she'll still feel secure and close to you. One hand is also left free.

Many parents find themselves holding their baby this way. It allows them one hand free if necessary, with the baby securely held around the waist.

Once your baby can support her head, she may find this position soothing, especially if you gently swing from side-to-side. This can be turned into a game by swinging her higher and higher.

Cuddling and security

A toddler needs much less holding and carrying than a young baby, but there still will be times when she'll signal that she wants to be carried, just as she used to be. If you ignore these signals, she'll probably cry. You may find that she wants to be carried when she's tired; when you've taken her out for a long walk; when she's cutting teeth; when she isn't feeling well; when she's fearful, or when you've been away. Don't hesitate to give this kind of physical support and affection. She will give you a clear signal when she is reassured and has had enough, and will wriggle down and run off.

We never outgrow the need for physical affection. Always recognize this in your children; never scoff at it and always give it. My eleven-and-a-half-year-old son still likes a cuddle every now and then, especially when he's tired or when he's been scolded at school; or fears my departure or absence. "The world doesn't feel right," is the way he puts it.

Even when children are quite old they may still want to sit on your knee occasionally. In strange circumstances they may even like to sit on your knee while eating, particularly if strangers are present and they feel that they are under observation. Don't ridicule your child for wanting this. If it is convenient, let her sit on your knee; there is absolutely nothing wrong with it and a few moments of your touch will give your child the confidence to handle the situation in her own way. To my mind, a child should never have to go to bed without some cuddling; it will give her a sense of security and the reassuring feeling that you really do care. When your small child is hurt, worried, puzzled or frightened, always be there with an encircling, comforting arm and a sympathetic word. But do give such reassurances in the form that your child wants, and don't overpower her with your physical affection when she makes obvious signs that she doesn't require it.

Of course there are some children who don't like to be handled or cuddled very much. They usually show this from a very early age by stiffening their bodies and crying when you hold them. This can be quite difficult for a parent to cope with because it seems like rejection (see p. 206). These kinds of babies usually grow up to be children who avoid physical contact and who turn their heads away when you lean forward to kiss them. They make no physical overtures themselves and make it quite difficult for you to show love and affection to them in an overt way. They may never learn how to accept physical affection nor to be comfortable with it. If your child is like this, the only way to treat her is to not make her discomfort worse by thrusting physical affection on her. Respect your child's diffidence. Wait for her to come to you and only give your physical affection when she shows you that she wants it by *her* actions.

5 All about diapers

Until your child is toilet trained, usually during the third year, she will have to wear diapers both day and night. During the first few months life may seem like an endless round of diaper changing. But don't despair. As your child grows and gains more control over bowel and blad-der muscles she will go for longer intervals without excreting, and the number of diapers you need to change will decrease. By age two-and-a-half she will usually become aware of her need to go to the bathroom. It's at this point that you should start toilet training.

DIAPERS AND CHANGING   0–1

Diapers are now produced in a wide variety of styles and sizes, but your basic choice will be between disposable and fabric makes. Whichever kind you choose, you'll still use the same changing equipment, and the same general techniques for cleaning and caring for your baby's bottom.

Changing a diaper
You should change a diaper whenever you notice that it is soiled or wet. The number of times it needs to be changed will vary from baby to baby and from day to day. However, you will want to change the diaper when your baby wakes in the morning, when she is put to bed at night, and when she's been given a bath. In addition, your baby will need to be changed after every feed. This is because of the gastro-colic reflex which stimulates the elimination of feces when food is taken in.

Where to change a diaper
Always change your baby on a soft, warm, waterproof surface. Changing mattresses are ideal for this. They are usually made of a foam-filled, waterproof material, and have a slightly raised edge to prevent the baby from rolling off. They can be placed on whatever surface suits you best – floor, table or bed. As your baby gets older and starts to roll and wriggle while you change the diaper, you may find it safer to change her on the floor or on a low bed, with or without a mattress.

Putting on a diaper
Putting on diapers, even your first ones, will be easier if you are well prepared. Make sure you have everything that you need within easy reach (see list on p. 58). The last thing you want to discover is that halfway through the job you've left the baby lotion in the bathroom and the clean diapers downstairs.

There is no need to wash your baby's bottom with soap each change: just gently wipe away most of the feces with a front corner of the old diaper, and then clean the baby's bottom with oil or lotion. If your baby has only wet the diaper, use a water-soaked cloth or cotton wool. You don't need to use talcum powder; in fact, I disapprove of it. Powder can become caked and irritating in the skin creases, increasing the risk of diaper rash. When you change your baby, watch out for any redness and take appropriate action immediately (see p. 59).

Diaper changing sequence

1 Remove the baby's dirty diaper. Use the front to clean feces off the baby (see below). Fold the diaper so that the feces can't fall out, and place the diaper to one side of the changing mat.
2 Clean the baby's genital area, bottom and top of the legs, as shown below.
3 Put on a clean diaper, using one of the techniques described on pages 61 to 65.
4 Dress the baby.
5 Put the baby somewhere safe (like a cot or a baby bouncer), then deal with the dirty diaper (see p. 62 or p. 67). Wash your hands.

- Changing mat
- Clean fabric diaper, diaper liner, pins and plastic pants *or* a disposable diaper
- Cotton wool
- Baby lotion or oil
- Tissues
- Washcloth or flannel
- Bowl of water
- Diaper rash cream, if necessary
- Clean clothes
- Hamper
- Distracting toy

CLEANING A BOY

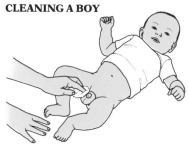  

1 *Using a wet cloth or cotton wool to remove urine, work from the leg creases in towards the penis. Don't pull the foreskin back.*

2 *Clean his bottom by lifting up his legs, and holding both ankles in one hand. Keep a finger in between his heels to stop his ankles from grinding together. Dry thoroughly.*

3 *If the diaper is soiled, remove as much feces as possible with the front of the diaper. Use lotion or oil with cotton wool – a different piece for each wipe. Wash your hands.*

CLEANING A GIRL

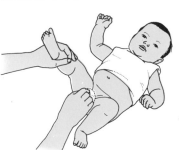

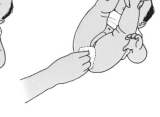
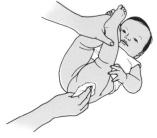

1 *Using a wet cloth or cotton wool to remove urine, clean the genitals and surrounding skin. Never pull back the labia to clean inside.*

2 *Lift up her legs, holding them as shown, and clean her bottom. Wipe from the vagina back towards the rectum to prevent the spread of bacteria.*

3 *If the diaper is soiled, clean with lotion or oil and cotton wool. Use a new piece for each wipe. Wipe from legs and bottom inwards. Wash hands.*

Diaper rash

Because passing urine is automatic, your baby's bottom will often be in contact with a damp diaper. Urine, if left for any length of time in a diaper or on the skin, is broken down to ammonia by bacteria from the baby's stools. Ammonia is an irritant: it burns the skin and causes diaper rash. Diaper rash can range from a mild redness to an inflamed area of broken skin and pussy spots. The bacteria which produce diaper rash thrive in an alkaline medium. The stools of bottle-fed babies are alkaline, unlike those of breast-fed babies, which are acid. For this reason, bottle-fed babies are more prone to diaper rash. To minimize the possibility of diaper rash:

□ Change your baby's diaper regularly; never leave your baby lying in a wet diaper.

□ Put a one-way disposable diaper liner next to your baby's skin. The urine will pass straight through and be absorbed by the diaper below, the skin will stay dry.

□ Use a fairly thick barrier cream. There is no need to buy an expensive one. Simple zinc oxide or a diaper cream are usually good enough if applied generously.

□ Leave the baby's bottom open to the air whenever you can. Let the baby kick happily without a diaper after a bath or at feeding time. Just slide a diaper underneath her bottom to catch any mess.

□ Pay particular attention to washing diapers. Make sure they are well washed and rinsed to remove all the ammonia (see p. 67).

□ At the first sign of broken skin start using a special cream for the prevention of diaper rash. Those which include titanium salts are especially good.

□ At the first hint of diaper rash, stop using plastic pants. These help to keep the urine close to the skin and promote the formation of ammonia. Stop washing the baby's bottom with soap and water, which dry the skin and can cause it to become cracked.

Treatment of diaper rash

You may find, despite your precautions, that your baby develops a sore bottom. If you are satisfied that your baby doesn't require specific treatment (see chart below), then follow the tips listed above. Also:

□ Change diapers more frequently.

□ At night, use a disposable pad inside a terry one for extra absorbency. This is especially useful for older babies who are sleeping through the night and will there-fore not be changed from evening until morning.

□ Do not apply barrier creams when changing the diaper, as this prevents air from getting to the skin. It also keeps the skin dry, but it is more important that the skin be well aired when your baby has diaper rash.

DIAPER RASH CHART

Appearance	Cause	Treatment
Redness and broken skin in the leg folds.	Inadequate drying after bathing.	Meticulous and thorough drying. Do not use powder.
Rash which starts around the genitals rather than the anus. Strong smell of ammonia.	Ammonia dermatitis.	General diaper rash treatment, above. If this doesn't work, check with your doctor.
Spotty rash all over the genitals, bottom, groin and thighs, which eventually leads to thick and wrinkled skin.	Extreme form of ammonia dermatitis.	Check with doctor for advice after trying general treatment (above) first.
Rash which starts around the anus and moves on to the buttocks.	Thrush.	Check with your doctor. You will probably be given nystatin cream and medicine.
Brownish-red scaly rash on the genitals and buttocks and anywhere the skin is greasy.	Seborrhoeic dermatitis.	Ointment for rash, prescribed by your doctor. You might also get a special lotion if the scalp is very scaly and sore.
Small blisters all over the diaper area.	Heat rash.	Don't use plastic pants, and leave off the diaper as much as possible.

DISPOSABLE DIAPERS   0–1

If you can afford them, disposable diapers are the answer to every parent's prayers. There is no cleaning, washing or drying involved – you simply put on the diaper and then discard it when it is wet or dirty. A disposable diaper is also much easier to put on the baby, as it needs no elaborate folding, diaper pins or plastic pants. You may also feel more at ease using them because there will be no risk of hurting the baby with a pin.

Even if you've chosen to use the fabric variety, keep a stock of disposables in the house. They're a useful back-up if you've run out of your usual diapers, or if your baby develops a rash because of your washing methods. They are much more practical than fabric diapers when you're travelling, since you don't need as much room in which to change them, and you don't have to carry as many accessories with you. Also, if you go visiting, used disposables can be thrown away in a suitable receptacle; fabric diapers, which may be both soaked and smelly, will have to be taken home with you to be washed. Disposables are also practical for toddlers, since they are less bulky to walk with. The disposables are also neater looking than fabric diapers.

The disposables may be more practical, but, because they can be used only once, you have to make sure to have a constant supply at home. To save time and energy, buy them in as large a batch as possible: wholesalers and discount warehouses are ideal for this, especially since their prices for bulk purchases are cheaper.

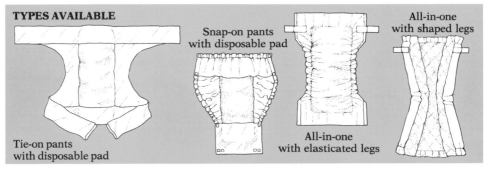

TYPES AVAILABLE

Tie-on pants with disposable pad

Snap-on pants with disposable pad

All-in-one with elasticated legs

All-in-one with shaped legs

Types available

There are basically two styles of disposables: two-piece and all-in-one. The two-piece diaper consists of an absorbent pad which slots into specially designed plastic pants. These pants are either T-shaped tie-ons or snap-on pants. Most parents find the tie-ons more suitable for newborns and small babies. The pads are available in a *standard* size which can be used with the pants, as a diaper, or inside a fabric or all-in-one diaper to provide extra absorbency. *Graded* pads are available in varying sizes and thicknesses, and fit newborns to toddlers. Rolls of pad, which you cut to the size you want, are also available. The

plastic pants can be re-used. The two-piece diaper is cheaper to buy than the disposable all-in-one.

As their name suggests, all-in-one disposables function as diaper, liner and pants, but in a single unit instead of three. They are available in a variety of sizes, suitable for newborns to toddlers, and in a range of styles. The best have elasticated legs for added protection against leaks. They all have a plastic outer covering and an absorbent inner layer topped with a one-way diaper liner (see left), and are secured with adjustable adhesive tabs. They are the most expensive variety of disposable diaper.

HOW TO PUT ON A TWO-PIECE DISPOSABLE

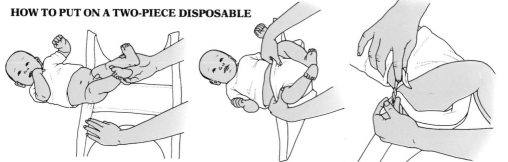

1 *Insert the pad into the pants, smooth side upwards. Lift the baby's legs and slide the diaper under so that the top aligns with the baby's waist.*

2 *Bring the pants up between the baby's legs. If you are using tie-ons, wrap the two front ends around the baby so that they cross at the back.*

3 *Twist the ends over each other so that they are secure but not tied in a knot which would be uncomfortable.*

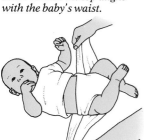

4 *Bring the other two ends forward to tie at the front. If you are using snap-on pants, just do up the snaps.*

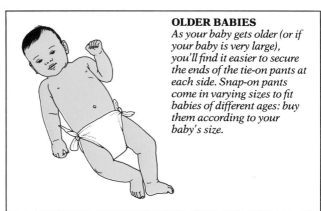

OLDER BABIES
As your baby gets older (or if your baby is very large), you'll find it easier to secure the ends of the tie-on pants at each side. Snap-on pants come in varying sizes to fit babies of different ages: buy them according to your baby's size.

HOW TO PUT ON AN ALL-IN-ONE DISPOSABLE

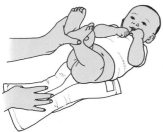  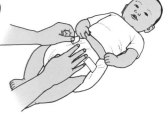

1 *Open out the diaper with the adhesive tabs at the top. Lift the baby's legs and slide the diaper under so that the top aligns with the baby's waist.*

2 *Bring the front up between the baby's legs and smooth the sides of the diaper round the baby's tummy so that they tuck under neatly.*

3 *Unpeel the adhesive tabs and pull them firmly over the front flap to secure the diaper. They should be quite taut.*

CHANGING TIPS

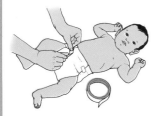

● Even though they have a one-way liner, it's useful to put a paper liner in, too. Feces can then be lifted out with the liner and easily disposed of.

● If you've torn the adhesive strip to remove a diaper, only to find that the diaper is clean, use a strip of household masking tape to re-seal the diaper. The same applies if the tape fails to stick.
● If your baby has an upset stomach or a very sore bottom and you therefore have to change the diaper very regularly, use disposable pads. This costs less.

● If you use all-in-ones without elasticated legs, you can gently pull out the leg area for a better fit.
● Keep a supply of fabric diapers just in case you run out of disposables.

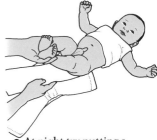

● At night try putting a standard pad inside an all-in-one disposable for extra absorbency.
● If you split open the back of an all-in-one disposable, you can slip a disposable pad between the padding and the plastic layer for extra absorbency.
● If you're really worried about leaks and you're going out, put a pair of tie-ons over the all-in-one.

Disposing of a disposable

All disposable diapers are designed to be thrown away. The entire all-in-one diaper, plastic backing included, can be discarded; in a two-piece diaper the pants are retained and the pad is replaced. Despite many manufacturers' claims to the contrary, disposable diapers have a nasty habit of getting stuck in the drain, so you will have to find an hygienic alternative to flushing them down the toilet. I suggest that you flush away as much of the feces as possible, then wring out the excess water and put the diaper in a strong plastic bag. Plastic trash bags are ideal. When you throw the bag out, make sure that it is firmly secured at the neck.

FABRIC DIAPERS   0–1

Although initially more expensive to buy than all-in-one disposables, fabric diapers made of terry cloth or muslin work out to be less expensive over the years. Since they have to be rinsed, sterilized, washed out and dried after use, they involve much more work than disposables. Because they have to be washed regularly, you will need a minimum of 24 fabric diapers. Obviously, the more diapers that you can afford to buy, the less frequently you'll have to wash them, and the larger and therefore more economical your batches will be. Buy the best quality that you can afford. They'll last longer and be more absorbent.

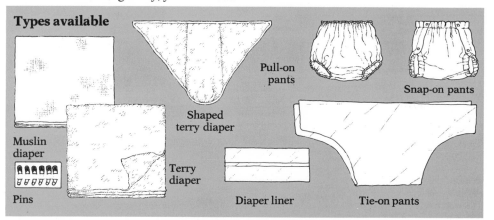

Types available

Pull-on pants

Snap-on pants

Shaped terry diaper

Muslin diaper

Pins

Terry diaper

Diaper liner

Tie-on pants

Terry squares
These traditional diapers are thick and absorbent and will fold into a variety of shapes according to your baby's size and needs (see pp. 64–65). Buy them ready-hemmed to avoid fraying when they are washed. They are more absorbent than the majority of disposables and are therefore very suitable at night. They can be bulky on very small babies and newborns.

Shaped terry towelling
These T-shaped diapers are made of a softer, finer towelling than ordinary squares and have a triple-layered central panel for added absorbency. They are shaped to fit neatly around the baby's legs and are easier to put on.

Muslin squares
These are about the same size as towelling squares, but are soft and filmy. They are ideal for newborns because they are so comfortable against their skin. However, they are not very absorbent, and have to be changed frequently.

Diaper liners
These are placed inside the diaper and go next to the baby's skin. The best variety is made of a special material which lets urine pass through but which remains dry next to the baby's skin. This minimizes the risk of a sore bottom caused by friction or moisture. They also catch most of the feces and prevent the diaper from getting badly soiled. When it comes time to change the diaper, the liner can be lifted out with any feces and flushed down the toilet.

Diaper pins
Specially-designed for fabric diapers, these pins have a self-locking head which makes it impossible for them to come undone accidentally. Buy at least twelve.

Plastic pants
These pants, which come in several designs, are used over fabric diapers to prevent wet or dirty diapers from soiling clothes or bedding. Buy six initially. You'll need to replace them as they get old and unusable.

63

Folding diapers

Not long ago, most parents were taught to use the simple triangle or rectangle methods. Both methods are easy to use, but neither is very efficient. The triangle is baggy around the legs, and the rectangle, although absorbent, is very bulky and suitable only for small babies. I therefore suggest that you use other methods which make the diaper neater and more absorbent. Use the triple absorbent fold for your newborn. It has good absorbency because of its central panel, and it is also very

small and neat when worn. Another method you can use for a newborn baby is the diaper skirt. Put a muslin diaper on the baby, then lay the baby on an open terry square. Fold the square around the baby like a skirt and secure it at one side with a diaper pin.

When she grows too large for the triple fold, use either the kite or the parallel method – whichever suits her best. The kite is usually easier to adapt to your growing baby since you can adjust how much you fold in towards the center.

TRIPLE ABSORBENT FOLD

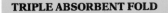

1 *Take a diaper folded in four, with the open edges to the top right. Pick up the top layer by right-hand edge.*

2 *Pull out the top layer to form an inverted triangle.*

3 *Carefully turn the whole diaper over so that the pointed edge is at the top right-hand side.*

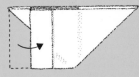
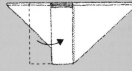
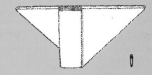

4 *Fold the two middle layers in to the center by one third.*

5 *Fold in another third to form a thick central panel.*

6 *Put a diaper liner in the middle and have a pin ready.*

PARALLEL FOLD

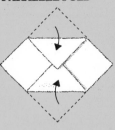
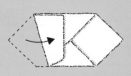
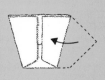

1 *Lay out diaper in a diamond shape. Fold top point in to the center; fold bottom up and over the center.*

2 *Pick up the left-hand point and align it with the top edge.*

3 & 4 *Fold in the right-hand edge in the same way. Place a diaper liner in the middle and have two pins ready.*

KITE FOLD

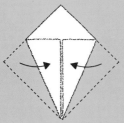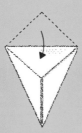

1 *Lay out diaper in a diamond shape. Fold sides in to the center to form a kite shape.*

2 *Fold the top point down to the center, leaving a straight edge at the top.*

3 & 4 *Fold the bottom edge up to the center, according to the baby's size. Place a diaper liner in the middle and have a pin ready.*

HOW TO PUT ON A FABRIC DIAPER

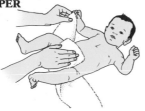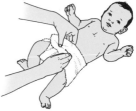

1 *Slide the diaper under so that the baby's waist aligns with the top edge.*

2 *Bring the diaper up between the baby's legs. Hold it in place and fold first one side, then the other, over the central panel.*

3 *Secure the diaper for a small baby with one pin in the middle; use two side pins for bigger babies.*

Triple absorbent fold

Parallel fold

Kite fold

CHANGING TIPS

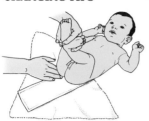

● If your baby is wriggly, have a toy handy to act as a distraction. Older children can be distracted by holding the cream or looking at a book.

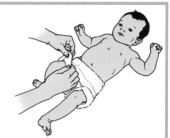

● Use a disposable inside a terry diaper for extra absorbency at night. Also use this method if you're travelling and want to avoid a difficult change.
● Use stretch towelling pants over plastic pants – they look neater than plastic pants by themselves. Frilly and patterned plastic pants are also available if you want something fancier.

● Boys often urinate when changed, so cover penis with a clean diaper as you take old one off.
● Always keep your fingers between the diaper and the skin when inserting a pin.

● When you've put on the diaper, run your fingers round the legs to make sure the diaper is not too tight.
● To save time, fold all the diapers ready for use and put the diaper liners in position.
● Make sure the diaper fits snugly around the baby's body. It will gradually stretch as the baby wears it. If you've pinned it too loosely it will slide down.

Diaper washing and sterilization

Diapers must be thoroughly washed to remove all traces of ammonia and fecal bacteria which would otherwise cause irritation and possible infection (see p. 59). Special diaper sterilants are now available which make this process much easier and less time-consuming. After soaking in a sterilizing solution for a specified length of time, the soiled diapers are washed with powder, and the wet diapers are thoroughly rinsed. Whenever you wash diapers, use pure soap flakes or powders. Avoid strong detergents and biological enzyme powders, as these will irritate the baby's tender skin. If you have to use a fabric conditioner because the towelling has become stiff, make sure that you rinse it all out; despite manufacturers' instructions to the contrary, this too can cause irritation. Unless the diapers are very stained, or have turned grey, there is no need to boil them. After using sterilizing tablets, hot water is sufficient for both rinsing and washing. Never add colored clothing to

the sterilizing solution – the color will run. Even if the clothing has been soiled, just remove the worst of the mess, rinse the item, and wash as normal.

Diaper washing routine

To balance the chores of feeding, changing, and diaper washing, try to develop a routine whereby you wash the diapers in sufficiently large loads. The prerequisite of this routine is a large supply of diapers – I suggest no less than 24. In order to sterilize the diapers, you will need two plastic bins: one for soiled diapers, one for wet ones. The bins should be large enough to hold at least six diapers, plus solution, and they must have lids and strong, reliable handles. Don't, however, buy such a large bin that you can't carry it fully loaded to the washing machine or bath. Special diaper bins are sold, but any bin of a decent size with a lid is suitable. Bins designed for beer-making are ideal and also quite cheap.

Each morning fill the bins with the

required amounts of water and solution. Rinse a urine-soaked diaper in cold water, squeeze out the excess moisture, and put it into the bin. Shake the loose feces into the toilet, then hold the soiled diaper under the water as you flush it to remove the excess. Wring out the diaper and submerge it in the solution. After the required time, wring out both sets of diapers. Rinse the urine-soaked ones thoroughly in hot water before drying them. Put the soiled ones through the hot cycle of a washing machine, then rinse and dry them. Alternatively, wash them out in a bath with hot water.

Washing plastic pants

If they become soiled or wet, they should be washed in warm water with a little mild soap. If the water is either too hot or too cold, the plastic hardens and becomes unusable. Pat the pants dry after washing and leave them to air before using. One way of softening them is to tumble dry them with a load of towels.

WASHING TIPS
● Some buckets have special holders for air-fresheners. If yours doesn't, hook a piece of wire through a freshener and attach above water line.
● Keep plastic gloves near the bucket for lifting diapers out. Alternatively use plastic tongs.
● If you use powder, always put the water in before the powder. Otherwise, you will inhale the powder as it spreads through the air.
● Drying diapers in the open air or in a tumble drier keeps the fabric softer. Avoid using radiators to dry diapers – they tend to harden the fabric. If you don't dry diapers outdoors or in a tumble drier, invest in a retractable clothes line or a rack which can be placed over the bath.
● Keep diapers changed at night in a separate bucket, or in a large plastic bag, and add them to the new day's solution the following morning.

USING DIAPERS   1–3

A one-year-old child still urinates automatically, but because the bladder can hold an increasing amount of urine, your child will remain dry for longer periods. You will therefore use fewer diapers – an average of 50 per week as opposed to the 80 used on a newborn. If you hesitated to use disposables before because of the price, you may want to consider them now. Your increasingly mobile child will find it difficult to walk with a cumbersome fabric diaper between her legs, and may prefer the neater and less bulky disposables. If you continue to use fabric diapers, fold them in the least bulky way – using either the kite fold or a shaped terry. When it's time to change the diaper, you'll find your toddler far less willing to lie still. Make sure that you've got some books or toys as distractions (see p. 266) or you'll find that each change becomes a battle. Clothes which give easy access to the diaper save you time and energy, so buy dungarees which have snaps or zippers in the crotch, or use pants which you can pull down quickly.

At some time during her third year, your child will probably gain conscious control over her bowel and bladder muscles and your days of frequent diaper changes should be over. When your child stays dry during naps, start leaving off the diaper during that time (see p. 134). Once again, I'd suggest that you use disposables. As part of your toilet training you may also want to use trainer pants which can be pulled down quickly when your child tells you that she wants to go to the bathroom. These are basically plastic pants lined with towelling. They're comfortable to wear and provide some protection against the inevitable accidents which will occur. Buy at least six to begin with, because they're not absorbent.

6 Bathing and hygiene

Part of your daily routine will be to keep your baby clean. This will be reasonably easy when she's very small, but as she becomes more active, you'll have to bathe her more often, and cleaning her will require more effort. By the time she's two, however, she'll begin to wash her own body.

WASHING YOUR BABY   0–1

Most young babies don't need bathing very often because, apart from their bottoms, faces, necks and skin creases, they don't get very dirty. Regardless of what you were encouraged to do in the hospital, there's no reason why your baby can't go a day or two without a bath, so long as you clean her face, hands and bottom every day. You can do this without even putting the baby in the bath by "topping" and "tailing" (see p. 70).

Some parents feel apprehensive the first few times they bath their baby. However, if you set aside half an hour, have everything you need around you, and try to relax, you will probably enjoy it. After the first two or three times it will become fairly routine and you'll wonder what your nervousness was all about.

Where to bath your baby

Until your baby is big enough to go into an adult bath, you don't have to use a bathroom to wash her. You can use the baby's room, the kitchen, or any other room that is warm and spacious enough to lay out all that you need to bath your baby in comfort. The baby's bath can be filled in the bathroom and then carried to the chosen room (make sure you don't fill it too full or the water will splash out as you walk from room to room).

A small baby can be washed in a specially designed, sculpted plastic bath with a non-slip surface (see p. 21). Since it will be more comfortable for you if you don't have to bend too much, the bath should be placed on a table or worktop at a convenient height. Alternatively, you can place it on an adjustable stand (although they tend to be rather flimsy) or on a rack which straddles the bath.

As a practical, inexpensive alternative to a baby bath, you can simply use a plastic household tub. Like the baby bath, it can be carried anywhere you choose. Kitchen or bathroom sinks are also practical because they are generally at a comfortable height and they often have additional counter space to the side. However, you must make sure that the taps are well out of reach of your baby's kicking legs. If they aren't, the taps should be wrapped with clothes or towels so that they can cause no harm. If the "bath" surface is too slippery, either use a plastic suction mat or line the bath with a small towel or diaper to provide traction for your baby's bottom.

Topping and tailing

This method allows you to wash those parts of your newborn baby that really need it, with a minimum of disturbance and distress to the baby. As your baby gets older, you need not use boiled water; warm water will do.

- Boiled or warm water
- Cotton wool
- Washcloth
- Towel
- Clean diaper
- Diaper liner
- Plastic pants, if used
- Diaper changing equipment
- Clean clothes

 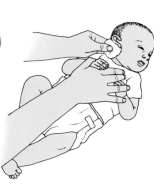 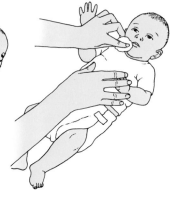

1 *Lay your baby on a firm surface. Taking a moist piece of cotton wool for each eye, gently wipe from the bridge of the nose outwards.*

2 *Wipe outside and behind the ears with cotton wool. Do not poke about or clean inside them.*

3 *Wipe your baby's face with damp cotton wool to remove any milk or spittle. If left, this will irritate the baby's skin.*

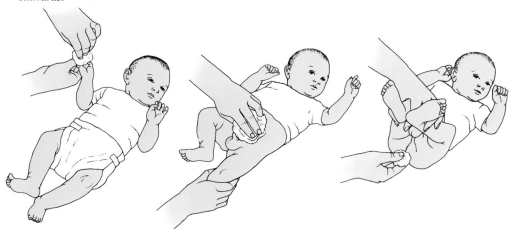

4 *Use a new piece to clean your baby's hands. Dry with a towel. When your baby's older you can use a washcloth.*

5 *Take off the old diaper. If he's just wet, wipe the area with a washcloth or damp cotton wool.*

6 *If he's soiled, remove as much as you can with the diaper, then use baby lotion and cotton wool to clean the diaper area (see p. 58).*

70

Giving a sponge bath

If you're a bit scared of giving your new baby a bath, or if she really hates being undressed, you can use the sponge bath method of washing. This way, the baby is held securely in your lap and only the minimum amount of clothing is removed. You could alternatively wash your baby on a mat, using the same techniques.

- Bowl of water
- Cotton wool
- Washcloth or sponge
- Towel
- Soap
- Baby shampoo
- Clean diaper
- Diaper liner
- Plastic pants, if used
- Diaper changing equipment
- Clean clothes

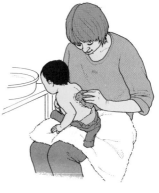

1 *Have a bowl of warm water on a table near your chair and put a towel across your knees. Remove the top half of your baby's clothing but keep the legs covered. Gently soap the baby's front.*

2 *Rinse off soap using squeezed out cloth, making sure all the soap is removed from the skin creases. Pat your baby's skin dry, paying special attention to the skin folds.*

3 *Lean your baby forwards over your arm so that you can wash his back. Rinse and pat dry. Put on a clean undershirt.*

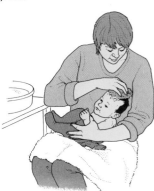

4 *If you want to clean your baby's hair, do so before you put on the undershirt. Sponge the head gently with water and then use a non-sting baby shampoo. Rinse carefully.*

5 *Remove the bottom half of your baby's clothing and then take off your baby's diaper. Use baby lotion to clean the diaper area (see p. 58).*

6 *Wash the legs and feet using a damp cloth. Rinse and pat dry. Put on a clean diaper and dress your baby.*

Giving your baby a bath

- Bath
- Large towel
- Soap, if used
- Washcloth
- Cotton wool
- Clean clothes
- Clean diaper
- Diaper liner
- Diaper changing equipment

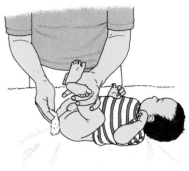

1 *Fill the bath. The water should be as warm as your baby's body temperature (85°F/ 29.4°C). Always pour cold in first; hot water first may make the bottom of the bath too hot.*

2 *Before putting your baby in the bath, test the temperature of the water with your elbow, or the inner side of your wrist. It should feel neither too hot nor too cold. You can also use a thermometer.*

3 *Undress your baby on a flat surface, but leave his undershirt on. Clean the diaper area with baby lotion (see p. 58). Once in the bath, all he'll need will be a good rinse with water.*

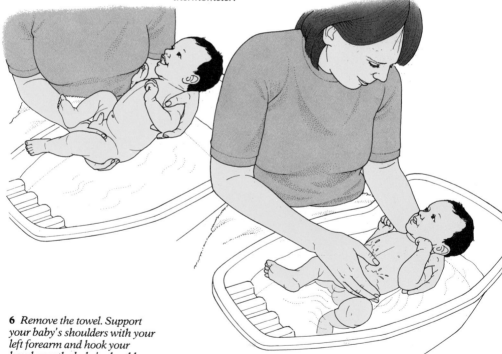

6 *Remove the towel. Support your baby's shoulders with your left forearm and hook your hand over the baby's shoulder and under his armpit. Cradle the baby's legs with your right arm, holding onto one thigh. Gently place the baby in the bath so that you are facing him.*

7 *Keep your baby in a semi-upright position so that the lower half of his body is immersed and his head and shoulders are clear of water.*

Use your free hand to wash the baby; the order is up to you. Chat and smile all the time you are bathing him.

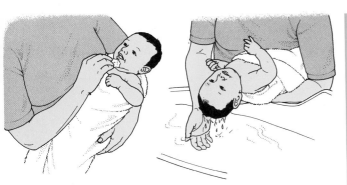

4 *Remove the baby's undershirt and wrap him in a towel so that he doesn't panic at being undressed. Clean the eyes, ears and nose (see p. 70).*

5 *Using the football carry (see p. 75), lean over the bath and wash the baby's head. Rinse well and pat dry.*

TIPS
● Make sure that you have everything that you need for washing, drying and dressing close by.
● Wear a waterproof apron to protect your own clothing but also lay a large, soft towel across your lap and up your front so that when you cuddle your baby after the bath she will feel warm and comfortable.
● Very young babies can't regulate their own temperatures very efficiently, so keep the time she's undressed to a minimum.

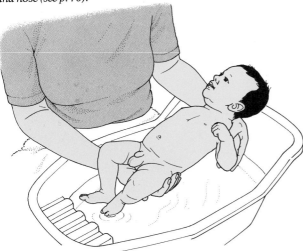

8 *When your baby is clean and well rinsed, put your free hand under his bottom and, gently supporting his bottom, lift him onto the towel.*

9 *Place your baby diagonally across the towel. Fold the bottom corner over the feet, followed by the two sides. Pick your baby up for a cuddle while you dry him. Pay particular attention to the skin creases, drying them gently but thoroughly.*

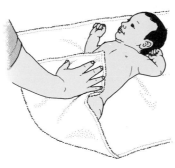

● For an older baby try using one of those towels with hoods. It will make her feel even more secure and snug – especially if the towel has been left over a radiator to warm.
● Until you get used to bathing your baby, fill the bath with only a couple of inches of water.
● Never use baby powders. They are unnecessary. When drying a baby's delicate skin, they may cake in the creases, causing irration and rashes.

73

Using a bathtub

Between the age of three and six months your baby will outgrow most small baths and you will have to start using an adult one. If you think that your baby may be frightened by the size of this new bath, continue to use the small bath but place it inside the large, empty one until she gets used to it.

It is much more awkward to wash a baby in a big bath, but you must still hold on to her arm until she can support herself. Don't bend over the bath or you'll strain your back. Instead, kneel by the bath and have everything that you need next to you on the floor. Use a plastic suction mat on the bottom of the bath to prevent the baby from sliding about. Keep the water shallow (no deeper than 4–5 inches). It doesn't take much for a wriggly, kicking baby to slip under the water, so you must be alert at all times. Never, ever, leave your baby alone in the bath, even for a moment; don't even turn away to attend to something else in the same room. If the phone rings, either ignore it or take your wet baby with you. Leaving your baby unattended, even for a second, is just not worth the risk.

As your baby gets older, she'll spend more and more time crawling about on

the floor and, as a result, will need to be washed more often; baths will become a regular feature of the day. By this time she should no longer be scared of being undressed and should feel quite secure in the water. In fact, she should enjoy her bathtime. It is therefore your job to make it as fun and trouble-free as possible.

As soon as your baby can sit up, always set aside a period near the end of the bath when she can enjoy splashing and playing with toys. Have some boats, ducks, sponges or unbreakable containers on hand so that she can experiment with them and see what they do. If you have two children, try bathing them together occasionally so that your older child can share games and can teach your younger one about the things that water does. It will be exciting for your baby to see how containers can be filled and emptied or how water pours from one to the other. She'll love watching how some toys float and others sink slowly to the bottom of the bath.

Even if your baby can sit unsupported, keep a light grip on his thigh, just in case he should slip.

BATH TOYS

Many household items can be adapted for bathtime. Babies love seeing water pour out of objects and this makes plastic fruit boxes with their air holes, ideal. Other good toys include measuring spoons, small watering cans, ice cube trays and colanders.

BATHING TIPS

● Never, ever, leave your baby alone in the bath. If you turn around, even for a moment, she could slip under the water and drown.

● Don't let the baby stand up in the bath without your support – she could fall.

● If your child starts to jump up and down – no doubt rejoicing in a newly found skill – be very firm about making her sit still; she could easily topple without your support.

● Cover up hot water taps with a cloth or towel so that she won't get scalded.

● Don't pour more hot water into the bath with the baby in it – she may get scalded.

● Don't see if she can sit unsupported. She could easily tumble under the water and get a bad fright – bad enough to go off bathing for a while.

● Don't pull the plug out when the baby's in the bath. She may be both frightened by the disappearing water and the noise.

● Don't dust your baby with talcum powder after a bath – it's very drying to the skin.

● If you're at work during the day, make the most of bathtime – it can be a great time to play and relax with your baby.

● Make sure that you pick your baby out of the bath with your back straight, taking the strain with your thighs.

Care of the hair

To prevent cradle cap from forming, wash your newborn's head every day with a soft bristle brush and a small amount of baby shampoo. To prevent scales from forming, you should comb through the hair, even if she has very little. If cradle cap does appear, smear a little baby oil on her scalp and wash it off the following morning. This will dissolve the scales, making them soft, loose and easy to wash away. Don't be tempted to pick them off with your fingers.

After about twelve to sixteen weeks, wash your baby's head with water every day and once or twice a week with baby shampoo. You can use either a football carry (if the baby is quite light) or you can sit on the edge of the bath with the baby across your legs, facing you. (This method is especially useful if she's scared of the water.) Make sure that you use a non-sting variety of baby shampoo, but still take care to avoid getting it near her eyes. Don't worry about the newborn's fontanelles. They are covered with a very sturdy membrane and you can do no harm if you are gentle. You need not scrub the hair. Modern detergents get dirt and oil off hair within seconds, so you just have to bring the shampoo to a lather, count to twenty, and then rinse it off again. One wash is quite enough to get your baby's hair clean.

To rinse your baby's hair, simply dip the towel into the basin of warm water and wipe it over her head. Try to get as much soap off as possible, but if your child is complaining, it won't hurt to leave slight traces on her hair. Dry your baby's head with the end of the towel, taking care not to cover her face or she will become very distressed and panicky.

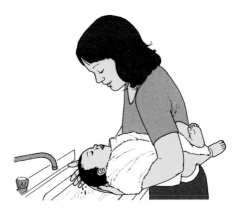

Pick up the baby in a football carry by tucking the legs under your armpit and supporting the baby's back along your arm. Fan out your fingers to cradle the baby's head. Wash the hair using mild, non-sting shampoo.

75

Care of the skin

A newborn's skin is too delicate for soap, which is a defatting agent. Since she needs to preserve all her natural oils, use only water for the first six weeks. Then, any soap will do. You may want to try a special liquid soap which is simply added to the bath water and needs no rinsing off. Make sure to wash folds and creases properly by running a soapy finger along them. Rinse well. Dry the skin thoroughly – moist creases may cause irritations. Never use powders.

Care of the eyes

When you wash your baby's eyes, squeeze two cotton wool balls in warm water. Use a different one to wash each closed eye, starting from the inner part of the eye and working to the outer.

Care of the nose and ears

Since the nose and ears are self-cleaning organs, you should never try to push anything up them or in them. Do not interfere with them in any way. Pushing something the size of a cotton bud up a baby's nose or into a baby's ears will only push whatever is there further in. It is much better to let whatever is in the nose come down naturally. Never put drops into the ears or nose except under a doctor's instructions (see p. 93). Never try to scrape wax out of a baby's ears, even though you can see it. Wax is a natural secretion of the skin lining the canal of the outer ear. It is antiseptic and prevents dust and grit from getting near the ear drum. Some babies make more wax than others. Removing it will cause the baby to pro-duce even more. Removing wax irritates the skin, so leave the wax alone and consult your doctor if you are concerned about it. Wash your baby's ears and nose with a soft washcloth (see p. 70).

Care of the nails

There is no need to cut a newborn baby's nails for about three or four weeks, unless your baby is scratching her skin. Nails are easiest to cut when they are soft, so have a pair of small, blunt-ended scissors nearby when you take your baby out of the bath. If you cut the fingernails and toenails im-mediately after a bath, you'll be able to finish the job in less than half a minute. If, however, you are worried about cutting your baby's nails, try doing it when your baby is asleep. Or bite them off yourself – your mouth will be sensitive to every move she makes and it will be impossible to hurt her.

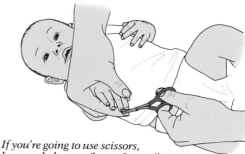

If you're going to use scissors, lay your baby on a flat surface, talk soothingly to her, and then gently cut the nails, following the shape of the fingertips.

Care of the navel

When your baby is born, you'll probably be advised to wipe the umbilical cord gently with surgical spirit and sterile cotton wool, and then to put sterile gauze over it. But you don't have to wait for the navel to heal before you give your baby a bath, so long as you dry the navel thoroughly afterwards.

Care of the genitals

You should never try to open the lips of your baby girl's vulva to clean inside; there is no need. Just wash the exterior of the diaper area (see p. 58), taking care to wipe from the front back towards the anus. This minimizes the risk of bacteria spreading from the bowels to the bladder, causing infection.

An uncircumcised baby boy should not have his foreskin pulled back for cleaning. Just wash the exterior of the diaper area as described above; the foreskin will retract naturally at about age four.

POSSIBLE PROBLEMS 0–1

Fear of undressing

Many young babies become extremely distressed when they are undressed. They hate the feeling of air on their bodies, preferring instead the security of being fully clothed or swaddled tightly. When your baby's very small you can get around this by giving sponge baths or by topping and tailing.

Fear of bathing

If your baby is absolutely terrified of having a bath, skip it for a couple of days and then try again, very gently, using only a little water in the bath. Until your baby is ready to go back into the bath, give sponge baths or top and tail.

If, after some time, she still doesn't like being bathed and remains frightened of water, try to overcome this fear by introducing an element of play. In a warm room (not the bathroom), spread out a towel beside a large plastic bowl full of water. Put some floatable toys and plastic containers into the bowl, undress your baby, and encourage her to play with the toys. She'll gradually get used to the idea of being near the water.

When she seems happy and confident, help your baby to paddle in the water. If your kitchen is warm, put a towel on the draining board, fill the sink with warm water, and let your baby dangle her feet while sitting on the towel. Make sure that you keep a firm grip on your baby with one hand while you play with toys and containers with the other, and that all the taps are wrapped in protective cloth.

Do this a couple of times, then swap the bowl or kitchen sink for a baby bath and let your baby play in the same way as before. You'll know she's overcome any fear when she struggles to get into the water with the toys. Let your baby do this twice before you turn it into an occasion for washing as well.

Fear of the big bath

Once your baby is splashing about and making a mess in the small baby bath, she is ready to go into a big bath. However, if your child is frightened of getting into a big bath, you'll have to build up to it gradually. Place the baby bath inside the big bath and put a towel or a rubber mat next to it so that she can't slip. Sit her in the big bath along with some toys and fill up the baby bath with warm water as usual. Then let her climb into the baby bath. Once she is happy doing this, pour a few inches of water into the big bath, leaving the towel or rubber mat in the bottom with all the toys, and the baby bath full of warm water. She should then climb in and out of the baby bath and quickly get used to sitting in the big bath in just a few inches of water. You can then increase the amount of water in the big bath, leaving the baby bath there until she is no longer interested in it. This will boost your baby's confidence, and make the transition fairly painless.

Dislike of hair washing

A baby who thoroughly enjoys having a bath may hate hair washing. She will probably develop this dislike when she is eight or nine months old. Even though you may be gentle and take every precaution to make sure that your child isn't frightened by hair washing, it may remain a problem until your child is of school age. It's therefore worth getting the technique right from the start.

☐ Young children hate to get water in their eyes, let alone soap, so do everything you can to keep your baby's face and eyes dry throughout the whole operation of hair washing.

☐ Never pour water over your child's head just to prove that it won't hurt. Few children under the age of six can stand this; if it's done suddenly they find it extremely unpleasant. Don't continue the washing operation if she screams or struggles and *never* forcibly hold your child so that you can get her hair washed. You may have an accident, like getting some soap into her eyes, which will make everything even worse. It will also make all future attempts to wash your child's hair very difficult for both of you.

☐ Once your child strenuously objects to hair washing, give up and don't try again for three or four weeks. Bathtime is generally happy for most children, so it is better to dissociate hair washing from bathtime if it's unpleasant. If you find bits of food in your child's hair, simply sponge them out or wait until they are dry before brushing them out with a soft, damp brush. It really doesn't matter if your child's hair is greasy; it will come to no harm.

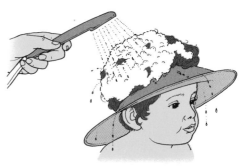

☐ Another way of keeping the water from your baby's face is to use a specially-designed headband. This fits like a halo around the hairline and allows you to rinse off any shampoo without getting soapy water all over your baby's face.

☐ You may find that your baby will let you wash her hair so long as she's being held by you. Sit with the baby on your lap next to a basin of warm water, and use a cloth to wet the baby's head before using a non-sting shampoo. So that no water gets onto the baby's face, rinse the water off with a damp washcloth, *not* by pouring water over the head. She won't be disturbed by this because she'll feel no water trickling over her head or body.

WASHING YOUR TODDLER

As your child gets older she will probably regard bathtime primarily as playtime. You should therefore keep bathtime as cheerful as possible – a pleasant moment of the day in which to relax before being put to bed. Encourage your child to wash herself by having a special sponge that she can use. Until she's developed adequate co-ordination, she won't make a perfect job of it, so be prepared to go over the same areas with another washcloth. Soap both your child's hands by holding a bar of soap between them, and show her how to spread the soap over her body and arms.

Daily routine

Most children need a wash in the morning, but it's probably best to postpone it until after breakfast. A child is often ravenously hungry when she wakes up, and you'll only have time to change the soggy diaper before food becomes imperative. After your child has eaten, she'll be more willing to sit still and to have face and hands washed, teeth brushed (see p. 201), and hair combed. By the time she's about one-and-a-half she'll be able to rinse both hands under water. With improved co-ordination, she'll learn to soap them. Do remember, though, that she will some-times forget the routine of hand washing: sleeves may not be rolled up, clothes may get wet, and soap may slip out of tiny fingers. Always be close by to lend a hand should she need it.

Hygiene

Start hygiene routines young and, where possible, teach by example. Washing before eating should become automatic, for example, from the day that your child starts to crawl and get her hands dirty. If you start by washing your hands with your child (and I mean *with*), by getting your hands soapy together and washing each other's hands, it can become fun. While teaching your child how to wash, you can make a game of blowing bubbles with the soap film that forms between your fore-finger and thumb when you make a circle. Afterwards, let your child inspect your hands, and then study hers.

Starting early makes it easier to apply hygienic rules later on. For example, hands should always be washed after going to the bathroom. But you should start at the "potty" stage and do it with your child every single time.

DAILY HYGIENE
Encourage your toddler to wash her hands from an early age. She may find it easier to rub both hands with a soapy washcloth.

If your child objects to washing her face, suggest that she use a sponge. This is both fun and much softer on the skin.

Give your child a soft toothbrush and encourage her to use it after meals, especially once the molars are through (see p. 202).

Handling pets requires special rules. Stop your child from kissing a pet, especially near its nose or mouth. Encourage washing after playing with the pet: it should be a rule not to touch food or eat anything after playing with a pet. If your pet gets worms of any kind, stop your child from playing with it until the problem is successfully treated. The same applies to any animal infestation, such as fleas or ticks.

POSSIBLE PROBLEMS 1–3

Fear of hair washing

If your child really hates having her hair washed, keep the hair very short so that it needs only sponging to keep it clean (see p. 78). One of the major reasons why children hate having their hair washed is that they're afraid of water going over their faces. To overcome this, you'll have to encourage your child to believe that neither hair washing nor rinsing will hurt.

☐ Make a game out of hair washing. It will be much more fun for your child if you join her in the bath and wash your hair, too. Rinse it with a plastic jug of water, acting as though it's great fun pouring water over your head.

☐ If you have an older child, you could prove that hair washing doesn't hurt by letting the younger one help you wash the elder's hair. Once you've lathered up the

shampoo, hold the frightened child and let her rub both her hands through the bubbles. When possible, get the younger child to help pour the rinsing water, too. Alternatively, wash a doll's hair in the bath with your toddler's assistance. Let your child help with the rinsing and then suggest that you do it to her hair. With any luck she'll consider it part of the game. Alternatively, encourage your child to wet her own hair with a washcloth and put a tiny bit of shampoo into both hands so that she can participate.

☐ An older child is also useful in proving that a wet face isn't unpleasant. For example, the elder child may well be proud of holding her breath under water; once your younger child is about three, she might want to join in with this game, even if it means only putting her nose and mouth under the surface for a count of five.

☐ Another way of getting your child used to water on her face is to take her swimming. Once she's used to splashing and getting her hair wet, you'll be able to start hair washing. This is especially easy if you take a shower after swimming. You can then gently and deftly introduce the idea of having a shampoo in the shower with a non-sting baby shampoo. A quick shampoo should take no longer than a couple of minutes. You can also use the shower attachment at home, encouraging the child to play with the spray, directing it up to her shoulders and eventually on to her hair and face. Once again, when she's used to wet hair, you can quickly shampoo and rinse it.

Fear of water

A few children hate water, and bathtime for them and their parents will be very distressing. The easiest way of overcoming this fear is to make bathtime as happy and relaxing as possible, with plenty of playtime included. Try to find out what is frightening your child. Is it the size of the bath? Is it the amount of water in it? Is it related to an incident, such as slipping and suddenly being ducked under the water? If it is the size of the bath that causes the

worry, introduce alternatives, such as the kitchen sink or a large washing-up bowl. Your child will probably sit quite happily on a towel on the draining board, playing and dipping her feet into the water (see p. 77). This should also help if she's scared of the volume of water. Also helpful is playing with a shower attachment or a garden hose (as long as the water is coming out gently).

Ironically, swimming can be used to overcome your child's fear of water, although you'll have to introduce her to it slowly. If you can, take advantage of swimming classes which allow you to join your child in the water and do most of the teaching (with help from an instructor if you need it). Being able to swim may save your child's life. You should try to make sure that she can swim before she goes to school.

7 Feeding

Remember that the first principle of infant feeding is to *feed the infant*. Breast-feeding is undoubtedly best for your baby, but if you can't or don't – for whatever reason – you will have to bottle-feed her. Don't feel guilty if you make this decision. Concentrate on the needs of your baby. The love and affection you give her are at least as important as your method of nursing. The important rule is to take your lead from your child. So long as you offer a wide variety of foods she doesn't have to have "essential" foods every day. Remember, above all, that nursing and feeding should be a pleasure.

NUTRITIONAL REQUIREMENTS   0–1

A baby's growth is more rapid during the first six months than at any other time during her life. The majority of babies double their birth weight in about four months and triple it by the time they are one year old. All parts of the body develop quickly and gain tremendously in size. Your baby may grow from 20 to 30 inches during the year, and her nutritional needs will change accordingly.

In order to grow, your baby needs to take food; for your baby to be healthy that food has to contain adequate supplies of protein, vitamins, carbohydrates and minerals, whatever age she is. Until she's at least four months old your baby will receive these supplies in the form of milk. After this, when she's started on a solid diet, you will provide her with all she needs if you give her a sensible, well-balanced diet.

Calories

The energy needed to perform all bodily functions comes from food. The energy content of food is usually expressed in calories, and in an infant the calorie requirements are about two-and-a-half to three times those of an adult. During the first six months, slightly more than 50 calories per pound are needed every day. From six months to one year, slightly less than 50 calories per pound are required.

A baby weighing seven pounds at birth will therefore need in the region of 570 calories a day. If the same baby doubles its weight in six months, to 14 pounds, she will need 740 calories a day. At 12 months, if the baby has tripled its birth weight, she will need about 1000 calories a day.

Protein

Most of the protein a baby takes in is used for growth. The protein requirements during the first 12 months are correspondingly higher than at any other time of life; they are three times as great as those for adults. Milk, as long as it is given in adequate amounts, provides all the protein that a newborn infant needs.

Vitamins

Breast milk is short of nothing except vitamin D. The main source of this vitamin is the sun, which stimulates the skin to manufacture it. If you live in a sunless climate, or if your child has very dark skin, you may need to give vitamin D supplements; ask your doctor for advice. If you bottle-feed your baby, all vitamin requirements will be satisfied by the formula.

Minerals

The rapid growth of bone and muscle during the first year means that babies have a greater need than adults for minerals like calcium, phosphorous and magnesium. All babies are born with a supply of iron that will last for up to four months; after this, iron has to be added to the diet, usually in the form of solids, but possibly as iron supplements. Breast milk and cow's milk are both pretty low on iron; formula milk usually has iron added to it, but once again you should check the ingredients.

Trace elements

Your baby needs traces of certain minerals like zinc, copper and fluoride. The first two are present in both breast and formula milk. Fluoride, however, is not. Since infants need fluoride to protect them against dental decay in infancy and childhood, you should check with your nurse or doctor about giving your baby a fluoride supplement (of about 0.5 milligrams per day). You can give it as drops until your baby is old enough to take a tablet each morning (incidentally, it is to better to chew tablets, since this will coat teeth with fluoride and aid in their protection). If fluoride is added to the drinking water in your area you won't have to give fluoride supplements to your children. If in doubt, contact your water authority.

Fats

The body needs minute traces of fatty acids for growth and repair. The fat content of both breast and formula milk is about the same, but in human milk the droplets of fat are smaller and therefore more digestible.

Carbohydrates

These are major energy providers. Both breast and formula milk contain the same carbohydrates, although the carbohydrate level is slightly higher in breast milk.

BREAST-FEEDING   0–1

Human breast milk is tailor-made for a baby: it contains just the right amount of protein, carbohydrates, minerals and vitamins to sustain her growth. Don't be put off by the bluish, watery appearance, or worry that it can't possibly be "good enough" because it's not as creamy as cow's milk: your milk is rich in every foodstuff that your baby needs.

Apart from its nutritional worth, breast-feeding makes sound sense for the following reasons:

☐ Breast-fed babies are less prone to illness than bottle-fed babies. Antibodies which babies receive through breast milk result in fewer cases of gastroenteritis, chest infection, and measles. All babies receive some antibodies from their mother's placental blood, via the umbilical cord, but these are supplemented by antibodies in both the colostrum (see p. 86) and the mother's milk. In your baby's first few days of life, these antibodies exert a protective influence on the intestine, reducing the likelihood of intestinal disturbance. Because they are also absorbed into the bloodstream, they form part of the body's protection against infections. Some antibodies, such as those that protect against poliomyelitis, are in the breast milk, so the mother can actively protect her newborn while she is breast-feeding. She does, however, have to repeat this immunization when the baby is three- to nine-months old.

☐ Breast milk is more easily, and quickly, digested than cow's milk. Breast-fed babies don't get constipated. If they pass stools infrequently, it is because the food is so efficiently and completely used up. Their stools are always soft and comparatively odorless, and don't contain the bacteria which generally cause ammonia dermatitis, so your baby is less prone to diaper rash.

☐ Breast-fed babies rarely become overweight. Each baby has its own appetite and metabolic rate, so don't worry if your baby is fatter or thinner than your neighbor's. She'll be the right weight for her own body.

☐ Breast-feeding is the most convenient method. The milk is always at the right temperature, you don't have to waste your time sterilizing bottles and making up formula, and you save money by not having to buy all the equipment. Breast-fed babies have less wind and sleep longer. They spit up less, and the milk they spit up smells less unpleasant.

☐ Breast-feeding is good for your figure. Research has shown that most of the fat that is gained in pregnancy is shed if a woman breast-feeds. During breast-feeding a hormone called oxytocin is released which encourages the uterus to return to its normal size, as well as stimulating the production of milk (see p. 86). Your pelvis returns to normal more quickly and so does your waistline. Contrary to popular belief, breast-feeding does not affect the shape or size of your breasts. Breasts may get bigger, smaller, or sag after pregnancy, but none of these changes is contingent upon breast-feeding: they are due to being pregnant.

☐ Breast cancer is rarer in parts of the world where breast-feeding is traditional. Breast-feeding may provide some protection against the disease.

☐ If you breast-feed your baby, your body will respond by producing the hormone prolactin, which activates the production of milk. It also suppresses ovulation. Although it is unlikely that you will conceive while breast-feeding, you should *never* rely on this as a means of contraception. See your doctor for advice.

Supply and demand

All mothers are anatomically equipped to feed their babies. There is no such thing as mother's milk which is unsuitable: the milk that the breasts produce is the baby's natural food and she will not reject it. Nor is there such a thing as a mother physically incapable of feeding her baby: the size of your breasts bears no relation to the amount of milk you can produce. Milk is

produced in deeply buried glands, not in the fatty tissue of the breasts, so don't worry if your breasts are rather small: they *are* adequate. The actual amount of milk that you produce is dependent on how much your baby takes, hence the expression supply and demand. If your baby's appetite is not very great, for example, then your breasts will not produce very much milk because they're not being stimulated by your baby to do so. If your baby is an eager feeder, however, your breasts will respond and produce more. The amount of milk available for your baby will fluctuate throughout the whole time that you breast-feed, according to how much your baby takes. Even if your baby is hungry half an hour after being fed, don't worry. Your breasts will have produced some milk for your baby to feed on, and they'll soon build up a supply for her new needs. When the need for more milk slows down, the breasts will correspondingly produce less.

A newborn baby requires between two and three fluid ounces of milk per pound of body weight, so a seven pound baby will need between 14 and 21 fluid ounces per day. Your breasts can manufacture one-and-a-half to two fluid ounces of milk in three hours, in each breast, so your daily output of 24 to 32 ounces is ample.

Preparing to breast-feed

You should decide whether or not to breast-feed your baby well before delivery so that you can prepare and plan for it. At one time women were advised to harden their nipples by, among other things, rolling them between their fingertips or even scrubbing them with a nail brush. This is no longer considered essential. The only time you have to take special action is if you have an inverted nipple. In such cases the nipple is completely flat, so the baby has nothing to hold on to. This condition is quite rare, but if you do have an inverted nipple you can wear breast shells to make the nipples protrude more. Most women, no matter how small their nipples, are perfectly able to feed their babies.

If you are having your baby in a hospital, tell the nursing staff that you intend to breast-feed as soon as you are admitted. Be very firm about asking for help from them. Don't be intimidated by busy nurses who seem to have no time for you. Demand to see the staff nurse or sister if necessary. Ask her to sit with you for an entire nursing and to give a running commentary on what you should or shouldn't be doing. The best way to learn is to have someone who knows a lot about breast-feeding watching and encouraging you. In the small families that we have today, very few girls see babies being breast-fed.

The first contact

It's good for both you and your baby if you try nursing as soon as the baby is born. If you are in a hospital, ask for the baby to be put to your breast in the delivery room. There are two important reasons for doing so: first, nursing naturally stimulates the production of oxytocin, a hormone which, among other things (see p. 85), makes the uterus contract and expel the placenta soon after birth; and second, nursing helps to form a very strong bond between mother and baby immediately after birth. Incidentally, you needn't worry about your baby choking. The natural reflex to suck is very strong, and she is able to swallow at birth.

Colostrum

During the 72 hours after delivery the breasts don't produce milk. Instead, they manufacture a thin, yellow fluid called colostrum. This consists of water, protein and minerals and it takes care of all your baby's nutritional needs during the first days of life before the milk comes in. Colostrum also contains invaluable antibodies which protect the baby against intestinal and respiratory infections, and diseases like polio and influenza. It has an additional laxative effect which stimulates the excretion of meconium (see p. 15). Your baby should be put regularly to the breast in the first days, both to feed on the colostrum and to get used to fixing on the breast (see p. 88). If you're in a hospital where they have "rooming in" (where the baby is left with the mother all the time), and where they actually encourage demand feeding (see p. 85), so much the better. Whenever she cries, you can put her to either breast, but for only a couple of minutes at first, so that the nipples don't get sore. If your baby is automatically put into the hospital nursery, tell the staff that you want your baby brought to you for feeding and that she's not to be bottle-fed.

The let-down reflex

When your baby nurses at the breast, the pituitary gland in the brain is stimulated to release two hormones: prolactin and oxytocin. Prolactin activates the actual manufacture of milk in the milk glands; oxytocin is responsible for passing the milk from the milk glands to the milk reservoirs behind the areola. This process happens within seconds and is known as the let-down or draught reflex. You may feel this reflex very powerfully: in fact, the very sight or sound of your baby may trigger it off, and milk may actually shoot out of your nipples in anticipation of feeding.

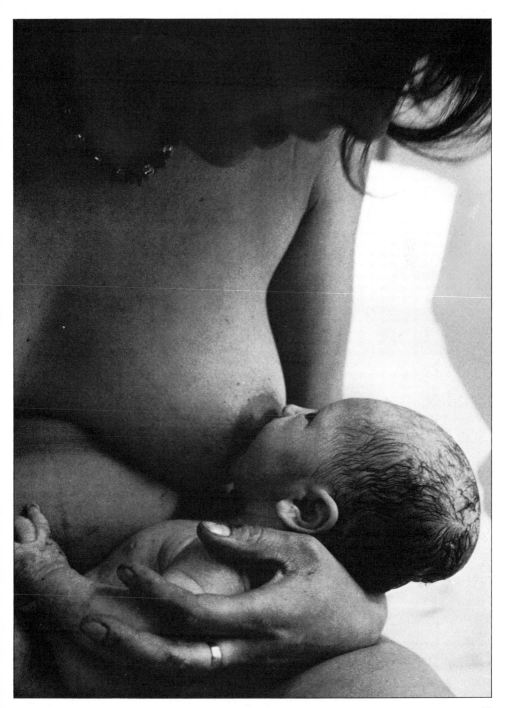

How to hold the baby

Cradle your baby in your arm, with the head in the crook of your elbow, and her back and bottom supported by your hand. Never bend or strain forward to lower the nipple into your baby's mouth. If she's too far away from the nipple when held in your arm, try laying her on a pillow on your lap, still supporting the head in the crook of your arm. Alternatively, cross your legs and use your knee as a prop for the arm that's holding the baby. Leave her arm free to touch your breast – she'll enjoy the sensation of your being warm and close.

The rooting reflex

The first few times you put your baby to the breast she may need some encouragement and help to actually find the nipple. Cradle your baby in your arms and gently stroke the cheek nearest the breast. This will elicit the rooting reflex. Your baby will immediately turn towards your breast, mouth open and ready. If you put your nipple in now, she will happily clamp both lips around the areola and settle down to nurse. Many babies lick the nipple before they take it into their mouths. It sometimes helps to express some colostrum as an added incentive.

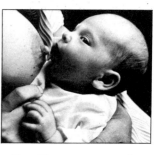

So that your baby turns to your breast, gently stroke the cheek nearest to you.

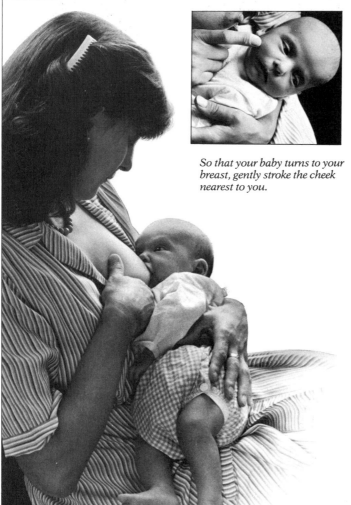

She will turn to your touch, open-mouthed, searching for your nipple.

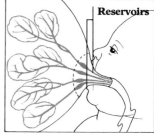

Cradled in your arm, mouth surrounding the areola, your baby settles down to nurse. As you can see (above), your baby squeezes down on the reservoirs while sucking so that the nipple elongates and milk comes out.

After a few days your baby will need no artificial stimulation and will happily turn and latch on to the breast as soon as she is picked up and held close to your body.

Never try to guide your baby's head to the nipple by holding both your baby's cheeks between your fingers, or by squeezing the mouth open. The baby will become very confused by the conflicting stimuli of both cheeks being touched and will turn from side to side in a desperate bid to find the nipple.

Putting the baby to the breast

Each time you put your baby to the breast (also called "fixing") try to get your nipple well inside the baby's mouth. This is important for two reasons. First, unless she takes a good proportion of the areola into the mouth, the milk will not be successfully sucked from your breast. (Your baby extracts milk from the breast in a kind of chomping, sucking motion: the baby's mouth forms a seal around the areola, and, as she sucks, the tongue pushes the nipple up against the roof of the mouth. The milk is then drawn out in a rhythmic combination of sucking and squeezing. It can only be done successfully if the baby can exert pressure on the milk ducts behind the areola.) Second, if you position the nipple well into the baby's mouth, you minimize the chances of developing sore or cracked nipples (see p. 98). Your baby has a very strong sucking action and if only the nipple is in her mouth she will effectively shut off the openings of the milk ducts and little milk will get out. Your nipples will become extremely sore and your milk supply will eventually be reduced because the milk is not being drawn out (see p. 85). The baby will quite naturally become frustrated and bad-tempered with hunger.

Bonding

Once your baby is happily sucking at your breast, settle down and *look* at her. If her eyes are open, make eye contact. Smile, talk and chat softly while she is feeding so that she associates the pleasure of feeding with the sight of your face, the sound of your voice and the smell of your skin.

BREAST-FEEDING TIPS

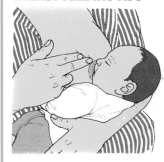

● If your let-down reflex is too efficient, you may find that your milk pours out too quickly and chokes the baby as soon as she sucks. You can slow the flow down by expressing a little milk first (see p. 96). If you have a lot of milk, reduce the flow by applying pressure above and below the areola.

● Your baby must be free to breathe while she feeds. If you have very large or full breasts, or if there is any risk of smothering the baby, gently pull your breast back from the baby's face, just above the areola.

● If milk is gushing out of the breast that's not being used for feeding, press the heel or palm of your hand over the areola. This should stop it.

How long on each breast

Your baby's sucking will be strongest in thefirst five minutes, when she will take 80 per cent of the feed. As a general rule, keep your baby on the breast for as long as she shows interest in sucking, but not usually longer than ten minutes or so on each breast. Your breast will probably have emptied by this time, and your baby may just be enjoying the sensation of sucking. You'll find that your baby will lose interest in her own individual way: it may be that she starts to play with your breast, slipping her mouth on and off the nipple; or she may turn away or fall asleep. When she appears to have had enough of one breast, gently take the baby off your nipple (see right) and put her on to the other breast. If your baby falls asleep after feeding from both breasts, she's probably had enough: you'll soon learn whether she's going to wake, hungry again, after ten minutes or so. Similarly, if your baby appears to have taken all she wants from just one breast, don't worry. You can begin the next feed on the breast she didn't drink from.

Removing the baby from the breast

Never pull your baby off the breast – you'll only hurt your nipple. To remove the baby, loosen her mouth by pressing gently but firmly on her chin. Alternatively, slip your finger down between the areola and your baby's cheek and put your little finger into the corner of the baby's mouth. Both these techniques will make her mouth open and allow your breast to slip out easily, instead of being dragged off by suction. This is very important during the first few days, because the nipple is rather soft and needs a chance to harden.

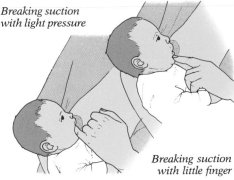

Breaking suction with light pressure

Breaking suction with little finger

WHAT TO WEAR TO BREAST-FEED

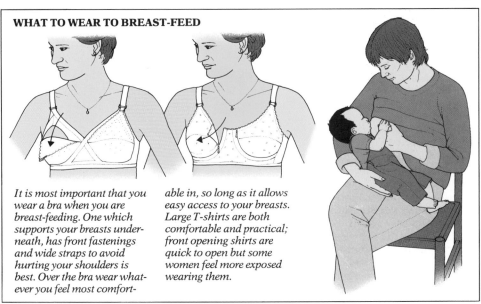

It is most important that you wear a bra when you are breast-feeding. One which supports your breasts underneath, has front fastenings and wide straps to avoid hurting your shoulders is best. Over the bra wear whatever you feel most comfort-able in, so long as it allows easy access to your breasts. Large T-shirts are both comfortable and practical; front opening shirts are quick to open but some women feel more exposed wearing them.

Breast-feeding positions

You can feed your baby in whatever position you choose, so long as your baby can fix on to the nipple and so long as you are comfortable and relaxed. Some of the most popular methods are shown right. Experiment with them and use whichever feels most natural. Try to change positions throughout the day – this will ensure that your baby exerts pressure on more than one part of the areola, and also minimizes the risk of a blocked milk duct.

If you are going to sit down to feed your baby, make sure that you're in a comfortable position, with your arms and back supported with cushions or pillows if necessary.

It's also quite nice to lie in bed to feed your baby, especially in the first few weeks and at night. There's no reason why you shouldn't do this. Lie on your side, propped with pillows if that's more comfortable, and gently cradle the baby's head and body alongside you. You may need to lay a small baby on a pillow so that she's at the right height for your nipple, but a larger baby should be able to lie on the bed next to you. Make sure that the muscles under your arm aren't strained or taut, as this will slow down the flow of milk. An alternative method is to lay your baby on a pillow under your arm, with her feet tucked behind you. Your hand can support your baby's head as she faces your breast.

The position you choose initially may be affected by the type of delivery you have. If you've had an episiotomy, for example, you'll probably find it extremely uncomfortable sitting down, so any position that lets you lie on your side will be more suitable. Similarly, if you've had a Caesarian section your stomach may be too tender for your baby to lie on, so try the position with your baby's feet tucked under your arm. Alternatively, use the position with your baby lying on the bed alongside you.

Sitting position in low nursing chair

Sitting position with back propped against furniture

Lying position with baby alongside

Lying position with baby propped

Ensuring a good milk supply

☐ Rest as much as you can, particularly during the first weeks. In your condition, you should sit rather than stand, and lie rather than sit.

☐ Tenseness will affect your milk flow, so go through your pre-natal relaxation routines and make sure that you have a period to yourself every day when you can lie down.

☐ Go to bed as early as you can. You will be quite tired anyway and your sleep patterns will probably be broken by your baby.

☐ As far as the house is concerned, let the housework go, or get the rest of the family to do the work for you. Don't do anything but the most urgent things.

☐ Whenever you can, give yourself a few treats; feel free to relax with a glass of wine at the end of the day.

☐ Make sure your diet is well-balanced and sufficiently rich in protein. Don't eat a lot of highly refined and processed carbohydrates (cakes, biscuits, sweets, chocolates, etc.).

☐ You may need some iron supplements and possibly some vitamin supplements, so ask your doctor about this.

☐ Drink about six pints of fluid every day while you are breast-feeding. Some women even need a drink while they are feeding, so keep one by you, if necessary.

☐ Most of your milk is produced in the morning, when you are rested. If you constantly rush about or become tense during the day, you'll find that by evening your supply is poor.

☐ If your baby doesn't take all the milk available in the early feeds of the day express the remainder off. This will ensure that the supply continues throughout the day.

☐ Get help and support from everyone around you who is positive and optimistic. Use your nurse or doctor; speak to friends who have had babies and get reassuring advice from them.

☐ If you are unable to nurse your baby because you're away or because you're ill, express the milk off to keep the supply going.

☐ Avoid using contraceptive pills for the first five months after delivery, as they decrease the supply of milk. Discuss alternative methods with your doctor.

Frequency of feeds

Babies need frequent feeding because of their body size. Breast-fed babies may need to be nursed more than bottle-fed babies because they absorb their milk more quickly.

Babies should be fed on demand (see p. 85). Parents will quickly learn to recognize the cries that mean their baby is hungry (see p. 155). Newborn babies may need to be fed every two hours, with as many as eight to ten feedings a day. After about one month, babies are usually taking food every three hours; at two to three months, approximately every four hours. Every baby is different, however, because each has its own needs and appetites.

By the time they are three months old, most babies sleep through the night after their late evening feed, but don't even consider dropping the night feed until your baby indicates her willingness by sleeping through.

FREQUENCY OF FEEDS

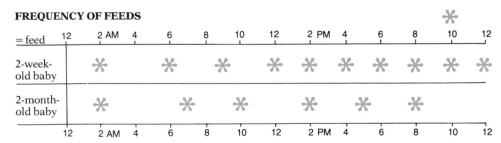

Supplementary bottles

Even though you may be committed to breast feeding, there are occasions when you may have to give supplementary bottles; for example, if you have a very sore nipple or a blocked duct (see p. 98). If this does occur, feed your baby from the unaffected breast first to satisfy some of the hunger, and then give the bottle. You will also have to use supplementary bottles if there is any risk of the baby being underfed (see p. 95) – though if you're breast feeding, this is highly unlikely.

Whenever you have to give a bottle, make sure you sterilize all the equipment and prepare the formula according to the instructions given on page 99. The amount of formula you should use will be specified on the container, according to your baby's weight.

There are certain disadvantages in using supplementary bottles. Babies used to a mother's nipple tend to dislike plastic ones. Unfortunately, if she rejects the bottle you won't know if she just dislikes the nipple, or if she's not hungry. If you persist, however, she'll eventually get used

> **STAND-BY FEEDING EQUIPMENT**
>
> ● Large plastic container with lid
> ● Two plastic 8 oz bottles
> ● Two shaped nipples
> ● Sterilizing tablets

to the bottle, especially if she's hungry. By this time she may not want to go back to the breast, since it requires less effort to get milk from the bottle.

Relief bottles

These are bottles of your own expressed milk which can be given to your baby when you are ill, extremely tired, or leaving the baby with someone else. Expressed milk can be frozen and kept for up to six months (see p. 96).

POSSIBLE PROBLEMS   0-1

All will probably go without a hitch from the beginning, but you should be prepared to be a bit clumsy at first. Your baby may not suck very vigorously or very long during the first 24 to 36 hours, and your breasts maybe a bit sore.

Refusing the breast

One of the most common reasons why a baby has problems taking the breast is that she has difficulty breathing. Your baby can't breathe through her nose and swallow at the same time, so make sure that your breast is not covering her nostrils (see p. 88). Your baby may also have trouble breathing because she has the sniffles or a stuffed nose. Your doctor can prescribe nose drops which should be used to clear the nostrils before every feeding.

Your baby may be reluctant to take the breast if there was a delay in breast-

feeding after birth. The sooner you start the better – both for you and the baby. Babies learn to take the breast quickly during the first 48 hours but find it increasingly difficult as time passes. This does not mean that your baby will never take to the breast; it just means that you will have to be patient and persevering. If your baby is premature, for example, you can ask the hospital to give her your expressed milk and when you get home, introduce the breast.

If your breast is engorged (a) as opposed to just being full (b), your baby won't be able to latch on successfully, so gently express some milk before feeding.

a   b

93

Another reason your baby may refuse to take the breast is that she's fretful. If she's woken up anxious to nurse, only to find that she's ignored, fussed over, or changed, she may be too distressed to take your breast. If this happens, you'll have to hold her firmly and talk soothingly to her, not even trying to nurse her until she's calmed down.

Babies that love to nurse

Many babies find sucking on their mother's breast the most pleasant experience of the day. You'll soon learn to distinguish between sucking for food and sucking for comfort. While nursing, you may see and feel your baby making strong, rhythmic sucking movements – look closely, though, and you'll notice that she isn't swallowing. There's no reason why your baby shouldn't suck as long as she wants, so long as you're happy and your nipples aren't sore.

Sleeping through feeds

During the first few days your baby may not be all that interested in feeding. Don't be put off. Continue to try nursing her for about five minutes on each breast, at each feeding. If your baby goes to sleep at the breast, don't worry. It's a good sign that she's contented and doing well. She won't come to any harm if she sleeps through a feeding and will make up for it the next time.

Don't stick to a rigid routine. If your baby sleeps through a feeding, wait for half an hour and then wake her up gently and offer her your breast. If she wants to go on sleeping, let her: just nurse her when she wakes. If she's hungry, she'll perk up when food is offered.

Startled babies

Most babies are easily startled during their first few weeks. When you pick your baby up to nurse her, hold her firmly and talk soothingly all the time. Lower your head toward her so your face and eyes are all that she sees and concentrates on. Make sure there are no disturbing noises.

Whenever possible, pick your baby up *before* she starts to cry with hunger.

Biting

This is a natural impulse, and your baby may well bite you even before her teeth have come in. When it happens, you will automatically jerk back and may even let out a cry. Your baby will be startled by this. If you say "NO," quite firmly but without shouting, she will soon learn not to do it – even at a very early age.

If you become ill

So long as you feel like breast-feeding you should continue to do so – even if you have to be hospitalized. You may have to make special arrangements with the nursing staff, but if this is what you want, you should argue firmly for it and not be dissuaded. However, if you have to have an anaesthetic you will not be able to breast-feed – not only will you be too groggy afterwards, but the drugs you take will pass into your milk. If you have an advance warning of an operation, try to express and freeze your milk, so that your baby will not miss it, even though she may miss the pleasure of having you nurse her.

If you are merely confined to bed with a bad cold or 'flu, you can still express your milk so that your partner can feed the baby when you feel too weak or tired. If you are too ill even to express your milk, however, your baby will have to be given formula milk by bottle or by spoon. She'll probably protest at first but will acquiesce the hungrier she becomes.

Anxiousness on your part

If you meet a minor obstacle such as your baby's refusal to be nursed, try not to get worked up about it. Nervousness may create more difficulties, which will discourage you even further and turn you away from breast-feeding. Nervousness may also affect your milk. Don't see breast-feeding as a race you have to win. As far as your baby's health is concerned, even a few days of colostrum and breast milk give her a good start to life, and are better than none at all. Never get worried about your baby going without food – you can always fall back on bottle-feeding. Don't let small problems lead to hasty decisions. Mothers are easily upset during the first few weeks after delivery, and it would be a mistake to give up breast-feeding when you are in this rather unsettled state. Try and persevere and ask your nurse or doctor for advice and suggestions.

If you are worried about breast-feeding, make it as easy on yourself as you can. If it embarrasses you, make sure you are not in a public place at nursing time. Don't invite visitors to the house unless you're prepared to nurse your baby in front of them, should the infant want food in a hurry.

Overfeeding

You cannot overfeed a breast-fed baby. She regulates how much she wants (see p. 85), so unless you give something other than breast milk (like improperly prepared supplementary bottles), her weight will be correct.

Underfeeding

Although it is highly unlikely, it is possible to underfeed a breast-fed baby. The first sign of this will probably be her desire to continue sucking, even though she's finished feeding from both breasts. The problem is that this doesn't always signify hunger; it could mean that your child is thirsty or simply likes sucking. After nursing her, therefore, try giving her about an ounce of cooled, boiled water (from a sterilized spoon), in case she is thirsty. If she's still fretful or crying, go to your doctor or clinic to have her weighed. If she has not gained weight as quickly as expected, you'll know that you haven't been producing enough milk. This can happen if you overexert yourself and get tired and run down. You can rebuild your milk supply (see p. 92), but it may take a few weeks to get full milk production, and in the meantime you may have to give supplementary bottles (see p. 93). If you are at all worried, contact your doctor.

CARE OF THE BREASTS   0–1

Take good care of your breasts – they are going to be working quite hard for the next few months! The first step is to buy yourself a few of the best maternity bras that you can afford. Ask the assistant to measure you and to make sure the bra gives you good support both below your breasts and on your shoulders. The drop-front kind (see p. 90), is very good because it makes feeding quick, convenient and hygienic and your breasts are never left to sag. Toward the end of the first week, when lactation becomes well established, your breasts may be so full of milk that they become full, sore, hard, and tender to the touch. A good bra will minimize discomfort; so will expressing (see p. 96).

Pay attention to the daily hygiene of your breasts and nipples. Cleanse them every day with water or baby lotion. Don't use soap because it dries to the skin and can aggravate a sore or cracked nipple. Always handle your breasts carefully; pat them dry gently after both feeding and washing. Leave your nipples open to the air whenever you can: continue to wear your bra for support, but leave the front flaps down. Use a spray or cream on your nipples if you find that it helps.

Once the milk really starts to flow, quite a lot may leak out during the day. Put breast pads or clean handkerchiefs inside your bra to soak up the leaking milk. Change the pad frequently for cleanliness.

Expressing milk

There is no need to feel tied down with breast-feeding, since you can express milk from your breasts and keep it either in sterile containers in the refrigerator or in the freezer. This will enable your partner or baby sitter to feed the baby your own milk in your absence.

You can express milk from your breasts with your hands or with a breast pump. Most women find hand expression easier and more convenient than a pump. Before you start, get a bowl, a funnel and a container that can be sealed, and sterilize all of them, either in a sterilizing solution or in boiling water. Hand expressing is almost always a bit difficult during the first six weeks, as the breasts have not reached full production. But do persevere! The best times to express milk are in the morning, when you have the most milk, and in the evening, after your baby has finished her night feeding. You should be able to get one or two ounces without too much trouble then. If your baby is premature, you'll need to express your milk at least four times a day to maintain your milk supply.

EXPRESSING TIPS

● Expressing can be quite back-breaking if you have to lean over a low surface. If you haven't got a high enough table or work surface, put the container on a pile of books.

● Expressing milk should never hurt. If it does, you're not doing it correctly; stop immediately.

● Every piece of equipment and all containers should be sterile; your hands must be clean.

● If you're worried about your baby not going back to breast-feeding once she gets used to the bottle, try feeding the expressed milk from a cup, with a spoon. Both should be sterilized before use.

● Milk must be stored correctly, otherwise it will go bad just as bottled milk. Feeding your baby this milk will make her ill. As soon as you've collected your milk, put it straight into the refrigerator until it's needed; it will keep for 48 hours. You can also freeze expressed milk for up to six months. Put it into sterile plastic containers which can be sealed. Don't use glass – it might crack.

EXPRESSING BY HAND

1 *Wash your hands. Cup your breast in both hands with the fingers underneath and the thumb encircling the breast above.*

2 *Squeeze the outer part of your breast between your fingers and thumbs, gently and firmly. Repeat this ten times, moving around the breast as you do.*

3 *Repeat the squeezing movement ten times between the outer part of your breast and the nipple area. This stimulates the flow of milk down the ducts to the milk reservoirs in the areola.*

EXPRESSING BY PUMP

Bulb pump

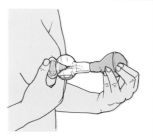

1 *Place the opening firmly over your nipple to form an airtight seal.*

2 *Squeeze the bulb rhythmically until the milk comes out to fill the reservoir. Empty the bulb when the reservoir fills and start again.*

Syringe pump

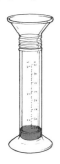

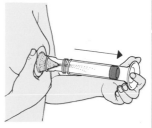

1 *Assemble the cylinders according to the instructions and place the opening firmly over the nipple to form an airtight seal.*

2 *Hold the end against your breast and gently pull the cylinder away from you with a downward movement.*

4 *While holding your breast in one hand, place the tips of your thumb and forefinger on either side of the areola.*

5 *Press your thumb and fingers back into your ribs, then squeeze them together gently and rhythmically. If milk doesn't flow immediately keep on trying.*

6 *Move your hand around the areola, so that all parts are compressed, and keep going for five minutes or so. Repeat on the other breast, then go back to the first and repeat the whole procedure.*

Sore nipples

The new stimulation of your nipples by your baby may make your nipples sore, especially if you are very fair-skinned. However, you can minimize soreness by always making sure the baby has the nipple and areola well into her mouth, always taking the baby off gently, and keeping your nipples as dry as possible between feedings.

If you notice that a nipple is becoming sore, give that breast a rest from feeding for 24 hours or until the soreness has gone, and avoid comfort sucks. Feed your baby from the other breast and express milk from the affected one. Smear some cetrimide cream on the sore nipple two or three times a day to prevent the nipple from becoming cracked. You could also try using a nipple shield when you feed your baby. Made of soft rubber, it fits over your nipple but allows the baby to suck through a small rubber nipple on the front. It should be kept in a sterilizing solution before use.

If you suddenly experience a sharp pain in your nipple as you put your baby to the breast, your nipple is probably cracked. This happens when a sore nipple is not properly treated.

BREAST PROBLEMS

	Description	Prevention	Cure
Cracked nipples	Shooting pain when the baby is feeding.	Feed little and often in the first days. Keep the nipples dry by using disposable breast pads or clean hankies.	Don't feed from the affected breast until the crack heals. Express the milk by hand (not by pump), and feed the baby by bottle or by spoon.
Engorgement	Extremely full and painful breasts with a swollen areola.	Feed your baby frequently and try to encourage her to empty your breasts regularly.	Have a hot bath and gently express some milk, or encourage it to flow by massaging toward the nipple.
Blocked duct	A hard red patch on the outside of the breast where the duct lies. This can often occur as a result of engorgement, or when your bra or clothes are too tight.	The same as for engorgement. Wear a properly fitting bra and feed the baby in different positions throughout the day.	Frequent feeding, offering the breast with the blocked duct first so that it is properly emptied. Express the breast if necessary.
Mastitis	Acute infection of the milk ducts resulting in a pus-filled lump.	(The same as for a blocked duct.)	Antibiotics prescribed by your doctor. If this fails breast will have to be drained surgically. You can, however, continue to nurse, even if you need an operation.
Breast abscesses	This infection, which results from an untreated blocked duct, often makes you feel feverish, as if you're coming down with 'flu; you may have a shiny red patch on your breast.	(The same as for a blocked duct.)	The same as for a blocked duct, although your doctor will probably prescribe antibiotics. Unless instructed otherwise, you can continue to feed your baby from the affected breast.

BOTTLE-FEEDING   0–1

Once you make the decision to bottle-feed, stick to it and don't feel guilty about it. The majority of babies are bottle-fed – including those who started out on the breast – and they are just as happy and well-fed as infants who are breast-fed. Just make sure your child gets the same attention and closeness at feeding times that she would get if you were breast-feeding. If you decide not to breast-feed, you will probably need to have your milk suppressed by hormones.

Mother's milk is important to your baby, but it is not as important as your love. Fill the hours you spend with your baby, particularly feeding times, with your love, affection and care. These are just as important to your baby's physical and emotional well-being as your milk.

Many women feel pressure to breast-feed their babies, and worry quite a lot if they decide not to – but there are several good reasons for deciding that breast-feeding is not for you. Despite your best efforts, you may simply not be successful at it. In that case, the best thing is to forget about it and concentrate on giving your baby a good bottle-fed diet: she will do just as well. Other women find it emotionally or psychologically difficult. Some feel that a breast-feeding routine will tie them down and curtail many of their activities, including return to work. Some couples are opposed to breast-feeding because it excludes the father.

One of the good things about bottle-feeding is that the new father can be just as involved as the mother at feeding times. Make sure that your partner feeds the baby very soon after you get home from the hospital, so that he gets used to the technique and isn't afraid to handle the baby. The sooner the better. If possible, your partner should share the feeding equally with you. If not, he should give at least two of the six feedings a day.

Choosing the bottles

You should choose unbreakable bottles which have a wide neck so that they're easy to fill and to clean; the 8 oz size is most suitable. The nipple should ideally be shaped to fit the baby's mouth. Disposable bottles are useful for travelling, and for when you accidentally run out of sterilized bottles.

Sterilizing the bottles

Buy your feeding equipment well in advance of having your baby so that you can practise with it before going into the hospital. Major department stores and chemists sell bottle-feeding packs which contain all the essential equipment.

Keep your sterilizing equipment in the kitchen, preferably near the sink. You'll soon develop your own routine of sterilizing and making up bottles, but I'd suggest that you always sterilize and make up a full batch (see p. 100), and keep it in the refrigerator until it's needed. Once you've finished a bottle, rinse it in warm water and put it to one side. When your stock of made-up bottles is down to two, sterilize more bottles. Continue to sterilize all feeding equipment until your baby is at least four months old.

Sterilizing units usually hold only 4–6 bottles. Because your newborn baby will need about seven feedings over a 24 hour period, you'll have to sterilize and prepare the bottles twice a day – morning and evening – so that you have enough formula ready whenever she wants it. As your baby grows, the number of feedings will decline and you'll be able to prepare all the bottles you need in a single batch.

EQUIPMENT	
• Sterilizing bath	• Bottle brush
• Sterilizing tablets	• Measuring jug
• 6–8 bottles	• Long-handled spoon
• 1 dozen nipples	• Salt
	• Knife

Sterilizing the bottles

1 *Put all the bottles into warm, soapy water. Use the bottle brush to remove all traces of milk from the bottles.*

2 *Rub the inside of the nipples with salt to remove any milk that might be trapped.*

3 *Rinse the bottles and nipples thoroughly in warm water.*

4 *Half-fill the sterilizing unit with cold water. Add a sterilizing tablet and wait for it to dissolve.*

5 *Put the bottles, nipples, measuring cup, and spoon into the unit. Fill the bottles with water as you put them in so that they don't bob about. Pour in enough cold water to fill unit.*

6 *Make sure all the equipment is submerged and leave for the required time. Leave the feeding equipment in the solution until you need it.*

ALTERNATIVE STERILIZING METHODS

● Boil all the equipment for at least 25 minutes in a large covered pot. This does, however, cause rubber nipples to disintegrate rather quickly.

● Put the bottles, cup and knife into the dishwasher on the normal cycle. Boil the nipples separately in a covered pan.

● Put all the equipment into a large plastic container with a lid, and use sterilizing tablets and water, as discussed above.

● Use the terminal method which sterilizes milk and bottles at the same time. Wash out and rinse the bottles as before. Mix the formula with cold water, put it into the bottles and screw on the lids loosely, so that steam can get in. Stand them in a large pan with about three inches of water, cover and boil for 20 minutes. Leave to cool down for two hours. Tighten the lids before storing in the fridge.

Making up the formula

You can use one of two kinds of infant formula: powder, which you mix with boiled water, or liquid concentrate, which is usually mixed with equal parts of cold water.

Making up a powder formula

1 *Boil water. Wash your hands while you wait for the water to cool slightly.*

2 *Remove all the equipment from the sterilizer and drain it; there's no need to rinse it.*

3 *Check the formula to see how much water you need, according to your baby's age and weight. Pour this exact amount into the measuring cup.*

4 *Fill the required number of scoops with powder, levelling them off with the back of the knife, and put them into the measuring cup.*

5 *Stir the solution thoroughly with a sterilized spoon so that all the powder dissolves in the water.*

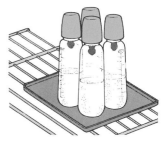

6 *Fill the bottles with the formula, according to how much is calculated for each feeding. Never add any extra formula to the bottles.*

7 *Put nipples, top first, into the bottles, and secure them with the screw-on lids.*

8 *Put all the bottles into the fridge immediately. If they keep falling over, put them on a tray or in an empty six-pack.*

Preparing a liquid formula

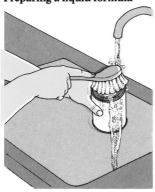

1 *Wash your hands, then wash the can top with a brush and soapy water to remove any grease.*

2 *Boil water and pour it over the can lid and a can opener.*

3 *Open the can, making two holes so that the milk pours out freely.*

4 *Pour out the specified amount of milk into a sterilized measuring cup.*

5 *Add the required amount of boiled water, stir, and then pour it equally into the bottles.*

6 *Put the nipples into the bottles and secure them with screw-on lids. Put the bottles into fridge.*

HYGIENE AND PREPARATION TIPS

● Always wash your hands before sterilizing equipment, and before preparing and giving feedings.

● Follow all sterilizing instructions.

● Sterilize every piece of equipment that you use.

● Once you've opened a packet of formula, keep it in the refrigerator.

● Prepare the formula according to the instructions. *Never* add anything extra.

● Once the formula has been made up, cool it immediately by putting it in the refrigerator. Never put warm milk into a thermos flask – it will breed germs.

● Keep all bottles in the refrigerator until required.

● Give warmed-up milk to a baby immediately.

● Throw away any milk that's left after a feeding.

Warming the bottle

When you're going to use a bottle, simply bring it out of the fridge half an hour before you need it and allow it to warm up to room temperature, with the top still on.

Although there is no need to heat the milk up, many parents want it to be as similar to breast milk as possible. To warm up your baby's bottle quickly, run it under the hot tap or stand it in a bowl of hot water for a few minutes. You can heat a bottle up even more quickly by putting it in a microwave oven for half a minute or by using a bottle warmer. *Never* keep warm milk in a thermos, and never leave a bottle standing overnight in a bottle warmer. This will only encourage any germs which are present to multiply. Test the temperature on your wrist before feeding the baby: it should be neither hot nor cold to the touch.

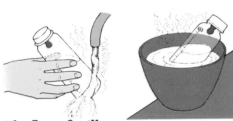

The flow of milk

Milk simply runs out of the breast at the beginning of a feeding, so there is hardly any need for exertion when your baby is sucking. Bottle-fed babies will find feeding just as easy if the hole in the nipple is large enough to let drops fall in a steady stream when the bottle is inverted. If it takes a few seconds for a drop to form, then the hole is too small; if the stream is continuous, it is too big.

☐ To make a hole bigger you need a fine, red-hot needle. Simply insert it gently through the hole in the nipple and the rubber will melt. Have a few spare nipples around, since it's not as easy as it sounds. You may end up with half a dozen nipples with oversized holes – I certainly did the first time I tried it.

☐ It is worth spending a little time getting the size of the hole just right, because if it is too large your baby will get too much too fast and cough and splutter. If the hole is too small, your baby will get tired from sucking before she has taken a full meal, and she may also swallow too much air.

☐ Buy shaped nipples if possible. These are shaped to fit the baby's palate and allow the baby more control over the flow.

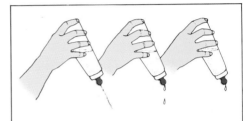

Check the flow of milk by inverting the bottle. The hole is too big if it comes in a steady stream; it is just right when several drops come out per second.

The first feed

There is no artificial equivalent to colostrum. Even if you're not going to continue to breast-feed, you will be giving your baby a great head-start if you put her regularly to the breast in the first few days (see p. 86). If you choose not to do this, however, your baby should be given some sugared water four to eight hours after delivery and then a formula feed after about 48 hours; this will be organized by the medical staff.

Don't worry if your baby doesn't gulp down all that's in the bottle. It's perfectly normal for all babies, breast- or bottle-fed, not to take too much in their first 48 hours – it takes a while for them to get into the swing of it. Like a breast-fed baby, yours will let you know with a cry when she wants to be fed. Follow your baby's lead and develop the supply and demand system explained on p. 85, just as for a breast-fed baby.

Feeding with a bottle

Make sure you have a quiet, comfortable place to sit and that your arms are well supported with cushions or pillows if necessary (see p. 91). Lay the baby in your lap with the head in the crook of your elbow and the back supported along your forearm. Make sure your baby is not lying horizontally. She should be half sitting so that she can breathe and swallow easily, without choking.

Just before you start feeding, test the heat of the milk by letting a couple of drops fall on to the inside of your wrist.

The milk should feel neither too hot nor too cold. You should already have tested the flow of milk (see p. 103). Loosen the cap of the bottle slightly so that air can enter to take the place of the milk your baby sucks out. If you don't do this, quite a lot of negative pressure can build up inside the bottle which will flatten the nipple and make sucking very hard work. Your baby may become angry and refuse the rest of the feeding. If this happens, gently pull the bottle out of your baby's mouth so air can get in, and then continue feeding, as before.

Always check that the milk's not too hot by letting a few drops fall on to your wrist.

To ensure that the milk comes out and that there's no vacuum inside the bottle, loosen the cap slightly before the feeding.

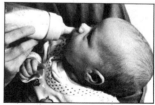

Settle down comfortably with your baby and prepare her for the feed by eliciting the sucking reflex. Gently stroke the cheek nearest to you and she'll turn to you and the bottle.

To trigger the baby's sucking reflex, so that she takes the bottle, gently stroke the cheek nearest to you. As she turns to your touch, you can gently insert the nipple into her mouth. She should hold on to a considerable portion of the nipple so that the tip is far back into her mouth, as a mother's nipple would be. Be careful, however, not to push it so far back that she gags on it.

Let your baby set the pace of feeding. She might want to pause mid-feed to look around or play with the bottle, and she should be allowed this pleasure. From the very beginning, make feeding times as pleasant as possible. Face your baby and make eye contact. Don't sit in silence: talk, sing, chatter, make any kind of noise you like. Just make sure that your voice sounds pleasant, happy and responsive. This is the first conversation that your baby will enjoy, so react to movements, gestures and smiles.

Half-way through the feeding, move your baby to your other arm. This will give her a new view, and your arm a rest; you may also want to burp your baby at this point (see p. 107).

Removing the bottle

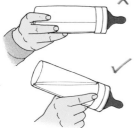

Always make sure the nipple is full of milk by holding the bottle at a sufficient angle. Unless you do, the baby will swallow air with the milk.

a

The only reason you have to take care when removing your own nipple from a baby's mouth when breast-feeding is that, unless you do, the nipple could become very sore. With a plastic nipple this problem doesn't arise. When you want to

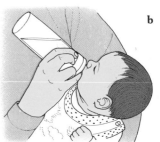

b

remove the bottle from the baby just pull the nipple away gently but firmly and your baby will release the bottle (a). If she doesn't, gently slide your little finger into the corner of her mouth to break the suction (b).

BOTTLE-FEEDING TIPS
● Don't feed your baby lying flat; it's very difficult to swallow in this position and your baby may gag or get sick.
● Never leave your baby with the bottle propped up on a pillow or cushion. Not only is this very dangerous – your baby could choke – but she could become very uncomfortable if she swallows a lot of air because of the angle at which the bottle is propped. More-over, your baby misses out on the cuddling and affection that she should enjoy while she nurses.
● Don't try to force your baby to finish the bottle after she has stopped sucking: she knows when she's had enough.
● Don't try feeding your baby if her nose is blocked. She can't swallow and breathe at the same time, so ask your doctor for nose drops which can be used before each feeding.

● Even if you think the milk formula doesn't suit your baby, don't change it without first consulting your doctor. It is very unusual for a brand of milk to stop a baby from feeding; however, on rare occasion a baby is allergic to cow's milk, and may need to use a soya formula. Seek medical advice first!

Bottle-feeding patterns

Bottle-fed babies tend to need less feedings than breast-fed ones. This is because formula milk takes longer to digest; it also contains slightly more protein, which provides more calories and delays hunger. After the first two or three days, bottle-fed babies usually settle on a four-hourly regime. They will therefore need six feedings a day – one less than if they were being breast-fed. When your baby is first born she will probably take not more than two ounces at each feeding, but as she gets older the amount will increase, and the number of feedings per day will decrease.

Let your baby determine when she's to be fed; never, ever, feed your baby according to the clock. Nurse her when she tells you with cries that she is hungry, not when you think she should be.

Don't feel that your baby has to finish the bottle at each feeding. Your baby's appetite – like everyone else's – will vary,

Approximate age of baby	Mixture for a single feeding			Feedings in 24 hours
	Level scoops	Warm water fl oz	ml	
0–14 days	3	3	85	7
2–6 weeks	4	4	115	6
2 months	5	5	140	6
3 months	6	6	170	5
4 months	7	7	200	5
6 months and over	8	8	225	4

so if she seems satisfied don't make her continue, even if some milk is left in the bottle. She will only get over-fed and spit it back up (see p. 108). What's more, she may become fat. On the other hand, if your baby seems ravenous, give her some extra milk from another bottle. If she regularly wants more milk, start to add the extra amount to every bottle.

POSSIBLE PROBLEMS

Overfeeding

Fat cells are produced by an infant in response to the amount of fat in her diet. Once produced, these cells can't be removed and will remain with her as an adult. If you overfeed her she will grow an excessively large number of these cells and become fat, which is not only an embarrassment but a health hazard.

It is easier to overfeed a bottle-fed baby for two main reasons: first, it is tempting to put extra formula into the bottle. (You should *always* follow the instructions to the letter (see p. 101), otherwise you'll be giving the baby unseen – and unrequired – calories.) Second, because you can see the amount of formula the baby is taking, it is hard to resist encouraging her to finish the last drop. (You should always let your baby decide whether she's had enough or not.) Giving your baby sweet, syrupy drinks and introducing her to solids too early may also contribute to obesity.

Underfeeding

This is rare in bottle-fed babies, but it can happen. Your baby should be fed on demand (see p. 85), and not according to the clock. Although most babies will be ready for a feeding every four hours by the time that they are 2–3 months old, their individual appetites may vary from day to day. Say, for example, that your baby's at the age when she can take five 6 oz bottles per day, but at one feeding she takes only 4 oz from the bottle. If you insist on feeding to a schedule, and don't put any extra milk in these scheduled bottles or allow any of the interim feedings that your baby will be crying for, she will never be able to catch up with the botal volume of milk that she needs, and will not gain weight.

You should be flexible in the amount of formula you prepare. The figures on the packages are given as a general estimate; should your child consistently drain each bottle and still remain fretful and upset, she may still be hungry. Make up an extra 2 oz of formula and see if she wants it. If she does, without your forcing her, then she needed it and won't put on weight.

If you find that your baby is demanding frequent feedings but doesn't take much and remains fretful, check that the nipple hole isn't too small. She may be having a hard time sucking the milk out of the bottles, and therefore not getting enough nourishment.

BURPING AND SPITTING UP 0–1

Burping

The point of burping is to bring up any wind that has been swallowed during feeding or crying prior to feeding. The reason for bringing up wind is to prevent it from causing your baby discomfort. Babies vary a great deal in their reactions to this, and in my experience the majority of them aren't noticeably happier or more contented for having been burped.

Babies also vary a great deal in the amount of air that they swallow during feeding. Some – including all breast-fed babies – swallow very little. Bottle-fed babies tend to swallow more – but even then it doesn't seem to be a problem. If very small quantities of air are swallowed during feeding they form small bubbles in the stomach which cannot be burped up until they have coalesced into a large bubble – and this can take a great deal of time. Small bubbles in the stomach are very unlikely to give rise to discomfort.

The one point in favor of burping is that it makes *you* pause, relax, take things slowly, hold your baby gently and stroke or pat her in a firm, reassuring way. This is very good for your baby and very good for you, too.

My attitude towards burping, therefore, is this: by all means do it, even if it is just for your peace of mind, but don't become fanatical about it.

Don't pat or rub your baby too hard, since this may cause her to spit up her meal. A gentle upward stroking movement is usually preferable to firm pats.

Most authorities advise that you stop the feeding halfway through to burp the baby. I don't think there is any need to do this. Wait until your baby pauses naturally in the feeding, and take advantage of this pause to try burping her. As your baby gets older, she should finish the whole bottle quite comfortably without needing to be burped.

BURPING POSITIONS

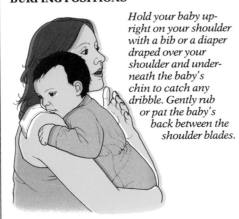

Hold your baby up-right on your shoulder with a bib or a diaper draped over your shoulder and under-neath the baby's chin to catch any dribble. Gently rub or pat the baby's back between the shoulder blades.

Sit your baby up on your knee with the chin supported between your finger and thumb; pat or rub her back.

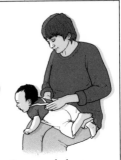

Lay your baby on your lap, face downwards, with the head turned to one side, and gently pat or rub her back.

Spitting Up

Some babies never spit up at all. Others do it with surprising frequency, which can be quite a cause of concern to parents. My youngest son was a child who had a tendency to spit up his food. If he took a bit too much, he would always bring back the last few mouthfuls. If he cried for longer than a few seconds, the exertion made him cough and then spit up. Whenever he had a cough he invariably brought back his food. I always knew he wasn't ill – he seemed too content. But I worried that perhaps he wasn't getting enough to eat. If he spit up a lot, I simply followed my own instinct and offered more food. If he took it, I assumed he needed it. If he refused, I assumed he had spit up what he didn't require. In very young babies, the most common cause of spitting up is overfeed-ing. This is another reason why you should never coerce a bottle-fed baby into finishing his meal.

If your bottle-fed baby shows a tendency to spit up, check the hole in the nipple. If it is too large, she may be taking too much, too quickly. If it's too small, she may have had to suck very hard and in the process taken in a lot of air.

As an observant parent, you should always be able to tell whether spitting up is serious. Forcible vomiting, especially if it occurs after consecutive feedings or if it continues for more than a day, should be reported immediately to your doctor. Vomiting in a very small baby can quickly lead to dehydration, and you should have medical advice as soon as possible.

NIGHT FEEDINGS

0–1

Because you'll respond to all your baby's demands for food, you may find that feeding takes up quite a lot of your time – at least 30 minutes per feeding, or a total of three hours out of every 24. With night feedings on top of all your other responsibilities, you may get extremely tired and tense. The problem won't be so much the number of hours of sleep you lose, but the way in which your sleep patterns are broken over long periods. It's very important that you get adequate rest both day and night, and this means that your partner has to give you a hand, and do more than his share of chores. The responsibilities of child-rearing should be divided equally between you. If you are doing most of the nursing, it's only fair that he take over some of the other jobs. Even if you've decided to breast-feed, the night feeds shouldn't be entirely your responsibility. If the baby sleeps in another room, ask your partner to bring her to you as soon as she cries, and get him to take the baby back and change the diaper after she's been fed.

TIPS

● Feed your baby in bed so that you're warm and comfortable.
● If you're very tired, express enough milk for the night feeding, put it into a sterile bottle, and arrange for your partner to give it to the baby.
● Keep some diaper changing equipment in your bedroom so you can feed and change the baby with a minimum of disturbance.
● It's easy to get cold sitting up in bed, so have a sweater or robe nearby.
● Have a drink by your bedside in case you get thirsty while feeding.
● If the baby's in another room and you're scared of not hearing her cries, invest in a baby alarm which will relay any loud sounds she makes.

Reducing night feedings

Until your baby weighs about ten pounds she won't be able to sleep for more than five hours at a time without waking with hunger. Once this weight is reached, however, you can try stretching the time between feedings, with the dual aims of giving yourself about six hours of undisturbed sleep, and of painlessly getting your baby to end her early morning feedings. She will have her own routine, but as a general rule, it's sensible to try to juggle your baby's last feeding so that it's given at about the time you go to bed. But *do* be flexible; your baby may not want to drop the early morning feeding, and, no matter how hard you try to alter her routine, will still wake up and want to be fed. In this case you'll just have to make the night feedings as simple as possible and look forward to when she drops them.

HOW FEEDING FREQUENCY CHANGES

This chart shows the varying times at which four four-week-old babies wanted to feed.

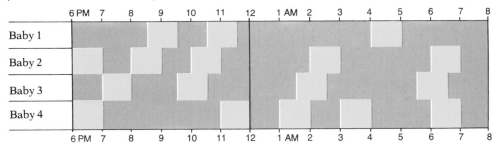

Feeding
Sleeping

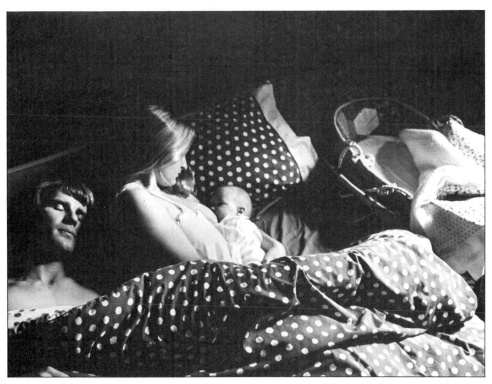

INTRODUCING SOLIDS   4–6 m

At some stage during the first year you will have to start to wean your baby off milk and on to solid food. There is quite a lot of pressure on parents to start giving solids before the age of three months, and in the United States many babies are started as early as six weeks. You should, however, resist *all* such pressure for the following reasons: First, breast milk (or its formula equivalent) is the only food your baby needs in the early months. Second, the introduction of solids too early can lessen a baby's desire to suck. Breast-fed babies will reduce the amount taken from the mother's breasts which, in turn, will begin producing less milk. Whether your baby is breast-fed or not, she'll end up with a diet that fails to satisfy her needs. Third, babies are incapable of digesting and absorbing complex foods until they are at least three months old. If you introduce solids before this time, not only will they pass through largely undigested, but you will be putting an increased strain on the baby's immature kidneys.

When to introduce solids

In the early months milk provides all the calories required to make your baby grow: the more she grows, the more milk she'll therefore need to drink. But your baby's stomach can only hold a certain amount of milk at each feeding, and she will eventually reach a point when she's drinking to full capacity, but still won't have enough calories to keep going. This is the point at which you'll have to introduce solids. You'll recognize her readiness when your baby starts to demand more milk and appears very unsatisfied after each feeding. She may suddenly demand a regular sixth feeding, for example, although she had been quite content with five. This happens to many babies at about four months – an ideal time to start on solids because it coincides with a lessening of her intense desire to suck.

What foods to give

Until the fourth month, your baby's diet is limited to milk. It's therefore only sensible to start with bland, semi-liquid, milk-like foods. Unsweetened purées of fruit (bananas, dessert apples, ripe pears and peaches) and vegetables (potatoes, carrots and cauliflower) and gluten-free rice cereal are ideal. Although specially-manufactured "first foods" are available, it's better to prepare your own. It will be cheaper (especially in the small amounts you'll be using initially), and you will know exactly what is in the food, and not have to worry about additional sugar, salt, or preservatives.

Cook the fruits or vegetables in a small amount of water until soft, and then purée or strain them. Your baby will find it easier to cope with foods of a smooth, heavy, creamy consistency, so add some expressed milk, boiled cow's milk or water if the consistency is too thick. Rice cereal should be mixed up with expressed milk or boiled cow's milk.

By the time your baby is ready for weaning, you don't have to sterilize all cooking utensils meticulously – but you must follow the general principles of good hygiene. Wash your hands before preparing the baby's food and before feeding, and make sure that all utensils are clean and that any prepared food is kept in the refrigerator. Purées of fruits and vegetables will keep safely for two days in the refrigerator; alternatively, they could be frozen in individual portions.

Giving the first solids

Start off by giving your baby one or two teaspoons of food along with a normal milk feeding; the one around mid-day is ideal because your baby will be quite alert and not ravenously hungry. Although your baby is ready for the calories that solids provide, she will be hungry for what she knows is satisfying – milk – so feed from one breast first, or give half the usual bottle. As she gets more used to solids, she

may want them before she takes the milk.

Prepare the small amount of solids you'll need, and then settle in your normal position to feed the baby. When you've given half the milk, sit the baby in an upright position on your lap. Scoop up some food with a small spoon and place it gently between the baby's lips so that she can suck the food off. Be very careful not to push the spoon in too far or she may gag on the unexpected food on the back of her tongue. She's bound to be messy at first –

pushing more food out than she manages to take in. Gently scrape the excess off the baby's face and place the spoon between her lips as before. Your baby will signal that she's had enough by turning away from the spoon with lips shut, maybe even crying. *Never* force your baby to take any more food than she wants. When she's taken the solid food, give her the rest of the milk.

111

TIPS

● Give your baby only one new food at a time, and then wait for several days to see if it suits her.
● Use dry infant cereals which you have to make up rather than ready-mixed cereals; they contain more iron and are more nutritious.
● Only give cereal once a day.
● If the baby doesn't like taking food from a spoon, try dipping a clean fingertip into the food and let your baby suck it off.
● If you find it awkward to feed the baby on your lap, put her in a baby seat on the floor or on a table.
● Keep plenty of kitchen towels nearby to mop up any mess.
● Even early solids can stain clothes, especially banana, so put a small cloth bib on the baby.

SAMPLE WEANING CHART

Stage 1	About 4 months
1st feeding	
Breast or bottle feeding, as usual	
2nd feeding	
Half breast or bottle feeding. Try one or two teaspoons of purée or cereal, then give remainder of the milk.	
3rd feeding	
Breast or bottle feeding, as usual	
4th feeding	
Breast or bottle feeding, as usual	
5th feeding	
Breast or bottle feeding, as usual	

Stage 2	About 4½ months
1st feeding	
Breast or bottle feeding, as usual	
2nd feeding	
Half breast or bottle feeding. Two teaspoons of cereal, then remainder of milk.	
3rd feeding	
Half breast or bottle feeding. Two teaspoons of vegetable or fruit purée, then remainder of milk.	
4th feeding	
Breast or bottle feeding, as usual	
5th feeding	
Breast or bottle feeding, as usual	

ESTABLISHING SOLIDS   6 m–1

Once your baby happily accepts one or two different solids, it's important to introduce a variety of textures and tastes. As the year goes on she'll be able to deal with foods that had only been mashed or chopped, and will learn to enjoy chewing and sucking on chunks of food. She'll soon move from milk feedings with "tastes" of solids to three established solid meals a day, accompanied by drinks of water, diluted fruit juice or milk.

The amount of solids you give your baby can be gradually increased over the weeks until she is getting most of the calories she requires for growth from solid foods and not from milk. As the number of solid meals increases, the amount of milk your child wants will correspondingly decrease. Thirst will be satisfied by water and diluted fruit juice, not by milk alone. It's difficult to specify the amount a baby should be eating because every baby has different requirements and appetites. You'll be the best judge of how much your baby wants, but if you have any doubts, prepare food according to the recipes on p. 120 and feed as much of each individual portion as your baby wants.

An example of how to build up your baby's intake of solids is shown opposite. The list includes the foods considered most suitable for the first year.

What foods to give

By the time your baby has been taking fruit and cereal for a month she'll be ready to try some meat, fish and dairy products other than milk. In fact, your baby can slowly start to have foods which you normally eat, with a few exceptions (see right).

What you have to make sure of is that your baby has a balanced diet. Until this point, milk alone will have fulfilled all her nutritional requirements – now you will have to meet these requirements with other foods as well. This is perfectly simple to do, so long as you give your baby a diet of the type outlined on page 122, which includes daily helpings of protein, fresh fruit, vegetables and carbohydrates.

Don't give your baby:	
Very spicy food	Rhubarb
Sugary foods or drinks	Raisins, sultanas and currants
Smoked fish or meat	Fruit with seeds
	Whole nuts
Salt beef, pastrami or salami	Chunky peanut butter
Oily fish	Yeast extract
Shellfish	Coffee or tea
Unripe fruit	Alcohol

Stage 3   About 5–6 months

Early morning
Breast or bottle feeding, as usual

Breakfast
Two teaspoons of cereal, followed by a lightly boiled egg yolk, and a solid.

Lunch
One teaspoon of puréed meat or fish with three teaspoons of strained vegetables. Try giving a drink of water or well-diluted fruit juice instead of milk.

Mid-afternoon
Try some mashed banana or other soft fruit in addition to the regular feeding.

Dinner
Give the breast or bottle feeding if your baby's still hungry.

Stage 4   About 6–7 months

Early morning
Breast or bottle feeding, as usual

Breakfast
Two teaspoons of hot or cold cereal with a lightly scrambled egg. Offer some milk from a cup instead of the usual breast or bottle feeding.

Lunch
Try giving minced or mashed food instead of puréed food. Give meat or fish with some vegetables, then offer some yogurt and fruit. Offer a drink of water or well-diluted fruit juice.

Late afternoon/dinner
Offer a cheese or some other healthy and tasteful wholegrain bread sandwich, then some fresh fruit and yogurt. Try giving milk from a cup instead of the usual feeding.

Stage 5   About 7–8 months

Early morning
Offer a drink of water or fruit juice instead of the usual feeding.

Breakfast
Cereal and then a boiled egg with wholegrain bread and butter. A drink of milk.

Lunch
Cheese, fish, minced meat, chicken or liver with mashed vegetables. A milk pudding or fresh fruit with a drink of water or fruit juice.

Late afternoon/dinner
Wholewheat bread and butter with a cheese. Fresh fruit and a drink of milk.

Stage 6   About 9–12 months

Early morning
Drink of water or fruit juice

Breakfast
Cereal, then bacon, egg or fish with wholegrain toast and butter. A drink of milk.

Lunch
Chopped, instead of mashed, meat, fish or cheese, followed by a milk pudding or fresh fruit. A drink of water or fruit juice.

Late afternoon/dinner
Meat or cheese sandwiches with a drink of milk.

Preparing food for babies

● Blender, liquidizer, food processer or strainer ● Small pan for heating food up	● Steamer or pan with tightly-fitting lid ● Grater

You'll probably already have a liquidizer or processer; if you haven't, buy a cheap easy-to-use, hand-operated blender. You'll only have to purée food for the initial months of your baby's new diet; thereafter it can be mashed or chopped finely. At the beginning you may find it easier just to strain the food, especially when you're not preparing big batches. If you've frozen portions of food, a small pan is ideal for heating them up quickly.

For thinning down your home-prepared foods, simply add water. The water in which you've steamed fruit or vegetables (with no additional salt or sugar), is ideal, but you can also add expressed milk, cow's milk, soup, tomato, orange or apple juice. For thickening, use cottage cheese, yogurt, mashed potato, or ground, wholegrain cereals. If you feel that you need to sweeten foods, use naturally sweet fruit juice or dextrose. Never use refined sugar – brown or white. Our bodies don't need it, it's bad for our teeth, and it only encourages a sweet tooth which is bad for general health.

PREPARATION TIPS
● Always peel fruits to remove bits which may choke the baby and cut them into fairly small pieces before steaming and puréeing them. Do the same for vegetables.

● Give your baby meat, cooked any way you like, and then puréed. You need not give red meat more than twice a week. Don't forget, chicken, chicken livers and certain types of fish, which are relatively cheap and easy to prepare. Thin down meats with vegetable water or soup.

● Always choose the freshest looking vegetables (not wrinkled or dull-looking ones), and cook them as soon as possible.

● Handle fruit and vegetables gently. Don't cut them until you have to and don't crush and bruise them, as this destroys the vitamin C.

● Cook vegetables and fruit in as little water as possible, with a tightly-fitting lid. They will retain their vitamins better when steamed.

● Cook soft-skinned fruit and vegetables in their skins because this helps to retain the vitamins and it will also give your child fiber. Remove the skin if it's tough and therefore likely to choke the baby.

● Use cast iron cooking pots. A little iron is absorbed into the food, which helps to replenish your child's iron supply.

● Always make the food a suitable consistency for your baby's age – for example, a thick milk for your four-month-old; a thick cream for your six-month-old, and a slightly chunky mash for your nine-month-old.

● Don't use copper pans for green leafy vegetables. Copper breaks down the vitamin C.

● Don't cook tinned foods for too long – you will destroy the vitamins.

● Don't add salt or sugar to anything you have cooked for a child. The immature kidneys can't handle a heavy salt load, and you will be doing your child a favor if you don't encourage a sweet tooth.

● Avoid using too many saturated fats in your cooking – use safflower or corn oil.

● Don't prepare vegetables or soak them in water a long time before you cook them or you will destroy the vitamins.

● Don't wait for your baby's food to cool slowly. Put it straight into the refrigerator, which will discourage bacteria from growing.

Prepared foods

Whether you mix your baby's foods yourself (see left), or buy prepared foods is up to you. Bought foods are certainly convenient if you're travelling or in a hurry, but they are more expensive and not always nutritionally sound. If you are going to use them, especially on a day-to-day basis, follow the guidelines listed below.

SAMPLE LABELS

INGREDIENTS: WATER, BEEF, CARROTS, POTATOES, SWEDES, TOMATOES, MODIFIED CORNFLOUR, PEAS, HYDROLYSED VEGETABLE PROTEIN.

INGREDIENTS: SKIMMED MILK · SUGAR, TAPIOCA · MODIFIED CORNFLOUR COCOA · SUNFLOWER OIL · NATURAL FLAVOURING

INGREDIENTS: WATER, PORK, POTATOES, WHEATFLOUR, HARICOT BEANS, TOMATO PUREE, DRIED ONIONS.

Check the list of ingredients on the tin or jar. They are listed in order of concentration, so never buy anything in which water is listed first.

Make sure the jar is vacuum sealed when you open it, otherwise it may be contaminated.

If possible, buy meat and vegetables separately and then combine them when you want a "mixed dinner."

Don't keep opened jars in the refrigerator for longer than two days. Throw them away after that.

Don't buy anything which has added salt, sugar, modified starch or monosodium glutamate (MSG).

Don't buy mixed dinners; they usually contain a lot of thickener.

Never store food in opened tins; put it into a dish or bowl and keep it covered in the refrigerator.

Don't heat the food up in the jar – it may crack.

It is very unhygienic to feed the baby from the jar and then to keep some for a second meal, as it will have become contaminated with saliva. It's okay to feed your baby from a jar if she's going to eat all of it.

Giving drinks

While you're introducing solids, milk will remain an important part of your baby's diet, and will make up a large part of the daily caloric intake. By the time she's six months old it will be safe for her to have cow's milk, either from a cup or in food. Although the milk doesn't have to be boiled, the containers you serve it in have to be thoroughly cleaned every time the baby drinks from them.

As soon as your baby is having any quantity of solid food she will need water as well as milk to drink. Start her off with half an ounce of water or diluted fruit juice between and after feedings (if you don't want to use a bottle, try serving it from a cup, see p. 116). Thereafter, she can be given liquids whenever she's thirsty during the day. Bear this in mind, especially in summer or when she's been rushing around. Syrup drinks of blackcurrant or rosehip are traditionally given to babies, but they are very high in calories and bad for their teeth. Avoid squashes and colas and any drinks that have sugar or saccharin added to them – stick to water or natural fruit juice.

Weaning your baby on to a cup

At about six months you should start your baby drinking from a cup as part of the process of weaning her from breast or bottle. The best feedings to begin using the cup are the two closest to mid-day when she'll probably be hungry for solids as opposed to milk. Give the solids first and then the cup.

There is a variety of special cups on the market (see p. 23). Cups with spouts are best at the beginning, since the liquid drips out and the baby has to half suck and half drink to get anything. Hold the cup yourself, offering only a few sips of milk at first, and releasing the cup as soon as she wants to take it from you. As she gets more dexterous, you can use a two-handled cup; the ones with specially slanted lips are ideal because they don't have to be tipped very far before the liquid comes out. Some babies go straight to an cup.

Your baby will gradually wean herself off the breast and by six or seven months will have dropped the morning feeding. She'll still want a breast or bottle feeding before bedtime until she's at least a year old – more for comfort than for food.

Where to feed your child

Until your baby is six months old, you will probably feed her on your lap or in a baby chair. But once her back muscles are strong enough to support her, you can consider using a high chair or feeding table (see p. 24). Because it's closer to the ground, a feeding table is safer than a high chair, although you do have to bend down to feed the baby until she can do it alone. A feeding table on wheels is more convenient because you can wheel it around the room, to wherever it suits you. But it does take up more room than a high chair, and it may be more expensive.

Initially you may have to prop your baby up with cushions. Many high chairs have harnesses to stop the child from slipping or falling out. These safety features, however, could also prevent you from getting to your child quickly if she were choking. Because you should never leave your child alone while she's eating, leave off the straps and keep a close eye on your baby instead. If she does gag on some food – and she's bound to at some stage – pat her firmly on the back until the food that's caught dislodges itself. When you give your child food with a new texture, she may gag out of surprise. Talk soothingly while you gently rub her back, and she'll be able to swallow whatever was worrying her. It's essential to know how to react quickly in any situation like this. Should the child's choking be severe, or if she loses consciousness, you must know what to do (see p. 302).

Feeding your child

Your baby will soon look forward to solids – not only to eat, but to play with. Feeding times will become messier, so it's advisable to put newspaper or a plastic sheet below the high chair or table to catch the worst of the mess. Keep your baby well away from expensively covered walls – remember, she can throw food now.

After a month on solids, your baby will have grasped the technique of getting food successfully off the spoon. By the time she's taking two solid meals a day, she'll be prepared to open her mouth to take the food.

Self-feeding

Your baby will leave you in no doubt when she wants to feed herself: she will simply take the spoon from you. Let your baby experiment, and be prepared to put up with the mess. Encourage all attempts at self-feeding because it is such a huge step forward in your baby's development, both physically and intellectually. It will give your baby a feeling of accomplishment and confidence. It will help her to become manually dexterous and to coordinate muscles and movements. There is nothing that will speed up the coordination of eye and hand faster than getting a spoonful of food to the mouth.

☐ Your baby will take several months to become proficient at self-feeding. In the meantime, food will be a plaything and you will worry because most of the food seems to be going on the floor and not in your baby's stomach. Don't worry; nature has arranged for babies to begin self-feeding at a time when their growth rate is decreasing, and less food is required.

☐ Until she can manage to get food successfully into her mouth, use two spoons, one for each of you. When she can't scoop the food up, swap your full spoon for the empty one.

At six months this baby tries to get the food to his mouth more quickly by trying to grab the spoon, although he can't hold it himself.

By the time the baby's eight months old he's using the spoon himself with reasonable, if messy, success. He can also handle a cup.

SAFETY TIPS

● You should still take care not to give your child food of a size that might stick in her throat or be inhaled. Avoid peanuts and fruit with seeds. Fruit with tough skins must be peeled.

● Don't leave your child eating or drinking alone in a room, ever. If she gags, chokes or vomits, she needs immediate help.

● Don't be obsessive, but be careful about mealtime hygiene. Have clean utensils, a clean high chair and a clean bib.

● When you are storing food in the re-frigerator, never store cooked and un-cooked meat together.

FEEDING TIPS

● Tuck a pile of tissues under the neckline of the bib to stop the baby's neck from getting wet as she practises drinking.

● If a baby won't wear a bib, put a colored scarf around her neck so that the clothes are protected.

● If your baby is going to sneeze, get out of the way or you'll be covered with food.

● Fit a paper towel holder on the back of the high chair or near it so that you have supplies on hand for emergencies.

● Keep the high chair well away from any walls unless they've got a washable sur-face – your baby will be quite capable of throwing food by now.

Finger foods

If self-feeding with a spoon seems to frustrate your baby, but her appetite is good, try the following finger foods. Your baby will be able to handle them easily, and get them to her mouth using only her hands and fingers as implements. If the food is hard, your baby will suck it.

Fruits and vegetables	Grains and cereals	Protein	
Sliced fresh fruit that is easy to hold (bananas, etc.), with skins and pits removed.	Small pieces of sugarless dried cereal	Smooth peanut butter on bread	Any kind of meat in pieces that are easy to grasp
Any vegetable that you can make into a stick or shape that is easy to grasp (tomatoes, carrots, etc.)	Little balls of cooked rice	Cubes of soft cheese	Chunks of firm fish, taken off the bone
Mashed potato	Wholegrain bread and toast (without the complete grains)	Macaroni and cheese	Sliced hard boiled eggs
	Wholemeal rusks (without the complete grains)	Strips of cheese on toast	
		Hamburgers and patties cut into small pieces	
		Scrambled eggs	
		Cottage cheese	

Be flexible about feeding

Try not to get tense at meal times. This will be easier to do if you don't spend so much time preparing food that you're resentful if it isn't eaten, and if you take a few precautions that reduce your cleaning-up time. The most important rule of all is not to pit your will against your baby's. In the end there is no way that you can force a baby to take food – and you should never even try. Don't worry that your baby isn't eating enough – she is. If she doesn't want to eat, then she doesn't need to. If she's hungry, she'll always eat to satisfy her need. A period when she eats little will usually be followed by a period when she eats a lot.

Think in the long-term. Don't consider your baby's nutritional intake in terms of what she has eaten that day, but in terms of what she has eaten that week. For two days your baby may refuse everything but cereal, and then on the third day go on a fruit-eating binge, or want only cheese. A baby, like most animals, is self-regulating. She knows what she wants and when she wants it. As in many other instances of child-rearing, you should take your lead from your baby. Rest assured that her chosen diet is a balanced diet, lacking nothing, so long as she is given the correct food.

Regardless of the guidelines already given, or of what some baby books say about nutrition, your baby doesn't have to have every kind of food at each meal. She can take a whole day's supply of protein at one meal, and a whole day's supply of carbohydrates at the next. Try to let go of the urge to control your baby's diet! Don't think that being a good mother means that she has to eat "good" food at every meal.

Your baby won't need more than one or two big meals a day. In between, she'll simply need a snack. Don't confine eating to meal times; a stubborn baby will turn them into pitched battles. Of course you should encourage your baby to have regular feeding times, but if she is going through a difficult phase, bend a little and supplement a small meal with a snack later on.

If your baby stands up or tries to get out of the high chair, take her out and forget about the feeding. She will come back to the food or ask for it when she's hungry. If you argue, you'll get upset, your baby will get upset, and meal times will become unpleasant. Your baby will come to associate unhappiness with meal times, and this will only make feeding more difficult.

RECIPES FOR ONE- TO THREE-YEAR-OLDS

Potato, cheese and tomato hash

1 medium-sized potato	*2 oz grated cheese or cottage cheese*
2 fresh tomatoes	*1 carrot*

Peel and wash the potato and scrape the carrot; cook them until soft. Pour boiling water over the tomatoes, remove the skin, and strain to remove all seeds. Mash the vegetables, return to the heat, and mix in the cheese, egg and tomato until the egg is slightly cooked and the cheese has been absorbed.

Spaghetti and meat sauce

¼ lb spaghetti	*Pinch of thyme and oregano*
½ lb tomatoes	*¼ lb mince*
2 tablespoons tomato purée	*½ chopped onion*
½ pt stock	*2 tablespoons oil*

Cook the onions until transparent. Add the mince to brown it, then add the remaining ingredients; cook for about ¾ hour. Cook spaghetti, then place the sauce on top (freeze any remaining sauce). Blend if necessary, or cut up before serving.

Poached chicken

1 chicken breast	*Chopped parsley*
¼ pt milk	

Simmer the ingredients until the chicken breast is cooked. Remove breast then reduce the cooking liquid to about a tablespoon. Pour over the chicken and either chop up or blend before serving.

Fish and vegetables

1 small fillet of white fish	*3 oz green beans or*
1 tablespoon milk	*leaf spinach*

Steam the beans or spinach until tender. Poach the fish in milk until cooked. Blend or chop up before serving.

Quick crumble

½ lb stewed, strained fruit (apples, black-berries, peaches)	*2 tablespoons of cookie crumbs*

Put the fruit (sweetened if necessary) in a buttered dish. Sprinkle the crumbs over the fruit and cook for 20 minutes at 350°F.

Fruit jelly

1 cup fresh fruit juice	*1 oz gelatine Chopped fresh fruit*

Dissolve the gelatine according to packet instructions. Cool slightly before stirring into the fruit juice. Add the fresh fruit to the jelly and stir gently. Put into the refrigerator until set.

Beef stew

1/2 lb stewing beef, cubed   1/2 pt stock
2 medium-sized potatoes   Flour
1 stick celery   Garlic
2 carrots, chopped   Oil
Mixed herbs

Roll the meat in flour and brown in hot oil. Add the stock and bring to a boil. Add the garlic, if desired, and the herbs; simmer for an hour. Add the vegetables and continue cooking until both meat and vegetables are tender. Blend or chop up.

Liver and vegetables

1/2 lb liver   1 chopped onion
2 tomatoes   1/2 pt stock
1/2 lb carrots

Slice the liver and put into a casserole. Pour boiling water over the tomatoes to skin them; chop them up. Scrape the carrots and chop them. Add all the ingredients to the casserole, pour on the stock and cook on top of the stove for 40 minutes, or until tender. Blend or chop up before serving.

Tuna salad

1 small tin tuna (preferably in water)   Finely chopped onion, if desired
2 oz cottage cheese   Grated lemon
Finely chopped cucumber

Flake the tuna fish and mix in all the remaining ingredients.

Hamburgers

1/4 lb minced beef   Pinch each of cumin and oregano
1 egg yolk
1/2 finely chopped onion
1 tablespoon tomato purée

Mix all the ingredients. Form the meat into patties and grill them. Chop up or mash before serving.

Baked egg custard

1 pt milk   2 tablespoons clear honey
2 eggs

Beat the eggs together then add the milk and honey. Pour into a baking dish and place this in a pan of water (the water should come about half way up the side). Bake at 325°F for an hour, or until set.

Apricot mousse

1/2 lb apricots   1 tablespoon plain yogurt
1 egg yolk
lemon juice

Cook and purée the apricots. Beat the egg yolk into 2 to 3 tablespoons of purée, add a few drops of lemon juice and then bring the mixture to a boil, stirring carefully. Let it cool slightly before stirring in the yogurt. Cool in the refrigerator before serving.

121

FOOD AND EATING   1–2

For your toddler to be strong and healthy she must have a diet with sufficient amounts of protein, carbohydrate, fats, vitamins and minerals (see below). She will get this if you provide her with a wide variety of foods. The amount your child eats will be determined largely by how active she is and whether her body is going through a period of rapid growth. An infant's growth slows down around the first birthday, but speeds up again when she learns to walk. By the age of 18 months she'll require about three times the number of calories per day that an adult does because of the speed of growth. To provide enough energy for this each day, your child should receive roughly 45 calories per pound of weight. She'll also need 25 grams of protein a day, which is less than what an infant needs, but twice the requirement of an adult.

What foods to give

By the second year your child will be able to eat more or less the same diet as you. There is no one essential food your child *has* to eat in order to be healthy – she just has to have a plentiful supply of sensibly-cooked, fresh foods from which to build a balanced diet. Milk will remain an important part of the diet since it's a useful source of protein (one cup of milk = 8

grams of protein), although drinks of water and diluted fruit juice should also be given when she's thirsty.

Give your child at least one nutritious protein dish at each meal, and at least four servings of fruit and vegetables a day. She'll be able to eat an increasingly large amount of food at each meal; exactly how large will depend on her appetite, although she'll probably be able to take one-third to one-half a standard adult portion.

Help your child to develop good eating habits by not sugaring or salting the food and by not giving "empty" calories in the form of cakes, biscuits and sweets. Don't give your child sweet puddings – fruits, yogurts or fruit purées are much better.

Don't give your child:
Whole nuts
Popcorn
Very rough wholegrain bread, with pieces of whole grain
Small pieces of raw fruit or vegetable
Fruits (such as oranges) with pits
Unpeeled fruit with thick skin
Highly spiced dishes, unless child really enjoys them and specifically requests them
Excessively salty dishes
Sugary drinks

FOOD GROUPS	Food	Content
High protein	Chicken, lamb, beef, pork, eggs, cheese, nuts, vegetables	*Protein, fat, iron, vitamins A, D, B*
Milk and dairy products	Milk, cream, yogurt, ice cream, cheese	*Protein, fat, calcium, vitamins A, D, B2*
Green and yellow vegetables	Cabbage, brussel sprouts, spinach, kale, green beans, squash, lettuce, celery,	*Minerals, including calcium, chlorine, chromium, cobalt, copper, manganese, potassium and sodium*
Citrus fruits	Tomatoes, oranges, melon	*Vitamin C*
Other fruits and vegetables	Potatoes, beets, corn, carrots, cauliflower, pineapple, apricots	*Carbohydrates, vitamins A, B, C*
Breads and cereals	Wholegrain bread, noodles, rice	*Protein, carbohydrates, B vitamins, iron and calcium*
Fats	Butter, margarine, vegetable oils	*Vitamins A, D*

SAMPLE DIET FOR A 14 MONTH-OLD TODDLER

Day 1			
Breakfast	**Mid morning**	**Lunch**	**Dinner**
1 scrambled egg	1 cup diluted	2 oz white fish	5 oz baked beans
½ slice buttered	orange juice	½ brown bread roll	2–3 oz potatoes,
brown toast	1 apple	1 tablespoon green	2 oz grated
		beans	cheese
		1 cup diluted fruit	½ banana
		juice	1 cup milk

Day 2			
Breakfast	**Mid morning**	**Lunch**	**Mid afternoon**
1 cup diluted fresh	1 cup diluted fruit	1 cup milk	1 cup water
orange juice	juice	1 cup water	
4 oz yogurt	1 cracker	2 fish fingers	**Dinner**
1 tablespoon baby		1 tablespoon peas	1 egg omelette
muesli			with 1 oz cheese
½ tablespoon			1 tablespoon fresh
wheatgerm			green beans
Small amount of			1 cup milk
milk (2 fl oz)			¼ slice brown
½ mashed banana			bread

Day 3			
Breakfast	**Lunch**	**Mid afternoon**	**Dinner**
2 oz cereal plus milk	Egg florentine	2 cups diluted	Ham sandwich
1 cup diluted fresh	(2 tablespoons	apple juice	with wholegrain
orange juice	spinach,	1 oatmeal cookie	bread
½ banana	1 poached egg,		Cubes of cheese
	1–2 oz cheese)		Raw carrot
Mid morning	1 pear yogurt		Cubes of melon
1 cup water	(without sugar)		
1 apple	1 cup milk		

Eating patterns

By the time your child is walking, she will eat three smallish meals a day with a snack in the morning and the afternoon. Be prepared for your child's appetite to be a bit erratic during this year: she may seem to be starving one day and eat everything that you serve, but the next day eat hardly anything. Don't worry if suddenly your child will eat only one food, refusing all others: it's a perfectly normal occurence at this age (see p. 125). Similarly, don't be alarmed when she goes through periods of little appetite – your child knows exactly what she needs and will eat to keep pace with her growth.

GIVING SWEETS

I believe that it's wrong to deprive children of sweets. Deprivation very often leads to furtiveness and dishonesty. I believe, however, in the rationing of sweets. I am not beyond giving sweets as a reward, since this kind of reward is immediately understood by your child. In the case of my own children, I ration them to one sweet after lunch and supper. This scheme has worked with all four of them, encouraging them to develop self-control and good eating habits. They must brush their teeth afterwards.

Eating at the table

Introduce your toddler to family meal times by pulling the high chair up to the table when you have a meal. She'll be able to see everything that's going on and will gradually become accustomed to family meals and to meal time behavior and good manners. To make her feel included, give her the same food that you are eating, but prepare it in a way that she can spoon it or pick it up without your help. This will be easy if your child is neat. If she's messy, however, you may prefer feeding her before the rest of the family and bringing her to the table with a few favorite "finger" foods.

Don't expect your child automatically to adopt adult behavior, especially at the beginning. About the age of 12 months she'll be used to crawling and getting ready to walk, so don't be surprised if she is unwilling to sit still for long. If she insists on getting down, let her do so; she'll probably come back for more food in a few minutes and will soon learn that being fed means sitting still and eating. If she shows no signs of wanting to come back, however, don't insist that the food be eaten. She'll make up for it at the next meal.

Messy eaters

Some children take so much pleasure in the experience of eating that they find it hard to concentrate on the job of getting food successfully from plate to mouth. Try to be philosophical about the mess your toddler makes at meal times. It's a passing phase during which she will be learning coordination. She may seem to be learning this at your expense, but do try to stay cool and calm. Make meal times pleasant and minimize the amount of work you have to do by following the tips below. And remember, being tidy is nowhere near as

important as letting your child be happy and eat the way she wants to.

☐ Stand the high chair on a plastic table-cloth so that you can easily mop up what she spills. Otherwise just surround the high chair with newspaper which can be gathered up after each meal.

☐ Draw a circle some distance from the edge of the high chair tray to show your baby where the cup should go. Make the positioning of the cup into a game.

☐ Most toddlers don't like having their faces wiped with a cloth. Use your own hand dipped into water; for some reason, this is much more acceptable and will do

the job just as well.

☐ If your child is very messy, take her over to the sink to be washed. Make a game out of washing hands and let your child play some water games while you're at the sink.

☐ Let your child dip both hands into a bowl of water when she's still sitting in the high chair and then wipe them dry with a towel.

POSSIBLE PROBLEMS

Food fads

Between one and two, your child will begin to show pronounced preferences for certain foods. It is very common for children to have these food fads, eating one food and refusing everything else. She may, for example, turn away from meat and want to eat only yogurt and fruit. After a week she may turn from yogurt to cheese and fruit. Being a good parent means not making a fuss about any of this. There is nothing magic about any one food and there is always a nutritious alternative to the one that your baby rejects. Don't spend time cooking food that you think your toddler will refuse and then feel resentful when she does. Take the sensible way out and cook food you know she really wants, even if it's something of which you disapprove. Research has shown that as long as you offer your child a wide variety of foods, the diet she chooses will be a balanced one. There is, after all, no reason on earth why your toddler should eat only the food that you choose. Her tastes are not necessarily yours and, if it's your baby's happiness and well-being that you're concerned about, you will soon realize that it's more important for her to eat something she likes than not to eat at all. Do be flexible about what you give your toddler to eat.

Disliked foods

I really don't believe in camouflaging a disliked food by mixing it with a food that is well-liked, or of bribing a child to have a spoonful of a disliked food with a spoonful of one that is liked.

If your child dislikes one food, give an alternative one that provides the same nourishment. If your baby shows a profound dislike for a food, mixing it with a food she likes or bribing her may turn her off to other foods as well. Getting visibly upset will only encourage your child to prolong her odd eating habits, as a way of manipulating you. When you introduce a new food, do it when you know your baby

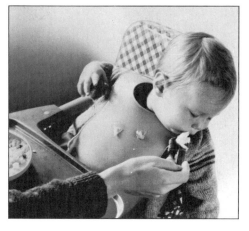

is hungry – she's more likely to take it then. The only thing to be on your guard against is that your child excludes all of one food group. If this happens, the diet will become unbalanced.

Weight problems

If a baby is offered the right kind of food, she will be neither underweight nor overweight, but will take in just enough to supply her needs at any particular time. Weight problems are the fault of parents, who are offering the wrong foods.

Overweight

Excess weight in a baby is nearly always caused by too much fatty meat, too many sweetened drinks, and refined carbohydrates (cakes, biscuits, jams and sweet foods) in the diet. It may also be caused by keeping your child in a pram or play pen and not allowing her to use up energy by crawling and walking. Always encourage your child to be active by playing games with her yourself – the livelier the better.

Underweight

Unless deprived of food, few toddlers are underweight in terms of their own development. They may be underweight compared to other babies of the same age and sex, but rarely in relation to their own physique and size. Many parents worry unnecessarily about having a small, thin baby – but some children are naturally small and thin, just as there are small, thin adults. If you are giving your baby a balanced diet and she is happy and developing normally (see p. 186), then you probably have nothing to worry about. If you are anxious, however, check with your doctor.

FOOD AND EATING   2–3

Your child's daily caloric requirements will continue to increase as she grows. During the third year she'll need roughly 50 calories for every pound of weight. Her nutritional requirements will remain the same and she'll need a variety of well-prepared foods.

What foods to give

Between the ages of two and three, children tend to prefer breads, cereals, and dairy products like milk, yogurt, ice cream and cottage cheese. They dislike, and may even reject, meat, fruit and vegetables. Don't get worked up about this; try, instead, to find some meats, fruits and vegetables that she does like and stick to them until your child signals that she wants a change.

Give your child two or three servings of protein, and four or more servings of fruit and vegetables a day. Provide four or more servings of bread – a serving being one-half a slice – and one or two tablespoons of cereal. Always serve whole grain bread and avoid high calorie, starchy foods.

Eating patterns

Your child may continue to have food "jags" (see p. 125) throughout this year, and may also demand rituals at meal times. A ritual is something your child has to have repeated. She may, for instance, insist on having her sandwich cut on the diagonal and refuse a sandwich which is cut in any other way. Some children will throw a temper tantrum if their plate is not set in a certain way. Approach these "rituals" with patience. After all, adults have food rituals, too: we sit in certain positions at the table, and may prefer our tables set in a certain way. As long as it is reasonable, your child's demand should be indulged. On the other hand, if it interferes seriously with the intake of food or disrupts the family, try to reason with your child and explain that such behavior is not fair to others. Be firm, but be prepared for it to take several attempts to break an undesirable ritual.

Organizing meal times

Your child should be getting quite familiar with the social aspects of eating, but don't expect too much from her. It will be very difficult for her to remain quiet and concentrate on eating with a spoon. You can't blame her for spilling a drink or making a mess while she is listening to what you are saying or trying to participate in the conversation. She is trying to learn so many new skills at once, it is not surprising that she gets a bit excited and, to break the tension, causes accidents. Be understanding and flexible!

TIPS
- Always make sure a meal contains at least one food you know your youngster likes.
- Always serve small amounts and allow second helpings. A plate piled with food is intimidating to a child.
- Keep foods simple. Children like to see what they are eating; they don't like messy foods.
- Always offer a variety of foods to guarantee a balanced diet.
- Liven up your toddler's meal by using brightly-colored food.
- Until your child is going to school, include a "finger" food in a meal where possible.
- Include foods that are fun to eat like jello, salt-free potato chips, and ice cream made without preservatives.

MAKING MEAL TIMES FUN
As with all feeding, the key word is flexibility. You and your child should enjoy yourselves, so give a little thought to making meal times entertaining for all of you.

- If she wants to use a knife, give your child a plastic or blunt-ended one.

- Ice cream cones don't have to be used just with ice cream. Fill one with cheese and tomato chopped together or a tuna fish salad. This allows you to give your three-year-old a snack on the move.

- Encourage your child sometimes to "build" her meal from sandwiches, cubes of cheese, vegetables and dried fruit. She could build a house or a car or a boat, and when it is finished eat it.

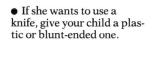

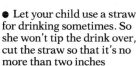

- Let your child use a straw for drinking sometimes. So she won't tip the drink over, cut the straw so that it's no more than two inches above the cup.

- Be open to innovation and occasionally serve your child's meal on a doll's plate or on a flat toy.

- Fill a cake tin with lots of different "finger" foods such as cubes of cheese, bits of cold meat, raw vegetables, fruit, potato chips, and tiny peanut butter sandwiches, and let your child pick out what she wants.

POSSIBLE PROBLEMS   2–3

The overweight toddler

Obesity in a young child is nearly always caused by lack of exercise combined with a poor diet which is high in "empty" calories. This includes highly refined starches and carbohydrates found in cakes, biscuits, sweets, chocolate, ice cream and sweet drinks. If your toddler is overweight, take the following steps:

☐ Reduce the amount of sugar your child is consuming. There is absolutely no need for her to take in any sugar in any form.

☐ If you have been adding sugar to food, stop. If necessary, use an artificial sweetener for a short time.

☐ Reduce the amount of food your child is eating as snacks. Switch to low-calorie, safe snacks (see below).

☐ Cut down on the amount of fat you use. Stop using butter and margarine; your child will probably not even notice. Don't fry in fat, but grill. Buy the leanest meat available and trim off any fat. Cut down on cheese.

☐ Make sure your child is getting every opportunity to play. Encourage active sports. Have friends to the house for a game of kickball or go outside with your child and play an active game with her.

☐ If your child is consuming a lot of protein, plus a lot of milk, she is probably getting too much. Cut down.

☐ Try giving your child more home-made and uncooked food. Pre-packaged foods, especially snacks, are often high in calories.

Refusing to eat

Refusal to eat is one of the first signs that your child is not well, so observe her carefully. Is she more clumsy than normal, rather pale and fretful? If so, check her temperature and, if you're worried, get medical advice. Sometimes your child may not be hungry at meal time simply because she had too many snacks beforehand. If she's had a drink of milk an hour before the meal, it's not fair to expect her to eat with her normal enthusiasm.

Sometimes your child may appear to refuse food for no reason at all. What you must never do in a case like this is force her to eat. Don't be taken in by her seemingly capricious behavior. Be casual about it and move on to something else. If you try to make her eat, her meal time can quickly become a battleground, and in the end you always lose. If you ignore your child, she'll eat when hungry; if she doesn't, don't worry. She will almost always make it up at the next meal.

SNACKS   1–3

Studies on the eating habits of children show that babies between the ages of four and five prefer to eat – indeed, their bodies require them to eat – frequently throughout the day. This is largely because their stomachs can't cope with three adult-sized meals a day, so we shouldn't try to impose an adult eating pattern on them. The actual range of eating-times for children is quite wide – from three to 14 times a day, with the average of about five to seven times. The size of the meal a child wants will vary throughout the day, but, as a general rule, the more often she eats, the smaller her meals will be. On average, children take in the same amount of nutrients, regardless of the number of times they eat in the day. What is important is not how often your child eats, but *what* she eats.

Sensible snacks are those which provide adequate calories in a nutritious form but contribute little to tooth decay. They include fresh fruits and vegetables, cubes of cheese, peanut butter and cheese sandwiches with wholegrain bread and fruit juice. Most commercial snack foods, especially those bought from vending machines and fast food stores, are highly refined and processed, and contain a lot of calories and very few nutrients. Don't over-do foods like biscuits, sweets, cakes, ice cream sundaes, raisins and other dried foods.

Planning out snacks

Snack foods should contribute to the whole day's nutrition, so don't leave them to chance; plan them out carefully. It is important to introduce variety since snacks can become just as boring to children as meals. Here are some ways to do this:

□ Coordinate meals and snacks so that you don't duplicate foods.
□ Try to make the snacks amusing. Place a tomato on top of an open wholewheat sandwich so that it looks like a smiling face, for instance, or cut up pieces of fruit in unusual shapes.
□ Try to involve your child in planning and, more important, in preparing part of the snack.
□ Take advantage of the activity to make the snack exciting and even educational. Your child can help you shell peas or make bread, for instance, and then eat what she has prepared.
□ Serve an ordinary food in a different form. Yogurt, for instance, may be unpalatable straight from a container, but frozen, like ice cream, it becomes a treat.
□ Drinks make nutritious snacks, particularly if they are milk-based (preferably with low fat or skimmed milk), because they contain protein, calcium, iron and many of the B vitamins.
□ Natural fruit juice is very nutritious since it contains natural sugars and lots of vitamin C, but doesn't promote tooth decay.

Snacks and tooth decay

Food encourages the development of tooth decay. Every time we eat, small amounts of food are left on and between the teeth, and these particles, particularly if they are starches, are broken down to acid by bacteria. It is these acids which dissolve the outer enamel layer of the tooth and cause the decay.

Carbohydrates and starches form the major food source for bacteria in the mouth. Refined sugar (sucrose) found in sweetened drinks, cakes and sweets is more easily converted to acid by bacteria than any other form of food. It has been shown that the higher the sugar content of the food, the more acid can be made by the bacteria and the greater the likelihood of tooth decay.

Not surprisingly, sticky foods stay on the teeth longer, giving bacteria a longer time in which to convert the starches into acid. Sticky foods, therefore, give rise to more tooth decay than sweet foods, which don't remain in the mouth as long, or get trapped between the teeth as easily. A sticky toffee, for example, will lead to tooth decay more readily than the same amount of sugar taken in a drink. This applies to other chewy foods, too.

When feeding your child snacks, you must consider the effect they will have on tooth decay. Start early in your baby's life by never adding sugar to her food. No person needs white sugar; the body can manage perfectly well without it. Do your children a favor and don't encourage a sweet tooth!

What you should encourage your child to do is to brush her teeth after eating any food (see p. 201). In addition, avoid ending meals with sweet desserts. It is much better to finish off with fruit or, best of all, a piece of cheese. Cheese is alkaline and neutralizes the acid in the mouth, therefore helping to prevent tooth decay.

8 The bladder and the bowels

Your child reaches a great milestone when she learns to control her bowels and her bladder, and manages to stay dry and clean both day and night. This won't happen, however, until she's physiologically and mentally mature enough to cooperate. You can't speed up this process – you can only help your child as she gradually gains control over her own body.

PASSING URINE   0–1

In young babies, the bladder empties itself automatically. A baby will pass urine frequently during the day and night because her bladder is unable to hold urine for any length of time; as soon as it contains a few ounces, the bladder wall is stretched, and it begins to empty itself. This is perfectly normal. You cannot expect your baby to behave any differently until the bladder has developed sufficiently to hold urine. This rarely happens before the age of 15 months.

BOWEL MOVEMENTS   0–1

During the 24 hours after delivery, your baby will excrete a sticky black substance called meconium. This filled the intestines when the baby was in the womb and has to be eliminated before normal digestion can begin.

Your baby will soon settle into a regular routine, and the stools will become firmer. So long as your baby is healthy, happy and gaining weight, you should pay very little attention to her bowel movements. Don't become obsessively worried about them.

Babies vary a great deal in the number of stools that they pass, but the number always tends to decrease as they grow older. At the beginning, your baby may pass three or four a day, but at the end of a few weeks she may have only one bowel movement every other day. This is perfectly normal! In fact, all the following are normal: loose, unformed stools; a totally green stool; a bowel movement after every meal, or up to six stools in the first days.

Stools of the breast-fed baby

During the first day or so, the stools will be greenish-black, smooth and sticky; afterwards, the light yellow stools typical of the breast-fed baby will first appear. The number of stools per day is quite unimportant. Some babies have only a few, others have a bowel movement every time they feed. The stools may be pasty or they may be no thicker than cream soup, but they are rarely hard or smelly. Breast-fed babies seldom suffer from constipation. Because they absorb practically all of the milk they drink, they have very little waste, and therefore may not move their bowels more than once every third day. Remember that your baby will be affected by the food you eat and that anything very spicy could upset digestion.

131

Stools of the bottle-fed baby

A baby fed on formula tends to have more frequent stools, and the stools tend to be firmer, browner and smellier than those of a breast-fed baby.

Your baby's stools may be soft at times, like scrambled eggs, but the usual tendency is for them to be rather hard. The easiest way to correct this is to give your baby more water to drink: it's a good idea to add a few more ounces of water to the normal number of scoops of powder when you're making up the bottles. Also, try giving your baby an ounce of cooled, boiled water to drink in between feedings, tipping it gently into the mouth with a spoon. When your baby is several months old, you can soften the stools by adding a little prune juice to her drink, or by giving a few teaspoonfuls of strained fruit thinned down with water.

There is absolutely no need to add sugar to your baby's bottles, but if for some reason you do, or if the formula has a high sugar content, the stools may have a tendency to be loose, green and curdy. The first thing you should do is to stop putting sugar in the formula. If this doesn't work, contact your doctor.

Changes in bowel movements

So long as your baby is doing well, it really doesn't matter if the stools change in appearance from one day to the next. A slightly lighter or a slightly darker color doesn't mean anything serious, nor does a softer or harder stool. If you're ever worried, however, do consult your doctor for advice. Looseness of the stools *per se* doesn't indicate an abnormality or an infection. On the other hand, watery stools accompanied by a sudden change in color, frequency and smell should be brought to the attention of your doctor, especially if you feel that your baby is not feeling well (see p. 307). As a general rule, changes in the number and color of the movements are much less important than changes in the smell and the amount of water in the stools.

As your baby gets older, be prepared for the stools to change whenever you add a new food, particularly fruits and vegetables. If the stools become very loose after you introduce a new food, don't give it again for several days and then try it in a very small quantity.

Don't forget that beets can turn the stools red, and that it is quite normal for stools to turn brown or green if left exposed to the air.

Streaks of blood in the stools are never normal. Even though the cause may be minor, like a tiny crack in the skin around the anus, you should consult your doctor. Large amounts of blood, pus or mucus may indicate an intestinal infection, so contact your doctor immediately.

POSSIBLE PROBLEMS   0–1

Constipation

Constipation is caused by hard, infrequent stools. By infrequent I mean less often than every three or four days; and by hard I mean hard enough to cause discomfort or pain. Constipation itself cannot make a child ill, and old theories that constipation poisons the system were discarded long ago. Constipation without any other signs of illness is nothing to worry about. However, if your baby is straining a great deal to pass a hard stool, and it causes her discomfort, consult your doctor to see if a laxative is necessary. Doctors are loath to use laxatives or purgatives for a small child, and it is hardly ever necessary to resort to such treatments. In a very small baby constipation is rare and it is nearly always caused by not giving her enough water. It can usually be corrected, therefore, by giving her more drinks or by adding an extra ounce of water to each bottle. Don't try the old-fashioned remedy of adding a little more sugar to your baby's milk – she doesn't need sugar, and it will only encourage a sweet tooth.

By far the best way to soften the stools is to alter the diet and to add a bit more fiber and roughage. Two teaspoons of prune juice added to your baby's drinking water will help. When she's on solids, add two teaspoons of strained stewed prunes to the evening meal.

Once your child is on a varied diet, she should never get constipated unless her diet is lacking in fresh fruit, vegetables, whole wheat breads and whole grains (see p. 122). If your child is constipated, simply add more of these to the diet. In a small child, the bowels always respond to additional complex carbohydrates (which are contained in root and green vegetables), because the cellulose within them holds water in the stools and makes them more bulky and soft. There are really only two times when a child should become chronically constipated. The first is when an over-fussy parent becomes obsessive about the regularity of the child's bowel movements. The second is when a child who has previously felt great discomfort and pain when trying to pass a motion, retains the stools to prevent that pain from recurring.

It is fairly common for a child to have a few days of constipation after an illness with a high temperature. This is partly because she takes in very little food so there are no waste products to pass. It is also because water is lost when the child sweats with fever, and the body conserves all the moisture it can by absorbing it from the stools. This kind of constipation needs no treatment at all. It will correct itself when your child gets well and returns to a proper diet. Don't use patent medicines, laxatives, suppositories or enemas without consulting your doctor.

Diarrhoea

True diarrhoea – very loose, frequent, watery stools – is a sign that the intestines are irritated and that the food is "hurrying" along. Once your child is on solids, a change of diet, such as the introduction of a new fruit or vegetable, may be enough to cause it.

Diarrhoea in small babies is always dangerous because the intestines are not given sufficient time to absorb the water essential for life, and severe dehydration can develop quite rapidly. There is no need to be concerned about the odd loose stool if your baby remains well, eats normally and is perfectly happy. However, if she has stools that are watery, green and smelly, with blood or pus; if she refuses food; or if she has a fever of 100°F (38°C) or more and is listless, with dark rings under her eyes – then contact your doctor immediately; diarrhoea can be cured quickly if it is treated early.

If your baby is very young (under four months) go directly to your doctor or hospital emergency room as soon as possible. With an older baby, stop all food and just give drinks of water until you can see your doctor. If your baby has mild diarrhoea and no other symptoms, you can start treatment immediately yourself. If you are breast-feeding your baby, continue to nurse. Diarrhoea usually clears up well on breast milk. If you are bottle-feeding, make up the next bottle at half-strength, with half the regular formula to the usual amount of water. She may feel like having only small amounts at a time, so let her take as much of this mixture as often as she likes. If a mild diarrhoea doesn't improve within two days, consult your doctor even if your child seems well.

Once the diarrhoea has cleared up, start re-introducing food. The best foods to start off with are mild, milky ones like jello; diluted fruit juice; stewed apples; dried cereal with milk; strained vegetables; mashed potatoes; white meat; eggs; mashed banana and other fruit. Start off with one-third to one-half the usual serving on the first day and move up to one-half to two-thirds on the second. On the third day, if all is going well, and her appetite has returned, go back to regular servings.

GAINING BOWEL AND BLADDER CONTROL 1–2

To my mind there is only one way to approach the whole subject of bowel and bladder control and that is to take signals from your child and to *help*, not train, your child. Control over the bowel or bladder rarely begins before the age of 15 or 18 months; sometimes it starts considerably later.

Gaining bowel control

It is not uncommon for babies three months old to empty their bowels during a meal or very soon after. Some parents take this to be an early sign of readiness for toilet training. It is not at all. It is simply the working of the gastro-colic reflex which stimulates the passage of food down the intestines to the bowels when food is eaten.

Your child will be ready for your help when she can make the connection between inner sensations and the conscious need to pass urine and feces. You'll notice this awareness when, for example, she suddenly stops what she's doing and points to the diaper, or otherwise attracts your attention with a cry or a shout.

Your child's awareness of having a full rectum or bladder will probably occur at the same time, but her ability to deal with them will be different. Since it's much easier to control a full rectum than a full bladder, your child will probably achieve bowel control first. It's sensible therefore to begin teaching your child to use the potty for bowel movements. They're more predictable than urination, so you can help your child prepare for them. When she makes her special movements or sounds, suggest that she use the potty. Remove her clothes or diapers so that nothing hinders her from getting to the potty on time.

After she's been on the potty, wipe her bottom (front-to-back in girls) with toilet paper. Put the wipes in the potty and flush the whole lot down the toilet. Remove any trace of feces and rinse out the potty, then wash it with disinfectant, remembering to wash your hands afterwards.

Never force your child to sit on the potty – it will have the reverse effect, and when you next suggest that she use it, you may be faced with a point-blank refusal or even a tantrum. Instead of causing a confrontation, just forget about the potty for a few days and then re-introduce it in a casual way.

Gaining bladder control

For this to be successful, your child's bladder must be capable of holding more than a few ounces of urine without spontaneously emptying itself. The process will have to be gradual. One of the first signs of this development is a dry diaper after your child has been wearing it for a reasonable length of time (for example, after an afternoon nap). Once your child stays dry regularly throughout this nap, you can start to leave off her diaper during that time. Before you put your child down for her nap, encourage her to urinate. If she does, congratulate her; if she doesn't, don't make a fuss, just try it again another day.

When she is capable of indicating to you that she wants to go to the potty, start leaving off diapers completely during the day. Never start this, however, until she can wait comfortably for a few minutes while you take down her clothes.

There will be accidents, so be prepared for them, and always be sympathetic. Never scold your toddler: it's not her fault. Initially she probably won't be able to give you a clear signal, so unless you're quick to interpret what she wants, she'll have no alternative but to urinate without getting to the potty. Just mop up and change any clothing without a fuss.

TIPS
● Let your child develop at her own pace. There is no way that you can speed up the process – you can only be there to help your child along.
● Let your child decide whether or not to sit on the potty. You can suggest that she does, but you should never force the issue.
● Treat your child's feces in a sensible manner, and never show any disgust or dislike for them. They're a natural part of your child and initially she'll be very proud of them.
● Do not delay once your child has signalled her need, since control is only possible for a short time.
● Praise your child and treat her control as an accomplishment.

Toilet training

I am wholeheartedly against toilet training. I believe that there are no arguments in favor of it, there are only arguments against it. I feel so strongly because it is impossible to train a child to do anything unless the body has developed to a point where it is anatomically and physiologically able to perform the tasks that are demanded of it. It is impossible for your child to control either her bowels or her bladder until her muscles are strong enough to hold urine and feces. She also has to be advanced enough that, at a given order from the brain, the nerves to bowels and bladder can obey an order to evacuate.

If this level of development has not been reached, there is nothing your child can do to adhere to your training program. You can see immediately what a dreadful position you are putting your child in. She knows what you want, but her body is unable to perform the task. Her desire to please you overrides almost all other desires, and in this she is frustrated. She becomes unhappy at not being able to please you and may then feel inadequate, ashamed, guilty and finally resentful.

Insisting on toilet training when your child is not ready for it can only end in sadness. The relationship with your child will deteriorate. You will become a source of unhappiness, and toilet training will become a battleground of your baby's will against your nerves. It's a battle neither of you can win. You cannot make your baby pass a stool or keep a diaper dry. Try to do either of these things and you'll make your child suffer every time the inevitable accident occurs.

BOWEL AND BLADDER CONTROL   2–3

The procedure for helping your child understand her bodily requirements is the same, no matter what age she starts to control her bowels and bladder (see information on the previous page). If your child hasn't shown control yet, don't worry. If she has, you can expect her to continue to improve during this year. It has been shown that by age two-and-a-half, approximately 90% of girls and 75% of boys have complete bowel control and even go to the toilet alone. The same study shows, however, that more than half the children of that age are still wet at night, although they can go without a diaper during the day.

Staying dry at night

Bladder control at night comes last of all. It is often not possible for a two-and-a-half year old child to hold urine for much longer than four to five hours, and it is often much less than that. The signal to start leaving off the night-time diaper is when she wakes up regularly with a dry diaper. When this happens, take her to the potty and encourage her to empty her bladder before she goes to sleep. Leave a potty beside the bed and suggest that she use it if necessary during the night. Leave a night light on so that she can see what she's doing, and be prepared to give any assistance if necessary. It's a big step for your child to stop relying on you and to take the responsibility for using the potty herself. Encourage her as soon as she shows any signs of taking this responsibility, because it's important that you help cultivate in her a sense of confidence. Be prepared for accidents, but never get upset by them. You can minimize your own work by:

☐ Protecting the mattress with a rubber sheet, with your usual sheet on top.

☐ Putting a small rubber sheet on top of the child's ordinary sheet, with a half sheet over that. If there's an accident, you can quickly remove the half sheet and spare the rest of the undersheet.

☐ Making sure that night wear is free of zippers so that your child can take down her clothes without any trouble.

☐ Avoiding confrontation by not forcing your child in any way. Gentleness and understanding invariably pay off.

Getting used to the lavatory

Once your child is using the potty regularly throughout the day, it's sensible to introduce her to the idea of using the toilet. To help your child adapt to the larger size, and to give a greater feeling of support and security, use a specially-designed seat which fits inside the toilet rim (see p. 21). Your child should feel comfortable on this, but if she's worried, suggest that she hold on to the sides of the seat, and always stay near at hand. You'll probably need to put a small step or box in front of the toilet so that she can get up easily. Show your little boy how to stand in front of the toilet and be very specific in teaching him to aim at the bowl before he urinates. You could also put a piece of toilet paper in the bowl for him to aim at.

Your child may become very self-reliant and want to do everything alone, in private. Respect such wishes; however, teach your child how to wipe herself or himself – especially your little girl. She should learn that she must wipe from the front to the back to avoid spreading any bacteria from the rectum to the vagina.

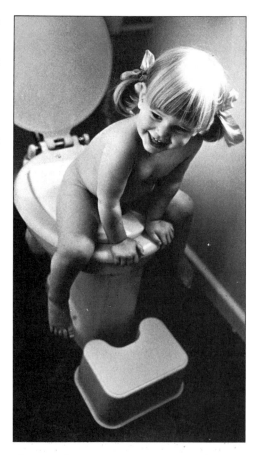

TIPS

● Whenever you travel, make sure to have a potty with you so that your child can go under any circumstances without having to wait. Put the potty on the floor in the back of your car so that you can stop anywhere along the road and not worry about finding a public restroom in a hurry.

● If she sits down and can't do anything, turn on the taps; this works for babies as well as adults.

● If you keep star charts for various accomplishments, keep one for "days without accidents."

● If you have a potty in the bathroom, you and your child could go to the toilet at the same time.

● Let your child accompany you to the toilet at an early age so that she can learn from watching you. This works particularly well with boys.

● Tell your child quite firmly and sympathetically that accidents will always be ignored and forgiven, and that she's not to worry about them.

● Get a potty well before you think your child will need it. You can explain why it is there and that when she is old enough she'll be able to use it. This may give your child an incentive to have a go.

● Don't flush the toilet when your child's with you – many get frightened, both by the noise and by the fact that "part of them" is being taken away.

POSSIBLE PROBLEMS   2–3

Late developers

Some children acquire bowel and bladder control much later than others. This may create problems for parents, but in nearly all cases it's wrong to blame the child. Often there is a family history of lateness in acquiring bladder control. Most doctors feel that if your child is wet during the day and night, there's no need to investigate this difficulty before your child is three years old. If she's wet only at night your doctor may feel that these investigations can be put off until she is five years old. Whenever you and your child go to see a doctor about a urinary problem, take along a specimen of urine so that he or she can look at it.

Bed-wetting

Some children, particularly boys, occasionally wet their beds well after the age of four. This is perfectly normal, particularly after a change of surroundings or routine, such as the arrival of another baby, an illness, or a spell of unhappiness. If your child has a bed-wetting problem, suggest lightly that she think about staying dry for the whole night – this positive thinking may help. But don't make a big thing of it – she'll worry and you'll have defeated your purpose. No matter how long bed-wetting goes on, always assure your child that it will eventually stop, because it does. She will just outgrow it, so stay calm and sympathetic at all times.

Regression

If your child suddenly seems to lose bladder and bowel control, and regresses to an earlier stage, she may be physically ill or emotionally disturbed. Sometimes the cause is perfectly obvious, such as a new baby in the house, which makes your older child feel dethroned and rejected. It would be quite normal for her to try all sorts of attention-seeking behavior to detract you from the new baby, including the wetting and soiling of clothes. Starting nursery school, moving to a new house, the absence of parents – these could all stimulate the same pattern of behavior. If there seems to be no explanation, however, consult a doctor. Your child may have an infection or a minor anatomical abnormality in the urinary tract.

9 Sleeping

A newborn baby spends most of the time asleep, but as he gets older, regular sleeping patterns will emerge. By the time he's three months old, he'll have one main wakeful period a day, usually at the same time, and quite often in the late afternoon or early evening. By the time your child's 12 months old, he'll probably be having two naps a day – one in the morning and one in the afternoon – and sleeping through the night. Although sleeping patterns will gradually come to resemble those of an adult during the second and third year, your child will still need a brief nap at some time during the day because of the amount of energy being used up both in growing and in play.

ALL ABOUT SLEEPING 0–1

Unless your newborn baby is hungry, cold or otherwise uncomfortable, he'll spend most of the time between feedings asleep. The amount of time he sleeps will depend on individual physiology, but the average is about 60% of the day. Don't, however, *expect* your baby to sleep all the time, and don't get worried when he doesn't. Some babies are naturally more wakeful than others right from the start.

Even though your baby will follow his own sleeping patterns it's important that he learn to differentiate between day and night. You can help him do this by darkening his room when you put him to sleep at night, and making sure that he is comfortable and contented. When he wakes up to be fed during the night, simply feed him without playing or otherwise distracting him. As he gets older and more aware of what's going on, develop an evening routine that includes the evening feeding, a bath, a story, games and songs before going to bed.

Occasionally a baby is sociable rather than sleepy after a meal. This is something you should enjoy, although it shouldn't stop you from establishing the same bedtime routine after the evening meal. If your baby is habitually wakeful after the meal, don't make everyone miserable by insisting that he stay in the cot. He'll only get upset and you and your baby will end up with frayed nerves. If you are a working mother like me and spend a good deal of your time away from home, your child will naturally see the evening as mothering time and will want to spend that time with you. You will probably want to be with him then, too, so why not be flexible? In our house, we were all far happier when we discovered that we had two sleepless young children, and abandoned the idea of a fixed bedtime. However, we didn't abandon bedtime routines.

Where your baby should sleep

So long as your baby is warm and comfortable, he'll be able to sleep almost anywhere. Most parents start their baby off in a crib or carry cot (see p. 26), because that way the baby is portable, and they can keep him close both day and night. When the baby outgrows these, however, he'll have to be put in a cot – preferably one with drop sides and an adjustable mattress (see p. 27), so that he can be picked up and put down easily.

Whatever room you put your baby to sleep in must be warm. An infant doesn't have full control over body temperature; in a cold room he'll lose body heat easily

139

but won't be able to generate it again by moving about or by shivering. Keep the room at a constant temperature of about 75°F (24°C). If you don't want to keep your whole house that warm, buy a thermo-statically-controlled heater (government approved), which will maintain your baby's room at a constant temperature.

Whenever you leave your baby to sleep outside, make sure she's not in direct sunlight. Either put the pram under a shady tree or use a fringed canopy. If there's a breeze, put the hood up and point the head of the pram into the wind so that there's an effective wind-break. Make sure you put a net over the front of the pram to keep out cats and insects.

MAKING UP YOUR BABY'S BED

To cover your baby use a washable quilt or light cellular blankets. Lie the blanket underneath the mattress, and pull the sides up over him when he's lying down.

Lay a muslin diaper where the baby's head is going to be to catch any dribbles.

Use flannel or terry towelling sheets with elasticized corners for easy bed-making.

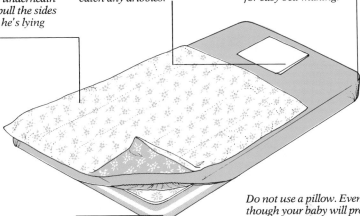

Baskets with oval mattresses can be made up with rectangular sheets, but make sure that the edges are tucked neatly underneath.

Whatever bed you use, protect the mattress with a thick, waterproof sheet.

Do not use a pillow. Even though your baby will probably roll free if his face gets covered, it's not worth taking the risk of making breathing difficult, should the pillow cover his mouth and nose.

BED-MAKING TIPS
● Buy special clips which hold the blanket or quilt in place to stop the baby from kicking them off.
● Avoid blankets with fringes – he may suck them.

● Buy closely-woven blankets otherwise your baby's fingers may get stuck in the holes.
● Supplement your supply of new sheets with your own old ones, cut to the

correct size. The more you have, the less frequently you'll have to do the wash.
● Use a pillowcase as a sheet – just slide the mattress into it. When one side gets dirty, turn the mattress over.

What your baby should wear

Young babies don't like being changed, so in the early weeks, when he's going to need changing quite frequently, you'll want clothes that give easy access to the diaper with a minimum of fuss. Nightdresses are therefore most practical initially, but once your baby has settled down – probably within a month – one-piece stretch suits are equally practical.

When your baby's about four months old, you may want to use a sleeping bag, especially in the winter (see p. 41). Your baby will stay warm and snug inside, and there will be no risk of the blankets or quilt being kicked off on a cold night. If the weather's very cold, put the baby in a

stretch suit first, otherwise just leave on the undershirt and diapers. In summer you may not need any covering other than the suit, although you may want to put a shirt on underneath.

Many parents worry about whether their baby is too hot or too cold once he's been put back in his crib. You can tell by touching the back of his neck, but make sure that your hand isn't too hot or too cold when you do this. If the back of the neck feels about the same temperature as your skin, then he's at the right temperature; if it feels damp and sweaty, he's probably too hot. If you've got blankets on, take one off; if he has a quilt, take off one layer of clothing. If the neck feels cool, add

141

an extra blanket or an extra layer of clothing. Never judge your baby's temperature by feeling the hands. Babies' extremities are often cooler than the rest of their bodies, and are quite often bluish in color. This is nothing to worry about.

Putting your baby down to sleep

When you lay your baby down to sleep (see p. 52), there's no particular position that is better than any other, except perhaps in the first few weeks, when it's advisable not to lay your baby on his back in case he spits up and inhales some of the curds. Put your baby down on his front or side. Change the position if he seems at all uncomfortable. When he's able to roll over (at about four or five months), he will take up the position of maximum comfort regardless of the position he's been put down in.

Put your baby down with his head touching, or close to, the top of the crib or cot. This, as when you wrap him in a blanket, makes him feel very secure. So that there's no danger of his head being hurt, put a quilted crib cover around the bed. Once your baby has fallen asleep don't change his position or he's bound to wake up. Similarly, don't keep on going into the room to check that he's all right. However, there's nothing wrong with carrying your baby around in a sling while he's asleep; after all, he slept in an upright position in the womb, and he'll be soothed by your constant closeness.

There's absolutely no need to keep the house quiet when you put your baby to bed. In fact, it's good to encourage him to go to sleep when all the usual household noises can be heard. Steady noises, like a voice on a television set, the sound of a vacuum cleaner, washing machine or spin drier, are quite soothing to babies and will soon send them off to sleep; only sudden changes in the level of noise are alarming. Over the ensuing months your baby will become an integral part of the family and will therefore have to get used to people living around him with all of their accompanying noise.

SWADDLING
Fold the shawl into a triangle and lay the baby on top with the head aligning with the longest edge (1). Fold one end across the baby and tuck firmly underneath (2). Repeat with the other edge (3). Tuck the bottom of the shawl under the baby's feet (4).

Getting your young baby to sleep

Your newborn baby will undoubtedly fall asleep whenever he's tired, and in almost any situation, but there are a few precautions to take to guarantee this:

☐ Wrap your baby in a blanket before he's put down, at least during the first month. He'll feel much more secure and contented with something firmly wrapped around him.

☐ Darken the room at night.

☐ In the winter leave a hot water bottle in the bed for half an hour before he's put down.

☐ Make sure that the room is warm enough (see p. 140).

☐ Place your hand on your baby's back or on one of the limbs to soothe him; rock the baby slightly.

☐ Use a musical mobile.

Getting your older baby to sleep

By the time your baby's about nine months old, he'll be able to keep himself awake, even when he's actually quite sleepy. As a result, he can become over-tired and so tense that sleep is impossible. The main reason he does this is his attachment to you: you provide love, security and excitement, and he doesn't want to lose these, even for a moment. Another reason, also linked to the desire for security, is his dislike of changes in routine, such as staying in a room that is not his own. Whatever the cause, this period of clinginess and insecurity will be brief, so treat it as calmly and sensibly as possible. Remember, your child isn't the only one in the world who refuses to go to sleep!

SLEEPING TIPS

● Keep pre-bedtimes as happy and pleasant as possible.

● Try nursing him, whether from the breast or the bottle, just before he's put to bed.

● Develop a routine and stick to it. Don't just put your baby straight to bed: work out a routine of play, bath, bed, story and song. After saying goodnight, don't leave the room; quietly tidy up so that your baby learns that he can drift off to sleep without actually "losing" you.

● Let the baby develop comfort habits (see below).

● Rock the baby's cot if he finds that soothing.

● Play the musical mobile. Many babies are fascinated by the movements they make and are soothed by the sound.

● Don't take the baby out with you in the evenings, even if you had no problems doing this earlier. He'll be used to his own routine and his own room, and will be frightened by being moved somewhere else.

● When he cries, always go back, but don't pick him up immediately. See what's wrong first – he may just need you to change his position.

Security objects

By about nine weeks, your baby may be showing signs of attachment to a security object such as a blanket, a handkerchief, a doll or his own thumb. He may choose to twist a piece of hair, to pull an ear, or to rock rhythmically and persistently. Child-care books used to frown at these habits, but there's nothing wrong with *any* of them. There's no particular age at which comforters should or shouldn't be used

and, like bed-wetting, children outgrow them. So, if your baby takes up a security object, don't try to prevent it. If you still feel dubious about letting him use one, look at it in this way: it is letting him cope without you and therefore developing self-reliance. The time when you should question your baby's use of a security object is when he uses it all the time, even when you're there. If he clings to it occasionally when he's very tired or coming down with

143

an illness, that's understandable. But if he persistently uses it, there's a good chance that you're not providing the kind of comfort and love that he needs, and he is having to resort to an artificial source of comfort to replace what he is not getting from you.

Naps

Once your baby sleeps through the night he'll need to take one or two naps during the day to restore his energy. What time he takes the naps depends on the individual baby – it may be after breakfast, it may be mid-morning, after lunch or at four o'clock. In the beginning, the time may change from day to day and from week to week. By the end of the first year a set pattern will probably emerge. Apart from special occasions (when, for example, you want your baby to be awake at a special time), the length of the nap should be left to your baby – some sleep only 20 minutes a day, others need four hours. If, however, he wants to sleep through the afternoon and then stays up most of the evening, encourage him to wake up earlier so he'll

go to sleep at a more convenient time for you. This won't harm your baby, and having his schedule conform to yours will make life easier for the whole family.

Going out at night

Until your baby is about six months old and requires a regular routine at bedtime, you can take him with you whenever you go out at night. Parents – especially mothers – need to have some relaxation during their child's first months, and infants will sleep anywhere. Once he starts sleeping through the night, however – especially toward the end of the first year when sleep isn't always predictable – try to stick to a regular bedtime routine. You can't expect infants to be as adaptable as adults, and if you want trouble-free bedtimes, you're going to have to follow a consistent routine.

POSSIBLE PROBLEMS   0–1

Early wakers

From the very beginning, try to encourage your baby to be happy alone in bed when he wakes. Put an interesting mobile just above the cot that will swing in the air and make patterns for your baby to watch whenever he's awake. Put a round-edged mirror on one side of the cot so that he can look at his own reflection and not feel lonely. Once he can reach up, put a string of objects within arm's reach so that he can move and play with them. These need not be expensive; they can be simple household articles, such as a small wooden spoon, an empty spool, or clothes pegs strung on a length of string and attached to the cot. It will also help to put a few favorite toys in the cot so he will always have something interesting to play with, and not need to scream for your attention. Make sure the room isn't too dark in the

mornings so that he can see what he's playing with. If the room is very dark, leave a night light on near the cot or hang thinner curtains.

You can help to train your baby to stay happily in bed by training yourself first. Don't lie there waiting for the first wakening murmur and then leap out of bed to see if he is all right. Let your baby chatter to himself as long as you can, and only go to him if he appears to be getting restless and upset. Always wait to see if he quiets down; it will be teaching him self-reliance and independence, even at this early age. If he becomes fretful, however, go immediately and give all the comfort and affection that you can.

KEEPING YOUR BABY AMUSED

Unless your baby is hungry or uncomfortably wet, he'll lie quite happily so long as he has something to hold his attention. The shapes within photographs or pictures pinned around the cot or crib stimulate young eyes, as do mobiles which sway and swing in the slightest breeze.

Night wakers

Young babies

It is absolutely essential that you get enough rest. If you have a baby who wakes at night, you and your partner should bear the burden equally from the very beginning and take alternate nights on and off duty. Whatever the cause of the crying, you should always go to your baby immediately. If you don't, he'll become increasingly distressed and difficult to pacify, and you'll become distraught.

Until your baby stops his night feeding and sleeps through, you're always going to have to get up at some point during the night. To cope with this, try the following:

☐ Work out a routine with your partner so that you can go to bed early at least once or twice a week.

☐ If you are bottle-feeding your baby, make the night feeding as little trouble as possible by preparing everything before you go to bed.

☐ If you are bottle-feeding, get your partner to do it every other night.

☐ If you are breast-feeding, and your milk is well-established, prepare a bottle of expressed milk for your partner to give at night. There is absolutely no reason not to do this, although your baby may not readily accept the rubber nipple (see p. 93).

☐ If you breast-feed your baby, make sure your partner helps you by bringing you the baby if he's in another room, by changing the diaper after feeding, and by putting the baby back to sleep.

☐ Many mothers find it difficult to get back to sleep once they have been woken up. Don't lie there fuming with resentment: try some relaxation exercises, read a book, tackle some work, or get up and do something that you've been putting off.

☐ If you've lost sleep during the night, you must make it up the following day. Completely relax your routine and do as little in the house as possible so that you can have a nap when the baby's sleeping.

Older babies

By the second half of the year, your baby should sleep through the night. However, there may be occasions when, for whatever reason, he wakes up. Try the following:

☐ Make sure that he's not too hot; if he is, remove either some covers or clothing.

☐ If he's cold from kicking off the covers, use a sleeping bag (see p. 41), more bedclothes, or leave a safety heater in the room to provide a constant temperature.

☐ Check that he doesn't have diaper rash; the discomfort could wake him up. Deal with the rash immediately (see p. 59).

☐ Don't constantly go into the baby's room to check that he's sleeping well – your anxiety will be more of a disturbance.

☐ If he's had a nightmare, provide comfort and stay until he's asleep again. If it happens on two successive nights, look for some external reason. Are you getting excessively upset with him? Is he being watched by a new baby sitter? Is he disturbed by your absence during the day?

Wakeful babies

Some babies just don't need as much sleep as others, and, as a result, are much more demanding of their parents' time and energy. Such babies should never be left lying alone in their cots with no diversions. They should have either mobiles or "amusement centers" (see p. 145), and should be carried about as often as possible. Put your baby in a sling as you work or move about the house. Put him in a bouncer in the doorway of the room you're in, or prop him up near you with cushions (see p. 53). Whatever you do, don't fret because your baby sleeps less than anticipated. When he's awake he's learning all the time, and you'll inevitably be rewarded with a bright and eager child.

ALL ABOUT SLEEPING   1–2

Most toddlers will sleep an average of 11 hours each night, and make up any extra sleep they need in naps. If your baby needed a lot of sleep during the first year, he'll probably continue to need it in the second; conversely, if he needed little sleep, this trend will continue, too. Although he sleeps through the night, he'll still need two naps a day. How long these naps last will depend, as noted before, on your baby. What may change this year are the times at which he wants to take the nap. His 9:30 nap, for instance, may get later and later, until he wants to sleep immediately after lunch, at 1:30 or 2. On other days, however, he may take a nap late in the morning, but then not want another one until the middle of the afternoon. In dealing with these changes, you have to take the lead from your baby; there's no point in trying to make him sleep to order, and you'll have to accept that napping patterns will vary from day

to day. Fit into the baby's routine so that, should he establish a pattern of getting sleepy towards 11.30 and wanting a nap around noon, you will begin lunch about 11.30. He'll then be able to have a satisfying nap after lunch, and you'll have a much less grumpy baby. Alternatively, you could wait until he wakes up before having lunch – it all depends on your baby.

About the age of 15 months, your toddler will reach a period where two naps a day are too many and one nap a day is too little. He'll happily play through the first nap but, because he can't last without sleep until the second one, he has to have a nap later than usual. This inevitably means that he's alert enough to miss the usual afternoon nap, but then needs to go to bed early. As with everything else in child care, you have to be flexible. The period where he has to drop one nap will be brief and he'll soon sort out his own

napping routine. By the end of the second year, he'll probably take a single nap at the end of the morning or in the afternoon.

Until he settles into a napping routine, make sure he is having adequate rest during the day. Even if he doesn't seem to be that tired, and rushes around, eager to learn new games or play with exciting toys, it's quite easy for him to become over-tired. Keep an eye on your child and if he becomes bad-tempered or fretful, or shows a sudden lack of coordination, make sure he rests or plays a quiet game.

Whenever your toddler takes a nap, let him wake up slowly and gently. It may be a restorative sleep, but he's unlikely to wake up perfectly refreshed and active. He'll need to be cuddled and talked to quietly for 15 minutes or so before he's ready to be active again. If you have to go out after your toddler's nap, try not to leave until he has recovered his good spirits.

Bedtime routines

Your baby's bedtime routine will change this year, requiring more diverting games and more of your attention. Give your baby both. The essential thing to remember is that bedtimes are play times and happy times. Even though you may be worn out, try to be calm and relaxed. If you are not, your baby will pick up your anxiety and you may have to spend twice as long putting him to sleep as when you gave him an extra five minutes of your undivided attention.

Where your toddler should sleep

At some time during this year, your baby may try to get out of his cot to come to you. Obviously a fall from the top of a cot could be dangerous, so either lower the mattress so that the top of the rails are out of reach, or put your child into a single bed (see p. 27). Specially-designed beds with safety rails are available and may be advisable if your toddler is quite small when he's first put into a single bed.

HELPING YOUR TODDLER TO SLEEP
During the day
● Fill a nap time play box for your child with favorite toys and books which he can look at as he gets sleepy. Don't leave good or expensive books – they may get ripped up. An imaginative alternative is to make up your own books by pasting interesting pictures from magazines on to board and then covering them with clear acetate.

● Give your child a treat by letting her take a nap in your bed, or on the couch or somewhere else near you.
● If your child won't take a nap, make sure that he has a rest time where he is calm and quiet.
● If your toddler won't go to sleep, put on a long-playing tape. Teach your child that the rest time is not over until the music stops.

HELPING YOUR TODDLER TO SLEEP
In the evening
● Don't put your child to bed immediately after an exciting game or rough-and-tumble – he will have great difficulty settling down, which will be frustrating for you. Give him ten to 15 minutes to quiet down, sitting with you watching TV or looking at a book.
● Even an infant likes looking at a book in bed. If your child seems happy, leave him with a favorite, non-scary book.
● Put a dab of your perfume or aftershave on to your child's pillow and suggest that he breathe it in deeply. Deep breathing is relaxing and calming and will help your child fall to sleep.
● Give your toddler a bath before bedtime, followed by a warm drink and bedtime story.

POSSIBLE PROBLEMS   1–2

Waking in the night

The estimated 15% of all two-year-olds who wake regularly in the night can be a source of great worry to parents, who also need their sleep. No matter how often this happens, or how irritating it may be, don't leave your child to cry; go to him immediately, provide comfort, and try to find out what the problem is. It may be something easily remedied – he may be cold because the blanket or quilt has fallen off; he may be too hot; he may be thirsty; he may be teething. On the other hand, it may be something less tangible: he may simply have woken up with a bad dream. The difficulty is that he can't explain what's upsetting him, and you can't tell him that he's got nothing to fear. What you should *always* do is provide love and affection, without any fear of spoiling him.

Dealing with a sleepless child

I'm very sympathetic to parents with sleepless children, having had two myself, one of whom became sick if he wasn't comforted within a minute or so after he started to cry. I would like to give the parents of such children a hopeful message. You may not enjoy an unbroken night's sleep for many years, and on many days you'll feel almost too tired to drag yourselves around. But you'll get through it! When I look at our two affectionate children I sometimes think I wouldn't have had it any other way – we gave them love in the night, they gave us five hundred times as much back every day.

At the time we were so desperate for sleep that it became our overriding priority; once it did, our worries were half over. We decided to do anything to ensure a full night's sleep, at least now and then. I could never believe that taking my baby into my bed and staying with him when he needed me could do either of us any harm. So I followed my instincts and threw any so-called rules to the wind. If you want to do the same, try it sooner rather than later. I'm convinced you're not buying problems, you're only being a good parent to your child.
☐ My husband and I took alternate nights "on duty," the other remaining asleep and undisturbed unless there was an emergency.
☐ We put a rollaway bed next to the baby's cot, so that we could put out a reassuring hand and pat him as he started to cry. This way, neither of us really woke up at all.
☐ We gave the child 15 minutes to settle down, then we took him into our own bed – a sure fire success.
☐ We only gave water or fruit juice at night, never milk.

TIPS FOR EARLY WAKERS
● Put a pile of cloth or homemade board books at the bottom of the cot or bed for early morning "reading." Make sure there is enough light to see by; if there isn't, leave on a low-wattage night light when you put your toddler to bed.
● Beside the baby's bed or cot put a soft box or plastic bucket filled with small toys, crayons, paper, bits of cloth or interesting household articles. He can sort through and play with them in the morning.
● Leave a paper bag with some fresh fruit or bread at the bottom of the bed; for safety reasons, never put the food in a plastic bag.
● Leave a drink in a cup within reach of your child.

Refusing to go to bed

According to the correspondence I get, there are more "difficult" babies around than most people realize, and they pose great problems for their parents. The baby who doesn't go to sleep at night is classically intelligent, physically very active, interested in everything that is going on around him, and openly affectionate. During the day these difficult children are delightful and very rewarding – but *you* pay the penalty at night.

Two of my four sons were sleepless, demanding babies, so I devised a few guiding principles for coping with them. Let me say first that the standard advice given in baby books did not work. If you have a difficult baby be prepared for this, and you'll feel less frustrated and inadequate when it happens. Begin by getting your priorities straight: no one can function properly for long without adequate sleep, and you, as a parent, are no exception. The trouble with some baby books is that they fail to consider the needs of parents. If you have a difficult sleepless child, you must think of yourself, too. Sleep is too important to miss for long, so why not adopt a few pragmatic rules, as opposed to the old-fashioned, dogmatic ones:

☐ There is nothing magical about bedrooms. Let your child go to sleep where he is most comfortable: at your feet on the floor, on a couch, in your lap.
☐ Be flexible about bed times. Left to themselves, most children go to sleep at seven or eight o'clock in the evening, whether you put them to bed or not. Why should they be unhappy upstairs in a room on their own, instead of happy in your company downstairs?
☐ Give your child an early evening bath. This often relaxes them and makes them sleepy.
☐ If your child is proving difficult to get to go to bed, still put on his nightclothes before he's brought downstairs. If he falls asleep you won't have to wake him up again, but can put him straight into bed.

Sleeping in a strange bed

If you're going to take your child away from home, on holidays or just to a friend's house for the night, give some thought to making the night in a strange bed a happy one. Don't be secretive and spring the trip on your child at the last minute; this will only increase his feelings of insecurity. Take along a favorite toy and a familiar blanket; be prepared to read his favorite book and play a favorite game once he's in bed. If he still clings to you, stay with him until he falls asleep. Leave a night light on and go to him as soon as he starts to cry. For the first few days of a holiday, put the cot or bed in your room, or very near it, until he's used to the surroundings and feels more confident. If your child gets upset don't force him into bed and don't ever leave him alone or lock the door. If your child's very upset, keep him on your knee until he falls asleep. Great distress should make you question whether it's a good idea to change the bedtime routine by taking him out in the first place.

By the time your child is two years old he usually needs 12 hours of sleep at night and one or two hours of napping during the day; once again, the actual amount will depend on the child. In general, the nap or rest time will shorten during the year, but the amount of time your child sleeps at night will remain the same until he's about six years old, at which time he'll reduce it half an hour per year.

About the age of three many children stop having naps, although the majority still need a rest period indoors after lunch until they are five or six.

Sleep routine

Children about the age of two and three sometimes begin to use delaying tactics at bedtime. They may want to go to the toilet or to have a drink – or they may just appear at your side with no excuses, wakeful and charming. In these circumstances, decide how to act according to what your previous routine has been. If you have been pretty flexible about bedtimes, never insisting that your child go to bed in his room, cot or bed, then you can't suddenly change tactics when your child is two or three: he simply will not accept the inconsistency, and will quite rightly balk at the new regime. In these circumstances, it is better to be practical and let your child play in the room with you until he is tired. Let him fall asleep beside you and then carry him up to bed.

On the other hand, if the bedtime routine has been carefully set and this new behavior is a departure from the norm, then your child will only benefit from your being firm about the re-establishment of routine. No doubt you will get a few whimpers and a few doleful pleas, but you have presumedly already established that you are loving and will come if he's in real need, so you can afford to be firm. If you have credit to draw on, your child will learn this lesson quickly, and soon return to his old routine. If you give in, however, your child will certainly begin to take advantage of you.

The way you handle these situations depends largely on how much energy you have left at the end of the day, and how prepared you are to have your evenings interrupted. If you are with your children all day, you will probably feel, with some justification, that night times are your own. If you've brought your children up to recognize this, you can be quite firm in insisting on it.

Keeping bedtimes happy

It is important to keep bedtimes happy. Personally, I am prepared to make quite a few concessions to make sure that my children are content when they go to bed. So that they won't fall asleep with the memory of my angry voice ringing in their ears, I forgive certain misdemeanours which would normally be punished earlier in the day. I try to avoid upsetting them or making them cry. It is worth making pre-bedtime activities especially joyful and friendly: as your children get older, spend the time between supper and bed (about 30 minutes) in their company – even if you are only sitting in the same room, reading a newspaper, or knitting, your physical presence will be very comforting and consoling, and will put your child in a happy mood when he makes the transition from the living room to the bedroom. Try to watch a suitable television program together, or read a book or play a game before you take your child to the bedroom.

Bedroom rituals

Most children like a bedtime ritual. My children have always had half a dozen favorite songs they like me to sing, and a story book they like their father to read. When we're at home together my husband will share the bedtime routine: ten minutes with me on songs and ten minutes with him on a story. We both try to stay in the bedroom. Since there are three children going to bed, bedtime is a communal experience, with the children sitting or lying on each other's beds. It's a family time. My husband lies on a bed while I sing my songs; I lie on a bed while he reads a story. When the story and songs are over, it's lights out, except for a low night light, although we often stay and talk over what has happened during the day. Sometimes we lie under the blankets to give our children the extra loving feeling of companionship.

In our house this rather protracted but worthwhile bedtime routine works. The last thing we do is switch on the landing light so the children can see their way to the bathroom or to our room, should they need us during the night. It's useful to have a light with a dimmer switch so that no doors have to be shut.

TIPS FOR MAKING BEDTIME EASY

● Mark the approach of bedtime with an alarm or a timer, so your children can have five minutes' warning.

● For a young child, have a toy clock next to the real clock and set the hands of the toy clock to bedtime. When the hands of the real clock match up with those of the toy clock, it's time for bed.

● Keep bedtime as close to the same time as you can every night to help establish regular sleeping patterns.

● Children are quite often not sleepy at their bed times. They like to have time to slow down just lying in bed looking at a new toy, reading a new book, or chatting to one another. It's usually a good idea to have children who are near each other in age sharing the same bedroom until they require privacy.

● Once your children get into a proper bed, snuggle down under the covers with them before you leave them to go to sleep. It's very nice for them; it warms up the bed, and their last memories are of your closeness. I do it with my children and I nearly always drop off to sleep before they do! We started the tradition when they were young and we still continue to do it even though the youngest are ten and eight.

POSSIBLE PROBLEMS   2–3

Delaying tactics

Your child may try to stop your leaving by saying that he simply doesn't want you to go. Here again, you have a choice of action. You can stay with your child until all fears are gone and he is feeling calm enough to go to sleep – either with or without you. Or you can call your child's bluff and leave. I think the latter action is dangerous, as it can frighten your child to the point of hysteria. This is bad both in the short term – he will have great difficulty going to sleep that night – and in the long term – he may develop a fear of sleep that lasts for several years. I would never advocate it.

An alternative is to say, "If you lie still for five minutes, I'll come back," and then return in exactly five minutes. Make sure that he is comfortable. If he's still awake, promise to return again – and do. In your absence, leave some music playing or let your child continue to read his book or to enjoy the game he has been playing. Don't leave him alone with fearful thoughts, waiting for you to return. On the third or fourth occasion you will probably find that your child has gone to sleep.

As a last resort, take your child into your room with you. Rest assured that there's absolutely no harm in this, although you will have to be prepared for it to become a long-term habit. It will make for some very rewarding family evenings, so long as you don't get too tired and aren't too jealous of your privacy. Use the method most suitable for you both.

Fear of the dark

If your child delays going to bed because he's fearful of being left alone or of being in the dark, you yourself can allay these fears. If he's scared of the dark, sit with him and distract him by reading a story, playing a game or singing nursery rhymes. Pat his back until he's calm and sleepy, or until he has quietly dropped off to sleep. Fear of the dark is perfectly normal and reasonable in a small child, so don't insist on the bedroom being dark. A low-wattage night light will be a comfort to him and also help you to see your way in the child's bedroom late at night.

Bad dreams and sleep walking

Your child probably won't have a nightmare before the age of three, though children sometimes wake up with a scream and a frightened look, which suggest that they have had a bad dream. An occasional nightmare is quite normal, although it can be frightening for the parent if the child doesn't become conscious straight away. Nightmares are not abnormal unless they occur frequently or are accompanied by regular sleep walking. This behavior suggests that the child is having to exercise a great deal of self-control to overcome anxieties when he is awake, and only loses this control when he is asleep. Try to find out the cause of the tension and remove it. If the cause isn't obvious – like the arrival of a new baby in the house, or the beginning of nursery school – talking things over with your doctor may be of help. If nightmares are a real problem, your doctor may recommend a child psychotherapist.

During a nightmare your child's eyes may be open although he won't actually see you. He may shout abuse at you in a strange, garbled language and be extremely rude and angry. Ignore all of this; he is not in control of himself and during the nightmare he'll be very frightened.

Very often there is little you can do to relieve your child's fear, even though that is your greatest wish. There's no point in trying to speak to him rationally about what is going on; in most cases he won't be able to understand you. During the nightmare don't ask your child to do anything – it will put further pressure on him and only increase his anxiety. The only way for you to behave – even though the nightmare may last as long as half an hour – is to remain by his side, entirely sympathetic, calm, softly spoken and caring. Never, ever, leave a child who is having a nightmare; stay until it is over. Your nearness and comfort are all that is required. Speak soothingly and quietly about anything you like; don't suggest that he try to pull himself together. Never raise your voice and *never* scold your child – it may make him hysterical.

Locked doors

One thing you should not do is lock your child's door to keep him away from you. This is just admitting your own failure to handle your child and is quite cruel. Locked doors and other barriers shouldn't be used in child care. There's no substitute for teaching your child, even as early as two years old, about the need to respect other people's privacy, including your own. A three-year-old child is open to reason and you should be able to explain to him that he cannot get out of bed whenever it pleases him, and that you will put him back no matter how often he does it. If you are firm but reasonable, your child should respond.

One thing you must do, for your child's own safety, if he habitually gets out of bed is to put a guard across the top of all stairs.

10 Crying

A newborn baby will always be in one of three conditions – asleep, awake and quiet, and awake and crying. Many newborn babies cry quite a lot, so be prepared for it. If you expect your baby to cry, and treat it as normal when she does, you will find it easier to cope with. If your baby doesn't cry much, be thankful!

In order to understand why your baby is crying, and how you can provide comfort, you have to understand that what upsets a baby and what provides comfort for her changes as she develops. A two-week-old baby may cry when she's clumsily undressed for a bath; a one-year-old may cry because she's unhappy when you leave the room. The two-week-old baby will be comforted by being snugly wrapped up in a towel; the one-year-old will be comforted by your return.

ALL ABOUT CRYING   0–1

Your newborn baby has a limited repertoire for communication, and crying is almost her only way of telling you that something is wrong. Remember that for many months she's been floating gently in the dark, with a constant temperature and a constant food supply, so bright lights, hard surfaces, cold sensations and hunger are quite a lot to cry about! However, the cry doesn't necessarily mean that your baby is in danger.

Recognizing different cries

Mothers and fathers become increasingly adept at distinguishing among different baby cries during the week following birth. This is not a one-sided distinction; babies become increasingly able to anticipate their mother's responses to their cries. Most parents worry quite a bit about their baby's crying, and the interpretations seem endless. Is it hunger, boredom, anger, loneliness, overtiredness, stomach pains or colic? Does she want a cuddle or is she just plain miserable? After the first four weeks mothers interpret the crying in terms of other information, such as the last time the baby was fed, and how much she ate.

Responding to crying

The way you respond to your baby's distress can affect how your baby behaves and how she grows up. The way you comfort her can influence the bond that grows between you. The issue goes beyond that of spoiling to the central question of how your child's early experiences with you affect later development.

Some fairly recent work with newborn babies has shown that over the first few days of life a slow response to crying may lead to more, rather than less, crying. Another study found that babies whose crying is ignored early on tend to cry more frequently and more persistently later in the first year, and that after the first six months this persistent crying further discourages the mothers from responding. The same research showed that mothers who respond quickly have children who are more likely to be advanced in "communication skills" (as measured in terms of the range of facial expressions).

Further studies found that a mother's sensitive and prompt response promotes a harmonious relationship with her child, who in turn, becomes more content, obedient, secure and competent. This research supports the belief that mothers are programmed to respond immediately to their babies. Some psychologists see insensitive mothers, who do not respond promptly, as "going against nature." They attribute the difficulty mothers have with demanding children largely to the erosion of a natural mother-baby relationship – an erosion caused largely by anxiety about spoiling.

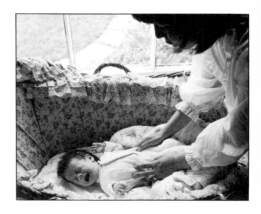

Never leave your baby to cry

Parental apathy is the most important factor in a child's failure to develop deep, loving relationships. This failure to respond to the needs of children may even cause more lasting distress than physical violence.

I have heard mothers say, "If she is clean, dry, and well fed – let her cry." Or, "He needs to cry for an hour – it's the only exercise his lungs get, so leave him alone." I am very strongly against these attitudes. In my opinion, a baby should *never* be left to cry. In the first place, a crying baby may swallow air, which will cause discomfort and make feeding difficult. Prolonged crying may make your baby feel very tired, even exhausted, and she will become extremely irritable and difficult to soothe. More important, she will quickly learn that pleas for attention go unheeded, and that there is no loving human response when she needs it.

All the research I have cited supports the belief that you should not let your baby cry. Ignore her, and she will soon stop asking for attention, which may seriously damage her ability to ever form relationships with others while growing up. A baby's pattern of behavior, first with the mother, then with the father, and later on with family and friends, begins to form during the first six weeks, and continues to develop during her first year of life. If friendship is denied to a child in these early weeks, she may grow up introverted

and withdrawn, hesitant to display affection, and repulsed by physical contact. Don't give your child such an unfair start in life.

Spoiling your baby?

A baby cannot be loved too much. I don't share the belief that too much physical contact or nursing will spoil a child. If picking up, nursing, loving and cuddling mean spoiling, then a child under one year old cannot be spoiled enough. A child who is picked up and nursed is learning about loving, human behavior. The model for this behavior, which she'll retain for life, is the early relationship with her mother and father.

What we tend to call spoiling is both the natural response of a mother to a distressed child, and the natural need of the baby. A mother's behavior is "built-in," just as much as the behavior of the baby. A mother is genetically programmed to respond to her baby's crying, though she may suppress her instinctive response with a learned response which interferes with her natural drives. Her natural inclination is to pick up, soothe and nurse her crying baby. Society has suggested that she will spoil her baby if she does this, and so she is torn; she should not be. She should follow her natural instincts. The protective instinct in a mother (which is what she displays when she picks up and tries to soothe her crying child) is the basis of her mothering instinct, and essential to

her biological function as a mother. Babies require this physical contact with a soft, warm, loving human being. The need for this is so strong that it almost overrides the need for food.

Crying, and your prompt response to it, undoubtedly play an important part in the way your baby becomes attached to you. Every child in a family will become attached to both parents, but the quality of the attachment depends on the sensitivity of the mother. It is the promptness and appropriateness of the mother's response to her child's distress – in other words, how attuned she is to the needs of her child – that constitutes the most important part of this sensitivity, and it is critical for the development of a stable and happy relationship both between baby and mother, and between baby and other people as she grows up. So my answer to the question, "Is it possible to spoil a baby?" is an unequivocal "No."

Crying spells

Spells of crying are likely to go on for three, four or even six weeks, while your baby becomes acclimatized to the outside world. When she establishes a routine with regular likes and dislikes, she will usually cry less frequently.

All parents find it harder to cope with a child's crying during the night. Patience and stamina are much greater during the day, when you're feeling strong and awake; but when sleep is interrupted, you can expect to feel a great amount of impatience. Such feelings are not abnormal; everyone experiences them. When your baby starts to cry at night, don't panic. It's inevitable that she will, and your tenseness will only make matters worse.

If you feel that your baby is crying a lot, take comfort from research which has shown that babies may cry quite independently of any discomfort they may feel or of the effectiveness of the comfort you give. The report showed, for instance, that babies whose mothers were given general anaesthesia during delivery took longer to calm down after birth. They were also more easily startled and less anxious to be cuddled. Babies who were born after a long labor, or whose mothers were given drugs during labor, were more likely to cry frequently and to sleep for short periods.

Mothers who were highly anxious during pregnancy have more irritable and difficult babies. It is also well-known that male babies are more vulnerable to stress at the time of birth than female babies. At least one American study has shown that boys at the age of three weeks are more irritable than girls.

Cultural differences are a factor, too. Chinese/American babies were found to be calmer, and more passive in their responses to unpleasant stimuli than European/American babies. The Chinese babies were also easier to soothe, and stopped crying immediately after they were picked up and spoken to. They were also better at quieting themselves.

Another study undertaken in America has shown that babies differ in the amount that they cry, even though they are cared for under the same conditions. One has to accept the fact that all babies are simply not the same!

THE CAUSES OF CRYING   0–6m

Hunger

This is the most common reason why young babies cry, and parents soon learn to recognize the sound. Studies have confirmed what every parent knows – that babies cry more before feeding than after. Experiments have shown that it is the actual feeling of having a full stomach that brings the most comfort, and not the act of feeding, swallowing or being held.

What to do
● Nurse on demand. Don't be inflexible about feeding times, and never nurse by the clock. Remember, she's very young and may want feeding every two or three hours. Nursing her 15 or 30 minutes earlier than expected will do her no harm.
● If your baby seems to want only to suck, give her an ounce of boiled water as a drink between feedings (off a sterilized spoon).
● Use a pacifier (see p. 22). Hold it in the baby's mouth if necessary so that she can suck on something. You can also use a clean finger.

Temperature

Temperature and humidity both have important effects on the amount of time a baby sleeps, cries and is active. Young babies kept at a rather high temperature – between 88F and 90F (31°C and 32°C) cry less and sleep more than when they are kept at 78F (26°C). Wet or dirty diapers don't in themselves cause crying unless the wet diaper gets cold, too, in which case the drop in temperature will cause her considerable distress.

What to do
● Make sure your baby's room is at the desired temperature.
● Feel the back of your baby's neck to test whether she's too hot or too cold (if she's sweating, for example, she's too hot [see p. 141]). Add another layer of clothing if she's too cold, or take one off if she's too hot.
● Check your baby's diaper to see if it's wet; change it if necessary.

Lack of contact

Some babies cry whenever you put them down in their cots, but stop as soon as you pick them up again. This is a perfectly natural instinct, and means that your baby feels happiest when she is physically close to you. In many cultures babies are constantly swaddled or held in close contact with their mothers' bodies, and these babies rarely cry.

What to do
● Pick your baby up as soon as she cries.
● Carry your baby around with you in a sling or a shawl (see p. 53), so that she can hear your heart beat.
● Rock your baby until you get tired, then let your partner take over until the baby's calm again.
● Wrap your baby tightly in a receiving blanket (see p. 142). The texture of the cloth should be warm and fluffy – cool fabrics are far less effective.
● Lay your baby across your lap, tummy downwards, and massage her back and limbs.
● Lay your baby across a warm hot water bottle on your lap or on a bed.

Undressing

Most babies hate being undressed, even when their room temperature is controlled and they are awake and contented immediately beforehand. This aversion to undressing gets worse during the second and third weeks. As soon as the baby senses that her clothes are being removed, she tenses up. Her discomfort is greatest when the clothing nearest her skin is removed. The cause is not the cold, but the fact that the skin is no longer in contact with the familiar and reassuring texture of the clothing.

What to do
● Keep undressing to a minimum in the early weeks. Try giving sponge baths (see p. 71), so that you only have to undress the baby a bit at a time.
● Whenever you have to undress the baby fully, lay a towel across her body – the contact with the fabric will reassure her.
● Always talk soothingly and reassuringly and try to get the undressing over as soon as possible.

Pain

This is a very definite cause of crying, although the actual cause of the pain may be hard to determine. It may be the pain of colic (see p. 160); it may be something quite obvious like an open diaper pin or a tightly fitting garment. If it's caused by ear ache, you'll probably see your baby putting her fist against the affected ear.

What to do
● Go to your baby immediately. Hold her close, cuddle and talk soothingly to her.
● Remove the source of pain if it's easily discernible.
● Stay with your baby until she's completely calmed down.
● If no amount of comforting works, and your baby seems ill, seek medical advice.

Violent or sudden stimulation

Sudden changes in the level of stimulation – light, noise, jerking movements, rough play, or the sensation of falling – will cause your baby great distress. Thinking she is about to fall, for instance, your startled baby will throw out both arms and legs in the Moro reflex (see p. 14), and will invariably begin to cry.

What to do
● Hold your baby close to you and use the general pacifying methods of contact, movement and sound.
● Avoid moving your baby in such a sudden way next time.
● Avoid sudden stimulation with bright lights, loud noises or sudden, jerky movements. A baby can stand quite loud noises or bright lights over a long period of time, but a sudden change will cause immediate distress.

Tiredness

Many babies cry when they are tired. It took me almost two weeks to understand this! "Clever baby," I thought, "Dumb mother." Some babies (like adults) twitch or jerk just as they are dropping off to sleep. This may cause a baby to wake up again and, if it continues, will result in a fretful sleep.

What to do
● Lay the baby in a quiet, warm, dimly-lit room.
● If your baby's particularly twitchy, wrap her up firmly before she's put down to sleep.

Misreading your baby's signals

Failure to read your baby's signals –
whether they be "I'm hungry," "I'm tired,"
"I want to be cuddled not played with" –
can result in tears. If your baby is ready to
be fed, for instance, but you give her a bath
first, she's bound to cry. If, while you're
breast-feeding, you fail to notice that your
baby can't suck properly because she's
being smothered by your breast, then she's
bound to cry.

What to do
● Be alert. Look at your baby, listen to
her gurgles and grumbles, and
interpret what she's saying to you.
You will understand what she is saying
if you are attentive enough to listen.
● Take care of the problem
immediately.
● Use the general crying cures.

Colic

Many young babies have a crying spell
sometime during the day – often about
6 o'clock, just before or after the evening feeding. This is quite normal. However, if the crying differs from the usual
hungry or lonely cry and is basically a
scream; if your baby's face becomes
very red, and she draws both of her legs
up to her stomach as if she's in great
pain; if every effort you make to pacify
her is unsuccessful – whether it's feeding, burping, swaddling or cuddling –
then the likelihood is that she has colic.
No one knows why it occurs, but it
usually starts in the first three weeks
after birth and lasts until the baby's
three months old, when it stops as
suddenly as it started.

Colic has been attributed to many
causes such as underfeeding, overfeed-
ing, allergy, constipation, diarrhoea,
too much wind in the bowels, being
picked up too much, being picked up
too little, mild indigestion, intestinal
cramps, and, finally, tension.

All pediatricians agree that babies
who cry a great deal in the evening
seem otherwise healthy. The world-
famous pediatrician Ronald Illingworth has commented, "The outstand-
ing impression given by the colicky
baby, except in the evening, is that he is
a well, happy, thriving, well-fed, well-
managed baby with nothing wrong
with him." Although Illingworth found
no evidence to support the causes listed

above. After studying 100 babies, he
stressed that spoiling was unlikely to be
the original cause of regular evening
crying.

The tension theory seems to me the
most likely cause, although there is no
real proof. The late evening is quite a
busy time of day. You will be expecting
your partner home from work, and
there will probably be an evening meal
to prepare. The baby has to be fed,
bathed, played with and put to bed.
You will probably be feeling worn out,
and your sympathy will be at a low ebb.
Your baby is very quick to pick up
tension and may well respond to your
evening hypersensitiveness with a fit of
crying.

What to do
There are no known remedies for colic.
Although gripe water is a traditional
remedy, its usefulness is unproven.
Since crying is so frequent an occurrence in a young baby, I'm against
using any kind of medication, even
specially formulated drugs. Take heart
from Illingworth's studies, which show
that babies with evening colic are
otherwise perfectly healthy. Try to
comfort your baby, using any of the
methods previously described, but
don't expect miracle cures. Remember
above all, that screaming fits come *only*
at night and last eight weeks out of a
whole lifetime of pleasure that you'll
have with your child.

General crying cures

Most babies are soothed by sound and movement, and many parents find themselves relaxed by them as well. But if your baby continues to cry, try some or all of the following remedies:

Movement

● Rock your baby – rocking chairs and swings are ideal for this.

● Walk or dance with your baby.

● Bounce the baby gently in your arms or on a bed or in the cot.

● Put your baby in a bouncing seat that will move gently.

● Take your baby for a ride in a car, pram or sling, even at night.

● If you are by yourself, put your baby in a sling and let her cry while you get on with whatever you were doing. Try to ignore the crying until it stops.

Sound

● Talk, sing or hum to your baby.

● Put on the radio or television.

● Put on the vacuum cleaner, or let a tap run forcibly into the sink for a few minutes.

● Give your baby a noisy toy. Shake it and rattle it.

● Play tapes or records of calm music.

Your baby will continue to cry if she's hungry, in pain, or too hot or too cold. The cures for these problems will remain the same as for newborns (see p. 158); as she gets older, however, she will also be distressed by new things.

Boredom

Your baby will spend longer periods awake during the latter half of this year and may cry out of sheer boredom if she's just left unattended in a cot, with nothing to look at or play with. During this period, she'll be anxious to stay with you and see what you're doing at every moment. You're a constant source of amusement and affection, and when you leave her – especially if she can hear you elsewhere – she's bound to cry.

What to do

● Always have mobiles or similar toys above your baby's cot so that she can touch them and watch how they move (see p. 145). Leaves on trees, curtains blowing by an open window, lampshades moving – these all provide amusement for your baby.

● You'll have a more contented baby if you keep her near you whenever she's awake.

Anxiety

Your baby may become increasingly wary and scared, especially of strangers and of your going away. During the second half of this year she will be extremely clingy. Her increasing dependence on you will be paralleled by growing attachments to security objects, like her own thumbs, a blanket or a doll. The source of comfort varies from child to child, but the need for it is common to all of them. The intensity and persistence of these attachments can last for two to three years. The objects can usually be sucked or stroked, and children use them when they are anxious and tired to simulate the effects of continuous physical contact.

What to do
● Understand that this is just a period in your child's development – one that she has to go through.
● Never force her to go to a stranger if she really can't stand it.
● Let your baby have a pacifier. She'll grow out of it in time.
● Give your baby lots of cuddles.

Frustration

Your baby's increasing physical capabilities may well lead to tears of frustration. Once she starts crawling she'll be able to move away from you more quickly and will want to explore her surroundings. What this in fact means is that she'll frequently have to be stopped from doing what she wants to do both for own safety and to protect whatever it is she's trying to explore.

What to do
● Make your home as "child-proof" as possible by removing objects from low tables and shelves, and by using the correct safety fittings throughout (see p. 293).
● Remove the baby from the source of frustration. If, for example, she keeps going up to a dog and pulling it's tail, remove one or the other from the room. Your baby's memory is very short at this point in time, so she'll soon forget the object of her curiosity.
● Distract your baby with other games.

ALL ABOUT CRYING   1–2

Among one- and two-year-olds, most crying is due to emotional disturbance: to fear, anxiety, separation, deprivation of mother and mother-love.

Insecurity

Between the ages of one and three, children spend less and less time physically close to, and touching, their mothers. But in contrast to this apparent independence, there will be moments when she becomes frightened and anxious. When she reaches the age of one, you may notice that she's quieter and less mischievous than usual; that she has become very shy of strangers and unusual situations, and clings desperately to your legs. She may even seem to lose interest in food. These are all general signs of anxiousness to which you should respond immediately.

What to do
The best way of coping with these anxieties is to give your toddler extra affection. Encourage her to be curious and adventursome, and to develop a sense of self-confidence. Praise and reward each feat, each new achievement. Your toddler requires your approbation and will do almost anything to get it, so it really is

quite easy to encourage her to be independent.

A child who is securely attached to a parent, uses that security as a base from which to explore – and to explore with confidence. Much research has demonstrated that the presence of the person with whom the child has a secure attachment enables her to cope with new, possibly fearful, experiences and with the accompanying anxiety.

Fear of separation

Because a toddler is so attached to his parents, separation becomes one of the greatest causes of distress, and fear of separation is one of the most potent causes of anxiety. When fear, insecurity, anxiety or separation cause great distress, then crying ensues. The degree of distress varies according to several factors: your toddler's age (it often decreases from age 10 months to age 15 months); the way in which you actually leave her; and the strangeness of the situation in which she is left. If also depends, of course, on how frequently your child has been separated from you. If it was unpleasant the first time, she is likely to find it more unpleasant the second time.

Children undoubtedly don't like being left. In a way, the better parent you are, the more your child is likely to cry when separated from you.

What to do
Never be scornful of fears; always try to be sympathetic and supportive. Reassure your child, more by actions than by words, that you are to be trusted and relied upon. If you say you will come back in half an hour, do so. If you say you are just going into the next room, go no further. If you say you will pop back in five minutes to check on a game, return as you promised. One of your baby's greatest sources of confidence is knowing she can trust you to keep your word!

In your attempts at sympathy and reliability, do your best not to be overprotective. This will only curb whatever adventurous spirit your child has, and stop her from building self-confidence.

Frustration

Toward the end of the second year, your baby's adventurous spirit will almost certainly outstrip her powers of coordination and mobility. She will attempt tasks that are beyond her dexterity, sense of balance and physical strength, and this will cause great frustration. It's inevitable that you, too will become a source of frustration, since, for her own safety, you'll have to stop her from doing certain things she wants to do.

What to do
Try to be patient. The best form of support you can give is your help. Help with her painting. Help her build a tower of blocks. Help with climbing, making sand castles, propping up soldiers or farmyard animals. If frustration at her own inability causes crying, you can easily distract her by introducing her to another favorite game.

If she gets frustrated when she tries to copy older children's games, or tries to do something which an elder child can do easily, suggest that you play a game together that you know she can physically cope with. It's important for your child to try new things, and to continue trying when she doesn't immediately succeed. But too many defeats could have a retrogressive effect.

Don't be drawn into battles with your child – whether they're over using the potty or eating a certain food. She'll want to assert independence of mind and, where possible, you should respect this and not force the issue. Let your toddler decide whether she wants to use the potty, and don't worry if she wants to eat only green beans and ice cream. A calm acceptance of facts is better than arguing.

POSSIBLE PROBLEMS 1–2

Temper tantrums

A temper tantrum is an attention-seeking device. The tantrum will go on as long as you are giving your child your attention; it will end abruptly when you withdraw it. The best thing to do is to leave the room; your child will come to no harm. A breath-holding attack is self-limiting, and your child will take a breath as soon as she becomes at all short of oxygen. If she kicks and screams, simply move articles out of reach so that she can't be hurt, and leave her to kick and scream. Don't be tempted to cajole your child, to lose your temper, to hit her, or to threaten punishment. None will do the slightest good in stopping the tantrum, or in averting the next one. The only course of action is to leave your child alone.

Night-time crying

Quite a few babies cry as they are going to bed at night. You can do a lot to avoid this by establishing a bedtime routine. This doesn't mean that you are inflexible, but that you are giving the evening a rhythm both you and your baby can get used to. Bathing and going to bed should ideally be happy times. From the time your baby is six months old, she should be enjoying her bath – treat it as play time, and you're off to a good start (see p. 74). By the time the bath is over, your baby should be relaxed and getting sleepy. If supper is also casual, informal and happy; and if a story, game or song – whichever your child prefers – is followed by bed and a firm but loving goodnight, then your baby should go to bed without crying. As children get older, they express preferences for particular songs which they like sung in a certain sequence, or for favorite stories which they will follow with you in their story book. Some children will drop off to sleep while listening to music or while you sit by them quietly reading or singing. Find the bedtime routine that suits your child best and follow it *every* night without fail (see p. 147). Familiarity breeds security, and that brings a happy child at bedtime, more likely to go to sleep without a fuss.

Prolonged separation

The effect of prolonged separation varies a great deal with age. Before the age of six or seven months, babies usually do not show signs of distress when they're admitted to a hospital or separated from their parents for extended periods. From the age of six months to four or five years, however, children are acutely distressed by similar circumstances – boys perhaps more than girls. Young children who have had an unhappy first experience of separation are more likely to be upset by a second separation or by admission to a hospital. The longer the separation, the more disturbance the child will show, especially if the separation is from a mother, father or siblings.

The effects can be mitigated by mother-like care from another individual, say a foster parent or a loving nurse, especially if the surrogate mother does the following:
☐ Takes care to follow the baby's known daily routine and to respect the pattern of child-rearing to which she is accustomed.
☐ Meets and spends some time with the child before the separation occurs.
☐ Talks to the child about her family, so that her memories stay fresh.

ALL ABOUT CRYING 2–3

As your baby gets older, her reasons for crying become much more complicated. Her feelings will be influenced not just by the fear of separation, but by her understanding of the world and what is going on in it. She will develop insights into your motivations and recognize your more subtle expressions of approbation and disapproval. She will become acutely aware of her own position in the family, among friends, and in the world in general. She will develop new insecurities and anxieties. While she is gaining in self-confidence, she will also become more sensitive, and more likely to feel shame, resentment, frustration, anger, and jealousy – all of which will upset her and cause her to cry.

Fears real and imagined

There are so-called classical fears which affect all children between the ages of two and three. The fact that your child suffers from them is not a sign of abnormality. Two of them are described below.

Fear of the dark

Help your child by leaving a night light on in the bedroom. You don't have to go to any expense; just replace the standard bulb in your lamp by a colored one with low wattage. You can also help your child by showing her that darkness is nothing to fear. Go for a walk with her at night and point out all sorts of interesting things that you don't normally see during the day, like the stars or the moon, or some nocturnal animals (the nocturnal house in a zoo, which you tour in darkness, may also be a good idea). In the summer take your child in the backyard or in the park, and lie on the grass, covered by a blanket.

Fear of thunder

Most children are fearful of thunder and lightning. The best you can do is to distract your child until it's over. Tell a favorite story, turn the television set up loud, play music, or get out that game you bought "especially for a rainy day."

Dealing with fears

Encourage your child to talk about fears as soon as she is able to. Listen intently and show that you are interested and sympathetic. Hear her out even if she finds it difficult to put her fears into words. Help her find examples of her fears, and show that you identify with them. Never tease or shame your child about what she is feeling – that will only encourage her to hide it, and drive her away from you. Always be the sympathetic friend who will give help and comfort in a frightening situation. You are going to have to show your child how to face up to fears, and here are some of the ways that you can do it:

□ One of the best ways to reassure your child is to show her that you are, or were, exactly the same as she is. All children love hearing stories about when parents were little, like them. Tell your child some of the fears you had, and explain how you overcame them with *your* parents' help.

□ If your child becomes fearful of a piece of household equipment, such as the washing machine, help her to overcome it by explaining what it does and how it works. Tell your child that a washing machine is nothing to be afraid of, and to prove it, hold her in your arms while you fill it, and give a running commentary on exactly what you are doing. Go through the routine of putting in the powder and switching the machine on. Put your hand on it to feel the vibrations, and then, slowly and gently, put your child's hand on it with yours on top, so she knows you're not frightened, and that with your support she needn't be frightened either.

□ If your child is scared of getting lost or of being in an accident, talk her through it. You might say, for instance, "If you get lost, what's the first thing you could do? ... Well, I think probably the best thing would be to go to the first house with a light on, knock on the door, and say, 'I am Jane Brown. My address is ... my telephone number is ... Please will you ring my mummy and daddy?'"

□ Never, ever brush off a fear as though it weren't serious. It *is* serious to your child, and you should treat it as such. If, for example, your child is worried by the ominous shadow her bedroom lamp casts on the wall, move the bed to a position where there are no shadows.

Dealing with irrational fears

One of the best ways to deal with irrational fears is to dispel them with some kind of physical activity. If your child is afraid of monsters or ghosts, tell her you are a parent who can do magical things to them. Tell her you are able to blow them away, and give a big blow; promise that you will be able to get rid of them with the vacuum cleaner, and switch it on; or guarantee that you can flush them down the toilet and do so. Some people say you should not pretend to believe in monsters and ghosts, since this will only encourage your children to believe in them, too. But that assumes your childrens' fears are rational – which they're not.

Separation anxieties

Children well over the age of three still dislike being separated from their parents, even if you are only going out for the evening. Until the age of five or six, it is quite usual for a child to shed a few tears until she is given some reassuring details about the evening. Tell her what time you're going; whom you'll be with; what you'll be doing and what time you'll return. Explain the evening in terms she can relate to. Tell for, for instance, that you're going to spend the evening with a relative who lives about as far away as your child's play group, and that you'll just be having a meal and sitting around talking with friends. Reassure your child that at 11 o'clock you will be returning home.

Making separation easier

☐ Always spend a few quiet, enjoyable minutes with your child before you leave. Start getting dressed 15 minutes early so you will have this time to devote entirely to your child before leaving the house. Never rush off without proper leave-taking!

☐ If you make a promise to be back by a certain time, keep it. As you are going, remind your child that you will always come back. If you are delayed, telephone to explain why, and say that you will be home in a short while.

☐ It is a nice idea to have a goodbye ritual – to tell a story or play a game, to give a hug, to blow a kiss as you get into the car, to wave to your child as she stands on the step, or to honk your horn as you leave.

☐ Be imaginative: kiss your child's palm, fold her fingers around it, and tell her that if she needs a kiss while you're away, there is one there for her to have.

☐ Never keep the fact that you are going to go out a secret from your child. In fact, talk about it well ahead of your absence – at least the day before. Mention it again casually the morning of the day you're going out, and once or twice during the afternoon. Suggest that your child come into your bathroom while you bathe, and even help you to get dressed. All children love playing with jewelry, so give your child the free run of your jewelry box.

☐ When your child is very small, don't use a time scale that she can't grasp; instead, compare time with some favorite television programs. If you are going to be away for an hour and a half, for instance, tell her you will be gone for the length of three science fiction programs; if you're going out for half an hour, tell her you'll be gone for as long as it takes to watch four cartoons.

☐ If you are going to have a babysitter, ask her to come a good half hour before you leave so she can get involved in some kind of activity with your child before you go. If you do this successfully, your child may not even raise her head as you leave, but simply say, "Bye, Mom."

Dealing with injuries

You don't want your child to grow up being babyish about minor injuries, but you should never underestimate one, especially if you can see the damage. There is no point in saying that a small scratch doesn't hurt, because the sight of blood will scare your child and she will use pain as an excuse for your attention. Whenever your child comes to you with an injury, give sympathy and support. The best medicine is a kiss, a hug, and a gentle word. Next, try a favorite drink or snack, then suggest a small treat – perhaps your child's favorite food for the next meal, or a game you can play together. Always keep your "magic" ointment by you. In our house it is 0.5% cetrimide cream – a simple antiseptic that can be used for all cuts and abrasions. It's very soothing, and if your child believes an ointment will take the pain away, why not use it?

Pre-school nerves

There are very few children who skip off happily to nursery school with a cheery goodbye to parents and hardly a look backwards. Be sure to prepare your child well in advance for nursery school, no matter how self-confident she appears to be.

The first thing you have to do is check out the various nursery schools in your neighborhood. This will require quite a lot of time and effort because you should visit each one, talk to the teachers at some length, and sit in on at least a few classes. Unless you are thorough, you won't be able to get a good sense of the atmosphere; of how interested the teachers are in the children, or of how much individual attention they are prepared to give during different activities. Is there a good rapport between you and the teachers? If not, there's no point in sending your child

there, no matter how good the nursery school appears to be.

Most good nursery school teachers will insist that you take your child along for a brief visit several weeks before she is going to start. Don't make a big thing of it. Fit it in between errands and don't stay any longer than about 15 minutes. Don't push your child into it. Make the point of your visit a chat with one of the teachers, and let your child look listen, observe and absorb. Let her wander around, touch, pick up and play with things, but don't force her to do so. Some nursery schools might like your child to visit more than once before she actually starts.

On the first morning, be prepared for a shaky start, and for the necessity of remaining in school with your child the entire morning. Many nurseries welcome this and encourage you to help your child by participating in her lessons and staying

quite near her. This may not be necessary. As soon as your child feels you are not going to leave, she will be quite happy if you sit at the back of the room. Take some work or a book along with you, so that your day is not wasted. If your child seems happy, tell her you are going to step out to get something from the car and will be back in five minutes. Return in exactly five minutes. If your child is distressed when you leave, don't go. If, on the other hand, she is quite content, let another half hour pass and then tell her you are going to do an errand and will be back in 20 minutes. Be back in time!

During the next few days, using your child's reaction as a guide, try to leave her for increasingly longer periods of time. Some children adapt very quickly to a nursery, and you won't need to stay after a few days. Others may still want you to stay for half an hour at the end of two weeks. Just fit in with their needs. The most important thing is that your child feels that school is a joyful place and does not associate it with the unhappiness of being separated from you. A good teacher – one who feels confident in herself – will very firmly suggest that you leave when she thinks the time is right. Being over-protective about your child at a nursery school makes it harder rather than easier for your child, especially if she's capable of coping without you. If you have good rapport with the teacher, you should feel happy taking her advice in this.

All of my children liked a ritual when they first arrived at nursery school. We used to either play games, try out new toys, draw pictures with new crayons, or draw on the blackboard. No matter what it was, we always did something together for about five to seven minutes before I said goodbye, and then they always came to the window and waved. These family rituals kept our children not yet three quite happy when I departed – so you may want to try a similar routine with yours.

Temper tantrums

A good method of handling temper tantrums when you are home alone with your child is to ignore them (see p. 164). Alternatively, you could distract your child by saying something unusual, amusing or silly, or doing something unpredictable, like switching the light on and off, or opening and banging a door several times.

As your child gets older, however, the chances increase that she will throw her tantrums in public, and you will want to deal with them in a different way. The majority of temper tantrums are caused by anger and frustration – anger that she can't have her own way or that her body isn't physically strong enough or well enough coordinated to do what she wants it to do. Every now and then your child, like everybody else, will need to give full vent to her anger and frustration. You can help her through this by doing some of the following:

☐ If your child is having a temper tantrum in a public place, don't get flustered; just take her into another room as calmly as you can. Take her from the shop into the street or car; or take her from the hotel foyer into the rest room. You can deal with the tantrum more calmly where there are fewer people about.

☐ Don't ever forget to congratulate your child and praise her when the tantrum is over and she has regained self-control. After all, it's only a stage she's going through at the moment.

☐ A lot of anger and aggression can be exorcised by physically active, outdoor games. Bicycles, skates and skateboards are such good toys because strenuous physical activity re-directs antisocial behavior.

☐ If your child is expressing anger by shouting, join in for a few moments, then gradually soften your voice, encouraging her to do the same, until you are both whispering. Then have a good laugh together.

☐ Give your child some paper and crayons or fingerpaints and ask her to put on paper exactly what she is feeling.

☐ Let your child release her anger by beating a drum, playing a musical instrument, or shouting a marching song.

☐ It can help your child quite a bit to talk about anger and to know that you consider it a reasonable and valuable emotion to feel. It lets off steam, but it also draws boundaries. Your anger tells her when she has overstepped the mark in all sorts of directions. Her own anger can be just as useful.

☐ Discuss with your child the causes of anger. Getting to the root of the problem together will teach your child about the importance of tolerance, love, kindness, thoughtfulness for others, etc. If you ever think such anger is justified, say so. Tell her why you think it's reasonable to be angry about something, and then discuss the different ways she might have reacted that wouldn't have been so hurtful and destructive.

☐ Show your child that anger is just as well expressed in words as in physical violence or destructiveness. Let her know that angry words are much more acceptable to you than blows or breaking things.

BREATH HOLDING TIPS

As your child gets older, she may try to express her feelings by holding her breath – which will make her face turn blue. In this instance, try the following:

● Blow gently on your child's face.

● Sprinkle a few drops of cold water onto her face or apply a cold cloth.

● Gently pinch your child's nostrils together for a second or two.

Phobias

A phobia is different from an ordinary fear. If, for example, your child is *afraid* snakes, she is only afraid when she meets one at fairly close quarters. The rest of the time she doesn't give snakes a second thought. However, if your child has a *phobia* about snakes, she will become hysterical, not only when she sees one, but when she sees a picture of one, when she thinks of one, or when something reminds her of one. One thing you must understand is that explaining a phobia to a child, even as she gets older, will not make any difference: she is not open to rational explanations. The only way you can help your child over a phobia is to convince her that the object of her fear is harmless. There are a variety of ways in which you can do this:

☐ Help your child realize such fears are unfounded by letting her know you don't share her fear – but talk to her in a way that doesn't make her feel inferior.

☐ Show her that her peers do not share her fears. If, for example, she has a phobia about dogs, ask one of your friends who has a dog to bring it to the nursery school at pick-up time when your child can see that no one else is afraid of it.

☐ Never, ever ridicule your child's fears. No matter how unrealistic they seem to you, they are very real to her. Give rational explanations wherever you can and *always* behave in a sympathetic and helpful way.

☐ If the phobia starts suddenly, look for something in your child's life which is causing stress. If the phobia's associated with a parent going away, the death of a pet or the start of nursery school, then there is a good chance that the phobia will be transient.

☐ Your child may be emotionally upset about something which is difficult to fathom. When her phobia is related to a specific object (as opposed, say, to a fear of heights), very gently introduce that object while she is doing something pleasant, like eating a favorite food such as ice cream.

Rows in front of the children

Of course your children have to grow up knowing the facts of life, one of which is that adults disagree occasionally, get angry and have rows, but for heaven's sake don't have rows in front of them too frequently! If your relationship is going through a difficult period, don't fight in front of the children. Children, of course, want their parents to inhabit an ideal world where there is no anger and no acrimony, and they begin to feel very insecure when the people they love most don't seem to love each other. After my husband and I had a fight, our four-and-a-half-year-old son snuggled up to me looking very doleful. When I asked him what was wrong, he said, "I don't know, but the world doesn't feel right."

Most children have the natural instinct to be peace-makers. As soon as they hear a raised voice or an opinion vehemently expressed, they start with diverting tactics like "Do you want a cup of coffee, Mom?" It is very hard to lose your temper when your small child is pleading with you to stay calm. Realizing the negative effect a fight can have on your children should act as a great deterrent.

Hitting your baby

Every parent at some time or other contemplates doing something physically violent to her/his children. Mothers who have to pace the floor all night trying to pacify a screaming infant, will confess that they have thought of doing *anything* to stop the baby from crying. When my youngest son was five days old I was in such bad shape that I actually did think of throwing him against the wall. It's not abnormal to think such things. It's only abnormal to do them.

The highest incidence of baby abuse among women is during the pre-menstrual period, and it is a well-recognized part of the pre-menstrual syndrome. Along with depression, irritability, tearfulness, lethargy and feelings of unworthiness goes a lack of sympathy and patience. Mothers who are ideal parents – very loving and caring, sympathetic and patient during the rest of the month – can become disturbed mothers for the few days prior to menstruation.

Most mothers know when they begin to lose hold of themselves and are able to control violent behavior against their children. But if you feel yourself sliding down the slippery slope, seek help, first from your partner or friend, and then from your doctor.

If you *ever* find yourself hitting your baby hard enough to leave marks and bruises, don't feel that it is an admission of failure to seek help from your doctor. It is *essential* that you do, both for your child's sake and your own. Don't stand by and let your partner injure your child: try to make him see that what he is doing is wrong, and if he is impervious to your pleas, seek help on behalf of both of you. Contact your doctor or the police immediately. If you think another adult is hitting a child, never stand by without intervening. If you have seen evidence of child abuse, don't take no for an answer from the authorities; be persistent.

11 Physical development

Watching your baby grow and develop is one of the most exciting aspects of being a parent, and during the first year you'll be astounded by how quickly your child changes. With each passing week he'll gain control over the various muscles in his body. As his coordination improves, he'll be able to sit, crawl, stand and, eventually, walk and run. His manipulative abilities will improve, and gradually, over the months, he'll develop fine control over his movements. Every child develops at his own rate – the ages which I give for various skills or degrees of coordination are only approximations. Don't force your child to go more quickly than he wants to – it will serve no purpose. Let him go at his own pace, while still providing all the encouragement and help you can.

GENERAL DEVELOPMENT   0–1

The main changes that occur in your baby's general appearance, besides those of size and weight, are in proportion, posture and body control. Your baby's head gradually gets smaller in proportion to the rest of his body, and his limbs lengthen and grow stronger. During the first year, your baby gains general control of his body, so that it's no longer floppy and he can move it purposefully.

Your baby goes through the fastest growing phase of life in the womb. Growth and weight will continue to be rapid during the first six months, but the rate will slow down toward the end of the first year. In general, a baby of average weight will increase its length by one-quarter during the first six months, and double its weight. In the first 12 months the head will increase in circumference by about twice as much as in the next 11 years.

Most size/weight charts plot the baby's weight in pounds or kilograms against the baby's age in weeks and height in inches (see p. 334). Except for the first few weeks of life, when weight gain is watched rather closely, it's best not to watch your baby's weight obsessively. If your baby looks healthy and acts in a healthy way, then it's highly unlikely that anything is wrong. It's the long term trends that are important. When considering your baby's weight, take account of different seasonal growth rates. Since growth is fastest in the spring and slowest in the autumn, a year is the minimum period over which you can study a child's growth realistically. And when you look at this growth, pay attention to the regularity of weight gain rather than the amount. So long as your baby's weight increases over the weeks, even if the rate is a bit erratic, and he shows signs of being happy, then you shouldn't worry about weighing him too often. Furthermore, all size/weight charts are constructed for an "average" child. This "average" child is a theoretical statistic. Your baby is unique, with patterns of growth and weight that will probably be different from those of any other baby. That doesn't mean he's abnormal.

Physical milestones

Milestones are "punctuations" in a baby's growth and development. These milestones occur with such regularity that it is usually possible to forecast with some accuracy when they will occur. This does not mean, however, that *all* babies will develop at the same speed. Physical capabilities develop faster in some babies than in others. However, there are a few general principles of growth which apply to all babies:

☐ All milestones are reached in the same order. Your baby will not usually go on to another milestone until the previous one has been reached.

☐ The rate of development is rarely constant; there are periods when it is very fast (growth spurts) and periods when it is very slow. Although development should be continuous, the pace can change. A big step forward is often followed by a small one.

☐ A primitive reflex or movement has to be lost before a baby can acquire a particular skill. For example, your baby has to lose the primitive grasp reflex (see p. 14) before he can acquire the skill of grasping an object purposefully.

☐ Development always proceeds from head to toe. The first milestone to be reached is control of the head, followed by the body, the arms, the trunk and the legs.

☐ When your baby is very young, his movements are usually jerky. As he gets older his movements become smoother and more precise.

☐ Generalized activities usually become more specific and focused. At six months your baby may be making rather purposeless leg movements which resemble walking, but they will be quite different from the movements your one-year-old child makes when he starts to walk.

☐ Development is measured not only in terms of *what* is done but *how* it is done. In other words, as your baby develops so do his skills.

☐ The brain and the nervous system control movement and coordination, so your baby can only reach milestones when his brain is ready. For instance, your baby will learn to pick up small objects between his fingers and thumb only when the nerve connections to the fingers and thumb are fully developed.

☐ While a new skill is being mastered your baby may appear to lose a previously learned skill. This is simply because he is concentrating on the new one. As soon as it is mastered, the old ones will return.

☐ Milestones can be affected by your child's personality. Independent, determined children nearly always try out and practise new movements more than other children, so it's not surprising that they master them earlier. A friendly, outgoing child often has a strong desire to communicate with others and may develop speech earlier than other children. You can encourage both of these characteristics in your child by the way you behave toward him (see p. 223).

BODY MILESTONES

At one month
Your baby will have lost his very newborn appearance, but his legs will still be bent. He may lift his head.

At two months
Your baby continues to stretch himself. He can lift his head to a 45° angle and hold it for a few minutes.

At three months
Your baby's body will be completely uncurled and his legs will be extended. He'll hold up his head.

At four months
Your baby will be able to roll from side to side and on to his back. He'll support himself on his forearms.

At five months
When placed on his stomach your baby will push his head well clear of the mattress. He'll roll from back to side.

MANIPULATIVE MILESTONES

At one month
Your baby's hand will be held in a tight fist; he'll reflexively grasp anything put in his palm.

At two months
He'll hold his hand open more often and his grasp will become voluntary.

At three months
His hands will generally stay open, although he may not be able to grasp anything for long.

At four months
Your baby will have discovered his own hands, which he'll suck and play with.

At five months
He'll be able to grasp objects between both hands and will love sucking his own feet this way.

175

BODY MILESTONES

At six months
Your baby will be able to twist in all directions. He'll probably sit unsupported for a few seconds.

At seven months
Your baby's ability to sit will improve, although he may have to bend forward to balance himself.

At eight months
Your baby will be able to sit up completely unsupported and will be able to turn round.

At nine months
Your baby will make determined efforts to crawl and may be able to support himself on hands and knees.

At ten months
Your baby will be able to crawl with straight arms and legs. He'll pull himself to a standing position.

At 11 to 12 months
Your baby should be able to totter when supported and will move about by himself.

MANIPULATIVE MILESTONES

At six months
Your baby will be able to hold an object between finger and thumb and may be able to rotate his wrist.

At seven months
The finger and thumb become completely opposable. Your baby can hold objects in both hands.

At eight months
Your baby's dexterity will improve and he'll use a pincer movement to grasp small objects.

At nine months
Dexterity continues to improve. He begins to use his index finger to poke into holes.

At ten months
Your baby will be able to hold two objects in one hand. He'll be a bit clumsy when releasing them.

At 11 to 12 months
Your baby can hold crayons, feed himself, give and take objects. Coordination will improve daily.

Control of the head

Up to the age of six months, head control develops in the following way:

WHEN ON HIS BACK
● *From birth to six weeks*

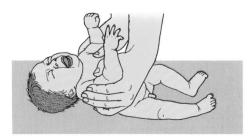

If you grasp your baby around the upper chest and lift his body from the mattress, his head will be so heavy and floppy that it will just hang back. This is why it is so important to carefully support his neck and head.

● *At six weeks*
If you lift your baby from the mattress by holding on to his hands, he'll be able to hold his head in line with the rest of his body for a second or so.

● *At three months*

If you pull your baby up from a lying position by his hands, he will keep his head up in line with the rest of his body without additional help from you.

● *At six months*
Your baby's head and neck will be so strong and well controlled that he'll be able to raise his head from the mattress and look at his toes.

WHEN ON HIS STOMACH
● *At one month*

Your baby will lie with his head to one side, with his bottom pushed up in the air and his knees slightly bent underneath his body.

● *At two months*
Your baby's body will be more fully stretched out, and he'll be able to lift his head from the mattress for a moment or so.

● *At three months*
He will now lie quite flat and will be able to raise his head and hold it in this position for a considerable time. He'll begin to take the weight of his shoulders and head on slightly outstretched arms.

● *At four months*

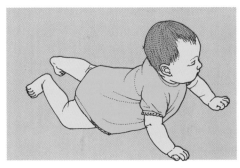

Your baby will be able to raise both legs off the mattress. He'll be able to support his chest and head by propping himself up on his forearms. This will allow him to see what's going on around him.

● *At five to six months*
Your baby will probably be strong enough to take the weight of his head, shoulders and torso on his outstretched hands. He'll also be able to roll over from his back to his side.

Sitting

Before your baby can sit up, he has to develop sufficient strength in his neck, shoulders and trunk so that he can control his head and keep his torso steadily upright. He also has to learn how to balance so that he doesn't topple over every time he tries to pick something up or twist around to see what's behind him; most babies don't achieve this before the age of eight or nine months.

● *At birth*

Your baby won't be able to sit up at all without support. If you hold him in a sitting position his back will be round and his head will loll forward. He'll be very wobbly, and will collapse immediately unless supported.

● *At one month*
Your baby's back will still be rounded and he'll only be a bit steadier. However, he'll try and hold his head up for a second or two when held by you.

● *At four months*

If you hold your baby in the sitting position, he will be able to sit with his head held up; the lower part of his back will still be rounded but the upper part will be almost straight.

● *At six months*
Your baby will be able to sit up without support, but only for a few seconds. However, by this time he will enjoy sitting up in a chair surrounded by cushions for support.

● *At seven months*

He will be able to sit alone, but will be very unsteady. His back will still be rounded and he will have to support himself with both arms, probably by placing them in front of his body as a kind of brace. However, in this position he won't be able to move his hands in any way because he'll be relying on them for balance. Any movement will result in his tumbling over.

● *At eight months*
Your baby should be able to sit up straight without using his hands for support. He will still be a bit unsteady, so always make sure that he is surrounded by soft cushions in case he topples over.

● *At nine to ten months*

Your baby's balance will be so well developed that he'll be able to swing his torso to look around and will be able to reach forward without losing his balance.

Helping your baby to sit up

Now that you know how a baby learns to control his head and sit up, you can help him by playing physical games similar to those played in the first months of life. This will introduce him to muscles used for grasping, pulling and pushing:

☐ From the age of about two months you can help your baby learn to sit up by supporting his tummy and shoulders. Talk to him so that he momentarily tries to raise his head to look at you.

☐ By the time your baby is three months old, you will find that he is able to control head, neck and shoulders, but that his back needs support because it's still rounded.

☐ At four months he'll be able to hold his head, neck and most of his back straight. All you'll have to do is hold on to his arms to keep his bottom steady and stop him from bending too much at the hips.

179

Propping your baby up

From as early as six weeks you should include your baby in what's going on by propping him in an upright position with pillows (see p. 53). He won't be strong enough to sit alone, but the pillows will provide all the support he needs. I found that, with my children, the bouncing cradle worked best. It's soft enough to conform to the baby's rounded shape, and it can be safely padded with soft pillows and cushions. Make sure that your baby is safely strapped into it to prevent him from slipping, and that his head is supported with a cushion or pillow. Because the cradle's so springy, it responds to both arm movements and kicking, and your baby is encouraged to try to make things happen for himself. And because the chair

is well-angled, he is propped up and can see all around him. The bouncing cradle is very portable; it makes it easy for you to carry your small child to a table or work surface next to you, where he will both learn from you and be reassured by your presence. The legs of the bouncing cradle are usually made of slippery metal, so it's a good idea to bind them with double-sided sticky tape. This will let you place your child safely on a shiny or slippery table. You can actually prop your baby anywhere, so long as there is a straight, firm slope between his bottom and his head. Make sure he's always well sur-rounded and supported by the cushions; if you're careful, he can be propped in an armchair, between the back and the arm of a sofa, or in his pram.

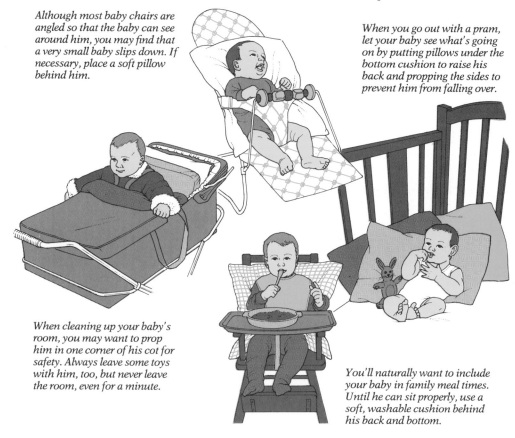

Although most baby chairs are angled so that the baby can see around him, you may find that a very small baby slips down. If necessary, place a soft pillow behind him.

When you go out with a pram, let your baby see what's going on by putting pillows under the bottom cushion to raise his back and propping the sides to prevent him from falling over.

When cleaning up your baby's room, you may want to prop him in one corner of his cot for safety. Always leave some toys with him, too, but never leave the room, even for a minute.

You'll naturally want to include your baby in family meal times. Until he can sit properly, use a soft, washable cushion behind his back and bottom.

Crawling

Before your baby can crawl, he has to be able to get into the right position; straighten his body so that his legs are outstretched; to gain adequate control of his head and neck, and to be strong enough to push up on both of his arms so that his chest and head are clear of the floor.

It's difficult to specify the exact age when a baby will start to crawl, so you should regard the times given below more as stages than as specific times. What's more, you shouldn't worry if your baby shows no interest in crawling. Babies who hate lying on their tummies – usually the same ones who love seeing what's going on around them – often leave crawling to a later stage. Some babies, in fact, never learn to crawl at all, but still go on to walk perfectly.

● *At birth*
Your baby will be born with a crawling reflex (see p. 14), but will lose this as soon as his body uncurls from the fetal position.
● *At about four months*

Your baby will probably raise both chest and legs off the floor while making swimming movements with his arms.

● *By about six months*

Your baby will be able to support the top half of the body on outstretched arms. You may see the first signs of crawling when he bends his knees up below his body. Although he's moving into the crawling position, he probably won't get the hang of it, and will merely rock back and forth.
● *By about seven months*
Within a month of the previous stage, your baby will probably begin to take his body's weight on one outstretched arm when he wants to.
● *By about eight or nine months*

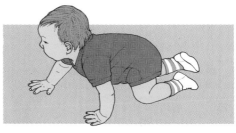

Your baby will begin to pull himself forward on the floor with his head held erect, making kicking movements.

Helping your baby to crawl

I am very much against *teaching* your baby to make orthodox crawling movements, but you can encourage him to start moving forward from a lying or sitting position:

☐ The best possible way is to sit a few feet from your baby and to encourage him to come toward you, possibly using a favorite toy as an enticement.

☐ Help your baby whenever you think he needs it, particularly when his unsuccessful efforts have left him tired and frustrated. Make sure that you always praise any efforts that he makes.

☐ As he becomes more adventurous, place a toy just out of reach so that he has to use all his own resources, including determination, to get hold of it.

☐ Babies learn by mimicry from a very early age, so once he starts trying to crawl, why not get down on the floor yourself and crawl with him?

☐ Slippery floors, although usually dangerous, can be encouraging for crawling babies because even the slightest movement is rewarded with forward motion.

Shuffling

To move forward your baby has to coordinate hand movements and knee movements. Initially he may find this difficult and may devise a unique shuffling movement to propel himself forward. This can be anything from a sideways, crab-like movement to a kind of shuffling on his bottom with one leg tucked underneath for purchase. It doesn't matter what kind of maneuver your baby works out – all are acceptable. The important thing is that he has mastered the art of moving forwards.

It's a great achievement, and he should receive a lot of praise for doing it. Don't discourage your baby from any odd movements he makes, but rather let him discover how to control and move his body in his own particular way.

The crawling baby

Once a baby has learned the knack of crawling (or shuffling), he can pick up speed very quickly and must be watched. He also needs a lot of room so that he can move about to the full extent of his capabilities. To encourage your child to be as curious and adventurous as possible, make sure there's enough clear floor space. Your crawling baby is also getting stronger every day, so beware of anything fragile because he'll break it very quickly. Your baby will also get much dirtier now, and will put any object he finds on the floor straight into his mouth, so make sure he doesn't go near a pet's feeding bowl or a trash can. Your baby's knees will take quite a bashing, so put him into dungarees or trousers. Try to keep the floor covered with something smooth or soft to prevent grazing. Your baby doesn't need shoes and should go shoeless until he's walking.

SAFETY TIPS
- Make your home child-proof.
- Never leave your baby alone.
- Remove all furniture with sharp edges and corners from his room.
- Remove anything breakable from surfaces which are less than three feet from the floor.
- Make sure there are no electric wires trailing across the floor.
- Electric outlets should be covered with safety plugs.
- Make sure that there are no switches less than three feet from the floor.
- All doorways and stairways should have adjustable safety gates.
- Try to keep the floor clear of small, sharp toys.
- Make sure all fires are guarded.
- Don't leave any cloths hanging from tables that a baby could reach up and pull.
- Make sure that all furniture and fixtures are sturdy and safely attached.
- Never leave anything hot on a table in the same room as your baby.
- Make sure that bannisters are too narrow for a small child to squeeze through.
- Make sure all cupboard doors are closed firmly and that the handles are out of a crawling baby's reach; if they aren't, lock them or seal them up with masking tape.
- Keep all containers with poisonous substances off the floor and out of reach.

Standing

Because a baby's development progresses from head to toe, control over the muscles of the knees, lower legs and feet is rarely achieved before the age of ten or 11 months. It's only at this time that he's strong enough and has sufficient balance to take the whole weight on his feet and stand up.

ATTEMPTS AT STANDING
● *At three months*

Once your baby can support his head, he'll love it when you hold him facing you with his feet touching your knees. When he's lifted up and down, he'll feel his feet in contact with your legs and will learn the sensation of taking his own weight. Even very young babies love to be held in this way, although you should take care to support the head.

● *At six months*
By now he'll probably make jumping movements by bending and straightening his knees and hips whenever he's held in a standing position.

● *At seven or eight months*
He may start a sort of dancing movement instead of jumping, and he'll also start to hop from one foot to another. Babies quite often place one foot on top of the other then pull out the underneath foot and repeat the whole movement over and over again.

● *About nine or ten months*

Your baby can take his full weight on his feet, but can't balance yet. If you support him firmly underneath the arms, he'll be able to take his weight on his legs and will try to move one foot in front of the other. Supported on your lap, he will try to take step or two forward. At this stage you must support your baby very securely to take most of the weight because his balance is still undeveloped.

● *At ten months or later*

The muscle control of the knees and feet will have improved and he will start pulling himself up on any nearby furniture, despite the fact that balance is still far from good.

Sitting down

Standing up is easy compared to sitting down, and it usually takes a baby three or four weeks to master the art of getting back down to the floor again from a standing position. He usually does this by sitting down backwards with a thump, or by sliding his hands down a support until his bottom's on the floor. Until he's mastered this he'll probably just stand still and scream for your assistance. There may be a three-week period of frustration for both of you before he learns to drop down into a sitting position. You can help by lowering your baby gently down so that he gains confidence in the movement and by not getting angry if you have to do it repeatedly.

The first steps

After your baby has gained sufficient confidence from pulling himself up into a standing position and getting back down again it will be about four weeks before he starts tottering about, holding on to supports. He does this by facing what he's holding on to and then gradually inching his hands along the support (a). He brings the rest of his body in line with his hands by taking small sideways steps, one foot after the other (b). As he gains confidence, he'll hold on to the support at arm's length and use it only for balance (c).

Once your baby has reached this stage, it's only a very few weeks before he will let go of the support and move forward to the next piece of furniture. These first few steps will be very unsteady. To keep his balance, he will spread his feet apart and hold his arms up and forward, with the elbows slightly bent. Not until your baby is quite proficient at walking will he bring his feet closer together and let his hands drop to his sides.

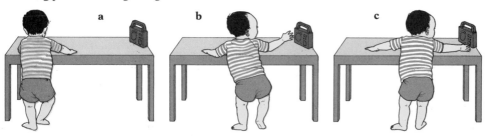

a   b   c

HELPING YOUR BABY TO STAND
● Don't put socks or shoes on your baby's feet. He has much better grip and balance when his feet are bare. If your house is cold, put bootees with suede soles on your baby's feet. Make sure that all his clothing is loose so that movements aren't restricted.
● All the furniture in the room should be heavy, firm and stable so that there's no risk of it toppling on the baby as he holds on to it.
● Resist the temptation to rush your baby into standing or walking. He'll do it in his own good time and nothing you do can hurry the process.

● Don't play tricks on your baby by suddenly removing your support. This will give him a bad fright and could damage his trust in you. Remember, until that moment, you were the one thing he could rely on.
● Don't start to use sleeping bags for the first time now – your baby will try to stand and will fall and may get hurt. If he's used to one, however, it's all right to continue using it.
● Make sure that all wires and flexes are tucked away or firmly tacked down. He may start by holding onto furniture, but a light flex may seem an ideal "hold" once he's on the move.

GENERAL DEVELOPMENT 1–2

During the second year your baby's body grows in length, loses its plump, pudgy appearance, becomes firmer, stronger and more muscular, and starts to take on adult proportions. Balance and coordination improve and fine movements are mastered. By the time he's two years old, your baby son will have grown to half his adult height; your baby girl will have to wait another six to nine months to be that tall.

Size and weight vary considerably from child to child, just as they do from adult to adult. Weight gain is proportional to your child's size, so small children gain less weight, less quickly, than large children. Some size/weight charts are given on page 336 to show the variations between small and large children. You can see that at age two there's a variation of almost 9 lbs (4 kilos).

BODY MILESTONES

At 13 to 15 months
Your baby should be able to stand unaided and take one or two steps to reach a support. However, he won't be able to get up from the sitting to the standing position without support.

At 15 to 18 months
Your baby will be able to raise himself to the standing position unaided. He will probably begin to walk without any support in the early position, with feet wide apart, elbows high.

At 18 to 20 months
Walking will become steadier and the arms will drop down by his side. Your child will almost certainly want to walk upstairs.

MANIPULATIVE MILESTONES

At 12 months
Your baby will have mastered the adult grip, which is a delicate movement achieved by bringing the finger and thumb together. He will be able to roll a ball across the floor. If you ask him for something, he will give it to you.

At 13 to 15 months
Your baby will be able to hold two small objects in one hand. He will be able to put one brick on top of another and may try to make marks with a pencil. When it's time to be undressed, he may start taking off his shoes.

At 18 months
Your baby can build a tower of bricks, possibly three or four high. He will be quite skilled at manipulating food with a spoon and will be able to turn over the pages of a book. If you show him how, he will open a zipper.

Walking

There is no right age for your baby to start to walk. He will probably take his first unsupported steps between the age of nine and 15 months, but he could start even earlier or later. The reason for this is not known, although there's often a family history of early or late walking. Though starting dates vary, all babies have to pass through several well-defined stages of development before they can walk with confidence and good balance (see below).

Babies can stay for various lengths of time in each phase, and you should never make the mistake of trying to push your baby too hard from one to the other. You will give the greatest help if you are there with encouraging words so that he doesn't lose heart. Learning to walk is one of the most difficult things he'll ever have to do, so make him proud of his achievement.

At 21 to 24 months
Your child will be able to maintain his balance and bend over to pick something up without falling over.

At two years
Your baby will have learned turning and screwing movements with his hands, so he'll be able to open a door by turning the door knob, and he may be able to unscrew a loose lid. He will probably enjoy washing his hands.

STAGES OF WALKING

1 *Your baby will probably start walking around using supports before he is one. He'll slide both hands along the support and bring up his feet to align with the rest of his body. Balance will be a problem.*

2 *He'll still need supports, but he'll stand further away from the furniture and take more of the body's weight on his feet. He'll start to move one hand over the other instead of sliding them together and, as he becomes more confident, he'll start to move both hands and feet together. This is a very important stage because, for a moment, your baby has gained the confidence and the balance to take all his weight on one foot.*

3 *Your baby will really enjoy the independence of moving around rooms, using any support he can. The next stage will be the negotiation of gaps between two supports. He will only do this if he can hold on to both supports at once. At this stage he still has to feel securely supported, and will only let go of one support when he's holding firmly on to the other.*

4 *Your baby will start to cross gaps which are wider than an arm's span. While still holding on to the support with one hand, he will move into the center of the gap and, having gained his balance, will release the support and take a step toward the next one, making a grab for it with both hands.*

5 *Your baby will now begin to waddle around. He will manage to stagger a few paces to reach the second support.*

6 *Your baby will now launch himself into an open space and take several unsupported steps with confidence. He may only take half a dozen steps before losing his balance and sitting down with a thud. However, you will find that he usually sets off to reach a goal and waddles rather bow leggedly to get to it.*

HELPING YOUR CHILD TO WALK

● Arrange the furniture around the room so that he can progress down one side, across the end, and up the other.

● Initially, the gaps between the furniture should be no wider than the width of your baby's arms so that he can hang on to a piece of furniture with one hand and stretch out the other to reach the next support easily. If the gaps are too big, your baby won't be able to reach the support that enables him to cross the gap.

● While your baby is learning to walk, make sure the floors aren't slippery – one bad bang may give him such a fright that he's put off walking for several weeks.

● Make sure the room is "baby-proof," and that there are no flexes or objects which can be pulled over (see p. 294).

● Shoes and socks are entirely unnecessary: bare feet are safer, not only because they eliminate the risk of malformed feet, but because your baby will be able to grip well and get used to the sensation of weight. In the winter, use slipper socks with suede or leather feet if it is very cold.

● A useful walking aid when your baby is holding on to supports is a baby walker. It is designed with a very stable, wide base so that it won't topple over and will only move at your baby's pace; it won't run away with him. Buy one that's fitted with a safety bar.

Your waddling child

When your baby first starts to waddle, he'll have little control over his movements. He'll be able to travel only in one direction, he'll be incapable of swerving, and he'll have great difficulty stopping once he's gotten up speed. By about 19 months, however, he'll be able to walk backward as well as forward and may even have mastered running. After he can run, he'll be able to jump. By two years he'll be able to veer and swerve while he's running, and will be able to glance over his shoulder without losing balance. He will be able to stop quite suddenly without toppling over and will have sufficient balance to bend over to pick something up without having to sit down first. If you encourage him, he will be able to kick a ball, although it will be a rather dragging kind of kick, since he can't maintain his balance on one leg for very long.

Your toddler will want, quite naturally, to race about as much as possible, but out of doors you'll have to be careful. He'll have no traffic sense as yet, so you'll either have to hold his hand or use reins. I believe that reins are the most satisfactory solution for both of you: they hurt neither your arm nor your toddler's and they give your baby far greater freedom than he would have holding your hand. Although your child's strength will increase during this year, don't expect him to walk much further than a few hundred yards at a time. If you're in a hurry, or can't bear the idea of constant stops and starts to look at things, then use a baby carriage.

If your baby is a late walker, don't worry. He's learning so much at the moment that it's quite understandable if he slows down in one aspect of his development to concentrate on another. His walking may also suffer a setback after an illness. Just relax and let him develop along his own lines.

SAFETY TIPS

● Remember, your baby can not only walk, he can also climb, so fit bars to all the windows. If you don't like the way they look, buy special fasteners which allow the window to be opened only a few inches.

● Keep possible hiding places, like cupboards or chests, securely locked so your baby can't disappear and lock himself in.

● Be sure that locks on room doors are out of reach.

● Do not allow your unsupervised child into a yard or park with open access to a road. The road-training drill should be taught as soon as possible.

● Unless taught how to negotiate stairs properly, your baby is bound to fall down them sooner or later. I taught all my children to go down stairs from the time that they could crawl, by sitting on the top stair, putting their legs down to the step below, and then following with their hands.

● All clothing should be non-flammable.

● Keep all the handles of pans turned away from the front of the burner.

● Never leave anything hot lying around to cool off; keep it out of your baby's reach until it's absolutely cool.

● A baby can't cope with swing doors, so don't have them.

● Glass doors should never be so clean that your baby bumps into them. Make them obvious by fixing stick-ons or colored paper on the glass.

● Keep all your medicines in an approved medicine chest, high up and always locked. Never carry medicines around in your handbag or leave them on your dressing table.

● Don't let your baby run around wearing socks but not shoes. He can slip on any smooth surface.

● Don't put rugs on polished floors unless they've been backed with double-sided tape or rubber backing to make them grip.

● Don't let your child near anything which is small enough to be swallowed or pushed up his nose or ears.

● All sharp instruments, including kitchen equipment, should be kept out of your child's reach.

● Never leave sewing materials around.

● Never leave your child alone near water.

GENERAL DEVELOPMENT 2–3

By your child's third year, his rate of growth and development will have slowed down. He will have almost complete control over his body, and many movements will have become automatic. He'll no longer have to concentrate or make an effort to do many things requiring fine physical skill or coordination. He will, for instance, have the coordination to build a tower of bricks. He will try to get dressed and undressed, and may even manage to undo buttons.

PHYSICAL MILESTONES

At two years
Your child will be able to go up and down stairs alone but will put two feet on each step before moving on to the next. He'll kick a ball successfully without falling over.

At two-and-a-half years
He'll be able to walk on tiptoe and jump on and off objects and in the air. However, he won't be able to stand on one foot yet.

At three years
He'll walk upstairs with a foot on each step. He'll have to put both feet on the same stair coming down but will jump off the bottom step. He'll be able to stand for a few seconds on one foot, but won't be able to skip.

MANIPULATIVE MILESTONES

At two years
He'll put on his own gloves, socks and shoes successfully. He'll manage to rotate his elbow accurately so that he can turn a door handle or unscrew a lid. He'll begin to draw pictures with pencils and crayons.

At two-and-a-half years
He'll take off his trousers and underpants by himself. He'll be able to thread beads on a string and to fasten large, easily placed buttons.

At three years
He'll dress and undress himself completely, so long as all the fastenings are within reach. He'll manage the buckle on his sandals. He'll draw and color quite accurately and will have mastered the complicated movement of using scissors.

COORDINATION

During the first six weeks, your baby's hands will be held in fists, although they'll probably open and close when he cries. By about eight weeks, your baby's hands will be open more often, and the grasp reflex (see p. 14) will be replaced by voluntary movement. Some parents get worried at this stage because their baby doesn't seem to hold on to objects as tightly as before. But there is nothing to worry about – your baby is simply learning a new skill, which he will perfect within a few months.

Up to the age of six weeks, he won't have tried to coordinate the movements of fingers and hands; instead, he'll spend a great deal of time discovering how they look, feel and move. He'll hold them open most of the time, and will move his fingers and watch them closely. It's as though he's assessing his powers before starting to use them.

Between four and five months, he'll have voluntary control over reaching – he'll probably move both arms toward an object and grasp it between his two hands.

At about six months, your baby will try to hold an object, either between two hands, or in one hand, squeezing it between the palm and fingers. There will be no fine control, but he will be able to differentiate between large and small objects and will open his hand accordingly. He'll love the *feel* of things, so provide lots of different textures to clutch and handle, as well as different shapes. When he's lying down, he'll probably reach out, grab his foot, and put it in his mouth. He won't know exactly what to do with all objects, so if you offer a cube he may hold on to it, but if you offer a second one, he may drop the first without thinking. About this time he'll start to explore how to use his hands during feeding. Hand/eye coordination will be sufficient for your baby to pick up finger foods and start feeding himself, although his efforts to get food to his mouth will be anything but accurate (see p. 119).

At about eight months, your baby will

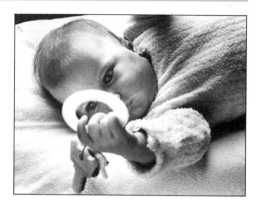

hold something out to you but will not yet have learned how to let it go and give it to you. He will not reach this milestone until he's about a year old, when dropping things deliberately from his high chair or stroller becomes a very entertaining game.

From now on your baby's ability to grasp becomes more and more refined. By the time he is nine months old he'll have stopped holding an object in the palm of his hand and will hold it between his thumb and the side of his index finger. By age one he'll be able to pick up quite a small object between the tips of his forefinger and thumb, and will usually point at it with his index finger before picking it up. He'll be able to pass an object from one hand to another, and to hold two objects at a time, one in each hand.

Between eight and ten months, your baby really learns to manipulate them. He squeezes them – slaps, slides, pokes, rubs, scrapes and bangs them. He explores every new substance with his hands, including food, and will mix, smear and splash anything that is liquid or runny. Most objects find their way straight to his mouth, whether they're feet, fingers, plastic lids or toys. As he gets more skilled at manipulation, the fascination of putting things in his mouth begins to wane, and he begins to play games like pat-a-cake. He'll also have developed the social skill of being able to wave goodbye.

Hand/eye coordination

Age	Skill	How to give encouragement
Up to eight weeks old	*Until he is about eight weeks old, your baby won't have learned to use his hands. He'll be learning to focus to a maximum distance of about 10 inches (25 cm).*	*Your baby will try to focus on anything which is moving, such as a highly-colored mobile. Your face, however, will be the most interesting object in his whole life, so make sure that he sees it often and close. Hang interesting objects within his line of vision, no further away than 10 inches (25 cm).*
Two to two-and-a-half months	*Your baby will have opened his hands and will watch them with fascination. Focusing distance is not much more than 12 inches (30.5 cm), so he'll bring hands and fingers close up to his face to watch them moving.*	*As soon as your baby's hands are open, they are ready to have things put into them. The most interesting toys are the ones that make a noise, like a rattle. These toys have the added advantage of helping your child make a connection between what his hands are doing, what his eyes are seeing, and what his ears can hear.*
Two-and-a-half to three months	*Your baby will watch his hands very carefully and with considerable concentration. Once he does this you'll know that he has made the connection between seeing and doing. At about this age your baby may make clumsy movements with either hand to get near objects.*	*Your baby is learning to judge distances and to move his hands to where his eyes think something interesting is happening. One of the best ways you can help is to put a string above the cot or pram with lots of interesting objects hanging from it. Let them swing freely so that your baby can reach up to make them move and, most important, to see them move as a result of his action.*
Three to four months	*Your baby will touch everything in sight, and will be learning how to measure distances using his hands and eyes. He'll look at an object and then confirm the distance by trying to reach it. He can reach objects, but now, instead of using an open hand, he tries to make a fist before touching them.*	*Your baby will now be too old for swinging things. Something that goes out of reach will only frustrate him, because he is longing to grasp it. Instead of having objects dangling from a string, secure them to the sides of the cot. Alternatively, hold out an object so that he can try to grab it. Always wait until he's touched it before handing it over.*

Hand/eye coordination

Age	Skill	How to give encouragement
Four to six months	*Your baby's eyes will be mature enough to focus on objects at any distance, and he will follow any moving object that catches his attention. As he approaches six months, he'll no longer have to measure the distance between hand and object by looking back and forth, from one to the other. A glance will tell your baby where the object is and where his hand is in relation to it. It will also tell him how big a movement he'll have to make in order to reach the object. At the same time, he'll be learning to grasp, so when he reaches out and touches the object he'll open his fingers and curl them around whatever he wants to hold.*	*Your baby needs lots of practice at reaching out and getting hold of things; he'll also have a great deal of fun doing it. You can encourage him to do this by holding out the most interesting objects you can find, such as anything that makes a noise or has an interesting shape (a plastic bottle, a ball of wool, car keys, and so on).*

Right- and left-handedness

If both you and your partner are left-handed, two of every three of your children will be right-handed. If both parents are right-handed, the chances of having a left-handed child are one in ten. There is, however, no natural law which states that one hand is superior to the other, so it should never bother you if a child is left-handed. Your child has no control over which of his hands is dominant; dominance is decided by the developing brain. Think of the brain as two linked halves, each of which controls different activities. One of these sides becomes dominant as your baby's brain develops. If it is the left side of the brain which dominates, the baby is right-handed. If it's the right side, the baby is left-handed.

During the first few months your baby may seem to have no preferences; it's a fact, however, that the majority of newborns turn their heads more to the right than to the left. As your baby's coordination improves and he starts to acquire manual skills, you may find that he starts to use one hand more than the other. Don't be worried however, if he doesn't do this – he will develop at his own speed. Never, ever, try to dissuade your baby from being left-handed. You may think that encouraging him to use his right hand instead of his left will be doing him a favor later in life – freeing him from such minor annoyances as right-handed potato peelers or scissors. You are not. Trying to alter what your baby's brain naturally wants to do may risk such psychological side-effects as stuttering or reading difficulties.

COORDINATION

By the time he's a year old, he'll be able to pick up something quite small, such as a button, between thumb and forefinger. If you make marks on a piece of paper with a pencil or crayon, he will take the pencil or crayon when offered it, and try to imitate the marks that you have made. By about 13 months, your baby will have learned to hold more than one object in his hand. Coordination will also be improving, so if you show him how to build a tower of blocks he'll follow your example, putting one block on top of another. He will also start to remove items of clothing (see p. 48), and will love pulling around a toy on a string, hammering pegs through holes, and fitting different shapes into the appropriate openings. By the time he's 15 months, he'll be able to feed himself without any help and without making too much mess. He will attempt to brush his hair if shown, and will be keen to help you around the house.

By about 18 months, your baby will be able to build a tower, four or five blocks high, and turn over the pages of a book, probably two or three pages at a time. By the time your child is two years old, he'll be coordinated enough to manage the complex movement of twisting something round in his hands. He'll be able to open a door by turning the door knob and unscrew a loose cap from a jar. Washing and drying his hands will be a favorite pastime. At age two, he should make his first attempt to dress and undress himself. He should be able to manage things like putting on shoes, but probably will need help with his socks.

Always remember that your child will proceed at his own pace; that he cannot develop muscular coordination faster than the brain and nervous system are developing, and that no two children develop at the same rate. Don't make the mistake of expecting more from your child than he is capable of doing. He has a tremendous desire to please, and if you constantly set goals for him that are higher than he's capable of reaching, he'll feel unhappy and demoralized because he has let you down. Even worse, he may become resentful and frustrated if he aspires to do things which are more complicated than his body will allow. Your primary role is therefore to help and encourage, not to set unachievable goals.

By the time your child is three years old, he will probably be able to do the following things: build a tower of bricks, up to eight or nine high; dress and undress himself with increasing skill; undo buttons which are within easy reach (although he may not be able to do them up), and help with any household task or chore that you suggest. He will also love playing games that imitate the kinds of jobs that you do, whether it's mending something, picking up a book or the washing up. He'll be perfectly capable of carrying plates and dishes to and from the table, and will be a much more cooperative and able member of the family.

How to improve coordination

Between the ages of two and three, your child will be a great experimenter. You should feed this curiosity by opening up his world and planning new discoveries. This is the age when children find out about, and understand the force of, gravity – that things always fall *down*. They discover that something round will roll, and that something square will not; that liquids flow and have no shape, but take on the shape of their containers. They learn that large containers hold more than small ones; that solids have shapes of their own, but that clay and dough can be squeezed and made into different shapes.

These discoveries can be made only if your child's coordination – not just of the hand and eye, but of the body and limbs – develops and matures. Toys which demand good coordination will help your child to develop it. You can help him improve balance simply by encouraging him to walk along narrow steps. Always stay close by, or he could lose his confidence and fall. You can improve ball sense by throwing and catching – initially with something large and soft, like a beach ball.

Children love jumping and somersaulting on soft surfaces, so put a mattress or a large piece of foam rubber down on the floor so that they can indulge in their love of acrobatics. (In our playroom we always had three very large, soft floor cushions for the children to tumble on.) A simple tree swing made from some stout rope and an old tire is wonderful for developing strength, coordination and a sense of adventurousness. Jungle Jims – so long as they are on a fairly soft surface, like grass, to cushion falls – provide a variety of physical activities that develop a wide range of movements requiring good coordination. A really sturdy one will give your child good service for years and years, and your child will use it in increasingly adventurous ways.

Encouraging adventurousness

Your child should become aware of, and enjoy, physical movement from very early on in life (see p. 262). There is nothing more natural than for a young baby to be tossed about. After all, he was constantly on the move inside the womb for nine months! Your child will get used to moving, and having to use his body in a positive physical sense, especially if he's carried around a lot while you go about your everyday life.

Once your child becomes mobile, it is better to encourage a spirit of adventure than to be over-protective. Of course, your child may have an accident once in a while – once or twice, that is inevitable – but an occasional accident is preferable to having a child who has no sense of physical freedom or confidence. Restraining him is also doing him a disservice, since his main pleasure for the next seven or eight years will be derived from physical activities. If he can't move with the same pace and accuracy as other children he will be left behind and excluded from many enjoyable activities. The over-protective parent, for example, will insist on holding her child's hand when he wants to climb along the edge of a low wall. A parent who encourages physical activity, however, will not only permit her child to balance on a fairly narrow surface, but will help him practice at home on a plank supported at either end by a pile of magazines.

One of the best ways of encouraging activity in your child is to join in and do it yourself. You are your child's favorite playmate and you should be the person to introduce him to new physical activities. You can also correct faults when they become apparent. Give your child tips on how to speed up and refine his coordination. Imitating your own physical movements will by itself teach your child new physical skills, without either of you knowing it.

VISION

It used to be thought that newborn babies could not see. It was thought that because they could not focus to any great extent their visual world need not be stimulating and could even be neglected. We now know that this is far from the truth. A newborn baby *can* see. The only difference between a newborn baby and an older one with mature eyesight is that the newborn baby cannot see as much, as easily, or as well. In other words, your newborn baby sees in a limited way but sees nonetheless, and you have to fit the visual world into a range that he can perceive.

Until your baby is between three and six months old, his visual powers will not be fully developed, and he won't be able to focus on anything further than ten inches from his face. As his eye muscles become stronger and he develops binocular vision, his acuity will improve greatly.

Even though your newborn baby's eyesight is limited, his eyes are very sensitive to two things: the human face, and anything that moves. If you bring your face to within eight inches of your baby's, his eyes will move and his expression change. Even a baby only a few hours old will be able to bring both eyes together on to an object (convergence) and follow it if it moves. As he gets older his whole body may react with excited jerking movements when your face comes into focus.

Color vision

When your baby is born the cells in the retina of the eye which see colors are not fully developed, so he can see the world only in terms of muted shades. The first colors that he detects are red and blue, and then green and yellow. For the first few months of life your baby can see only the brightest colors, so make sure he has brightly-colored objects around him.

Three-dimensional vision

Because your baby can only focus on objects which are closer than ten inches from his face, the world appears rather flat to him, and many details are not seen. Even at two weeks, however, a baby will automatically raise a hand to protect himself from something which is moving quickly toward him. It is necessary for your baby to have three-dimensional vision before he becomes mobile; he probably won't even crawl until he sees and understands this third dimension. Your baby may not develop a complete, three-dimensional picture of the world until he is four months old; and his vision may not be perfect until he's six months old.

Checking eyesight

During the first few months of your baby's life you are in the best position to check his sight, although you shouldn't become obsessive about it. By the age of four months even an inattentive or lazy baby should focus on a brightly-colored object held eight to ten inches from his face, if it is moving and if it makes a noise, like a rattle. One of the most joyful sights in your child's life is your face. By the age of four months, he should be reacting when you smile or nod your head. If he isn't, don't be too concerned, but mention it to your doctor when you see him next.

STIMULATING YOUR BABY'S EYESIGHT

● On one side of the baby's cot hang a fairly large photograph of your own face, your partner's, one of your other children's, or indeed any face cut out of a magazine, so that he can practise focusing on it. On the other side of the cot firmly attach a mirror so that he can look at his own face and see it moving when he wriggles.

● Put very simple, brightly-colored pictures around the rest of the cot within the baby's range of vision (no more than 12 inches away for the first month).

● Put a mobile over the cot. This doesn't have to be expensive. It can be a few balloons or household objects hung on a coat hanger or on a wooden pole attached to the cot.

● String some interesting objects on elastic across the hinges of the pram hood so that your baby can watch them when he is lying in the pram.

● If your baby's cot is near the wall, attach toys with rubber suction pads to the wall for your child to watch and focus on.

● As your child gets older, it's important that toys make noises and move. Dangle soft, light objects on strings so that they swing when your baby swipes at them. Anything that will jingle, such as a rattle or a toy with bells attached, will be entertaining.

● Put toys in the back seat of your car, or hang them from the side windows or roof. Make sure they don't cut down visibility.

● Your baby's never too young to go to museums or art galleries with you. If he's in a back pack, he'll be able to look over your shoulder at exactly the same things as you.

● When you leave your baby outside, either suspend some toys or mobiles from a tree bough or from a washing line or piece of string hung between two poles. Even a wash line will prove exciting to your baby if the clothes are blowing in the wind.

VISION

About the age of one, your child begins to see and follow rapidly moving objects. His vision is about as good now as it ever will be.

The main changes that occur in vision during your child's formative years have to do with his ability to *interpret* what he sees – in words, pictures and movements what develops, in other words, is not his ability to see *per se* but the ability of his brain to make connections between what he sees, thinks and does. As a parent, you should encourage the development of your child's eye/brain and eye/body connections so that he can reach his full potential. You can do this by providing him with stimulating ideas, stimulating books, stimulating toys and activities.

Regular eye check-ups are not necessary in a child who is developing normally, but be on the lookout for changes in the appearance of his eyes, such as a lazy eye, a drooping eyelid, or a squint. Be responsive to signs that your child can't see clearly, such as frequent bumping into furniture or an inability to follow the trajectory of a ball that's thrown to him. Seek medical advice at once; don't wait to see if the problem clears up. Like a disused limb, a disused eye deteriorates rapidly. Eyes need constant exercise and stimulation – that is how they stay healthy.

TEETH

There is no correct time for your baby to cut his first teeth. It's not unusual for babies to be born with teeth, or to have none at 12 months. It would be misleading, therefore, to give dates indicating when teeth will appear. It is possible, however, to generalize about the *order* in which they will arrive. Teething usually starts at about six months and continues until the end of the first year; the order in which teeth come in rarely differs among children.

HOW THE TEETH COME IN

1 *The first teeth to arrive are always the lower front teeth.*
2 *These are followed by the upper front teeth.*

3 *Upper side teeth come in next.*
4 *These are followed by the lower side teeth.*

Teething

If you're on the look out, you will probably notice your baby's first tooth as it starts to push its way through the gum and form a small, pale bump. The only normal symptoms of teething are fretfulness and dribbling. It's a myth that teething can cause fever, diarrhoea, vomiting, convulsions, rashes or loss of appetite. Don't make the mistake of attributing illnesses to teething, but if you're at all worried, consult your doctor immediately. No parent likes to see his child in discomfort, so do the following:

☐ Offer your baby something firm to chew on, like a raw carrot, or a cool teething ring. Your baby may find sucking rather painful, so let him drink from a cup instead.

☐ Gently rub your child's gums with your own little finger – this can help as much as anything. Certainly your attention and concern about his pain will bring comfort, too.

☐ Avoid taking your child out in a cold wind, since this often makes the pain worse. When you go out in the winter, cover most of your child's face and head with a warm hat or hood, and put a scarf around his neck and chin.

☐ Don't apply teething gels containing local anaesthetics. They only have a transient effect, and local anaesthetics can cause allergies.

☐ Don't use teething powders and teething medicines. Your baby has many teeth to cut, and regular use will expose him to large amounts of medication, much of which may be unnecessary and accompanied by harmful side-effects.

☐ Careless use of water-filled teething rings has been known to cause frostbite in babies. These rings can be used quite safely to cool down the mouth if they are kept in the refrigerator, not in the freezer.

☐ Avoid frequent use of baby aspirin or Paracetamol syrup. Both of these medicines are useful, but they should not be used with any regularity except under doctor's orders. Aspirin in any form certainly shouldn't be used frequently. Although Paracetamol syrup is the safest pain killer for a baby, it should only be used on occasion. If you need more than two doses of it, to soothe your fretful baby, consult your doctor.

Looking after teeth

When your baby has several teeth, get him to develop good habits early by encouraging him to play a game of tooth brushing. First let him watch you brushing your teeth so that he sees how it's done. Then offer him a soft toothbrush as something to play with. He will almost certainly want to imitate you, and will try to put the brush into his mouth and make the same kinds of movements to and fro. This shouldn't be serious business, but playful. You're teaching your child to enjoy caring for his teeth, so avoid censuring him, and make it into a game instead of a chore. To actually get the teeth clean, put some toothpaste on a gauze, and gently rub it across teeth and gums. It's important to clean the gums even if there are no teeth because it keeps the mouth free of the bacteria which cause plaque, and so provide a good environment for teeth to grow into. The easiest position will probably be with him on your lap, feet pointing away from you, mouth looking up at you.

Always use a fluoride toothpaste, and avoid varieties especially made for children, since they often contain a sweetener. Your baby may want to eat the toothpaste, but try to dissuade him. Clean the teeth once, if not twice, a day, and always after he's been given any medicine. Children's

medicines are often sweet and sticky to make them "more palatable."

Fighting decay

The three most important factors in the care of your baby's teeth are diet (the absence of sugar), good dental hygiene, and regular check-ups. One of the best ways to take care of your baby's first teeth is to see that his diet does not contain many sugary foods such as candies, chocolates, cakes, cookies and very sweet drinks. Sugar, be it white or brown, is the arch villain of tooth decay! It is not necessary for good health, and no child needs it. You will be doing your child a favor if you don't encourage the development of a sweet tooth, not only for his teeth but also for his weight (see p. 110). Never leave a bottle containing milk or a sweetened drink lying around for your baby to suck on endlessly. His teeth will be constantly bathed in a sugary fluid which will encourage decay.

Your baby's diet should contain plenty of calcium and vitamin D, since they are essential for the healthy formation of the permanent teeth which are already growing in your baby's jawbones. Foods which are rich in both of these nutrients are dairy products and fish. Fatty fishes like herring and sardine are particularly good.

Many people think that dental hygiene isn't important until their child has permanent teeth. This is not true, so make sure his teeth are brushed regularly and, as soon as he's about two, take him for regular check-ups (see p. 203).

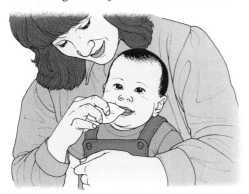

TEETH

At one time it was thought that milk teeth were not very important, but we now know that they are worth looking after. First of all, they guide in the adult teeth so that they grow in correctly. Second, if the primary teeth are lost through decay, the bone behind the teeth can be affected, eroding the support that the adult teeth need. Your baby will be teething during most of his second year, and you should be prepared for the molars to be a bit upsetting. The first molars usually arrive when your child is between 12 and 15 months. The upper molars appear first, followed by the lower ones. The second molars appear when your child is between 20 and 24 months, first in the lower jaw and then in the upper jaw. In general, the later teeth are cut, the less trouble they cause.

Once your child has all his teeth, you should encourage the development of strong jaw muscles by giving plenty of chewy foods, particularly fresh fruit and raw vegetables. These foods also happen to have a cleansing effect, as the fibers within them are shredded by the teeth. Maintain the health of your child's teeth and gums by making sure that he has regular checkups.

HOW THE TEETH COME IN

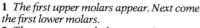

1 *The first upper molars appear. Next come the first lower molars.*
2 *The upper eye teeth then come in, one on each side.*

3 *These are followed by the lower eye teeth.*
4 *The second molars appear first in the lower jaw. And lastly the second molars appear in the upper jaw.*

Dental hygiene and care

The Royal College of Physicians in England has reported that children between the ages of two and 12 should take a fluoride tablet every day if the local water supply is not fluorinated. You should encourage your child to chew the tablet so that the fluoride coats the teeth as well as being absorbed into the bloodstream and strengthening the permanent teeth that are developing inside the jawbone. There is no evidence linking cancer with fluoride.

Until your child reaches the age of six or seven, he won't be capable of cleaning his own teeth thoroughly, so you should be responsible for the part of the tooth-brushing routine which actually cleans his teeth. He may object to this at first and clamp his jaws firmly shut. The best way around this is to use a "disclosing tablet," which will turn toothbrushing into a game. When chewed, the tablet exposes plaque as a dense area of color.

Dentists generally agree that it doesn't matter how a toothbrush is used, so long as it removes plaque. At one time we were encouraged to brush the top teeth downwards and the bottom ones upwards, so that the edges of the gums were protected. It has now been shown, however, that there is nothing especially effective about this method. What is more efficient, especially for children who don't have a great deal of coordination, is a gentle to-and-fro movement on all surfaces of the teeth. Make sure, however, that the bris-

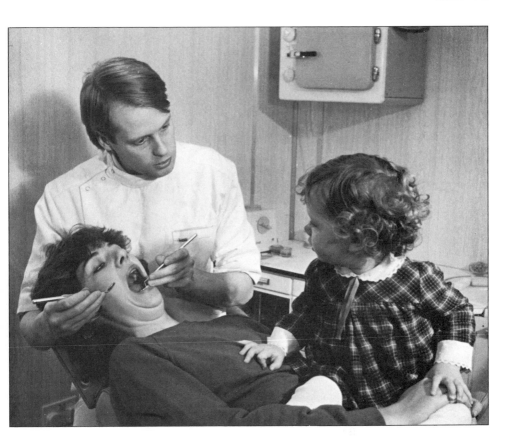

tles have rounded tips and that they aren't too hard. A very hard brush may cause the gums to bleed and recede, which will eventually loosen the teeth.

Always encourage your child to have a regular tooth-brushing routine. He should never leave for school or go to sleep without first cleaning his teeth. Most children will put up a fight if they have to brush their teeth every time they have a sweet drink or cookie, so give them a piece of cheese instead. This will make the saliva alkaline and counteract the sugary acid which erodes the protective enamel of the teeth and causes cavities.

Visiting the dentist

Take your child for his first dental check-up sometime around his second birthday. The visit should be as relaxed and pleasant as possible. Get your child used to the sight of the instruments and the smell of the surroundings by taking him with you when you go for your own check-up. If he can be trusted, and if your dentist has no objections, sit the child on your lap and let him watch while the dentist examines you. He'll no doubt watch with fascination and will be delighted to copy your example. Just before your child's visit, play a game of going to the dentist and look into each other's mouths. When you actually visit the dentist, arrange for him to look at your mouth before he looks at your child's.

12 Intellectual development

A baby is the most responsive and rewarding pupil you will ever meet. He wants to do more, explore more, and widen his horizons more than anyone else you will ever know. This plus his desire to please you give him an appetite for learning that should thrill every parent. From Day One he wants to learn everything! Don't forget, he has five senses and wants to learn through all of them – sight, sound, smell, taste and touch. One of the most important things to remember is that he's never too young to learn, but must be taught in a way that's tailored to his "own" level of development. You mustn't set him tasks which are beyond his capabilities, as this will lead only to frustration, loss of self-confidence and resentment towards you. Guide him in all things, but never try to force him.

LEARNING   0–1

Whatever you do, don't waste the first crucial six weeks of your baby's life. Many people still think that because the baby isn't making sounds or moving much he can't learn or respond to what's happening around him. We know this to be entirely incorrect! Your baby's emotions and intellect are developing during the first weeks of life, just as rapidly as his size, weight and coordination.

Initially, the most important person in a baby's life is the one who most consistently looks after him. In most cases, this is the mother. *You*, then, are his most important teacher.

As adults, we learn the most important and memorable lessons of our lives from people we like and have a special rapport with. If there's a special feeling of closeness and understanding, the lessons will have a profound effect on us, and remain with us for a lifetime. A child, too, will learn more, faster, if he establishes a strong bond with you, his teacher. Your partner will be an important influence, too. He should form as strong a relationship with his baby as he can, and get as involved in the teaching process as you are.

The teaching you give your child is not teaching in a formal sense; since there are no specific rules and no particular targets your child has to reach. You should "teach" your baby by making the world interesting for him. Introduce him to new experiences, explain everything that you see and, above all, join in with every activity so that the two of you can learn together. You have to give encouragement at all times, and praise your child even for the smallest achievement. You must give constant support, especially if your child fails to do something that he really wants to do. Without your support, he won't gain the confidence he requires.

What your baby understands

● *The newborn baby*
Your baby will concentrate on your face if
you bring it close to him. He can also
distinguish your voice from all others.
When he hears your voice, his eyes will
move in its direction, and he will try to
follow your face if you move it close to his.
He can recognize your face if you place it
less than 12 inches (30.5 cm) away from
the time he's 36 hours old.

● *Four weeks*
If your face is close enough for him to focus
on, he will watch you while you are talking
and will mimic you by opening and clos-
ing his mouth. He will also probably stop
crying when you pick him up because he
knows you to be a source of comfort. He
imitates the movements of your face: he
can use the right muscles to smile and
grimace.

● *Six weeks*
He will smile back at you. His eyes will be
able to follow a moving toy.

● *Eight weeks*
If you hold something brightly colored
above his head, he will take a few seconds
to focus on it and then follow it as you
move it from side to side.

● *Three months*
He will immediately see a toy held above
him. He will smile when you speak and
squeal and gurgle with pleasure. He will
show obvious signs of curiosity and interest in what is going on around him.

● *Four months*
At feeding times he will show signs of
excitement. He will laugh and chuckle
when played with. He will love being
propped up because he'll be able to see
what's going on around him. He will turn
his head in the direction of any sound.

● *Five months*
He'll be aware of strange situations and
can express fear, disgust and anger.

● *Six months*
Your baby will become very interested in
mirrors and in seeing himself in one. He
will begin to show preferences for certain
foods that you offer him.

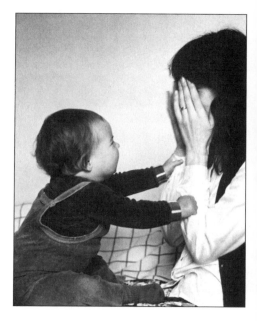

● *Eight months*
He will know his name and will understand the word "No." He will probably
have developed little sound signals like a
cough to attract your attention when he
reaches out for something he wants. He'll
probably want to feed himself.

● *Nine months*
He'll show a will of his own and may stop
you when you try to wash his face. He will
concentrate very hard on toys and games
and will even turn a toy over in his hand so
that he can examine it carefully. When an
object is hidden under a cloth, he'll lift the
cloth up to see the object.

● *Ten months*
He'll probably be able to clap his hands
and wave bye-bye. He'll show that he
understands a small number of words and
very short, simple statements.

● *11 months*
He'll have learned, and will enjoy, simple
games like "Peek-a-boo." His other favorite game will be dropping things and
having you pick them up. He'll become
very noisy and will want to shake, rattle
and bang anything that makes a noise.

● *12 months*
He will do anything to make you laugh and will repeat it over and over again. He'll enjoy "reading" simple books with you and will help you to undress him by lifting up his arms when you take off his clothes. He may know a few simple words like bottle, bath, ball, drink.

Look at your baby
In the early days it is imperative to face your baby. Facial contact is terribly important, since your face is one of the few things that a baby responds to visually during the first days of life (see p. 16). Your newborn baby has to see that face as close as eight to ten inches from his own, so bring your face up close to his and make it "interesting." Move your head as you talk; raise your eyebrows and, most important of all, smile. Look deep into your baby's eyes all the time, and make constant eye contact. It has been shown that mothers who face their children while they are feeding or playing with them, and look into their eyes, are much less likely to need to use corporal punishment to discipline their children as they grow up. It's hardly

surprising that the children of such mothers are much better able to form relationships with people as they get older.

Have conversations
Your baby holds his first conversation with smiles. The conversation goes something like this: you begin talking to him on a friendly subject, with your face about eight to ten inches away. You are animated and smile a lot. Every baby has the natural human desire to respond in a friendly way, and so he smiles back. You are delighted by his recognition and his friendly smile, and so you smile again, and laugh. You may cuddle him, and kiss him. He *loves* that, so he smiles more to please you. You do more things to please him, and so the conversation goes on.

From this interaction your baby learns two invaluable lessons. First, he learns that a smile is rewarded with a smile – even with hugs, kisses and words of praise. Second, he has found a way of pleasing you and interacting with you. He has learned that he can initiate this interaction and will continue to interact with other people.

Read to your baby
Children love books and will respond to them from a surprisingly early age if you look at them together and read to him. Reading books together will teach him different colors, the alphabet, numbers and names of simple objects. Your baby's never too young to be read to – your voice will be soothing to him, and you'll soon find that books at bedtime are a useful and pacifying part of your evening routine. As an unexpected bonus, your child may want to read them alone. You have thus not only taught him to entertain himself, but introduced him to the life-long pleasure of reading. This early start in life is invaluable.

I suggest you start off with board books which are brightly-colored and well-made. For variety, buy some pop-up books as well, but resign yourself to the fact that they will be treated roughly.

Learning spurts

Babies don't grow, develop and learn at a constant rate. During a learning spurt, your baby will gobble up new ideas, acquire new skills and put them into practice immediately. However, during these spurts he may stop certain activities or lose a grip on certain skills. Don't worry. They won't have gone for good. It's just that your baby is using all his powers of concentration to learn something new. Once he's learned it, he'll regain what he has lost.

When your child is learning quickly, you should try to make his life as interesting as possible. Of course, you shouldn't neglect activities that continue to be enjoyable. But he is ready to learn and absorb new information at a very fast rate, and you should introduce him to as many new things as possible. Don't be too discriminating; babies focus on what interests them and what they're old enough to understand, and let the rest go by. During the first year learning is entirely piecemeal, so you'll help your baby best by providing as wide and interesting a menu as possible.

Such spurts are invariably followed by periods when development appears to slow down. Treat them as recovery periods during which your baby can consolidate newly-learned skills and prepare himself for the next spurt. Don't get anxious about this – just let him practise skills he has already learned. You can help during these slower learning times by practising with him, saying things like, "Let's sing that song again," or "Why don't we try to push the peg through that hole again."

Letting your child guide you

All through life, the teachers who succeed are the ones who help us develop and reach our full potential. They maximize our strengths and minimize our weaknesses. As your baby's teacher, try to make the best of his good points and play down his bad ones. Give him the kind of help he needs when he needs it; help is worthless if the person who is being helped doesn't really require it. Be an active helper, not an interfering one. Your baby should not be learning what *you* want him to learn, he should be learning what *he* wants to learn, and this should be your first priority. Suppress any preconceptions of what a child his age ought to be doing, and respond to what he wants to do. Be guided by your child. It's your job as a parent to introduce him to as wide a range of interesting things as possible, not to decide which of those things he should find interesting. Having presented the menu, you must let him choose his own dishes.

LEARNING   1–2

During his first year, your baby focused on learning physical things: how to crawl, stand up, even take a few steps. These accomplishments brought with them a sense of physical achievement and independence. He was able to explore the world without having to wait for you to bring it to him.

During the second year he'll not only consolidate all the physical skills he acquired in his first year, he'll also master one of the most difficult intellectual ones – speech (see p. 222). Your child will be struggling to express his thoughts and desires through speech. His developing brain will allow him to see himself as a separate entity from you; he'll be aware of "self." He'll probably be quite frustrated this year, which may lead to tantrums. He'll need a lot of affection, much encouragement and constant support.

Intellectual development

● *12 months*
Your baby likes looking at simple books with you. He loves jokes and repeats anything that makes you laugh. He understands that he should hold up his arms when you dress him. He knows the meaning of simple, frequently used words like shoe, bottle, bath. Your one-year-old may even say a few intelligible words.

● *15 months*
He will show you that he wants to brush his own hair. He'll know what kissing means and will give you a kiss when asked. He'll want to help you with household chores, like dusting, and will be thrilled when he acquires any new skill. He can't understand individual words, but can understand quite complex sentences.

● *18 months*
When you're reading together, he will point to objects, like a dog, ball, or cow. He will recognize animals like cows, and identify them by name. He'll know the different parts of his body and will point to it – his hand, nose, mouth or eyes – if you ask where it is. He'll know the difference between his nose and Mommy's nose. If you ask him to fetch something, he will.

● *21 months*
He will come to you, attract your attention, and take you to things that he is interested in or has a problem with. He'll love scribbling with a pencil. He'll begin to understand and obey simple requests.

● *two years*
He likes his own company and will play happily on his own. Instead of just scribbling with a pencil, he'll make strokes up and down in imitation of writing. He knows the names of many familiar objects and toys, and will use these words with meaning. Once he learns the meaning of a word, he may repeat it continuously.

Learning and speech

Learning to talk is one of the most important intellectual lessons that your child will ever master. Without it, many other learning skills will be handicapped or may not even develop. Learning to speak is almost an act of survival; a child quickly learns that he has to communicate to get ahead.

Early communication, as we have seen, is not with words; initially it's with cries. The first conversation is usually with smiles; later it may be nothing more than a movement of the head. You may notice that your child just bobs his head to say thank you. Later he may stand close to something he wants and shout for your attention. Once he gets it he will point to the object. These early lessons in communication teach him that life will be a lot easier if he can communicate with the world around him in the language which is commonly used – a language of words, rather than gestures.

In learning to use words a child discovers a lot about the world around him and how people behave in it. Very often he'll try to guess at the meaning of a word from the general sense of what is being said and the tone of voice which is used to say it. In discovering language, your child makes connections between sounds and what he understands about the nature of things around him. When he first uses words, he'll use them generically – they'll have a much wider meaning for him than they do for an adult. (Many children call every man they meet "Daddy," because they don't yet understand the special nature of their relationship to their fathers.) "Nana" (banana) may be the generic name for fruit because that's the name he first learned for a single fruit. With your help, your child will soon learn to distinguish between a car and a truck, even though they both move on four wheels, or between a cat and a dog, even though they both have tails and are similar in size and shape.

Talk to your child

Your child is learning the art of communication, so make sure that you communicate with him. If he wants something, tell him you understand what he wants and give it to him, naming the object as you do so. Don't talk to him without looking at him. If he wants your attention, stop whatever you are doing, turn to face him, and listen. When your child first starts to learn a language he learns it in broad strokes, so while he may not understand individual words, he very often gets the gist of a sentence. Give him lots of clues to help with this. In the evening when it's time for bed, ask him to help you put the toys away, then go to the door and say, "It's time for bed now," and put your hand out for him. He may not understand the words, but he'll get the sense of what you're trying to say.

You can give your child a great deal of help in learning to understand language. Children love the sound of speech and they love your attention. Combine the two and talk to your child as often as you can. Look directly at him while you talk, and make eye contact. Slightly exaggerate your facial expressions and your gestures. Exaggerate the emphasis you put on words, the inflection and the tone of your voice. If you can, match your words with actions. For instance, when you say, "I think it's time for your bath," go into the bathroom and start running the taps. Say to him, "Let's comb your hair," and then pick up the comb and do it.

Learning and playing

To a child, play is learning; it's also very hard work. While he is playing, he is discovering his own strengths and limitations, and growing up. Play helps learning in many ways:

☐ It improves manual dexterity. Building a tower of bricks or, later on, doing a simple jigsaw puzzle, teaches a child that he can make his hands work for him as tools and prepares him for using his hands in delicate and complex ways.

☐ Playing with other children helps to

teach a child how important it is to get on with others. Having playmates to the house teaches him to overcome shyness and introduces him to the notion of sharing. It also presents him with problems he must solve without help from adults, and teaches him to control outbursts of antisocial behavior. Through a special friend your child may learn to love people and understand feelings that he can't easily put into words. At the same time, he will be learning to consider the feelings of others.

☐ Through play, a child learns to communicate. Playing with other children demands a more complicated use of language. Talking while playing may be one of the most challenging tests for your child, since the more imaginative the play, the more complex the ideas, and the greater the need to express these ideas in words that his friends can understand.

☐ Play undoubtedly helps develop physical coordination. In fact, it helps both physical and intellectual development. The freedom to swing, climb, skip, run and jump helps to perfect muscular coordination and physical skills. It also improves hearing and vision.

Provide the right games

Since your child makes no distinction between learning and playing, you can help him learn a great deal, by giving him the right kinds of toys and the best materials to play with. From a very early age, all four of my children loved playing with water, whether it was outside in a small washing pool, or just standing on a chair beside the kitchen sink with the taps running and an assortment of plastic dishes, cups and containers nearby. Water games were always good for an hour's diversion, and all the time my children were learning lessons: that water feels wet; that it will pour; that you can fill and empty things with it; that you can blow bubbles in it; that things will float on it, or sink through it; that vegetable dyes will dissolve in it and color it and that other liquids won't; that when the tap drips it forms drops, and that cupped hands aren't watertight.

Other activities and materials your child will profit from include:

☐ Anything pliable, like play dough, is interesting because it can be moulded by a child's hands. They will soon discover that it keeps its shape if left to dry out, or that it can be rolled into a ball and moulded again.

☐ Sand in a sandbox feels like a solid but pours like a liquid. If wet it will keep the shape of the bucket, and children can make sand pies; if it's dry, the sand pies will crumble.

☐ One of the most important concepts that a child grasps during his second year is that of classification – of sameness and difference. Toys can help the formation of this idea. Farmyard toys, with a variety of animals – horses, cows, chickens, and so on – allow your child to sort out the animals that look the same, especially if you help by showing him the differences and naming the animals repeatedly as you put them into little groups. The same procedure can be applied to many other objects – fruits, cars, shapes or tins.

☐ Children like participating in the domestic routine and can learn a lot about household activities and chores if they are allowed to contribute. A small child can be given a little bowl with some flour to mix each time you bake; he can help with carrying and, when it's time to clean up, he can have a dustpan and brush. If your dustpan and brush are not too big, give him a real one rather than a toy one.

☐ For years, an essential part of our playroom was the play box in which we kept all sorts of old clothes, uniforms, hats and shoes. Most children get immense pleasure from imitating other people. This is a very important learning step for a child because it teaches him to come to terms with the fact that there are other people in the world, and that we must learn to get along with them.

☐ Children of both sexes like dolls. Boys should have their dolls too: they are their imaginary friends and families, and they

help create an imaginary world into which all children can escape. While your child is playing with dolls – be it a soft, cuddly doll or a doll inspired by a comic book hero – he is learning about, and possibly mimicking, human emotions. He will mother the doll, talk to it very firmly, tell it off, rant and rave at it, smack it, then dress it, put it to bed and kiss it goodnight. Through this kind of behavior your child is working out the things that happen to him, trying to understand them fully, and preparing himself for dealing with parents and friends.

□ Long before he can write or draw, your child will love to scribble and use colors. A box of colored chalks and a blackboard and easel set at the same height as himself will be attractive because he'll be able to "draw," then rub out the scribbles and start again. Attach a sheet of paper to the easel, give your child a set of Inger paints, and let him make his own hand prints and finger smears on the paper. If you don't want to buy paints, make up your own (see p. 266). Body paints are also great fun, especially when your child is playing with friends.

□ Most children are musical and like to be sung to from the day they are born. Many children master the tune of their favorite song or nursery rhyme long before they can talk. As soon as your child is old enough, buy him a simple musical instrument like a xylophone or a toy piano so that he can make his own music. Encourage him by joining in with marching and clapping and singing. He'll enjoy it even

213

more if you have your own instrument to accompany him with.

☐ The best way to help your child learn is to join in with his learning activities, especially if you make suggestions about how to do something new with a toy and then demonstrate how to do it. You must do it tactfully and without interfering, however, and you must allow him to decide whether he wants to follow your advice or not. Many of your child's games will need to be played with a partner. You should volunteer yourself whenever you can, but only join in for as long as he wants you to; don't overdo it. Leave the initiative to him – he may ask you to fill the bucket of sand, but the last thing he'll want is for you to turn the bucket upside down to make the sand pie.

☐ Your child's concentration span is increasing, but he may still have problems concentrating on something which is difficult. You can help him by making the task easier or by giving him a helping hand. Showing him how the task is done will give him a goal to work toward. With your support and encouragement he will probably find the determination to go on longer than he would without you. The result will be a great feeling of achievement.

Let your child play alone

Some parents make the mistake of thinking that their child's every waking hour has to be filled with interesting diversions and stimulating activities. This is wrong and can even be harmful. One of the most important lessons your child has to learn – one he'll learn quite willingly if left to his own devices – is that he can be the source of his own entertainment. Very often a child wishes to play by himself, to make his own decisions about what to play, and for how long. Let him make these decisions alone – he'll ask for help if he needs it. Interrupting or introducing a new activity will not make his life more interesting, because it will deny him the opportunity of seeing any single activity through to completion. He will therefore miss out on

the sense of satisfaction and achievement which every child needs.

Another common mistake is to believe that children need to play with toys. Many of the most popular play activities don't involve toys at all. They may involve physical activities like swimming, climbing, running, carrying water to a sandpit and filling the moat or collecting pebbles and shells. Your child should be given the scope and the privacy to enjoy all these activities. If you don't encourage him to invent his own games, and to play alone, he will feel at a complete loss when you are not there to amuse him. This may lead to mischief, delinquent behavior or, even worse, danger. So be pleased if your child shows signs of self-sufficiency, and can entertain himself in your absence.

Leaving your child alone may mean, of course, that you ignore the mess he's making. If he's playing water games, cover the kitchen floor with towels that will soak up the water. If he's painting, cover the carpet with a sheet of polythene. If he's playing with mud or clay cover his clothes with a smock-style apron (see p. 45) and ignore the mess on his arms, face and hair; it can all be washed off when he's finished.

LEARNING

The way in which your child learns changes considerably during his third year, particularly in the second half of it. As a toddler, your child was learning about separate things, single events, one experience at a time. He may have satisfied his curiosity and explored that experience as far as he could, absorbing a great deal of new information in the process, but he rarely related it to anything else in his life. During his third year, however, he starts to think about the meaning of his experiences and to learn from them. Information is sorted and sifted, and viewed in the light of other experiences. Your child starts to think and plan ahead, and becomes much more creative and imaginative. Gradually all the information that he has absorbed over the past years becomes available to him to apply to any given situation. Your child suddenly has an orchestra of thoughts which he can command at will.

This new ability to think, imagine and create changes your child's world considerably. Many familiar objects in the house or garden no longer interest or excite him. He needs wider horizons; he needs to explore, to push the frontiers of his experience and knowledge further and further out.

Your child will become very interested in how things work, and his conversation will constantly be punctuated with, "Why?" He is avid for information and constantly asks questions. It's as though his brain wants more and more information to put into its computer to use immediately.

One of the most important steps in your child's intellectual development is understanding that time is not just in the present, but includes the past and future. The ability to plan ahead is a crucial function of our intellect, that distinguishes us from lower animals. It is during his third year that you will hear your child say for the first time, "I will eat that later," or "We can go tomorrow."

Intellectual development

● *two years, three months*
He will try to build houses and castles with bricks and will repeat new words when you encourage him. He knows who he is and can say his name. He'll begin to pit his will against yours, and may become rather negative. He'll say the word "No" more and more often and won't always fit in with your wishes.

● *two years, six months*
He loves helping you and will help with chores, putting things away, bringing things to the table. He'll know both his first name and his family name. He can draw horizontal and vertical lines and can name several common objects. A boy will have noticed that his sex organs stick out from his body whereas those of his mother, and of his little girlfriends, do not.

● *two years, nine months*
He'll know the differences between boys and girls. He'll begin to ask questions. He'll learn nursery rhymes and will be able to repeat them. He'll begin to understand numbers. He'll try to draw a circle but won't be able to complete it successfully without help.

● *three years*
He'll become increasingly sociable and will like to play with other children. He'll know several more nursery rhymes and will almost be able to draw a circle. He'll know the difference between such words as on, under, and behind and will be able to form quite complicated sentences.

Learning and speech

As your child grows older, speech will play an increasingly important role in communication between you and himself. Consequently, speech will become more and more important in helping him learn. By now your child has a sense of the etiquette of conversation. He knows, for instance, that people usually take turns at speaking. He knows when it is his turn, and doesn't try to dominate the conversation. He also knows that instead of accompanying words with gestures to explain what he means, he can vary the intonation of the words. He knows that an intonation which rises usually means a question, and that a falling pitch indicates a statement. When your child was younger, speech was part of a simple pattern of communication, telling you what he wanted or didn't want – it was used to greet you and to say goodbye and to give something a label. As your child's world widens, he needs more sophisticated ways to express his thoughts.

One indication of his progress is his use of the possessive – "*my* doll, Mommy coat, Daddy nose." Another is his use of negatives. As a younger child, he would merely have said, "No." Now he says, "Can't," or, "Won't." A little later he starts to express actions – "Dolly fall," "Dog bark," "Car bump." Another characteristic is the increasing use of questions combined with statements: "Daddy sleep, why Daddy sleep?" "Mommy must go shop, why Mommy go shop?" "Daddy gone out, where Daddy gone?"

By the time your child is three, he will be asking quite complicated questions that parallel the development of his thoughts. Consider the following sentences – they contain quite sophisticated ideas: "I go get pencil and draw." "What that on table?" "See, this one better. But this not better."

Don't "talk down"

The kind of language you use with your child is very important. It's well known that adults change the way they speak to children as the children get older. Sentences become more complex and contain longer words that describe abstract ideas. Don't fall into the trap of talking down to your child and avoid the redundancies of baby language. Throw into your conversation the odd word that you know is unfamiliar to your child, but which he can guess at from the gist of the sentence. This will teach him new words, and encourage him to become more articulate. Research has proven that children of articulate parents who don't "tailor" their speech to their children, use words more easily and freely at an earlier age than the children of parents who persist in simplifying their language.

Learning and playing

Play begins to teach your child about himself, and about his relation to the world he lives in.

☐ Play helps put the world around him into perspective. Playing with farmyard animals was once nothing more than sorting animals into different types and putting them in the right place. Now it introduces him to an aspect of life he knows is different from the one he leads. It also helps to reduce the world to a scale he can handle.

☐ Play increasingly becomes an outlet for emotions. Even an action doll – a cowboy, policeman, etc. – can bring out feelings of protectiveness and gentleness. The same toy can also help him get rid of aggressive instincts which, if directed against other children, would be frowned upon and considered antisocial.

☐ Play creates an interest in other people. If, for instance, the toy box has a cowboy's outfit and a nurse's uniform, your child can dress up and play a role. In a hat worn at an angle and a pair of high-heeled shoes too big for him, he can pretend to be say, his aunt. By acting out what he thinks she does, he can get an insight into her life and into other people's lives.

☐ Play develops a sense of territory and ownership. Safeguarding a new and cherished toy or his own private place to play teaches a child to respect the belongings and privacy of others. Play stimulates curiosity, independence, an adventurous spirit and intellectual growth. Mechanical toys and puzzles stimulate the development of analytical thought. Painting, drawing, making shapes with clay and fitting things together all encourage creativity. As your child gets older, toys like a microscope, telescope, chemistry set or magician's outfit allow experimentation. These kinds of toys teach him to meet challenges and master difficulties.

☐ As your child gets older, play helps to teach him how to cope with events beyond his control. He may break a treasured toy, he may fail to make a mechanical toy work or he may not have the competence to do what he wants to do. All these disappointments teach him to cope with his own limitations, and with the problems he will face throughout life. Play also teaches him how to face several difficult choices – and how to make the right one.

☐ Play helps your child get to know himself. Before he can interact with others, he has to understand himself – and play helps him determine his own physical and intellectual strengths and weaknesses.

☐ Play is an important aid in helping your child to mature. By the time he is three, he will have begun to develop a sense of planning. He will keep his traffic jam of toy cars under the surveillance of a police car, with a pick-up truck standing alongside. What better indication could there be that he has learned to think ahead! He will also show an ability to postpone pleasure when he begins to play with toys that need the glue to set or the clay to dry. If he's prepared to share one of his toys with a friend, who reciprocates by lending your child one of his, then he is learning the value of give and take.

Forming concepts

For your child to form concepts and put them to use, he has to learn to recognize similarities and differences, and to group things accordingly in his own mind. This accomplishment is a great intellectual leap forward. From 18 months to two years, your child will do this sorting automatically when faced with an array of different objects. All things that roll and are round are sorted into one group. All things that have edges and are rectangular, like bricks, are sorted into another. Things which have four legs and meow are cats. Things which have two legs and fly are birds.

By his third year, your toddler will give his concepts verbal labels (names). It would be extremely difficult for your child to develop without this facility for language. A younger child will use the word cat for every cat he meets, including the family pet, the cat drawn in a book, the cat he sees in a neighbor's garden and a toy cat. In his mind he uses a single label for all these different things. But by the time he approaches three, he'll have made several rather sophisticated distinctions. He'll know that all those animals are cats, so he'll have a concept of what makes "cat-ness." But he'll also know that there are subtle differences between "my cat," "your cat," "toy cat," and "paper cat."

Abstract ideas

When your child is two years old it is impossible for him to describe things which are not real – things that he cannot perceive with his senses. He doesn't know what pretty means. He can't quite distinguish between emptiness and fullness. He knows that when he blows bubbles they will float, but he can't yet distinguish between lightness and heaviness.

Your child may know the difference between "one" and "several," but he still has no idea of the magnitude of numbers, so anything more than one may be "lots." He has very little concept of time and can't visualize what tomorrow means, or last week. He has difficulty coping with the concept of "tonight," though his understanding improves throughout this year.

To have abstract ideas and to think in the abstract your child has to be able to picture things in his mind that are not actually there. If you ask him where a toy is, he has to remember when and where he was last playing with it; and then go and retrieve the toy. Once he can do this he can then make plans involving objects which are not actually there. When you ask him where his boat is, for instance, he'll have a mental picture of the boat lying in the garden and will say: "Boat in garden, me get it in a minute." He'll carry on with his painting, finish it, wash his hands and then go out and get his boat without prompting.

How to help your child develop

The most important way in which you can help your child develop is to listen to what he's saying. Because his world is expanding at a rapid rate, both physically and intellectually, it is very important that you communicate openly and freely with him. Listen carefully to everything he says, try to understand his thinking, and answer his questions in terms that he understands. Not only should he be asking you questions, but you should be asking them, too. This will keep you aware of what he is thinking and what interests him, and allow you to present information in the most interesting way.

market, and so on.

About the age of three your child becomes quite sensitive to what other people are feeling. He may show the first signs of sympathy by wanting to comfort you if you seem sad. Take advantage of this and start to teach him about the need to think of other people; that it is right to be kind and polite, helpful and thoughtful, cooperative and willing. Make sure he is introduced to people coming to your house like the window cleaner, the postman, and the handyman. Tell him about their jobs and the problems they have to cope with. Suggest some of the ways he can be helpful, such as taking letters from the postman at the door and bringing them to you.

Early reading

Some children have a natural bent for reading and writing, and turn to them long before their peers. If yours is one of them, encourage and help, but never push. Your child can master these advanced skills only when his brain and intellect are sufficiently developed. You won't know exactly when your child is capable of reading (and later writing), so wait to take your lead from him. Until this time, simply continue reading to him pointing out and naming objects in books, and encouraging him to repeat them.

I'm much against using "flash cards" when your child finds it an onerous bore. In this instance, you're only doing it for your own satisfaction and pride, which is always a poor reason for making your child do anything. If, however, your child is fascinated by new words and gets pleasure from remembering flash cards, do by all means encourage him as much as you can. Similarly you should not try to make him read; when he's ready, he'll start pointing out words; and then and then only should you start to help him.

Every time your child asks a question or has a conversation with you, you are given a golden opportunity to help him learn, even though the circumstances may be very casual and ordinary. If you're in the kitchen preparing lunch and your child asks why you cut the ends off carrots, you can explain to him how all plants have roots, because they need food in order to grow. And next time you are in a park or field, you can pull up a tuft of grass and show him its root system. Or if you're really ambitious, you could put some beans in a jam jar lined with wet blotting paper and show him how they begin to sprout. When you're out in the street, keep up a running commentary on what is going on around you: traffic lights changing, cars stopping at pedestrian crossings, a policeman who is stopping and waving on traffic, trucks carrying goods to the

Nursery schools

As your child reaches three years old, you should start thinking about whether he would benefit from attending nursery school. He will meet many new friends there, as well as interested and sympathetic adults who are trained at knowing how to widen a child's horizons. He will have the opportunity to try a variety of new and interesting activities. He will also have to learn to socialize and be a member of a group. Last, and most important, he will have to learn to manage without you.

The decision as to whether he's capable of managing without you for long periods of time will be an important factor when you are weighing the pros and cons of nursery school. If your child is very shy and clinging – fretting whenever you leave the room, and following you whenever you go – and if he doesn't talk easily to other adults and children, then you are going to have problems with nursery school. If your child is not toilet trained, most nursery schools won't accept him. Attending school for the first time is quite a traumatic experience for a small child – one for which you can't really prepare him because nothing similar has ever happened to him.

The decision – to send him or not – is a difficult one. You can, however, fall back on the knowledge that most children manage it and indeed thrive on it so well that they miss nursery school when they're on holiday. Bear in mind that with a little careful planning you can help your child get over the frightening first stages. There is no reason for him to feel deserted.

Assessing a nursery or playgroup

There are several different types of group for pre-school children, including play groups, nursery schools and day nurseries. Put together a list of all approved pre-school groups in your area and choose two or three to visit and assess.

Go about your assessment in a thorough way. Begin by talking to the teacher in charge. Make an appointment to sit in on some of the classes. If possible, spend a whole morning or afternoon there so you can get a feel for the routine, for the amount of discipline, and for the way the children are treated. Is the environment cheerful and informal? Do the children seem happy? Try to look over the facilities and talk to other mothers whose children go to the same school.

Once you decide where to send your child, ask to take him along to sit in on a session, so that he can get used to the environment. Try to arrange for several visits a few weeks before the start of school.

When he finally begins, make sure he knows who the teachers are and the sorts of things he will have to do. He may have a go in a sand box, do a jig-saw puzzle, look at books, or play with a variety of toys. Encourage him to play with other children, but if he becomes very shy, don't force him to be sociable. Many children get this way in strange situations and it's quite natural – let him take his time.

If your child seems worried or clinging, sit with him until he's happy to let you go. This may mean the whole session on the first day, a few hours on the second day, an hour on the third day, half an hour on the fourth day, and ten minutes on the fifth. Most nursery schools will welcome your staying. To see if your child's ready to let you go, just say that you want to pop off to the store and will be back in a few minutes. Make sure you are, so he can always trust you to return. For the first week or so, it's a good idea for you or your partner to take your child to the group and pick him up personally. Don't add to all his other worries by having him cope with a strange mother in a car pool. And when you go to collect him, don't be late!

SPEECH 0–1

The moment when your child first speaks is very exciting. For the first time you're given precise information about what he knows and thinks – it's as though language were a window with a privileged view into his heart and mind. It's also the tool through which he can learn. He'll no longer have to rely on crying to communicate.

Despite a great deal of research, we still don't know exactly how a child acquires language. What we do know, however, is the general sequence of development that all children follow. We also know that your baby learns a lot about language before he even starts to talk. Long before he knows what the words mean, he'll be aware of changes in sound, rhythms and intonations. Before he speaks, he'll also be aware of verbal rituals, such as the fact that first one person speaks and then the other.

Each month your baby will master new words and new grammatical rules. But learning to speak is infinitely more important than learning vocabulary and grammar. What your child is mainly concerned with is communicating and interacting with the people around him. Language both reflects and encourages the development of sensitivity to others.

Children develop at their own speed, and this applies to speech as much as to any other form of development. Don't get worried if your child doesn't seem to be as quick at picking up language as other children around you – give all the encouragement you can and let your child take the time he wants and needs.

How speech develops

Studies have shown that even a few days after birth babies will respond more to speech than to any other noise. Even very young babies can discriminate between different speech sounds – which is, after all, an essential part of learning a language. In one study, for example, one-month-old babies were observed to suck more rapidly from a bottle when they heard a new sound, especially if that sound was the human voice. The initial sound used in these experiments was "Pa." As the sound continued to be played, the baby got progressively bored until he lost all interest in sucking. But as soon as a new sound, "Ba," was introduced, his sucking rate increased once more. What's interesting is that the baby was able to distinguish between two such similar sounds as "Pa" and "Ba," before he could actually say them.

● *Up to six weeks*
As soon as your baby is born he'll start to make sounds. Initially they will be cries – cries of discomfort, or cries for food and affection. Along with these he'll start to make little gurbling noises as a mark of pleasure and contentment.

● *Around six weeks*
He'll begin to respond to your smiling face and your voice with a more exaggerated gurgling. Although he's not literally talking to you, he *is* communicating. What's more, he's learning to communicate in the way that adults do. On hearing your voice, for example, your baby will gurgle something at you, then wait for your reply before responding again.

● *Three to four months*
Your baby will make soft, cooing noises. At this stage the sounds will consist of single syllables with an open vowel sound. The first consonants he'll use will be *p*, *b* and *m*, so it's hardly surprising that he'll say "Maa" or "Paa," although he won't understand the significance of what he's saying at this time.

● *Seven months*
He'll be increasingly responsive to sounds, whether of the human voice or music. He'll expand his cooing into two-syllabled words by repeating the initial syllable: "Maama," "Beebe," "Daada." This stage will be followed by explosive sounds of exclamation: "Ai," "Imi."

● *Eight months*
Your baby will continue to babble, but he'll also learn how to shout to attract your attention. If he's near you when you're having a conversation with someone, he'll pay close attention to whatever you're saying and will then turn to watch any reply that's made to you. Since his babbling may become quite musical, he may try to imitate you when you sing a nursery rhyme to him, or join along when you open his musical box.

● *Nine months*
Your baby's speech will become noticeably more elaborate as he starts to combine syllables and pronounce them with sentence-like phrasing. So, with the rising and falling intonations of adult speech, he'll say things like: "Ca-mama-dah-ba." Once he starts to make up sounds like this, technically called *jargoning*, you'll know that he's just about to start talking.

● *Ten to 11 months*
Your baby will probably say his first "real" words some time during this month. The emergence of these first words is controlled as much by your baby's physical ability to articulate and make speech sounds as it is by his intellectual ability to make connections between objects and labels. The words he chooses will almost certainly be the names of things which are important to him: people (mama, dada); animals (dog, cat); objects (cup, ball).

Simplifying words

Your child's method of communication changes from babbling to words; from streams of uncontrolled sounds to planned, thoughtful, controlled speech. Furthermore, the sounds have to be in a certain sequence so that the words are understandable to other people. All this is rather much for a young child, so his pronunciation of early words is very often simplified.

Nearly all children reduce the number of consonants at the beginning (or the end) of words. Spoon becomes "poon" and smack becomes "mack." He may say "du"

for duck, "be" for bed, "ca" for cat. The mastering of consonants is one of the last basic language skills that children master. It is perfectly normal for children to have difficulty with consonants until they are four or five.

Another way that children simplify the pronunciation of words is to repeat the initial consonant sound. This accounts for the pronunciation of "doggy" as "doddy" or "goggy."

Children also like to substitute explosive sounds for less explosive ones. Your child may say "bie" for "pie"; "due" for "toe"; and "bop" for "pop."

Helping your baby to talk

☐ Among the first kinds of words your baby learns are label words identifying objects. In conversations with him therefore, stress the names of objects and repeat them frequently. When you're feeding your baby, talk repeatedly about the spoon – about putting food on the spoon and licking it off. Make an effort not to use pronouns. Say, "I'll get your coat," instead of "I'll get it." Say, "Here is the ball," instead of "Here it is." Your child is busy learning the difference between himself and other people, so use his name rather than "you": "William is a good boy," "Where are William's shoes?" and "William and Mommy will go into the car."

☐ Don't expect too much of your baby's pronunciation. If he can't say a word properly, but you understand what he means, don't insist that he keep on trying until he says it perfectly. He'll only get frustrated.

☐ Go to some effort to understand his own private, invented words or ones which are mispronounced. If he's trying to explain something to you, help him with a long list of synonyms until you find the word he actually wants. His pleasure in having communicated with you will be enormous and will encourage him to try again.

☐ Help your baby learn how to apply words by describing and talking about things which are actually in front of him. Repeat a word often enough and your baby will connect it with an object – especially if he can see, hold, touch and play with it. While you're playing with a ball, for instance, repeat the word "ball" as often as you can, and also discuss the innate properties of a ball – that it is round and that it will roll and bounce.

☐ In teaching your baby to talk, you have to be something of an actor, always bringing drama and interest to what you are saying. Exaggerate your pronunciation and intonations. Make it clear when you're asking a question. Show when you're pleased and when you're serious. Communicate through your actions as well as through speech and facial expressions.

☐ Your baby learns language from you more easily than from any other person, but don't expect him to pick it up from the general babble of adult conversation in which he's not included. He won't be able to distinguish the single sounds and sentences. Always look directly at your baby while you're talking to him. Stop what you're doing and look intently at him when he "talks" to you. Pay him the compliment of listening to his efforts when he tries to talk back.

☐ Ask your baby questions like, "Where's your teddy?" and, "Was that nice?" He may not be able to answer you initially, but he'll understand what you're saying and may point or nod.

☐ Don't oversimplify what you say to your baby – he needs the stimulation of adult speech, not a kind of pulpy baby talk.

☐ Take advantage of your baby's interests by talking about things on which he's already concentrating. He may not be interested in a story about a fictional character, but he will be riveted by a story in which he is the central character. He may not be interested in animals, unless they're discussed in terms of mother animals and their babies – he can relate to that.

☐ Encourage him to take the few words he has learned and use them frequently in your conversations. He will be delighted to hear words he knows, and this will encourage him to be adventurous with speech and to try out new words.

☐ Never, ever scold or correct early errors of pronunciation or understanding. In our house we said "aterator" for "radiator," "gamilla" for "vanilla," "binoclickers" for "binoculars" – and we all found the new words charming.

Bi-lingualism

Children seem to love learning two or more languages. When small babies are learning to talk they have the ability to make all linguistic sounds. They find new languages much easier to learn than we do. It also seems to be quite easy for them, not just to pick languages up, but to think and speak in two or more languages. Recently I watched a small godchild looking from her French mother, who was speaking French, to her English father, who was speaking English. She's just two-and-a-half years old, but she replied to her mother in French and to her father in English. I would encourage small children to be exposed to more than one language rather than be restricted to one.

Spotting when something is wrong

Don't worry if your baby doesn't speak this year. As in everything else, children develop speech at different rates. However, if your child is still not speaking by the time he's two-and-a-half you *must* seek expert help. If deficient hearing is responsible, then it's crucial to deal with it before he starts nursery school or kindergarten. If he has a real speech defect, you should consult therapists for children with speech disorders. Many problems can be treated if discovered early enough, and if expert help is secured.

This year your child will make great strides forward in terms of both physical and intellectual development. He'll increase his vocabulary, and his grasp of grammatical construction. In order to speak properly, he'll have to unlearn some of the habits he got into when his speech consisted of babbling – habits like dropping consonants and duplicating words.

The beginnings of classification

As your child learns to recognize and identify objects, he'll begin to classify and group them. At the beginning, however, this process won't be completely accurate. He'll look at several objects and use the same word to identify all of them if they have one or more features in common. This is referred to as overextension. He'll use a single word to describe various objects. The reason he uses words generically like this is because he lacks the proper powers of articulation. He has a strong desire to communicate with you, so he uses the only word he knows. Your child will link words together on the following bases:

Shape
Balls, apples or stones may all be called "ball."
Size
A handbag, a polythene bag and a shopping basket may all be "bag."
Sound
A whistle, a siren and a car horn may all be "beep."
Movement
A bicycle, a car, a bus and a train may all be "choo-choo."
Your child may call two objects by the same name, but he does know the difference between them. For example, he may use the word "guck" for truck and duck, and yet when faced with pictures of them both and told to point out a truck, he'll easily make the distinction.

In a similar way, children can underextend words. Most children, for example, associate the word "animal" with only those animals they see in everyday life; they very often have difficulty understanding that fish, insects and birds should be categorized as animals too. Whatever early words your child learns, he'll soon begin to use them to mean a variety of things. A single word can be used as a label for a greeting, a demand, or a question. At the beginning, your child may often add gestures to single words to give them meaning. Later on he'll learn to change his intonations to signal different meanings.

Expanding vocabulary

Your baby's vocabulary will continue to expand. The words he'll learn most readily will be those whose use affects his daily life, such as certain people, animals and foods. Early words nearly always include the names of animals like ducks, dogs, cats, horses, cows, plus the kind of noises that they make. Your child will also know the names of his favorite toys and – very important – the words he can use to change or regulate the world around him through interaction with you. So his vocabulary may include words like no, up, more, out and open.

Some children learn a slew of words as soon as they begin to speak, but it's more usual for them to acquire between one and three words a month. By the time he's two, he should be able to say about 200 words.

Helping your child to understand

Understanding always comes before usage, and your 18-month-old child will understand much more of the speech he hears than his own language suggests. To help him, you should make available far more information than your words alone provide:
□ Talk to your child as often as you can and always look at him when you do so. This will give your child the maximum number of opportunities for learning and understanding language.

□ Help your baby's comprehension by acting out what you are saying with facial expressions and gestures. Use words to accompany actions that involve him, such as, "Mommy will put on Jennifer's coat," or "Mommy will take off Mommy's shoes."

□ For your child to learn that communication is always two-ways, don't read long stories or use long sentences without giving him the opportunity to participate and contribute. Punctuate your conversations with questions that demand a response of some kind.

□ Your child finds it very difficult to understand language if there is a great deal of background noise that obscures speech sounds. So if the television is on while you are talking to him, keep the sound low and don't play your radio at the same time.

□ Give him the confidence to try conversation with strangers by acting as his interpreter. In this way he won't feel embarrassed and will have a go at it.

□ Give him as many clues as to your meaning as you can, even though you know that he can't understand exactly what you're saying. At bath time, for instance, take him into the bathroom, run the tap, feel the temperature of the water

and undress him – all the while giving him information about what you're doing. Then say, "Now you are ready for your bath." After all your actions and words, he will certainly understand your meaning.

The first sentences

Sometime before your child's second birthday he'll start to string words together. This is an important milestone because it shows that he's now aware of the relationship between objects. Your baby's first sentences will be limited in their meanings. They'll probably explain something that has just happened or describe what someone is doing. His sentences will be concerned with the following:

What's happening:	Me run
	Cow go moo
	Truck bump
Who possesses what:	My dolly
	Mommy dress
	Granny bag
Where things are:	Doll in box
	Daddy in garden
	Ball in bath
Repetition:	Me more milk
	Play again
Where something's gone:	Drink all gone
	No more toy

His sentences won't follow adult grammatical rules – that will develop later – but they will have a logical construction of their own. He'll learn fairly early that certain words are used in combination.

He'll repeatedly hear commands like, "Pick up," "Put on," "Go out," and will continue to use them as one word even when adding them on to others. And so he'll say, "Car pick up," and "Door go out."

His first attempts at tenses will be slightly awry. He'll make the past tense by adding "d" to anything – "I wented," "You goed,"

"I gaved." To make words plural, he'll add an "s" to the end – "Look, fishes," "Mouses," "Gameses."

The development of grammar

Your child learns grammatical rules in a specific order. The tense is indicated by adding -*ing* or -*ed*. Instead of just saying "carry," your child will say "carrying" or "carried." To distinguish between different spacial relationships, he'll start adding "in" and "on" to sentences. Next, he'll use *a* and *the* to distinguish between definite and indefinite objects. The next stage is to add the possessive "s," as in "Mommy's and "Daddy's." The final stage is to add the plural "s," as in "Mommy and Edward put on coats."

Helping your child with grammar

The best way to help your child learn and understand grammar is to keep a correct model in front of him. While your child may describe something in his own particular telegraphese, you should state the correct version for him. So when your child says, "Daddy comed home car," you will be helping him by repeating it to show that you understand what he is trying to say – but you should say it correctly: "Oh, Daddy has come home in his car. Let's go and meet him." Your child thus speaks his language and understands what you mean when you speak yours. But he will also understand the difference in the ways you express ideas – and, through this under-

standing, learn to speak correctly. You will be doing him no favors at all if you continue to respond to him in baby talk.

As with most other lessons your child is learning, all attempts, no matter how unsuccessful, should be rewarded with praise and not criticised. Don't interrupt what he is saying with the proper construction. He is having a good deal of difficulty both concentrating on the idea he wants to put into words and getting the words in the right order. He will feel frustrated, resentful and inadequate if you continually correct him, which, in turn, may inhibit him from trying to use new words and new speech patterns. Remember, it's your job to make language, conversation and communication exciting, not a chore. It isn't important that he speak everything correctly in the beginning – it's far more important that he learn about the excitement of communication and practise it with you.

During the third year, the structure of your child's sentences will become more complicated, and he will start to fit whole phrases together. He'll begin to understand and use negatives, not just simple "no's" and "not's." He'll make questions by using interrogative phrases, not just by putting "why" in front. For the first time, he will begin to fully appreciate the relationship between one object and another. He'll start to use adjectives – big, small, fat, thin – and then comparative

adjectives – bigger, smaller, fatter, thinner. He'll understand and use words that imply spatial relationships – this, here, that, there. He will learn the relationship between "I" and "my," "you" and "yours." He'll also learn how to use phrases with conjunctions like "and," "then," and "but."

Having conversations

In his third year your child becomes a natural chatterer, so take advantage of this tendency and show him how conversations are carried on. Teach him that conversations are two-way. Show him how to make subjects interesting with questions and how to move from one point to another.

One of the best ways of involving your child in a conversation is to ask him what he likes, what he's doing, and how things work. Having asked these questions, you have to show sincere interest in his response, so he learns that conversation is meaningful and worthwhile. Similarly, when he asks you a question, appeals for help, or just asks you to come and see something that excites him, you have to show a genuine interest in his request. If you respond to his baby talk with a series of absent-minded "mms," he'll not only learn nothing but assume you're not interested in him, and stop asking you for help.

You can help him learn from everything you do by giving descriptions that are slightly more detailed than you would normally use. For instance, if he is having difficulty getting his sweater over his head, say something like, "Oh dear, the opening in your sweater is too small for your head." This rather elaborate way of saying, "I'll help you," introduces him to at least three new words and ideas. If you can lift something that he can't, point out that you are able to because you're stronger than he is and the object is heavy. Talk about colors, shapes and textures whenever possible. ("You are going to have the *red* apple. I'll have the *yellow* one." "Look at the pretty blue flower with the long stem. Let's smell the flower." "Daddy's car has four wheels. This truck has lots of wheels, let's count. One, two, three, four, five, six, seven, eight.")

You can also help him out with conversation. If you ask him what he has been doing in the park and he can't quite get the words together, point him in the right direction by saing: "What did you make in the sandpit? ... How did you get down from the top of the Jungle Jim? ... Where did you go on your tricycle?" You can prompt his responses by asking, "What happened next?"

All my children loved it when I left a blank in the conversation for them to fill in with a word they knew. When they were playing, for instance, I would say, "Oh, you mean you slid down the ------," and my children would gleefully contribute "slide." In discussing what they had done in the sandpit I would say, "Oh, you made sandpies with your ------," and they would shout, "Bucket."

Helping with grammar

As your child begins to understand the more complicated forms of grammar, help him, as before, by simply repeating what he has said in the correct form. Let him hear you saying new words and expressions.

Negatives

With your help, your child can learn to put negatives where they belong. By listening to what you say, he will learn to use won't, can't, wouldn't, hadn't, wasn't.

Your child says, "I not eat biccit."
You say, "You haven't eaten your biscuit."
Your child says, "No cookies left."
You say, "Oh dear – there aren't any more cookies."

Questions

Using the same method, teach him how to arrange words so that they ask questions.
Your child says, "Go out?"
You say, "Where shall we go?"
Your child says, "More?"
You say, "Would you like some more ice cream?"
Your child says, "Coat on?"
You say, "How do you put your coat on?"
In the same way you can teach your child to use the "wh" words, such as what, who, which, where, and why.

Adjectives

One of the best ways to teach your child about adjectives is to point out the relationships between objects – particularly if they are opposites. If your child says,

"Big ball," show him a smaller ball, and introduce him to the concept of opposites like big and small. You will be able to show him that one is bigger than the other and that one is smaller than the other. In the same way, you can teach him the concept of wide and narrow, thick and thin, deep and shallow, heavy and light, hard and soft – always demonstrating with the appropriate objects, and, whenever possible, making it into a kind of game.

Possessive pronouns

When your child says, "I bring book here," you say, "Oh, you were over there and you brought your book to me here."

When he says, "I hate *this* biccit," *you say*, "Oh, then I'll have your biscuit and you can have my biscuit."

When your child says, "This Jennifer coat, that Mommy coat," *you say*, "Yes, that is *your* coat, this is *my* coat."

In this manner your child learns how to use the words "my" and "yours."

Asking and answering questions

When your child approaches his third birthday he will ask you questions continually. While you may get tired of answering the constant whys, you should be happy he is showing so much curiosity in what is going on around him and making so many attempts to express his ideas in words.

Your child's questions should always be treated seriously and you should always try to give the most accurate, truthful answers you can. Don't brush the question off with an answer like, "Because that is the way it is," or, "Things are just made that way." You have to give him information that adds to his knowledge in a form that he can digest. So when your child asks, "Why is it raining?" don't respond with, "Because it is." Try, instead, a simple explanation like, "Clouds are full of water, and the water is falling back to the earth in rain drops." If you don't know the answer, look it up.

Your child's questions are usually very simple because he hasn't learned to express himself fully. So you should examine his questions to see what it is he really wants to know. If he points to a ruler and says, "What's that?" he may want to know not only its name but its function. Tell him, "It's a ruler, and you use it to measure things – look, this book is nine inches long. A ruler is also used to draw straight lines; let's draw one together." He may often ask questions that are difficult to decipher at first, like "Why birds fly?" What he really means to ask, of course, is, "Why do birds fly?" Before answering, repeat his question: "How do birds fly? Why do birds flap their wings?" And then ask him, "Is that what you mean?"

If you don't know the answer to a question, be truthful. Tell him that you don't know but add, "Let's go and look it up in the book," or, "Let's go and ask Daddy," or, "Perhaps your sister will know."

Sometimes parents shy away from giving truthful and accurate answers to a child because they think he won't be able to cope with the truth. This is often the case with questions about death, and sex. You must *always* answer these difficult questions truthfully. However, don't make the mistake of thinking that when you tell the truth you have to tell the whole truth. You don't. Your child doesn't understand enough to cope with the complexities of a full and accurate reply. What you can do in awkward circumstances, however, is to supply that part of the truth which they can deal with and understand (see p. 252).

13 Social behavior

The foundations of your child's social behavior are laid down during infancy. The way you treat your child and the way he responds to you, and to the outside world, will become part of his permanent character. Social development in early childhood goes through fairly well-defined stages. From being a passive newborn, your baby will join in the surrounding social group by imitating others. He will first imitate facial expressions, gestures and movements, then speech sounds and, finally, patterns of behavior. One of his most important guides in this early period is the mother, or mother substitute. Babies who establish warm, loving, out-going relationships with these people are motivated to make friendly relationships with other people. There will be a slightly difficult time, probably in the second year, when your child will be struggling so hard to assert independence that he slips into an apparently negative stance, ignoring your wishes and doing only what he wants. Go along with your child on this. Realize that he's not turning into a monster, but still needs your help in his struggle for independence. Your job will be a lot easier if you use your wits to make it seem as though your child's getting his own way. In the end you'll have a lovable young child who has learned to respect the feelings of others, and who has an overwhelming desire to share happiness with those he loves.

Your baby is different from all others. He is unique, and no matter how many books you read, none can tell you about him. You are going to have to discover your baby for yourself and, little by little, with careful observation, paying close attention to all the signals, you will come to know and prize this individuality. It is one of the most precious possessions a child has, and one of your most important jobs will be to nourish it and help it to grow.

Getting to know your baby as a person is like reading an exciting story very slowly. You will gradually find out if he likes very gentle treatment or slightly rougher handling; you will find out if he has a ready sense of humor, enjoys a joke and is eager to join in with things, or whether he prefers to be quiet. It may take you several weeks to know how he behaves when he is well and happy, and until then you may worry a good deal about whether he's ill or not. It may even take a few months to know his crying patterns – which, in turn, will tell you whether he's going to be a fretful baby or a placid one (see p. 155). But don't worry. You will gradually come to know all of your baby's idiosyncrasies: whether he nurses quickly or slowly; whether or not he needs a lot of sleep; whether or not he likes to be cuddled.

While you're learning about your baby, you will have to make many reassessments and adjustments as you fit your daily routine to his needs.

Social milestones

By the time your baby is six months old he will have learned a lot about being a sociable human being. In ways that we do not quite understand, he will have become an expert at communication. He'll know how to start a conversation with you and how to get you to play. He'll know how to hold your attention by smiling, babbling or looking interested and curious; and how to end a conversation by looking away or appearing bored. The stages at which he acquires this ability are outlined below:

● *By three months*
He won't like to be deprived of social contact and will quite often cry when left alone. He will stop crying when an adult reappears and when he is talked to or diverted by a toy or rattle. He will turn his head when he hears human voices and will smile when an adult smiles at him or makes a kind of clucking sound. He will express pleasure when others are present by smiling, kicking and waving his arms. He will recognize his mother and other familiar people by acting sociably, and will show fear of strangers by turning away and possibly even crying.

● *By the fourth month*
He may lift his arms in anticipation of being picked up. He will focus on faces and will nearly always follow the direction of the person who leaves him. He will smile at a person who speaks to him and show delight when anyone shows particular attention to him. He will laugh when he is being played with.

● *Between the fifth and sixth month*
He will react differently to smiling and to a scolding tone of voice. Familiar people are greeted with a smile, and strange people with recognizable expressions of fear.

● *At six months*
Social behavior becomes much more active, so he may pull the hair of persons who are holding him or rub their noses or pat their faces.

● *At seven to nine months*
He will socialize by imitating speech sounds and gestures.

● *By 12 months*
He will refrain from doing things if told "No." He will show fear and dislike of strangers by rushing to his mother or crying when the stranger approaches. He may become slightly clinging at this age.

Responding to your baby's behavior

The generally accepted definition of a good baby is one who cries very little, settles down easily and sleeps for long periods; the definition of bad baby is one who does the opposite. On the basis of these definitions, all my friends had good babies and I had bad ones. However, I would not describe any of my babies as bad. They were demanding and occasionally difficult, but only because they wanted my attention – and this seemed perfectly normal to me.

During the first few weeks you and your baby have to get used to each other. Don't be put off by how your baby behaves initially. He has no control over how he responds to the outside world and may exhibit tendencies which will not remain beyond the first few months.

He may be jumpy, excessively wakeful or excessively sleepy. What you must do is deal with your baby's needs as competently and calmly as possible, giving all the love that you have.

"Difficult" babies

A baby who is really difficult, who cries, for instance, and cannot be comforted by any of the usual methods (see p. 158), is extremely hard to deal with calmly. The sound of a baby crying constantly is both irritating and upsetting. If your baby also rejects your efforts to comfort him, you may also feel spurned and inadequate. You may even become angry because you believe the baby is crying on purpose. This cannot happen, however – your baby cries because he is biologically programmed to do so until his needs are understood and fulfilled. Your failure to satisfy these needs starts a vicious cycle: you become tense because the baby won't stop crying. When you're tense you can't cope calmly with your baby who therefore cries even more. Ill-temper increases on both sides.

What to do
Try very hard not to lose your temper or to get too worked up.
● Share the responsibility with your partner and take turns dealing with your baby.
● Follow the advice on crying (see p. 158), and don't forget, yours is not the only baby in the world who is going through this "difficult" period. Whatever you think, it will be brief.
● Don't treat your baby's behavior as a deliberate rejection of you – at the moment he can't help behaving like this for he is desperately trying to adapt to a new world. You have to accept your baby as he is and deal with him accordingly; he will change as he grows.
● Accept any offer of help from friends and relations. You'll need your rest, and if friends can look after your baby, even for a few hours between feeding, you can recharge your batteries.

Sleepy babies

These babies are often called placid babies. They may sleep 21 hours out of 24. They make few demands on you and will rarely cry. They also seldom seem alert or aware of their surroundings. They may fall asleep in the middle of a feeding, fail to respond when talked to, and exhibit few emotions.

What to do
A placid baby is marvellous initially because he leaves you to regain your strength after delivery. However, he is missing an awful lot in life and should be coaxed into realizing that being awake is much more fun.
● Don't try to keep your baby awake forcibly. He knows how much sleep he needs and you should respect this. However, make sure that he doesn't go too long without food. If he can sleep through the night, for example, wake him up before you go to bed or he will go too long without liquid.
● Whenever he's awake provide as much stimulation and affection as possible. Surround the cot or crib with mobiles and photographs so that even if you're not there he has something to focus on and occupy him.
● Try carrying the baby in a sling so that he can respond to your warmth and smell, even though he's asleep.

Wakeful babies

Instead of sleeping the usual 16 of every 24 hours during the first few weeks of life, your baby may sleep as little as 12, and he'll take these in short bursts. He'll be full of life, interested in everything that's going on, and keen to learn. Wakeful babies are usually very sociable and affectionate. They may exhaust you, but they'll be very rewarding.

What to do
Until your baby's old enough to entertain himself, you and your partner will be his sole form of entertainment, and he may demand your attention all hours of the day

and night. If you don't work out some sort of shift system with your partner, you may become so fatigued that you can't carry on. Don't be resentful of your baby's wakefulness; try to accept it and take practical steps to make sure you get enough sleep.
● Carry the baby around in a sling.
● When you're at home take the crib or basket wherever you go and place it *safely* on a table or work surface so your baby can hear your voice.
● Have plenty of pictures and mobiles over the cot or crib so that he'll be occupied even when you're not there.
● Prop the baby up on a bed or in the pram from about six weeks (see p. 53).
● Keep the baby's room warm because this sometimes encourages sleepiness.
● Take the baby into bed with you (see p. 146).

Discontented babies

You may have a discontented baby, one who is irritable when he's hungry yet doesn't enjoy feeding. He takes the feeding slowly and with difficulty. Afterwards, he isn't very sociable and doesn't like to be held. When you talk to him he doesn't seem to take much notice; he seems tired but fretful, and not very relaxed. When laid down to sleep, he starts to cry.

What to do
Don't feel you'll never succeed in making your baby comfortable and happy or you'll begin to feel inadequate and eventually resentful. Try to keep all negative emotions out of your head. Your baby's behavior is aimed at the outside world to which he's not yet acclimatized, and not at you. Don't interpret your baby's unhappiness as personal criticism. Try very hard, no matter how much he rejects you, to get him to smile at you. Try to engage him in play; sit with him on your lap and try some physical exercises (see p. 262). Get your baby to respond. Once he does, you'll know you've turned the corner and can begin to get to know each other.
● When he cries, try all the crying remedies.

● Keep his room extra warm and cosy; try wrapping him up in a blanket (see p. 142) before he's put down to sleep so that he feels secure.
● Nurse him as often as he wants and *never* keep him waiting and crying.
● Put lots of mobiles above the cot to occupy his attention.
● Carry him around with you if that provides comfort.

Jumpy babies

All newborn babies are sensitive to loud noises and sudden, jerky movements, but jumpy babies over-react to quite normal stimuli. When he gets hungry he doesn't show hunger with the usual persistent cry but immediately begins screaming hysterically. When he's picked up, his body stiffens; when put down again, his body may jerk. He seems alarmed by any kind of noise or rapid movement.

What to do
● Understand, once again, that your baby's behavior is not a rejection of you as a parent. It's just an inability to deal with the new world that he's in.
● Keep the baby wrapped up (see p. 142) most of the time. When he's moved there will be no risk that his arms or legs will flop, giving him a sense of insecurity.
● Pick him up gently and slowly. When you bend down, speak softly and gently; you could even try singing a song.
● If he seems to feel more secure when he's near you, put him in a sling and carry him with you all the time.
● Don't give your baby baths, just wipe him clean every day (see p. 70). Never take all of his clothes off at once. Always leave his undershirt or diaper on and try to keep his body covered, even by a towel, for as long as possible.
● Don't leave him in a room with any loud stimuli. For example, avoid rooms which face noisy roads or schools, and rooms which have chiming clocks or telephones.

Your baby as part of the family

During the first few weeks of your baby's life the household will revolve around him, but from then on he'll have to learn to fit in with the household and with the needs of the rest of the family. It's important that your new baby learns to live with a group of people who have rules, customs and routines. Your baby can't be expected to fit into family routines if he isn't introduced to them, so, as early on as possible, include him in family activities like meals, games, outings, shopping, household chores, looking after pets and visits to friends.

Through his participation in family activities, he will learn about life and people in general. His behavior with his family will determine how he acts with strangers. Through his family he'll learn the social customs and attitudes of society. One of the ways a baby learns is by imitation – so watching you and copying how you behave will develop behavior patterns that will remain with him for a lifetime.

DISCIPLINE

Very few children under the age of a year need true disciplining. Up to this age, a child is not open to reasonable argument and your main form of discipline will simply be to say "No," and to separate your baby from something he shouldn't have if he refuses to obey. I don't believe young babies should ever be slapped or punished.

As they grow up, all young children need to be shown by their parents the boundaries of socially acceptable behavior. Many of these limits are implicitly set by the way members of the family behave to one another. Setting a good example is the best way to teach your child what good behavior is. But it is also your responsibility as a parent to give your child guidelines on behavior, and you should start to do this during his very first year. If you fail to do this, your child will soon find that other children and adults won't tolerate his bad manners and selfishness. You are going to have to keep to some guidelines in your home, as in any other organized group, if only for the sake of efficiency, justice and safety.

Understanding bad behavior

No baby behaves badly deliberately, although many a tired and exhausted parent feels convinced that they do. Your baby may cry constantly and be very irritable and grumpy, but this is usually because he is over-tired, hungry, ill, scared of losing you when you go out, or afraid of meeting strangers. This is not your baby's fault and he should never be blamed for what is really beyond his control. Nor should you blame yourself if you've done everything within your power to prevent or correct what is causing your baby's unhappiness.

Toward the end of this year, one of the major causes of "bad behavior" will be frustration. The more strong-willed he is, the more he will want to express his independence as he gets older. He'll no longer accept that you have total control over his life, and will assert himself by

challenging your instructions. Objections to your choice of food will be common, so let your baby choose what he wants to eat, and the order in which he eats it (see p. 119). Similarly, if he expresses a desire to wear certain items of clothing, let him go ahead and wear them. If you don't allow your baby some freedom at this time, he'll become extremely frustrated and angry.

Doing things alone will cause its own frustrations, since your child's ambitions will often exceed his capabilities. Because he won't be able to make his body do what he wants or manage the world in the way that he sees fit, he may cry or have temper tantrums (see p. 164). Try not to get annoyed at this – every child goes through similar behavior – but do give him your assistance. If you don't offer to help at this point, he may waste a lot of energy trying to do something that's beyond him, and repeated failure will be very demoralizing. When your baby is in poor spirits, bullying and pressuring him will simply cause more stubbornness. You have to be tactful, humorous even, and a little devious. If you let your baby feel that he is taking control, you'll find that he very often fits in with what you want. So, instead of saying "Don't" to your baby, when, for example, he is throwing plastic cups around the room, make the clearing up into a game. Suggest perhaps that he try to gather them all up before you finish the dishes.

When to say "No"

During your baby's first year there are very few reasons for saying "No." I prefer to keep the rules for my children to a minimum. I had only one unbreakable rule during their first year – that they do nothing that was unsafe for themselves or others. In these instances I would say "No" firmly, and at the same time remove the dangerous object from my child, or stop him from performing the dangerous activity. I did not wait for my child to stop, but to teach him rules of safety, I always tried to explain why I was stopping him from

behaving in a certain way. I simply stated what was dangerous, and repeated myself every time he did the same thing, in the hope that he would remember, learn, and not do it again. I did not chastise and I tried not to become angry. Only as they got older and learned the rule did I give them the opportunity to resist.

I believe many kinds of discipline are better taught by example and by praise and reward for good behavior. This will be successful, however, only when your child has the intellectual ability to recognize the difference between right and wrong behavior.

POSSIBLE PROBLEMS 0–1

Disliking your baby

Many mothers believe that mother love will be turned on like a tap as soon as their baby is born. It comes as rather a shock, therefore, when after two or even three days they don't feel anything for their baby that resembles love. They may feel tenderness and protectiveness towards this tiny new being that is dependent on them, but they don't feel a strong, binding love. This is very common and not at all abnormal. Until love develops – usually within one or two weeks – concentrate on enjoying your baby physically: the way he feels against your skin; the way he smells when you put your nose into the crease of his neck; the way he grips you tightly when you put your finger into his tiny palm.

Sometimes mother love never comes and – for whatever reason – a mother finds herself disliking, resenting and spurning her new baby. Sometimes a mother and baby are just what child psychologists would call "a bad fit." Neither is suited to the other. Society is accustomed to blaming the mother for this situation, censoring her for her assumed inability to adjust to her child's needs – but we now know that this is unfair. A woman can have powerful mothering instincts, a strong desire to look after a baby, and a great urge to love him.

237

But if love never develops, it's as much the baby's fault as the mother's; they are simply ill-matched. A mother who finds that she cannot relate to her baby with feelings of love should consult her doctor because she needs help, and so does her baby.

Antisocial babies

Just as there are taciturn adults who keep to themselves, so there are babies who can be described as antisocial. These babies don't smile very much, don't respond when talked to, don't enjoy playing games, and don't like being cuddled. On the other hand, they can become irritable when left alone in a pram or cot. They get upset easily. They tend to cry a lot and are slow, difficult feeders. When such a baby is tired, he is fretful but doesn't go to sleep. Nothing you do seems to make him happy, and you may wonder if it's worth lavishing so much love and attention on such a negative and unresponsive child.

The sad thing about this kind of baby is that he never learns the rewarding lesson that he will get back what he gives. A baby who smiles a lot and exudes joy gets friendship, love, companionship and help in return. The baby who is miserable or unresponsive gets nothing in return and often grows up into a somber and difficult individual. As a parent you *have* to do everything you can to make sure that your child outgrows or overcomes these negative feelings. It may be difficult, but you have to get your baby to look at you, listen to you, smile at you. If you can get to this stage, where your baby is responding to your overtures, most of his unhappiness – and yours – will be a thing of the past.

Backward babies

Babies develop at different speeds – some fast, some slow – and it can be difficult to distinguish normal slowness from backwardness. If you feel your baby is not reaching the milestones (see p. 232) appropriate for his age, consult your doctor. Minor defects may not show up for several months, so if you suspect that your baby is not developing normally, follow your instincts and, if necessary, seek early help. The sooner you get help, the greater the chances of dealing with the problem and preventing the baby and family from suffering unnecessarily.

If your baby is both socially and physically backward, the burden of looking after him can be enormous. Parents have to continue to care for such a child as if he were a newborn baby, seeing to his every need. When this causes great strain within the home, you must seek help. It's often comforting, as well as helpful, to talk to people in similar situations, so check your local directories for parent groups and national agencies.

Head banging

Toward the end of the first year some babies take to banging their heads against the side of the cot. This is rarely a sign of abnormality, and there's little risk of brain damage. Your baby should outgrow it quickly; in the meantime, minimize the risk by padding the sides of the cot with a quilted fabric. If the cot bangs irritatingly against the wall, pack the outside of the cot, too. Try giving your baby a relaxing bath before he's put to bed and give him an extra long cuddle (it's thought by some psychologists that such children may need more physical attention and stimulation than others). Music from a mobile or from a radio may also be soothing. If your baby continues to bang his head for several months, talk to your doctor about it.

PERSONAL DEVELOPMENT   1–2

During the second year, much of your toddler's behavior is attention-getting. He will try to do this by speaking, crying, hitting or doing things which he knows are forbidden. When he's successful at getting attention, he'll show his satisfaction by smiling or laughing.

Two-year-olds often seem to be very negative and their favorite word appears to be "No." This is a transitional stage between babyhood and childhood, during which he is trying to assert his independence. He'll want to do everything immediately, and demand that you keep to a rigid routine. Your toddler's mood may change frequently, and his emotions veer between extremes of love and anger. One thing you must do is tolerate your child's mood when he becomes negatively assertive.

Resisting his efforts at independence at this stage can lead to strongly negative behavior.

On the positive side, two-year-old toddlers become much more cooperative in play. Early play with adults teaches them how to relate to others – particularly if the adults are patient and teach their children how to share. Other children may share less readily, so encourage your children to persevere and don't ever stop teaching them by example.

Likes and dislikes

A child begins to show all kinds of assertiveness during this year, and dramatically demonstrates his preferences. He is very anxious to grow up and to show that he is growing up. He no longer sees himself as a mirror image of you; he now sees the two of you are separate people, and therefore finds no reason for doing exactly what you like. He is determined to exercise his independence and will refuse offers of help and shrug off your assistance, even when he really needs it.

Your child is developing strong likes and dislikes. He has a powerful urge to fulfil his own desires, even though they may not be the same as yours. The conflicts he initiates with you may also cause him unhappiness, since he is torn between the very strong drive to exert independence and the drive to be loved by you. Even when he is trying to win a battle with you, he needs your help and emotional support because he is too immature to manage without them. Your job is to take the middle road and try to balance his need for independence against his need for love and protection. It isn't always easy! Your toddler's thinking is immature; his memory is short, and his judgement unreliable. Because he cannot think ahead, he is impatient when things don't get done immediately. At the same time he is eager to control and dominate the world around him. His strength of will is ahead of his intellectual capacity, so you have to decide when to baby him and when to encourage and push him on, encouraging independence and adventurousness, while still guarding against any dangers. Be flexible in allowing your toddler to exercise these likes and dislikes, and don't enforce your will simply to win or to show your authority. You can always win by pulling rank, but don't be unreasonable just to show you're the boss. Judge each situation carefully. There are very few times when it's important for you to get your own way; unless your toddler's safety is at stake, let him do what he wants.

Personality

Your child's nature will assert itself within the first few weeks of life. However, there are certain social situations during early childhood which will also help form his personality – for better or for worse.

□ If your child has a strong desire for approval, he will be motivated to fulfil the expectations of those around him. The desire for your approval and the approval of other adults usually comes before the desire for the approval of friends. Whenever possible, get your child to do the "right" things for your approval.

□ Young children can express sympathy by trying to help or comfort a person who is sad or in distress. But they are unable to fully sympathize with anyone until they have been in a similar situation.

□ When children understand the meaning of facial expressions and speech, they develop the ability to empathize and to experience what the other person is feeling.

□ Children who tend to be rather dependent, who like to be helped and given attention and affection, are motived to behave in a socially approved way. Independent children are motivated less by the need for approbation.

□ Children who are friendly express their friendliness by wanting to do things for and with others. They express their affection through a wide variety of words and gestures.

□ Children who are not allowed to be constantly in the limelight, but who are given opportunities to share with others, grow up to be considerate of the needs of others. They care about more than their own interests and possessions, and do not always have to get their own way.

The timid child

Some children are naturally shy, keep to themselves, and speak infrequently. If your child is timid, don't immediately think he's retarded and become over-anxious and over-protective. A child who is quite talkative with you at home may be completely silent and withdrawn in a strange situation or when confronted with strangers. This happens to many children about the age of one. In a new situation, don't increase your child's difficulties by insisting that he join in immediately. Allow him to sit quietly on your knee or to stand by your side while he takes in what everyone is doing, and becomes familiar with it. After half an hour or so, when you can sense that he is feeling more comfortable, gradually encourage him to join in your conversation. Within an hour, even a shy child, if encouraged in this slow, gentle way, will join in with new friends and new games. Remember to introduce new experiences slowly and allow your child to get used to them before moving on to other ones.

If your child's very timid and shy, he may become very upset if you try to leave him with a sitter. Try to understand your child's needs, and respect them, no matter how irritating they may be. He'll grow out of this clinginess with your help, but he'll need to gain a sense of security first.

Playing and sharing

Your toddler should mix with others as early as possible. During the first year your child becomes used to interacting, not only with the immediate family, but with members of the extended family – grandparents, aunts, uncles, nieces, nephews, and cousins. Your toddler will be a great deal more comfortable with adults, including strangers, if he starts off feeling that every friend of yours is a friend of his, and that there are members of the extended family who care for him and can be trusted.

If you help your child accept others, then he shouldn't have much difficulty mixing with other children when he wants the company of others his age. At about the age of 18 months, children usually tolerate each other, though they won't necessarily play together. They may play side-by-side, doing the same thing, but rarely interact. Later, when they start to play with toys, it is not abnormal for them to hit and grab each other. If your child repeatedly does this, however, you must explain that it's not the right way to behave, and point out that he would not like the same thing done to him.

While your child has to learn to share, it is hardly realistic to expect him to automatically give up a toy to another toddler when the other wants it. This is not because your child is selfish or a bully; it is because he doesn't yet appreciate the concept of sharing. If your child grabs for a toy that another child is playing with, teach him about sharing by telling him he must reciprocate by giving one of his own toys to his friend. A child of two is usually able to understand the justice of reciprocity. You have to deal with the concept of sharing in very simple terms, because intellectually he is not grown up enough to understand. Not until two-and-a-half to

three can you use reason and expect your child to be more altruistic.

Encouraging generosity

Encourage your child to be generous from a very early age. As you are the most important person in his life, it is easiest for him to be generous with you. Take advantage of his desire to please you by encouraging him to perform small but meaningful acts of generosity (like giving Daddy a cookie). Continue to encourage unselfish behavior toward you and other members of the family. This should not be difficult, since it's only natural for a child to want to please people he cares for and who obviously care for him. Having accepted generous behavior as the norm toward members of his family whom he loves, it's just a matter of time before he acts generously to people who are just friends. If he finds a particular activity exciting and pleasurable, ask if you can join in and share the excitement with him. Then encourage him to share his game or toy with friends who come to the house. By the time your child is 18 months old, he should be able to share activities and treats with anyone whom he considers a friend. Once he can do this, he is well on the way to becoming generous and unselfish with his peers.

Only children

Although children in one-child families benefit from the constant love they receive from parents, there are few who don't confess to having wanted brothers and sisters at some stage in their lives. Whatever problems may arise – and they're rarely serious – can be mitigated by introducing your baby to other children of the same age. As your baby reaches the sociable age – about 18 months to two years – make a real effort to find friends for him and to have them visit you at home.

It's easy for parents to over-indulge an only child and to make him feel too important. You're going to have to curb your desire to give him all the things he wants and – just as important – all your attention. It's important that he learn to accept

that he can't have everything he wants and that he's not the permanent center of your world. Children in large families have to learn this, too (see p. 235).

You may be tempted to be possessive and over-protective, but this can only hurt you and your child. Either he will become independent and you will feel bereft, or he will cling to you forever. Of course, you mustn't shy away from disciplining your child – like all other children, he has to be shown the right way to behave it he's to develop a capacity to mix with others.

DISCIPLINE

It has long been known that children need discipline. In the past it was believed that discipline was necessary to protect the peace of mind of adults and to ensure that children conformed to standards that were socially acceptable. More recently it has been found that children need discipline simply to be happy and well-adjusted. Children like to know the boundaries of acceptable behavior. Discipline is essential to their development because it fulfils certain needs:

□ Discipline teaches children how to behave in ways that merit praise. They will thus be able to earn acceptance and love – both necessary for the growing child.

□ Discipline – when deserved – motivates children to strive to accomplish socially meaningful goals. These will bring a great deal of comfort and satisfaction throughout life.

□ Discipline, above all else, helps a child develop a conscience and sense of self-control. This inner voice will later guide him in making his own decisions and controlling his own behavior. Without it he will become indecisive and act in an antisocial way.

□ Children who do not learn to discipline themselves are often scolded. This leads to feelings of guilt and shame.

□ Discipline enables children to win social approval, which makes them feel happy and secure.

When to use discipline

Too much or too little discipline are equally bad for children, because both lead to insecurity. A healthy child cannot be ruled by fear, force, corporal punishment or humiliation. Reasoning with him, however, will have little effect until he is two-and-a-half or three, so discipline has to be very direct and easy for him to understand. Always discipline your child im-

Disciplinary guidelines

Remember that learning the rules of social behavior and learning about self control take time – not months but years. Don't expect too much from your child. Don't, for instance, expect him to remember what you said yesterday or last week. He isn't necessarily defying your earlier instructions – he may simply have forgotten them. A child of two has a very short memory, so be forgiving and repeat your instructions. Words never mean as much as actions, so you really do have to show your child how to behave. Here are some things you can do.

● Have as few "rules" – those instructions which can be broken under no circumstances – as possible. "Don't" is a very negative word; if you're not careful, by the time your child is two you could be prefacing everything you say by "Don't." "Do" is a very positive word, so encourage your child with positive "dos" and cut down on the negative "don'ts."

● Don't give vague instructions; be clear. Instead of saying, "Don't be naughty," tell him *exactly* what you don't want him to do.

● If you give your child an instruction, always give a reason why. If you tell him that his tricycle has to be put under cover when he's finished using it at night, explain that it may otherwise get rusty in the rain and not work. Try to refrain from saying, "Because I say so," when he asks you why.

● Always reward good behavior with praise and affection, possibly even with a treat if your child has accomplished something difficult. You can help him distinguish between good and bad behavior just by withholding praise and rewards from acts you don't approve of.

● There is no better way of getting your child to do something than to show that

mediately for what he has done, and make sure the punishment fits the "crime." If you frequently become extremely angry over something relatively minor, you will only bewilder your child – and eventually perhaps forfeit his love and affection. Reserve discipline for really serious misbehavior, like acts of wanton destructiveness, physical violence or lies. In this way your child will learn the difference between what you merely disapprove of and what is intolerable. Your child's memory is short; if you brood over what he has done he will simply not understand. He will think you are purposely withdrawing love from him, so make all discipline clear and swift – and then forget it.

Avoiding problems

Children are very receptive to fairness and justice, and if you adhere to these two principles you will probably avoid most difficulties in disciplining.

Corporal punishment will only lead to problems. I think it should be avoided at all costs. Research has shown that most children don't know why they are being spanked – they cannot remember what they did, so they don't associate the punishment with the crime, and the spanking fails to deter them from future misdeeds.

I think it's harmful to give a child the message that physical violence is acceptable – certainly not as retribution for something he has done. Not only is it an inefficient form of punishment, but it is extremely unkind.

Never punish a child as a calculated act. The child is much less damaged by a sharp word or a slap in the heat of the moment which is quickly forgotten when the air is clear, than by a protracted argument with punishment later on, when he gets home

you do it too. If you want your child to take off his dirty shoes at the door, or to put on boots before he goes out in the rain, do the same.
● Be consistent. Don't let your standards slide and give one instruction on one occasion and the opposite on another (although there is no harm in showing that under certain circumstances flexibility can be a virtue, too). There is no reason why your child shouldn't have several helpings of ice cream on his birthday, because he knows that that day is special, but he should learn not to expect the same on the following day.
● Always admit your mistakes, no matter how young your child is, and always be generous when you do something wrong. It makes your child feel the world is fair and just, so don't be afraid to say, "Naughty Mommy," or "Mommy shouldn't have done that," or "You are quite right, I won't do it again."

or, even worse, when your partner gets home.

You will not go far wrong if you are very clear with yourself about your motives for disciplining. Make sure you are acting for the happiness and safety of the child, and not simply as a means of impressing on your child your authority and superiority.

POSSIBLE PROBLEMS 1–2

The aggressive child

Aggression is usually an unprovoked act of hostility. Most children have feelings of aggressiveness which are expressed in verbal or physical attacks on other children, often on those who are smaller than they are.

Bullying and other forms of aggressiveness are modes of behavior that usually represent cries for help. They frequently result from parental neglect, absence, too much discipline (too much slapping and spanking), and too little discipline. A child who behaves in this way is really not at fault, although he may be very hard to help. It is worth remembering that a disagreeable little boy or girl is usually nasty because someone has been nasty to him. You shouldn't be too ready to blame them but should look beyond, to their home and their environment. Changing a child's normal pattern of behavior, and overcoming the distrust of adults, may take years because he has to unlearn so many early lessons and start again from the beginning.

If your child starts to show signs of aggressiveness, try to nip it in the bud. Don't punish or hit him – this will only make the aggressive behavior worse. Instead, show very firmly that you are not prepared to put up with it and that he will gain nothing but your disapproval if he continues. Show that if he can change he will be highly rewarded, and will gain lots of praise for all good efforts. If your child seems to be highly disturbed, or if you're at all worried by his behavior, seek medical help immediately.

Jealousy

Rivalry is a perfectly normal emotion for a child to feel. Sometimes it can have a positive effect, spurring him on to do his best. This may turn him into a more friendly and social individual. But if rivalry leads to quarreling and boasting, your child has a hard road ahead.

A child feels one of the strongest forms of jealousy when a new baby arrives. This is because he feels that he's been "dethroned" and has lost the special place he had in your life. He may try all sorts of attention-seeking devices and may even revert to such babyish behavior as losing bowel control, refusing to feed himself or refusing to dress alone. Or he may direct his jealousy directly at the baby and try to hurt it. Alternatively, he may feel unable to cope with these jealous emotions and

internalize them. He may become quiet and distant, and reject you altogether.

You must understand these emotions, and help your child prepare for the arrival of a new baby by showing him that his place in your affections is quite secure. Put aside a special time when he has all of your attention. Involve him in looking after the baby by asking him to help with certain easy tasks. Praise and reward all helpful behavior on his part, particularly when he shows love and affection for the new arrival.

Over-indulgence

It is very easy for parents to over-indulge or spoil a child. After all, you probably love him more than any other human being in the world. You have a natural desire to please him and make his life happy. It's therefore easy to err on the side of giving a child too much, of making life too easy for him and allowing him to become the center of your universe. For the sake of your child, you will have to control these desires.

One way to help your child not be egocentric is to make sure from early on that he's not always the center of your attention. He must learn that the world does not revolve around him. You will be doing him a favor if you let him know quite clearly that there are times when he's expected to manage without you and to do things alone. This does not mean that you should resort to cruelty or force. Give your child as much love as you have, but make him see that everyone has certain boundaries within which he must live. As your child gets older, teach him that you have a need for privacy, just as he does, but that you're always there if needed.

Don't make the mistake of thinking over-indulgence has anything to do with the number of possessions your child has or how much affection he gets. Over-indulgence means allowing your child to impress his will on you and on others by using power games such as wheedling or bullying. It is a parent's duty to prevent this from occuring.

Stuttering

Nearly all children of this age stumble over their words – which may on occasion turn into a real stutter. This may be because your child has so many ideas in his head that he can't speak as quickly as he thinks. It may also be that he is very excited and simply can't articulate proper-ly. Stuttering can appear for a short time and then disappear again. The most im-portant thing you can do initially is to remain calm and not draw your child's attention to the stuttering. Don't jump in with the word you think your child is trying to say, but simply accept your child's speech. Making your child feel nervous and self-conscious about the way he talks will only increase his tendency to stammer.

Temper tantrums

Between one and two years old temper tantrums are normal, attention-seeking devices (see p. 164). Children this age have more willpower than judgment, and clashes with parents are therefore fre-quent. If anger or frustration are excessive, they may culminate in a tantrum. Chil-dren usually throw themselves on the floor kicking and screaming because they do not have the maturity to overcome their prob-lem in any other way.

Far and away the best thing you can do is to stay calm. If you don't, your child will catch your mood and his behavior will deteriorate. Ignore your child and, if poss-ible, leave him alone. A tantrum loses much of its point for a child if there is no audience.

As your child gets older he will become better able to tolerate delays and accept compromises. At the same time you will become more expert at anticipating problems and finding distractions that forestall head-on clashes.

A "naughty" child

There are some children who are habitually naughty. There are some who are habitually disobedient. You ought to make a distinction between naughtiness and disobedience, because the two problems have to be handled differently.

A naughty child is one who is immature and unable to exert sufficient self-control to do what he knows is right. A disobedient child, however, is quite mature and knowingly flouts your wishes and rules.

A naughty child is often forgetful and simply forgets your remonstrances. You can scold him for doing something wrong and find him doing it again an hour later. He'll be genuinely surprised to find himself in the wrong again so quickly. Such naughty children frequently get so wrapped up in an activity that rules go by the board. You have to talk to these children more frequently, and with more sympathy and care. They are usually apologetic and contrite. Apologies and contrition should be received with warm acceptance and understanding; however, there does come a point when a naughty child needs punishing. Physical punishment should never be used; it is always preferable to with-

draw treats and pleasures, and reinstate them when a given goal has been achieved.

Your child may go on being naughty for a long time. Be prepared for this and don't become too angry. Sheer naughtiness is more of an irritation than a serious annoyance. If you can sympathize with your naughty child, don't be too hard on him.

Disobedience is another matter. Most of us feel little sympathy or patience with it. A constantly disobedient child rarely apologizes or repents. His negative behavior will lead to fights and disagreements, and make your life miserable. Guard against this if you can. A child has a limited repertoire with which to respond to your anger. Brutality on your part will lead to brutality in his. Physical punishment encourages violence, truculence and aggression. It won't be easy, but try a program of positive actions and words. Explain to him why he shouldn't be so disobedient. Let him know when his actions are dangerous or anti-social and suggest how he should behave. Outlaw punishments, reward all good acts. It often works. Whatever you do, don't alienate your child. You are all he has. Always show your love, always let him know he can come to you.

PERSONAL DEVELOPMENT 2–3

Your young baby was dependent on you because you were the center of his universe – the caretaker and the affection-giver. He couldn't get through life without your early help and support, and so he sought your approbation and affection.

As he gets older, however, and sees himself as an independent person, not just a reflection of you, he begins to recognize you as a whole person with a separate personality. This is only one of many new feelings and emotions with which he has

to become familiar. He also begins to experience real love for things around him: his favorite toy, pet, or grandparent. If he sees that you're tired, he is genuinely concerned; if you're unhappy, he is sincerely sympathetic. When he enjoys something, he wishes to share the experience with you. If you need help, he will offer it spontaneously. If you are upset or frightened, he feels profoundly sorry for you, and tells you so with words and expressions. He has a strong desire to make

you feel better and happier, and does so in the only way that he knows – by telling you that he loves you and by hugging you.

This unselfishness is quite a step forward in your child's personal development. Putting others first; genuinely loving and caring for them; trying to understand others and do what's best for them; trying to bring them pleasure and comfort – these are all grown-up feelings which should be praised and encouraged.

Imitation and identification

Your child first learns by imitation, but as he gets older he begins to learn by "identification," too. When he puts himself in your position and into the position of others and starts to behave as he would have others behave toward him, then he is starting to control and take command of himself. You may even overhear him scolding himself when he has done something of which he thinks you will disapprove. The difference is that he now disap-

proves of it in himself.

You will find your child observing and identifying with most adults who are close to him, and with other adults who capture his interest. He may give in to his imagination by dressing up and acting out roles, and by being all kinds of different people. But most of all he'll practise being you. He will play Mommy or Daddy with dolls and toys, and you may even hear him imitate the exact phrases you use, with exactly the same intonation you have in your voice. These are all ways of exploring and experimenting with the way he thinks the world works.

Making friends

Your child's galloping desire to learn brings with it the desire for the company of children of a similar age. During this year, he'll become gregarious and want to join in games with others. He'll need to be stimulated by the ideas and company of other children.

You cannot make friends for your child, but you *can* help him find friends. Since friendships develop slowly, introduce him to one friend at a time.

Start off on home ground first and invite a child who lives nearby so that your child is in familiar surroundings and has a sense of confidence about what he's doing and where he's doing it. Make sure you're near at hand to give him help and support should he need it. Encourage him to play, and join in if necessary. Once he has gotten over the first hurdle, and knows how to make friends, invite two or three children to the house at the same time. If it's summer, have a party in the park or around the wading pool.

Once your child becomes a member of a group of friends, make it clear to him that they are welcome at your home and that he can bring them into the house once he has asked your permission. As your child makes his first steps into the outside world, it's imperative that he feel comfortable and confident about his own place within it. Surrounding himself with a small group of good friends is an important step in the right direction.

Encouraging security

All children have fears and anxieties. These are perfectly normal emotions, but they make a child feel unhappy and uneasy. It will be some time before your toddler has the ability to cope with fears or avoid the things which make him afraid (see p. 166).

One of the most common early fears is of being abandoned by you. The easiest way to cure this is to show your child that you will always return as you promised, and when you said you would. Fear will not be cured by staying with your child; that will only make him more fearful because he will never learn to cope without you.

Your small child also begins to feel anxiety if he finds that his own feelings – frustration, anger, jealousy and so on – are beyond his control. The way to help here is to listen to your child and observe him as closely as possible, so that you can determine the cause of his anxiety and then reassure him. Just talking about some of the fears and explaining what is happening will give him the reassurance he needs.

Remember that whether your child's fear seems reasonable (thunder) or unreasonable (dogs), the fear is still real to him. Both fears have to be handled sympathetically and gently. Never suddenly present your child with things that frighten him. You wouldn't dream of asking your child to stay outside in a thunderstorm if he was afraid of thunder, so why should you expect him to meet a dog with a brave face? Whenever your child shows fear, accept that fear as real and don't brush it aside as nothing. Always tell your child when there is nothing to fear, but don't tell him not to be afraid, because he won't understand. Explain why there is no reason to be frightened, but tell him that you understand why he is. Sympathize with his fear. Ridiculing it will only make him secretive, and it will be much harder for him to cope with his fear alone, without your help.

Handling genitals

Babies usually become aware of their genital organs toward the end of the first year but handle them without any obvious pleasure. Handling eventually does bring a pleasurable sensation, and fondling becomes more like real masturbation. Most children of both sexes masturbate, and it's simply unreasonable to expect them not to. There are many misconceptions about masturbation but, despite the myths, it will not lead to blindness, homosexuality, insanity or any other such fictions.

It is perfectly normal for a boy to handle his penis. After all, he handles every other part of his body that sticks out, so why not that. Masturbation in young children is rarely done for any length of time or for any purpose. The pleasure it brings is more of a general pleasure than a specific sexual one. It is not until children are much older that they feel sexual excitement from masturbation.

There is no reason to discourage or try to stop masturbation. Trying to will only cause furtiveness, and worse, it may stop your child from talking about his genital organs later in life. Unless masturbation is an obsessional means of escaping from reality, the best way to treat it is by paying no attention to it at all. If it happens in public, distract your child, but never, ever, scold him for it.

Nudity and sexuality

A child's sex education begins with the first cuddle. All children take pleasure in physical contact and joy in their parents' reciprocity. They grow up realizing that people touch one another as an act of friendship as well as an act of love.

As your child gets older he will become pleasantly aware of his body, without being at all self-conscious about it. You can encourage this by having an open attitude to nudity within the family. Like everything else, a child learns patterns of behavior and attitudes from you. The child who sees his parents unclothed and unembarrassed will take nudity as a matter of course and is unlikely to grow up concerned about nakedness. On the other hand, if you're worried about it he will almost certainly worry too; if you're furtive, he'll be encouraged to be secretive too.

It is perfectly natural for a child to be curious about the differences between male and female bodies. Your child will probably be aware of differences in gender from the age of 15 months, and once he sees his parents naked, he'll be aware of sexual differences. Curiosity about his mother's breasts and his father's penis is best satisfied by a frank chat and a good look. Neither of these things is likely to stimulate sexual feelings; your child will be embarrassed only if you are.

Answering questions

Children who are encouraged to ask questions, and who are given explanations, take for granted that their parents will listen to them. These children grow up to be happier and less authoritarian than children whose questions are ignored and who are rarely supplied with explanations. Parents who try to answer their child's questions are teaching him that they consider him an individual with something useful to say.

In the early years your child regards you as omniscient and will naturally turn to you for advice on most subjects. If you remain approachable and welcome questions, your child will grow up feeling that he can talk to you about anything. Discouraging your child when he is young and uninhibited will only make him distant and reserved when he grows older. If you want to be the confidant of your children, keep the channels of communication open at any cost.

Don't avoid answering questions, even if they embarrass you. If you are concerned about when to tell your child about sex, wait until he asks you about it. A child's curiosity should always be met by your willingness to answer truthfully. It's much healthier for him to learn about sex in an accurate, matter-of-fact way from you than in a secretive, melodramatic way from friends who may well be misinformed.

From about three years onward, a child can handle at least part of the truth about sex, although he will not be able to understand the mechanics of sex until he is six or seven. I told my own children about fertilization, conception, the growth of a child in the womb, and childbirth whenever they asked about it. I left discussions about sexual intercourse until the age of six or so, depending on the child. All discussions on sex should include aspects of caring, loving and the responsibilities involved in intimate relationships.

DISCIPLINE 2–3

Don't expect blind obedience from your child. It is far better to reason and persuade. Never coerce a two-year-old; it will only lead to a battle of wills and resentment. As your child becomes old enough to reason, you should teach him the importance of self-discipline. Teach him that discipline requires a sense of mutual responsibility and should not always be imposed from without.

If you take the trouble to discuss why it is right or wrong to behave in a certain way, your child will be more likely to do what you want because he will understand your motivation.

On the other hand, don't make the mistake of talking over every decision. Don't, for example, over-burden your child with responsibility for his own conduct or safety. He is simply not old enough for that. When the situation warrants it, give a simple order, unless you feel your child is going to be recalcitrant, in which case a softer approach may be more successful.

For a child to develop self-discipline, you must sometimes allow him the freedom of choice. Carefully select the times when you are going to give him a choice. The options should be simple enough for your child to comprehend and you should be able to live with whatever decisions he makes. Never try to fool your child by giving him a choice when your decision is already made – you won't fool him.

When to use discipline

The times when you have to insist on discipline fall into a small number of categories:

☐ When your child's safety or the safety of another person is threatened. This will include dangerous games, toys and activities involving fire, electricity and sharp instruments. There have to be rules, for instance, whenever fireworks are used or whenever you make a campfire or have a barbecue.

☐ Children have to grow up learning that the wishes and comforts of other people must be honored. Be strict on matters where thoughtfulness, helpfulness, unselfishness and courtesy are concerned.

☐ There should be few concessions about honesty. With my own children, I have always been severe about lying and stealing. I have done this not by punishing them, but by proving to them that the truth is always better than a lie, no matter how dreadful the crime seems to be. The punishment for a lie should always be worse than the punishment for telling the truth or the admission of wrongdoing. Let your children know you appreciate the courage it takes to own up to something.

POSSIBLE PROBLEMS   2–3

Bed-wetting

It is perfectly normal for a child under the age of four to wet his bed occasionally (see p. 137). One in ten boys still wets his bed at the age of five. Remember that bladder control, like any other skill, develops at different rates in different children. As a child grows older, he learns to hold urine for longer periods of time, but it may take several years to learn to control his bladder for ten or more hours through the night (see p. 136). You can help in quite a few ways:

☐ Discourage drinks after six p.m.

☐ Make certain that your child empties his bladder before going to bed.

☐ Lift your child without waking him and see that he urinates before you go to bed.

☐ Put a potty by the bed so that if he should wake he can urinate without difficulty.

☐ Make sure the pajamas don't have difficult fastenings and can be taken down quickly.

☐ Leave a dim light on in your child's room so he can see what to do if he wakes up in the night.

Worry and anxiety are nearly always the root cause of your child's problem, and so it seems unkind to me to say or do anything to aggravate your child's sense of inadequacy. Never draw attention to wet beds or make a fuss about them. Never scold your child. Make sure that a wet bed causes a minimum of inconvenience to everyone by laying a rubber sheet on top of the ordinary bed sheet, and then putting a small sheet over the rubber sheet. This one can be whipped off and washed very easily and quickly while the rest of the bed linen remains dry.

Take your child for medical advice about bed-wetting only if he's willing. By the time you can establish that bed-wetting is a real problem and not just a variation of normal behavior, your child may be old enough to participate in the decision to seek help. If you talk it over frankly with your child and he really doesn't want to have medical tests and examinations, then don't subject him to them. All children outgrow bed-wetting, and yours will too. Make the process of reaching that grown-up stage as comfortable and unembarrassing as possible. If he agrees to have tests done, make sure they are thorough. Don't accept treatment without a full investigation.

Stuttering

Children often stutter for brief periods while they are learning to talk. Long-term stuttering or stammering usually have the same causes as bed-wetting: tension, anxiety or fear. They may start out of the blue after a severe shock or accident. Stuttering sometimes continues into adult life but, as we all know, it does not necessarily stop one from leading a normal, happy and fruitful life. I believe that stuttering should be treated in exactly the same way as bed-wetting. Accept it in your child when he is young, pay no attention to it, and never ridicule or draw attention to it. When he's old enough – say, five or six – you should be perfectly frank and unembarrassed to talk to him about it. If your child is very concerned and can't handle embarrassment at school or with strangers, and if you would like advice from a speech therapist, then seek it. If your child seems perfectly willing to continue stuttering, however, don't cause further unhappiness by dragging him from clinic to clinic in the hope that the stammering can be cured. One of my stepsons stutters, but he doesn't seem to mind, even when reading out loud in class. We've asked him if he wishes to see a speech therapist and he doesn't, so we haven't pushed him. Stutterers often don't stutter while singing or saying poetry, so if your child concentrates on giving his speech rhythm, it may help.

"Habits"

Nail biting, thumb sucking or carrying a security object are not abnormal in a young child. You should not try to stop them – either by force or ridicule. Almost half of all otherwise quite normal school children have these habits, and they are nearly always caused by some kind of

tension. For the most part they are unconscious, nervous habits, which you can help cure by developing in your child a sense of pride in his appearance. Most children stop nail biting when they become concerned about how it looks – particularly when they become interested in the opposite sex. At this age, social considerations begin to affect their personal habits. Thumb-sucking and the need for security objects may continue right on into the teens, but I see no reason to try to control them. As children get older, they sense what is acceptable, impose self-control, and only indulge their habits in private.

A cheeky child

It is not always easy to draw the line between cheek and impertinence. Occasional cheekiness is, to my mind, perfectly acceptable; I like it in a child. It suggests spirit, imagination and a healthy skepticism toward authority.

There is the mistaken belief that questioning decisions is being cheeky. This is because some parents feel it undermines their authority. But if you encourage your child to talk things over with you, you will not have to depend on your authority to discipline him. You will, on the contrary, encourage him to discipline himself and develop in him a respect for persuasive argument. If you demand that he blindly obey your decisions, and find his "cheekiness" unacceptable, then he will never get a chance to understand the reasoning behind your decisions.

The other good side of cheekiness is that it provides a verbal mechanism for getting rid of anger and frustration. Anger is a perfectly acceptable emotion in a child, but not if it expresses itself through aggression, destructiveness, and bullying. It is much better for your child to vent his anger with words than to hit someone. So when your child is cheeky, weigh his reasons, and if they are healthy, just make sure his cheekiness stays within acceptable bounds.

Insolence, of course, goes beyond cheekiness, because it flouts good manners. It ignores the feelings of others. If your child becomes insolent, you are going to have to teach him that his behavior is not acceptable.

Selfishness

All children are selfish, so you must teach them to do unto others as they would have others do unto them. Your child must learn that he can't always have the sweets he wants because they have to be shared with others. He may not get the biggest, rosiest apple because there is only one and another child may want it. He must learn how to lose because only one child can win and he won't always be the one. The most important way of convincing your child that he should not be selfish is to try to get him to feel how other children will respond to selfishness. If he can understand that all children feel as he does, then he will realize that people have to take turns at getting what they want, whether it's a prize, a ride on a tricycle, or a few more minutes on a swing. It's up to you, by your actions, to show your child the benefits of unselfishness.

An over-indulged child

An over-indulged child is a self-centered child. Here are some of the things you may have done to make your child egotistical:

☐ If you are over-protective, you can make your child feel that he is extra special. Children who are waited on hand and foot, or who are protected from day-to-day experiences grow up to expect others to take care of them and fail to make the efforts necessary to control their own lives.

☐ If you show favoritism toward a child, you encourage a sense of self-importance. If you neglect him, he'll feel inferior and develop a martyr complex. Either attitude encourages children to become self-centered, rather than outgoing and considerate.

☐ Some parents set too high a goal for their children, which can only frustrate them.

One of the best cures – possibly the only cure – for an over-indulged child is to let him go to school early. He really does need the levelling process of a nursery school or a kindergarten, where he will have to mix with other children and not get special treatment. Later in life he may respond well to boarding school. If you cannot afford these alternatives, you can still pull him down a peg or two by trying to choose bright, outgoing, intelligent friends for him. Contact with another sensible adult can also help your child overcome his sense of self-importance.

14 Playing

Until the beginning of this century it was thought that play was fun but a waste of time. When children reached school age they were expected to work, and play was kept for the time when work was completed or for holidays. It was thought that since young children were incapable of doing anything useful, they might as well spend their time playing. We now know that play can have a much more important role in your child's development. The last 50 or 60 years of research has shown that play develops important cognitive skills, and also sociable behavior. To learn to become sociable, a child has to have contact with children his age. This contact is usually made through group play. Most parents today encourage play in children and provide them with all sorts of equipment and toys, with an emphasis on their educational value.

PLAY   0–1

During her first year your baby will go through what is called an exploratory stage. Until she's about three months old, play will mainly consist of observing people and objects and of making rather random attempts to grab hold of anything that is held in front of her. After three months your baby will gain enough control over her hands and arms to enable her to grasp hold of, and examine, small objects. As soon as she can creep, crawl or walk, she'll be able to forage for herself and examine everything within her reach.

Suitable toys and games

Never in a person's development is play more synonymous with learning than in the first few years of life. Your baby is learning how to see properly, how to use her hands and how to master hand/eye coordination (see p. 193). She may learn quite a lot simply by watching and moving her own hands and fingers, but she will practise and perfect her newly-learned skills with any toys that you give her.

SUITABLE TOYS
- Mobiles
- Rattles
- Mirror
- Music box
- Large/small balls
- Soft toys
- Squeaky toys
- Flexible toys
- Activity center
- Books
- Cooking utensils

What toys to give

● *From about five weeks*

● *Six to ten months*

Her visual field will be increasing and she'll enjoy watching anything which moves, so hang mobiles above her cot and changing mat. They're easy to make from household items if you don't want to buy them (see p. 260).

● *Three months*

She'll love objects which make a noise so provide her with a rattle or any form of toy which she can shake or hit. Choose a lightweight, nonbreakable, washable rattle that has a small enough handle for your baby to grasp easily (at this stage she won't have the muscle strength or coordination to grip anything for more than a few seconds).

● *Four months*

Plastic containers filled with beans or water will also make interesting noises, and she'll be able to hold them between both hands.

Any object that is fairly small and has crevices, holes or handles that your baby can grasp or poke her fingers into will be ideal. Ideally, it should be brightly-colored and have bells or rings that make a noise.

Put a fairly large, specially-designed baby mirror in her cot – she'll love staring at her own face. Never be tempted to put one of your own mirrors in the cot – it could easily break.

Musical boxes provide endless fascination for small babies and can play a part in your bedtime routine (see p. 143). The best ones have a string which the baby can pull.

"Activity centers" which have a series of knobs and buttons which your baby can push or turn to make noises can be attached to the cot or bath. As your baby's manipulative abilities improve, she'll love playing with this.

● *Ten to 12 months*

Once your baby can pick up something small she'll be able to hold chalk, pencils, crayons and, eventually, paint brushes. She'll be more mobile now and will enjoy being able to pull or push toys like trains, cars or walking dogs. Provide her with toys on strings so that she can sit on the floor and draw them in towards her.

Games to play together

Play peek-a-boo with your baby, either when she's in her cot or when sitting on your lap. Vary the game by hiding your face behind a scarf or towel instead of your hands.

Buy a large inflatable beach ball and roll it gently toward your baby. Once she can sit unsupported she'll be able to bat a ball back to you with her hand. You could even throw a small ball gently into your baby's lap for her to "throw" back to you. Show your baby how to fill up a container with toy animals, plastic spoons, anything which isn't breakable. Encourage her to have a go and you'll soon find that she'll sit for hours filling up and emptying her container.

Babies seem to have endless patience for stacking containers or rings, both of which help her develop coordination. Though they come in a variety of styles, the basic principle is the same. The ones with large pieces are better for younger babies because they're easier for uncoordinated hands to grab hold of.

Making use of household objects

A baby under one year old doesn't need formal toys, although she'll inevitably be given some. Everything she comes across is interesting. Anything that smells, looks or sounds interesting will appeal to her, and many household items which adults take for granted will hold a world of excitement for her. Here are a few things you might do to entertain your child:

☐ Wooden spoons and spatulas, small saucepans and lids, colanders and strainers, funnels, a set of plastic measuring spoons, plastic cups with lids, plastic bottles of different sizes with their caps on, small plastic food containers, plastic ice cube trays, a whisk, an old egg carton, and a cookie tin. Just hand them to your baby and she'll discover what *she* wants to do with them.

☐ Anything which rolls: the cardboard tube inside a roll of paper towels or toilet paper.

☐ Round objects: balls of every type, balls of wool, balls of string, grapefruits, oranges, apples.

☐ Things which are very light: balloons, a sponge, foam rubber, polystyrene.

☐ Things which are flat and hard: a wooden plate, a table mat, a ruler.

☐ Things which stretch: a piece of elastic, an elastic band, a piece of cloth cut on the bias.

☐ Anything which has a hole that a child can poke his fingers through: a roll of Scotch tape, a napkin ring, a set of shaped plastic cookie cutters.

☐ Things which are quite large and heavy but perfectly safe, like a cushion, a football, a soft-backed book, rice or dried fruit in a tough polythene bag, a loaf of bread.

☐ Anything which rattles: transparent plastic jars with colored beads or paper clips inside (make sure the lid is firmly on).

☐ Ojbects with different textures: pieces of felt, strips of fine sandpaper, thick strands of wool, a fabric-filled bean bag.

SAFETY TIPS

● Never give your child anything to play with which is so small that she might accidentally swallow it, gag on it, or push it up her nose or into her ear.

● If you buy a toy that is painted, make sure the paint is lead-free. Young children put everything into their mouths and children have been known to get lead poisoning from toys or furniture covered with paint containing lead.

● Never give your child a toy that is made from a hard substance with sharp edges.

● Never leave your baby alone while she is playing, not even in a play pen.

● Always provide nontoxic crayons and pencils. For your own sake, make sure that crayons, pencils and felt tips will wash off sur- faces and fabrics.

● Don't buy toys made from thin rigid plastic. They break easily and leave dangerously sharp edges.

● When you buy soft toys, check for a safety label. If there's no label make sure no sharp pieces of wire are used to hold additional pieces on. Check that eyes and noses are firmly se- cured to the fabric of stuf- fed toys and dolls.

PLAYING EXERCISES

Help your baby's physical development from a very early age by playing simple games as part of your daily routine. These exercises should be, above all, entertaining. Think of them as an excuse to sit down with your baby and play together. One of the best times for this is after you've given your baby a bath and she's feeling calm and contented. There are, however, certain points to bear in mind:

☐ Never force your baby's limbs into unnatural positions.

☐ Always check that your baby is smiling and contented. As soon as she cries, stop.

☐ Exercise her on a soft carpet or towel, never on a slippery surface.

☐ Dress her in something comfortable. So long as the room's warm enough and she's not in a draft, her diaper will be sufficient clothing.

☐ Never exercise your baby when she's tired or hungry.

Cross-overs

1 (*top left*) Sit cross-legged on the floor with your baby on your lap, as shown.

2 (*bottom left*) Stretch your baby's arms out to the sides, no further than shoulder height.

3 (*bottom right*) Bring her arms back across her chest and then start the exercise again.

Flier

1 Lie on your back and put your baby on your shins with her chest on your knees.

2 Stretch her arms out to the side – as you do so, she should raise her head. Then bring her hands back to the original position.

Arm stretch

1 Put your baby on her back and let her grasp your thumbs. Move one arm above her head.

2 Lower the extended arm and at the same time raise the other arm above her head.

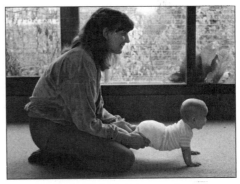

Push-ups

1 Put your baby on her tummy, with her arms out in front of her. Hold her lower half securely around the hips.

2 Slowly raise your baby's legs, so that her back forms a right-angle with her arms. Lower her legs and repeat after a short rest.

263

Bicycle
1 Place your baby on her back and hold both her legs.

2 Gently rotate her legs as if she were riding a bicycle. Make six rotations at first.

3 Then rotate your baby's legs six times in the opposite direction.

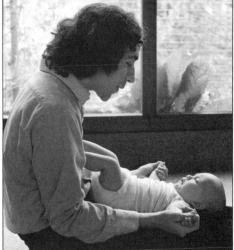

Sit-ups
1 (*top*) Lie on your back, knees up, your baby in your lap.

2 (*bottom left*) Sit up, slowly lowering your legs and the baby.

3 (*bottom right*) Raise your torso completely so you're sitting up and your baby's horizontal.

265

PLAY

Your child continues to develop in many ways, including her ability to play. The stage during which she plays with toys begins toward the end of her first year and reaches its peak when she is five or six. When children first play with toys, they just examine and explore them. As they get older they use their imagination to breathe life into the toys. They endow them with human qualities. They build houses, homes and farms with toys, and imagine that their toys are capable of feelings and speech.

Suitable toys and games

Your toddler's coordination will improve greatly this year, as will his manipulative skills. Toys which allow him to exercise new skills will eventually provide the most enjoyment. Some toys may prove too challenging at first, so begin with large, uncomplicated ones. Household objects will continue to be popular, but other toys will be needed to develop her mental abilities and her powers of concentration.

SUITABLE TOYS

- Post box
- Wooden blocks
- Building bricks
- Hammering table
- Push/pull toys
- Dolls
- Cars
- Crayons and felt tip pens
- Paints and brushes
- Blackboard
- Books
- Sand box
- Wading pool
- Slide
- Swing
- Jungle Jim
- Trolley

Manipulative toys

"Fitting" toys, which require your toddler to fit shapes into the appropriate holes, are ideal. The toy consists of a box with shaped holes cut into the surface. Your toddler pushes his blocks through the correct holes and has the pleasure of seeing them disappear with a clunk. Building blocks are also perennial favorites with children because they can be used as part of imaginary play to make endless shapes or objects – towers, forts, boats and houses.

Playing with paint

All children love to paint, even though during this year you may find it difficult to interpret exactly what's been drawn. Make sure to cover the painting area – the table or floor – with a waterproof covering or newspaper, and that you protect your child with overalls.

Two painting techniques your child might enjoy are block painting and butterfly painting. In block painting you have to provide the equivalent of a rubber stamp. This can be a small sponge, a ball of cotton wool, a cork, half an apple or a tomato – anything really, which your child can easily hold and use in a stamping movement. Prepare the stamp pad by sprinkling two tablespoons of powder paint on some moistened squares of kitchen paper which you've put in a flat dish.

Gently use the back of a spoon to mix the paint into the paper.

With butterfly painting, different colored paints are dropped on a piece of thick paper. Your child uses a straw to blow the wet paint into shapes. The paper is then folded in half, for a mirrored or butterfly effect.

Only keep paintings that you and your child both agree are worth keeping. Display them with magnets on refrigerator doors. If you find a place where your child's fingerprints always seem to mark the walls, such as down the sides of the staircase, or over his bed, cover these spots with your child's drawings. Your toddler's pictures make ideal cards to send to relatives, or "thank you" cards. They're also easy to make into calendars.

BLOCK PAINTING

1 *Prepare the painting area by covering it with newspaper. Give your child a sponge to dip into the paints.*

2 *Having dipped the sponge into the paint she should then blob (or smear) it on to the paper.*

3 *When she's done this a couple of times, give her another object to use with differently-colored paints.*

BUTTERFLY PAINTING

1 *Prepare the painting area. Make up some watery paint that your child can put on with a spatula.*

2 *If your child is old enough, give her a straw to blow the paint about on the paper.*

3 *Fold the paper in half but let your child open it up to see the mirror-image butterfly she has made.*

What paper to use

Inexpensive pads of paper, wallpaper, old envelopes, brown paper bags, even old newspaper – all can be painted on. Alternatively, buy a roll of lining paper and just cut off what your child needs. Make a reusable coloring board by covering a piece of cardboard with clear, washable fabric or paper. Paintings can then be wiped off with a damp cloth or paper towel (you'll probably have to experiment with paints to see which ones stick to the surface best).

What brushes to use

When your child begins to paint, use thick brushes so that he gets immediate, bold results. Let him use pastry brushes, cotton wool balls, ice cream sticks and pipe cleaners for variety. Let him use his fingers or his feet from time to time, because he's bound to love getting messy with the paint. A fun brush can be made using an empty roll-on deodorant bottle, which you fill with paint.

PAINT TIPS

● Buy powder watercolors and mix only the quantity you need; only buy blue, red, yellow and white.

● Keep paint in small plastic jars, preferably in the non-spill variety which have a hole in the top for the paint brush.
● Plastic egg cartons make a difficult-to-spill artist's palette for your child.
● Another useful kind of paint holder is a large piece of foam rubber in which you've cut holes for the paint pots.

● To thicken up powder paint without using extra powder, add some liquid starch.
● Children love making their own paint so put some liquid starch in a small container and add food color-

ing. They can add this until they have the color they require.
● A small amount of detergent in finger paints will make cleaning easier.
● Make a paint that will stick to a shiny surface such as glass or aluminium foil by mixing food coloring, egg yolk and dry detergent.

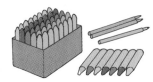

● If you buy your chil felt-tip pens or crayons make sure they're the fat, chunky ones because they're easier to hold.

Preserving drawings

You can preserve a crayon drawing by ironing it on to a piece of cloth. Lay it face upwards on the ironing board, cover it with a piece of lightly-colored cloth, and then iron it firmly at a low-to-medium temperature. The drawing will transfer to the cloth. Make sure you let it cool before you move it from the ironing board. You can also preserve drawings by spraying them with fixative or hairspray, or using a "magic" solution estimated to keep a drawing for 200 years! Dissolve a tablet of milk of magnesia in a quart of soda water and let it sit overnight. The following day soak a paper drawing in the solution for an hour; don't move it until it is completely dry.

PAINT STORAGE TIPS
● Take a fairly large block of synthetic foam rubber or polythene foam and make holes in it. Stand up all your child's bottles, brushes and jars in it.

● A silverware tray makes a very good store for bottles, jars and paint brushes.

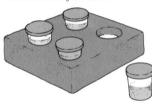

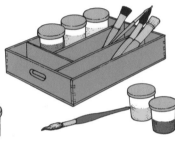

● Put drawing paper on a kitchen towel dispenser and attach it to the wall in your creative corner.

Creative materials

Fingerpaints
Mix two fluid ounces of liquid starch with either four drops of food coloring or one tablespoon of powder paint.
Glue
Mix ten fluid ounces of flour with one teaspoon of salt in a pan. Add 20 fluid ounces of water slowly until it's absorbed into a paste. Simmer for five minutes, then cool and refrigerate in an airtight container.
Modelling dough
Mix three parts of flour to one part salt, then stir in one part water. Color with food colouring.
Play dough
Mix together equal parts of salt and flour. Add a little oil and then add enough water to mix to a stiff dough. Knead until soft.

Playing with water

Most children love playing with water, and will have forgotten any fears they may have had by their second year. Help your child have fun by trying some of the following:

☐ Let your child play in the bath. All my children loved empty plastic bottles in the bath which they used as water pistols. As before, provide containers and colanders so that your child can create a variety of effects (see p. 74).

☐ Wading pools are ideal for summer, and they needn't be expensive. The small, round ones which you blow up serve the same purpose as the more elaborate, permanent ones.

☐ In the summer lay a tarpaulin sheet on the ground and play a hose or plant spray over it. When it's completely wet, it will make a perfect slide for your child.

☐ Make a small hole in the bottom of a plastic container and fill it with colored water. Attach it to the back of your child's tricycle (and later, bicycle). He'll be able to see the colored trail of water as he cycles along.

☐ All children love messy games, so if you have a tap in the back yard, put a container of soil near it so he can mix water with the soil and make up his own mud. It will be messy, but your child will adore it.

☐ Make an "iceberg" that can be played with in the bath or wading pool. This is done by putting water and food coloring in a balloon. Put the balloon in a pan just in case it bursts, and then place it in the freezer. When it's solid, prick the balloon and peel it off – you'll be left with a perfect, round "iceberg."

Playing with sand

Sand boxes are marvellous play areas for children. Whether you buy a ready-made one or make your own by adding sand to an old plastic wading pool, an old rubber tire, or a cement-filled hole, you should always use silver sand. Although more expensive than builders' sand, it doesn't stain as much. Always cover the sand box when not in use or every cat in your neighborhood may use it as a litter box.

Slides, frames and swings

As your toddler becomes more coordinated throughout the year, you may want to invest in a large piece of play equipment. If you decide to buy a swing, buy the style which your toddler has to be bodily lifted into and out of. If you buy a slide, make sure it has safety sides and *no* parts which will splinter.

SAFETY TIPS

● Never let your toddler go near or handle fireworks.

● Keep her well away from any kind of pool containing water. No matter how small or shallow it is, she should never be left unattended, even if she can swim.

● Take special care if you go to children's playgrounds with fast-moving roundabouts, and avoid the times when older, more boisterous children are using the equipment.

● Any game that involves metal implements (metal buckets, spades, toy pistols, etc.) is potentially dangerous. So is any game with sharp or pointed instruments (bows and arrows or toy knives).

Rough and gentle games

Not all children like the same sorts of games, nor does the same child like the same kind of game all the time. Some children have an obvious preference for more athletic, boisterous games, while others prefer quiet, contemplative activities.

I had four sons, two of the former type, and two of the latter. From an early age I indulged the two who preferred rough and tumble games by providing them with large, soft cushions in the playroom and foam-filled soft furniture for them to jump and leap about on for their acrobatics. Outdoors there was a rope to climb, a tree with a favorite way up and down, a Jungle Jim with rope ladder and netting for them to cling to, and a tire swing. They had their first tricycles about the age of 13 months. Ball games like soccer or baseball were always my favorites because they tired the children out.

With the latter two children, we had to provide lots of books and countless sets of paints, easels and drawing boards. At a very early age the children made toy ships or toy steam engines from household junk like empty egg cartons, toilet paper tubes, and plastic margarine containers. As they got older they went on to making paper airplanes. One of our sons became quite an expert at origami at the age of three. Both of these children loved musical instruments and had recorders, toy flutes, toy xylophones and toy guitars before graduating on to proper ones at a later age.

Are the toys creative enough?

There is hardly any toy or game that isn't creative for your child. Whatever he plays with or sees when he's awake will help him create imaginary worlds.

By far the most enjoyable and beneficial games available that don't need too much adult supervision. These games are usually totally absorbing because they allow children to follow their own fancy, and to use their own judgment. When children are constantly interrupted and told to be clean, tidy or careful, their interest inevitably wanes. They lose sight of the point his her game and become disheartened. This sort of adult interference can inhibit a child's ability to concentrate when she gets to school.

Is my child stimulated enough?

If you provide the right environment and equipment, you needn't worry about whether your child is being stimulated enough. At this stage, your child is developing basic attitudes toward play and what she needs most is freedom to follow new ideas as they occur to her. It's your job to provide the floor space, the tools and interrupted time – she'll do the creative thinking by herself.

Your child approaches play very much like an explorer and must be given privacy and time to herself with no interruptions (unless he asks for them). It's your job to be an assistant, to provide the equipment and make sure that she has all the facilities she needs. From then on it's up to your child – not you! – to decide what to do, and you shouldn't interfere.

How can you help

You can't teach your child to use her imagination, but you can encourage her natural gift for fantasy by doing the following:

☐ Play make-believe games with her.
☐ When you tell a story act out the characters' parts and make up all the various character's voices. If your child has a favorite, suggest that she pretend to be him.

☐ Play "What's this?" games. Get your child to shut her eyes, then gently stroke some object across her skin. She has to guess what it is.

☐ Help your child in her imaginary world by giving her some glove puppets – either bought ones or brown paper bags with faces drawn on them.

☐ Start to fill a play box. Put in some of your old shoes, shirts, skirts, dresses, hats and scarves. Add some special cheap jewellery as well. If you can find some authentic uniforms from second-hand shops, so much the better. Make a cloak from a length of fabric and attach a clasp at one end.

☐ Provide good fantasy toys like dolls: children of both sexes love dolls because they're so easy to incorporate into their imaginary worlds. Stuffed animals, house-cleaning tools and carpentry sets are also ideal.

☐ Play at being an animal. Get down on all fours and move about the floor making all the animal noises you know. This will show your child how to do it.

☐ Play at telephone conversations. If you've bought your child a toy telephone, pick up the real phone and pretend to have a conversation with her.

STORAGE TIPS

● Always save plastic containers with lids for storing blocks, marbles or small toys. Those made for ice cream or even margarine are ideal.

● Use brightly-colored red labels for easy identification of what's inside your containers.

● Large glass jars are good for storage because you can immediately see what's inside them.

● Never throw out any shoe boxes – they make good beds for dolls, as well as houses and barns.

● Loop a plastic mesh basket over the taps in the bath to store all bath toys.

● Use a flat-topped chest for storing larger toys. This can double up as a table.

● Your child's toys are bound to get strewn about your home. Try to keep a basket in each room to make for quick and easy tidying up.

● Keep a special bag or box of toys in the car at all times.

CLEANING AND PREPARING TOYS

● Buy machine-washable stuffed toys.

● Alternatively, use a carpet shampoo and brush to clean stuffed toys.

● Try to buy plastic toys which can be put into the dishwasher.

● If plastic toys have gotten out of shape, soak them in hot water and then re-mould them with your fingers

● Clean and deodorize smelly toys by sponging them with a cloth that has been wrung out in a solution of baking soda.

● You can dry clean your toys by shaking them in a bag containing a generous amount of baking powder or corn starch.

PLAY

Your child will probably still play with some of her existing toys although the ways in which she plays with them may differ. She may continue to play with building blocks but instead of just piling them on top of each other will use them as part of a larger concept: she may use them to form the wall surrounding an imaginary garage.

During this third year your child will want to imitate the way you behave and the way you look. Manipulative skills will be greatly improved so larger jigsaw puzzles will be popular.

SUITABLE TOYS
- Large-piece jigsaw puzzle
- Lego building bricks
- Scissors (blunt-ended)
- Glue
- Prams and strollers
- Tea sets
- Toy washing machines, cooking utensils
- Play house
- Tricycle
- Cars and trucks
- Jungle Jim

Imitative games

As part of her effort to imitate the adults around her, your child will create a little world of her own. you don't need to buy a proper play house for her to do this. A couple of chairs, or a small table draped with a large blanket, will make an instant tent or playhouse. So will an old playpen covered with a sheet. Children love playing in the dark, so draw the curtains if that's what they want. All of my children loved playing with cardboard boxes of any size, so long as the boxes were big enough to climb into. Small ones became boats and cars, piles of them were made into castles, forts and houses. Boxes laid on their sides became tunnels. Laid end to end, they became trains. More elaborate "houses" can be made by taking a large box or crate, removing all nails and strips of metal, and cutting out doors and windows. Your child can draw in curtains and put pictures on the wall inside. Outside she can draw shutters, a door and a knocker. If you put several stools or small chairs in a line across the room, your child will make them into a train, a boat or an airplane.

Manipulative games

Your child will use her hands to explore objects and discover what they do – it will be an important part of the learning process for her. All of the games and ideas listed below require good coordination.

□ During this year your child will have enough coordination to help with tasks around the house. She'll still see this as a form of play because she's so anxious to copy what you do. She'll be able to handle an electric mixer, as long as you keep an eye on her; she'll be able to snap the ends off beans and spinach.

□ Many children love taking anything mechanical to pieces, so don't throw away old clocks, old motors, cameras or record players; let your child have fun taking them apart. And if there's anything around the house that needs to be dismantled, such as an old wall or fence, or if there's stone to be broken up for paving, let your child join in.

□ Your child might enjoy spatter painting. To do this she places leaves, grass, coins, whatever shape she wants, flat on a piece of white paper. She then takes a toothbrush, well soaked with paint, and gently draws a knife across it so that the paint is spattered randomly across the paper. For more exciting effects she can continue doing this with different colors. When the paint is dry, she can remove the objects.

□ If you live outside the city, give your child a small plot in the yard which is

entirely hers. Provide her with her own trowel and watering can and help her plant bulbs or vegetables which grow quickly, like marigolds, radishes and beans.

☐ Your child will probably be able to deal with jigsaw puzzles of up to six pieces. Try to buy ones with easily-identifiable pieces when the puzzle's apart. Your toddler will find it much easier if she can see if it's a leg, an arm, or a tree rather than just a shape. Buy wooden jigsaw puzzles when possible: they're easier to handle and don't bend like cardboard ones. If your child has difficulty holding the pieces, make it easier for her by gluing on small plastic hooks from the hardware store. Start off with the inset puzzles, with pieces that fit into pre-cut areas on a tray. Your toddler will soon figure out how it's meant to work.

☐ With some jigsaws, you may have to show your child exactly how to assemble the pieces. Explain to her why certain pieces go together and interlock. "Look, this piece has two bumps which look like eyebrows ... This piece is for the head which always goes on top of the body." Once you've helped your child through it herself a few times, she'll happily sit and do it over and over again.

☐ Make a puzzle out of your child's favorite picture by pasting it on to heavy card and covering it with clear contact paper. With an artist's knife, cut the puzzle into about six pieces made up of triangles, diamonds and squares.

☐ Stop the puzzles from getting mixed up by marking the back of each piece with a specific color.

Learning through play

There is no time in your young child's life when play does not contribute to her development. Quite often her needs and desires can be fulfilled in play when they cannot satisfactorily be met in any other way. A child who is unable to be a leader in real life, for instance, may gain great satisfaction from being a leader of his toy soldiers or band of cowboys. For most children, play involves experimentation.

Through trial and error, they learn that they can create something new – something that never existed before – and this can be very satisfying. Once they have developed and fulfilled their creative interests in play, they can then transfer these interests to the real world.

At home and in school children learn what is expected of them. In pre-kindergarten or play groups they learn what they must do to become an accepted member of the group. Moral standards may be set more rigidly here than at any other time in their lives. There's nothing like a group of children at play for encouraging the development of desirable personality traits. By contact with friends, your child will be given lessons every day in how to be pleasant, generous, truthful and cooperative. These lessons are especially forcefully taught, because your child is constantly seeking the approbation of her friends and peers – particularly in her play group.

Learning about colors

Always mention the color of something you are using or looking for: "I'm looking for the green packet," "Where's that red tin gone?" "Oh, I've found the jar with the blue label," "I'm going to use this yellow pencil." Always describe the color of your child's clothes: "That's a pretty pink dress," "What a nice red jumper." Always point out the color of flowers, in your yard or in the park, show your child the different colors that animals and birds can have. Show her how colors are made: "Look, if we mix a little bit of red with this white we will get pink; yellow mixed with blue will make green." Teach her the colors of the rainbow – rainbows are magical to children.

Learning about letters

Make it easier for your child to learn letters by teaching her the alphabet song. Serve alphabet soup or alphabet spaghetti and help your child spell out her name with the letters. Buy your child magnetic letters that she can play with on the refrigerator door. (My children liked to recognize letters and words which we drew in the palms of our hands.) Play word games when you read a story: As you read a sentence, for instance, leave out a word and get your child to say what it is. Read to her, "The cat was sitting warming himself by the —." As you point to the picture of the fire, your child can shout out the word.

Learning about numbers

Always take the opportunity to count while you are doing routine things. Count from one to three, for instance, as you do up the buttons on your child's dungarees or jacket, or when you're washing her hands or feet. Help her learn numbers by counting things as you shop or put articles into the supermarket cart. Count bottles and jars and arrange them into groups, such as two bottles, three cans and four packets. Draw numbers on small sheets of paper and help your child use them to number her groups of toys, such as three balls, five blocks, seven farmyard animals. When you go for walks count the number of houses, gates, trees, or buses.

TELEVISION

Some babies are introduced to television while they are still in their cots. Their parents see television as a built-in babysitter because it keeps children amused when there is no one else to look after them. For many children, television is more popular and consumes more playtime than all other play activities together. Here are some of the reported facts on television:

● Television is at its least useful when a child is left to watch it alone. Even if she's watching a highly educational program she'll get less out of it if she watches it passively, with no feed-back from others. If she watches it with other children who comment on it, or with an adult who asks questions and makes observations, the program acts as a springboard for ideas and discussion.

● Some parents let television interfere with the usual eating and sleeping routines. This leaves them tired and puts a strain on their digestive systems.

● Watching television can curtail other play activities, especially outdoor play and play with other children. TV may reduce time available for creative play.

● Television often presents information in a more exciting and dramatic way than school books and school teachers. Children therefore often find books and school work boring.

● Television cuts down on conversation and other forms of social interaction in the family.

● Characters on television are often presented as exaggerated stereotypes. Children come to think that people they meet have the same qualities as the people portrayed on the screen. This influences their attitude towards them.

● Watching too many programs portraying crime, torture and cruelty may blunt a child's sensitivity to violence so that she accepts violent behavior as normal.

● Two groups of children were studied for the effects of violence on television. One saw violent programs, the other did not. The studies showed that the young children who were allowed to watch the violent programs were noticeably more aggressive, both with other children and with their toys, than those children who had not been exposed to the same programs.

● Children are great imitators. Since the law breakers often seem more glamorous than the heroes, children tend to identify with the villains.

● Light entertainment that children watch doesn't necessarily provide a good lesson in pronunciation and grammar. On the contrary, it encourages children to pick up sloppy habits.

● Television presents models for the behavior of the different sexes and for life roles and careers. These models give rise to expectations which are not always realistic or in the child's best interests.

● Children interested in programs they have seen on television are often motivated to follow up on what they have watched by reading or asking grown-ups about the subject.

15 Outings and travel

Your new baby can go everywhere with you. All you have to be is composed and well-prepared. If you're well organized and self-assured, outings with your baby can be a great joy, and the sooner you start the better.

For at least the first few months, most babies are looked after by their mothers, especially if they're being breast-fed. I have, therefore, addressed this part of the book mainly to mothers. Looking after a baby doesn't stop a mother from resuming the active life she had before. But new mothers shouldn't be too ambitious, or undertake strenuous shopping expeditions that involve walking long distances and carrying heavy packages. I made the mistake of doing this seven days after I had my baby, and I was so tired that I had to sit down on the pavement or I would have fainted.

LOCAL OUTINGS   0–1

Planning your outings

It's always worth spending some time planning how you're going to get to your destination, what you're going to need for the trip, where you're going to feed your baby, and how you're going to change him. Until you feel confident, take your partner or a friend along with you. An extra pair of hands to share the load, and an ally to share the novelty and any possible problems, will make any trip more enjoyable.

Make sure you have a place to feed your baby in peace. It's always advisable to know of some nearby rest rooms, restaurants or even parks, especially in the first months when your baby won't have settled into a predictable feeding routine. You'll have to change your baby as well, so if you know of a rest room with a table or shelf, so much the better.

What to take for a young baby
- A changing surface (which can be a fold-up changing mat or a fabric diaper)
- Disposable diapers and liners
- Pre-moistened sponge in plastic bag
- Baby lotion
- Cotton wool
- Breast pads if breast-feeding
- Bottle and formula if bottle-feeding
- Hat
- Sweater
- Toys for distraction
- Plastic bag for dirty diapers

What to take for an older baby
- A changing surface
- Disposable diapers and liners
- Baby lotion
- Cotton wool
- Pre-moistened sponge in plastic bag
- Bib
- Baby food
- Non-messy snacks
- Container with fruit juice
- Hat
- Sweater
- Toys for distraction
- Plastic bag for dirty diapers

281

Using a sling

Slings are one of the most convenient methods of carrying a baby; they're also one of the oldest. They hold your baby securely against your chest so that both of you have the security of being close to each other, and your hands are left free. Buy a washable one, because your baby is bound to spit upon it, and try the sling on before you make your final choice. It has to be easy to put on and wear. The shoulder straps must be wide enough to support your growing baby's weight comfortably, and both you and your partner must feel relaxed wearing it. It has been said that a baby shouldn't be carried in a sling until he can support his own head. This is not true. You can carry your baby in a sling as soon as you and he are happy about it – your baby will find close contact with you so soothing and reassuring that she'll probably curl up with her head quite well supported and doze.

PUTTING ON A POUCH SLING

1 *Clip the sling on around your waist, then swivel it to the back.*

2 *Pick up your baby and maneuver his legs into the leg holes with your free hand.*

3 *Pull one side of the sling up over the baby and on to your shoulder. Swap hands and repeat with the other side.*

PUTTING AN ENCLOSED SLING

1 *Put on the sling. Slip your baby comfortably on to the inner seat. Zip up the seat section.*

2 *With one hand still supporting the baby, pull the outer cover around him and do up the outer zip.*

LEANING FORWARD

Always cradle your baby's head if you have to lean forward or stretch to one side.

Using a stroller

If you don't carry your baby in a sling, a stroller becomes absolutely essential. Small babies fit quite snugly into the curved shape of the stroller, but do make sure that the baby is well supported with pillows on either side and that he's safely strapped in. Even a tiny baby, if awake, can be propped up to take in the interesting sights around him.

There will be plenty of occasions when you'll have to fold up the stroller – getting on a bus or shopping, for instance – so it's a good idea to practice before you make your first expedition. Make sure you can kick it shut, put it up one handed and, above all, operate the brakes.

SAFETY TIPS
● Never leave your baby unattended.
● Always make sure the stroller is fully extended and in the locked position.
● Never let go of the stroller for a moment without putting the brakes on.
● Always put the safety harness on your baby.
● Never, ever, put shopping on the handles of the stroller.
● From an early age teach your child to keep fingers away from the wheels.

STROLLER TIPS
● One disadvantage of strollers over prams is that in cold weather your child is more exposed. If you don't use leg muffs (see p. 29), lay a blanket over the stroller before you put the baby in. Once you've put him down, wrap the blanket over and around him.
● If your baby falls asleep before you get home, either put the stroller into the lie-back position or tuck him up comfortably with pillows.

COLLAPSING THE STROLLER

1 *Put shopping on the ground and take your baby out of the stroller. If you have a reclining stroller, slot the back into the upright position.*

2 *Grip one of the handles and put your foot under the collapsable strut. Pull your foot upwards.*

3 *Lean forward, pushing the handles down until they lock into position; this allows you to carry the stroller easily.*

Using a back pack

A back pack is a useful means of carrying an older baby who can sit up well and who has become rather heavy to carry in a sling. It leaves your hands free, and also allows your baby to see much more of what's going on around him. This becomes increasingly important the older your baby gets and the more aware he is of the world around him. Before you buy a back pack, do the following:

☐ Try on the back pack, with your baby in it.

☐ Check that the baby's seat comes half-way down your back. This is very important because it places the strain on your back and not on your shoulders; it also keeps the baby stable.

☐ Make sure the pack has a safety strap to keep the baby in place and a waist belt for you to keep the pack secure. Check that the shoulder straps are well padded.

☐ Check that your baby can hold his legs comfortably and that the leg openings don't restrict him in any way.

☐ Try to buy a pack with a built-in loading stand that you can put on without any help; such back packs often convert to free-standing seats.

Going shopping

Try to shop early in the morning when the shops are least busy. When you go to a supermarket and your child can sit unsupported, put him into your shopping cart and wheel it down the *center* of the aisles. Your baby will want to grasp or pull everything in sight – which can easily cause chaos in a supermarket! If you're still feeding your baby, plan to shop between feedings. If you're going to be out for a while, plan to have most of your shopping done before you have to find a quiet spot to nurse.

Having a car is one of the greatest freedoms a new parent can have. There's no worry about how to cope with public transport; there's no difficulty shopping, and it provides an ideal feeding and changing area.

Put the baby into the back pack and lift it up and against your partner's back. He can then slide his arms into the straps.

If you're alone, put the baby in the pack first, then rest it on a chair or table. Squat down and slide your arms into the straps.

SHOPPING TIPS

● When carrying your child in a back pack, remember that his grasping fingers can reach jars and cans in a shop.

● When you take your child into the supermarket you can keep him supported and under control if you use one of your own belts to buckle him into the shopping cart.

● For emergencies keep a few disposable diapers, wipes and plastic bags in the glove compartment of the car for quick changes.

● If you take toys on expeditions, attach them to the pram or cart so you don't have to keep picking them up.

● Shopping seems to make children hungry and therefore fretful. Bring snacks along.

● You can always use the back seat of the car, with a blanket laid over it, as a surface on which to change your child.

● Keep a spare changing bag in the car.

Eating out

In the first months your baby will doze off almost anywhere, so eating out will be quite easy. However, by the time he's nine months old he'll be capable of keeping himself awake; he'll be hungry for any new experience, and a restaurant, with strange people doing even stranger things, will fascinate him. Choose your restaurants carefully. Go to those which seem friendly toward both children and their parents, and which provide high chairs. In case they don't, always take along a portable high chair (see p. 25) and ask to be put at a table away from the main area of activity. Always take your own snacks with you, and, as soon as you've settled your baby in his seat, give him these to occupy him. Have plenty of toys for distraction as well (rearranging paper napkins is another pacifier). You may find it works better to feed your child before you and your partner start.

Using public transportion

My advice is, wherever possible, don't. Neither buses nor trains were designed for parents with young children. If you're shopping on your own, with a stroller, a changing bag and a grumpy baby, getting on public transportation can seem like the end of the world. There are some tips, however, to help you get over the worst problems.

☐ Always travel outside of rush hour, even if that means waiting in a coffee shop, or walking around a gallery for an extra hour; it's worth it.

☐ Where possible, carry your baby in a sling or back pack. This leaves your hands free. It also makes getting on and off a lot easier.

☐ Carry plenty of distracting toys.

☐ Never be embarrassed to ask for help.

LOCAL OUTINGS

By the time your child is walking, you may find that your greatest problem is keeping him safely restrained and happily occupied when you go out. You'll also have to be prepared for very slow walks with endless stops to look at the many objects which take your child's fancy. Most parents continue to use their stroller, although reins, back packs and bicycle seats (see below) are useful alternatives.

What to take	
● Toys	● Sweater/Coat
● Books	● Sun hat
● Drink	● Change of diapers
● Snacks	until toilet trained
● Comforter	● Potty,
	if necessary

Using the stroller

As your child gets older he won't be happy just sitting in the stroller, but will want to walk along with you. This may be inconvenient, especially if you're shopping, and you will have to do your utmost to persuade him to stay in it. The best way to do this is to take along one of your child's favorite toys as well as a snack. If he's so restless that he makes shopping impossible, then the only alternative is to take along a pair of reins and put your child in them (see p. 31). You can either stack your shopping in the stroller, leaving your hands relatively free, or you can collapse the stroller and carry it over your arm while you carry the shopping in the other.

Using a bicycle seat

If you have a bicycle you may find it easier and more fun to take your toddler on the back rather than wheeling him in a stroller or walking slowly with him. There are two kinds of bicycle seats – front-mounted and rear-mounted. These lightweight plastic structures fit neatly and securely on to the bicycle frame and can accommodate a child of up to 40 lbs (80 kilos). Make sure your child's feet are well away from the wheels and that there's a strong safety belt. You may want to buy a protective helmet for your child as well.

Shopping with an older child

As soon as your child can walk, you'll be faced with a new problem: how to occupy a lively young child, and keep an eye on him, while concentrating on what you have to do. The only efficient way of getting about, especially when shopping, is to take your partner or a friend along with you. In this way, one adult can get on with the shopping while the other occupies the child (there is also the added bonus of another pair of hands to help carry packages.)

The alternative is to keep your child on reins so that you can concentrate on what you're doing without having to worry about him all the time. It also helps to sit your child in the supermarket cart so that he can't run away. As you wheel him about, ask questions like, "Can you see the baked beans?" "Which is the largest can?" "Which apples do you want – the red or the green ones?" Most children love being involved in this way, and you can even let them choose their favorite foods and put them in the cart. My solution to the "supermarket problem" was to let my children put anything they wanted into the cart, and then to take it all out at the end, unbeknown to them. Time-consuming, but peaceful.

If you're going somewhere other than

the supermarket, still keep your child on reins but take along his favorite books. When you go into the changing room in a department store, sit him on the floor beside you and encourage him to look at the pictures, perhaps telling you what he sees or what the story is about.

SHOPPING TIPS
- Encourage your child to learn about shopping. Give him the wrappers or your own empty boxes of things on your shopping list and suggest he find them for you by matching them up with products on the shelves. It's a good game for both of you, if you give him a little help.
- Babies can get lost in shops. Dress yours in a brightly-colored coat or hat, so he is easy to spot.

- My father had a special whistle which he used to summon my sister and me. Since I can't whistle loudly enough, I used a referee's whistle on a string around my neck. We had a code: one whistle – come briskly; two whistles – run; three whistles – emergency.
- Any outing can be a lesson in disguise. In the supermarket you can teach your child about healthy eating habits (that beans are better than sugar) or

best buys (that large tins and large packets cost relatively less than small ones).
- Make sure your child can find his way home, should he ever stray, by repeating the same commentary as you approach your house or apartment: "And here's that big fir tree. Now we turn right, straight on past the church. Here's our own street. Our house is over there – one, two, three, the fourth house on the left."

MANAGING TWO CHILDREN

Double stroller. *The independently adjustable sections make it ideal for children of different ages.*

Partner and stroller. *Any trip will be easier if two of you go out together.*

Sling and stroller. *By carrying your youngest in a sling, your hands are free to push the stroller.*

Special excursions

Going out to the shops or to the park will probably be part of your toddler's daily routine, but there will be occasions when you want to plan a special excursion like a boat trip or a visit to the zoo. Bring along a variety of snacks – enough to last the whole day. Cater your plans to your child's personality. What's his attention span? Is he very active? If he is, don't plan to go anywhere where he's going to be confined to his stroller for long, or you'll ruin the day for both of you. If, when the day arrives, your toddler's in a bad mood, or you're not feeling up to it, postpone the outing.

CAR JOURNEYS   0–1

Travelling is a normal part of everyday life, and the sooner your baby learns about it the better.

Car safety

The most important aspect of travelling by car is the safety of your baby. Until he's old enough to go into a car seat (at roughly six months, when he can sit unsupported), you'll have to use cot restraints in the back seat. *Never* sit in the front with your baby on your lap. No matter how firmly you think you're holding him, he'd be flung against or through the window in a collision.

The movement of a car is very soothing to most babies and they often sleep soundly through long journeys and arrive more refreshed than you do. By the time he's old enough to sit in a car seat, he's going to need entertaining. This will be the most taxing part of any car journey you take.

Feeding your baby

Feeding is obviously easier if you're breast-feeding, because there's no need to prepare or sterilize a formula. If you're bottle-feeding, you're going to have to find some way of preparing your baby's formula in sterile conditions. *Never* keep pre-

287

pared milk warm for a few hours, since germs quickly multiply. If you can't get hold of disposable bottles of milk, either mix the formula with boiled water that you've kept in a sterilized bottle inside a thermos, or prepare the formula in your usual way and carry it in an ice bucket.

Once your baby's weaned you'll have to take along baby food, a plastic spoon, sugar-free crackers, a bib and a drinking cup with a spout. You can feed your baby directly from the jar, but whatever he doesn't finish you *must* throw away.

Changing your baby

Disposables are by far the easiest to use when you're travelling. If you have a hatch-back, you can change your baby on a mat laid out in the back; otherwise, lay your baby on a mat along the back seat. There's no need to do more than "top and tail" your baby when you're travelling, so either carry a sponge and a bottle of water, or use those specially designed wipes which come pre-moistened.

CAR TIPS

● Make it easy for your baby to sleep a substantial part of the journey by travelling at night, or by leaving just before his nap.

● Remove all loose objects from the back window ledge, just in case of accidents.

● Tie a variety of your baby's favorite toys on short pieces of string to the car seat. Stick pictures to the back of the front seats and the side doors.

● Always keep a bag with spare diapers and cleaning equipment in the car. Have a spare plastic bag for soiled diapers.

● Have a rug or cot quilt to put over the baby when he falls asleep.

● Have your baby's favorite tapes to play in the car.

● Keep some special toys for car journeys and introduce them one at a time.

● Have a large container of diluted fruit juice in the front with you, and give your baby frequent but very small drinks.

● Once your child is weaned he'll like to have a few snacks during the journey. Make these non-messy for your own sake.

CAR JOURNEYS

1–3

It's between the ages of one and two-and-a-half that car journeys become most difficult. Your child will hate being made to sit still in one place, at the very time when he's discovered the joy of walking and running. He'll also want to assert *himself*. A new sense of independence emerges at this time and he'll be anxious to express what he wants to do, especially when you don't want him to do it. It's your job to amuse him and keep him occupied – for everyone's sake. You will find it valuable to:

☐ Make an early start or travel at night.

☐ Pack soft clothing in such a way that it will do double duty. A raincoat in a pillow case will make a good pillow for a child to nap on.

☐ Be prepared to change seats so that all the passengers get varied views during the journey.

☐ Buy or make special covers for the front seats of the car with pockets which can carry games, snacks, drinks, or books.

☐ Curb restlessness by stopping for five minutes every hour or so, so the children can run about and stretch their legs and imaginations.

☐ To take full advantage of these stops, warn your children far ahead to put on their shoes, hats and coats.

☐ Stop your temper from getting frayed when there's a spill or accident by keeping in the car some spare clothes for the child and a plastic bag for soiled clothes.

☐ Always tape knives, forks and spoons to the inside of the food containers.

☐ To minimize mess, keep a supply of plastic garbage bags in the car.

☐ Keep a few *nutritious* snacks (raisins,

cornflakes, pieces of cheese, etc.) in plastic bags so you never have to say no if your child wants to nibble.

☐ Always take more drinks than you think you'll need, such as a thermos of fruit juice or small, sealed containers of milk.

☐ Most children love grapes (the seedless kind), which quench thirst as well as satisfying hunger.

☐ If you take toys in the car, tie them to coathooks or handles so they don't get trampled on the floor or roll under seats.

☐ To give your child some surprises, wrap favorite toys in several layers of paper. Unwrapping will keep him occupied too.

☐ Get your child to take some responsibility for his own entertainment by getting him to select a few of his toys and putting them in his own case or satchel.

☐ Magnetized games prevent bits from getting lost.

☐ Sew or stick Velcro to toys or games so they will stay in one place.

☐ A child listening to his favorite music in the car will give you half an hour of peace – so take a selection of tapes.

☐ Keep a stock of toys hidden away for the moment when your child gets grumpy.

☐ Play "I Spy" games. Ask your child to look out for a certain object: a cow, a red truck or a fire engine.

☐ Don't stand for any misbehavior like screaming or shouting or kicking. This can be very dangerous. If your child does this, pull off to the side of the road and tell him that you're not going any further until he behaves.

Preventing car sickness

Some children are more prone to car sickness than others. (The balance mechanism of their inner ear is more sensitive to the swaying movement.) Most children who suffer from car sickness grow out of it as they get older, but there are a number of things you can do to minimize the risks:

☐ If your child gets car sick, ask your doctor to suggest a suitable drug. These are usually given half an hour before you leave.

☐ Don't give your child rich or greasy food within a few hours of leaving.

☐ If your child wants a snack during the journey give him dry biscuits or hard candy sweetened with glucose.

☐ Don't become over-anxious. Children quickly pick up on their parents' moods and this can make them apprehensive and therefore more prone to car sickness. Excitement and apprehension play a part in sickness; it's been shown that children tend to suffer more on outward journeys than on return ones.

☐ Keep your child occupied.

☐ If your child goes very pale or very quiet, stop the car. Provide a plastic bag or bowl to be sick in, if necessary.

☐ Always keep water and towels to clean your child up and something tasty like mints for your child to suck to take away the bad taste.

AIR TRAVEL 0–3

Travelling by air is by far the easiest means of public transport to use, but you should still plan out your journey meticulously, especially if you and your baby are travelling alone. Things will not always go right, so you may on occasion have to simply grin and bear it. (I shall never forget making the journey from New York to London with my 18-month-old son crying the entire seven-and-a-half hours, despite all my efforts to quiet him down!)

When you make reservations, say that you're going to be travelling with an infant. Ask to be put on a flight that's not crowded and ask for a front row seat, because there's more leg room there. If they provide cribs, order one so your baby will be comfortable during the flight. Front row seats are advisable if you have a toddler, too, because you can lay a towel on the floor in front of you for him to play on. Carry a small baby on and off the plane in a sling so your hands are free. A stroller is useful too, since you may have a long walk to the boarding area, and trying to carry both hand luggage and a baby will be exhausting. If the airline doesn't provide strollers, bring your own – it can be carried on the plane as hand baggage.

Arrive at the airport early so you can check in before the lines start to form.

Carry everything you need for the flight in a lightweight shoulder bag – toys as well as diapers and changes of clothing – so that your hands are free.

What to take with you
- Child's passport and inoculation documents, if necessary.
- Lightweight bag for baby's equipment.
- Travel cot if cot is unavailable at destination.
- Stroller, carry cot or sling.
- Plastic sheet for diaper changing.
- Bouncing chair if used.
- Pack of disposables; buy supplies at destination.
- Diaper changing equipment (see p. 58).
- Potty if needed.
- Plastic bags for dirty diapers.
- Thermos bottle for days on beach.
- Bottle-feeding equipment if required.
- Non-spill cup and plastic dish if wanted.
- Toys and games.
- Security object if used.
- Quick-drying, non-crease clothes.
- Sun-hat, if necessary.
- Long-sleeved and long legged clothes.

MAKING THE BEST OF PLANE JOURNEYS
● Make sure your tickets are confirmed.
● Change your baby's diaper just before boarding the plane.
● Keep some food or drink ready to give your baby at take off and landing to help equalize the pressure in his ears and avoid discomfort.
● Shortly after boarding ask the most pleasant looking flight attendant for help. Find out when it will be convenient for him or her to warm your baby's food and drink.
● Make sure your inflight baby bag, with bottles, equipment and changes of diapers and clothing, is clearly labelled in case it gets mislaid during the flight.
● Don't try to eat or drink hot food while you're holding the baby. He could get scalded.
● Take along a few of your child's favorite toys but only bring them out one at a time and at intervals spaced through the journey.
● Let your baby play with all the inflight equipment – spoons and forks from the food tray, plastic safety instructions from the seat flap, earphones for the film or music.
● Amuse your child with the same kinds of games you would play in the car (see p. 288).

Toward carefree foreign holidays

Your baby's never too young to travel. (My mother took me on a camping holiday when I was six weeks old and I took one of my sons to Italy when he was barely three months.) Children usually rise to these occasions. My baby son lay gurgling in Rome airport for two hours while we went in search of our lost luggage. For the first three days of the holiday he calmly accepted a variety of milk formulas until we found an Italian mixture that suited him.

The type of holiday you choose is up to you and your individual tastes – it may be camping, staying in a luxury hotel, or swapping house with a foreign family. If you're planning to stay in a hotel, make sure they have adequate facilities for young children. Without them you're not going to enjoy your vacation very much! Check that they provide high chairs, wading pools, laundry (if you're using fabric diapers) and early meals for children. If you're going to a beach it's advisable to choose one which is sandy, with little surf.

Ask your doctor well in advance about health precautions, vaccinations, medication or special creams you should take with you. Check with the foreign government tourist office about food, facilities and hygiene in the country or area you're planning to visit.

If you're flexible about the family diet at home, let your child eat what he wants to abroad. If either of you is fussy or inflexible in your eating habits, and if you're not going to be preparing your child's meals for him, make early arrangements with the hotel to serve your child simple, plain meals. Don't introduce your child to exotic food for the first time in a foreign country.

SUNBATHING TIPS
● Never expose an infant's skin to large doses of direct, strong sunlight. A good guide for a child over six months is:
   5 minutes on the first day
   10 minutes on the second day
   15–20 minutes on the third day
   20–30 minutes on the fourth day
   45 minutes on the fifth day
   60 minutes on the sixth day
● Keep sunburn at bay by putting a film of sun-screen on all parts of the baby's exposed skin every three hours.
● Your child will easily get burned if he has a fair skin. (Any skin that freckles is fair.)
● Make sure your child wears a hat, T shirt and shorts all the time he's playing in the sun, even in the swimming pool.
● You must keep your baby cool in a hot climate with the minimum cotton clothing, a hat and a sun-shade. Place the carry cot or pram in a place that's warm enough but with a slight breeze.
● In a hot climate children need lots to drink.

291

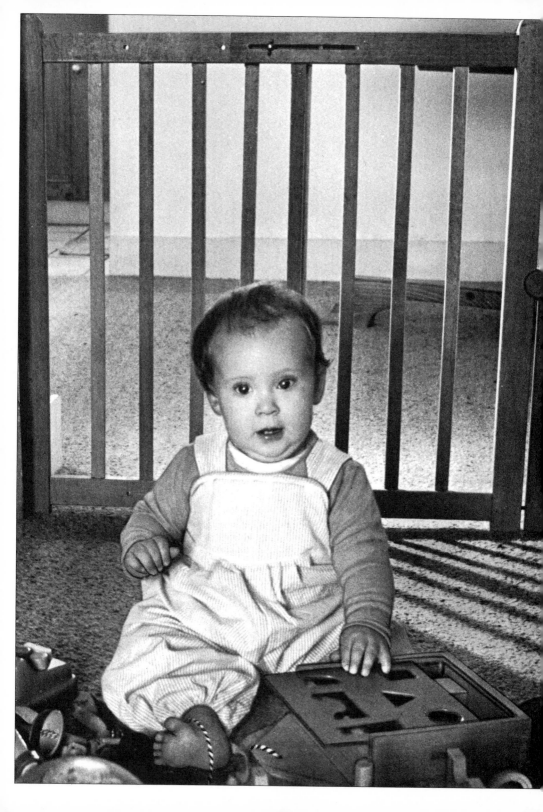

16 Home safety

Accidents in the home cause 37% of deaths in children between the ages of one and four. Most of them are avoidable, so take the time and care to minimize the chances of accidents in *your* home. Most accidents are caused by a chain of events, rather than a single occurrence. The chances of an accident happening are increased by the following:

☐ If your child is tired, ill or hungry.
☐ If the mother is pre-menstrual, tired or pregnant.
☐ If your child is considered hyperactive.
☐ If there's great excitement in the home, caused by an upcoming vacation, perhaps, or the arrival of a new baby.
☐ If you and your partner aren't getting on, or if you're actually fighting.
☐ If your child hasn't anywhere safe to play.
☐ If the correct safety precautions haven't been followed.
☐ If the equipment you use for your baby doesn't comply with safety standards.

SAFETY EQUIPMENT

As soon as your child becomes mobile you must protect him from potentially dangerous objects or situations in the house.

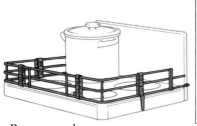

Burner guard

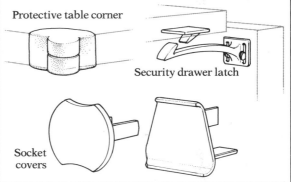

Protective table corner

Security drawer latch

Socket covers

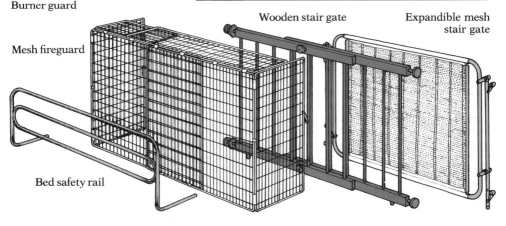

Mesh fireguard

Wooden stair gate

Expandible mesh stair gate

Bed safety rail

ROOM-BY-ROOM SAFETY

GENERAL TIPS

• Buy all medicines in childproof bottles, and always keep them out of the reach of your child in a locked medicine chest.

• Always keep medicines and chemicals in the clearly labelled containers they originally came in. Never put a poison into a bottle which previously held something harmless like lemonade or syrup.

• Store all drugs and chemicals as far away from food as possible.

• Don't leave aerosol cans lying around – your child could easily depress the nozzle and damage his eyes.

• Always keep a firescreen in front of a fire.

• Make sure the cords on electrical appliances are out of the reach of your child.

• All electrical cords should be in good condition and not frayed or otherwise damaged.

• Fit safety socket covers on all plugs.

• Cover hot radiators and pipes with towels or seal them off with pieces of furniture. Teach your child from an early age that radiators are hot and shouldn't be touched.

• Screen and bar all upper floor windows and never leave anything your child could climb up on near them.

• If you own a gun always store it, with its ammunition, in a locked cupboard.

• Keep pins, needles, matches, lighters, sharp knives and scissors out of the reach of your child, in a locked or childproof drawer.

• Buy flame-resistant clothing for your child.

• Your furniture should be too solid and heavy for your child to pull over.

The bathroom

☐ Make sure you can open your bathroom door from the outside.

☐ Medicines, scissors and razor blades should be out of your child's reach.

☐ Don't leave perfumes and cosmetics lying around.

☐ Keep the toilet lid closed.

☐ When you run your child's bath, always run the cold first so there's no risk of his being scalded; test the water before putting your child in.

☐ Fit handles to the sides of the bath.

☐ Use a non-slip bath mat.

☐ Have a non-slip floor surface.

☐ Teach your child how to swim as soon as possible.

☐ Windows should be barred and fitted with safety catches.

☐ The bathroom cabinet must have a childproof lock and be out of the reach of your child.

☐ Don't fit a bathroom cabinet above the toilet – your child could climb up on the seat and open it.

☐ Never leave your child alone in the bath.

☐ Electrical bathroom heaters should be fixed high on the wall.

☐ Hot towel rails should be covered with towels. Your child should be taught that they're hot at as young an age as possible.

☐ Don't mix toilet bowl cleaners with bleach, as they can give off dangerous fumes.

☐ Keep all cleaning agents, bleaches and disinfectants in a locked cupboard.

All heaters should be wall-mounted

Put heated towel rails out of your child's reach

Have a childproof lock on the medicine cabinet

Put safety handles on the bath

Have non-slip bath mats

Keep the toilet lid closed

Lock away all cleaning substances

The kitchen

☐ The floors should be non-slip.
☐ All work surfaces should be well lit.
☐ The floor should be uncluttered.
☐ Large doors and windows should be made of tempered, safety glass.
☐ Try to use sliding doors on cabinets. If this isn't possible, keep the doors closed and preferably locked.
☐ Keep drawers closed and locked if possible.
☐ Always wipe up spilled liquid at once.
☐ Keep work surfaces as clear as possible so that sharp implements such as knives can be spotted immediately.
☐ Fit a burner guard on the stove.
☐ Never leave a boiling pot or a hot frying pan unattended on the stove.
☐ Always turn the handles of pans toward the back of the stove.
☐ Never reach across a heated burner; you could knock a pan off the stove.
☐ Whenever using electrical equipment always follow the manufacturer's instructions exactly.
☐ Don't use tablecloths. Even a crawling baby can reach up and pull whatever's on the table on top of himself.
☐ Keep matches in a safe, cool place.
☐ Don't cook with your toddler around you. Arrange a play area in a special part of the kitchen so you can still talk to each other.
☐ Keep the cords on any electrical equipment short.
☐ Don't store things you use frequently on a high shelf. When you have to reach into a high place, stand on a well-made kitchen ladder, and make sure your balance is good before you reach up.
☐ Always keep cloths away from the stove in case of fire.
☐ Buy a dishwasher or washing machine with a safety lock on it.
☐ Keep a fiberglass cloth next to the stove in case anything catches fire.
☐ Keep plastic bags well out of reach of your child.
☐ Your child's fingers could easily catch in a swing door. Either remove it or secure it in an open position.

☐ Never leave a room with the iron on; it's all too easy for your child to topple both board and iron on top of himself.
☐ Glasses that your child uses should be unbreakable.

Never leave a boiling pot unattended

Keep a fiberglass cloth near the cooker

Always use a burner guard

Have childproof locks on dishwashers and washing machines

Have a special play area for your child

Keep your baby and his toys away from the immediate cooking area so there's no risk of your tripping and spilling hot liquid over him. Put him either in a play pen, baby bouncer or chair.

☐ If you put your child in a play pen in the kitchen make sure it's at least two feet away from your work tops.
☐ Store all cleaning materials – bleach or soap powders – out of reach of your child.

Store all cleaning substances out of reach

Keep knives away from your child

Put pets' bowls out of your child's reach

Make clear glass more obvious by putting transfers on it

Don't have long cords on electrical appliances

The living room

☐ Run electrical cords around the walls.
☐ Disconnect appliances when not in use.
☐ Keep wires on electrical appliances short.
☐ Don't place hot or heavy objects on low tables.
☐ All shelving should be securely fixed to the walls and should be well out of the reach of your child.
☐ Anything breakable should be out of the reach of your child.

☐ Use a fixed fire guard with a fine wire mesh.
☐ Fit safety glass to windows, especially French windows, so that it won't shatter even if your child falls on it.
☐ Never leave hot or alcoholic drinks lying around within reach of your child.
☐ Don't leave lighters or matches lying about.
☐ Keep the television out of reach.
☐ Make sure your houseplants aren't poisonous (see p. 300).

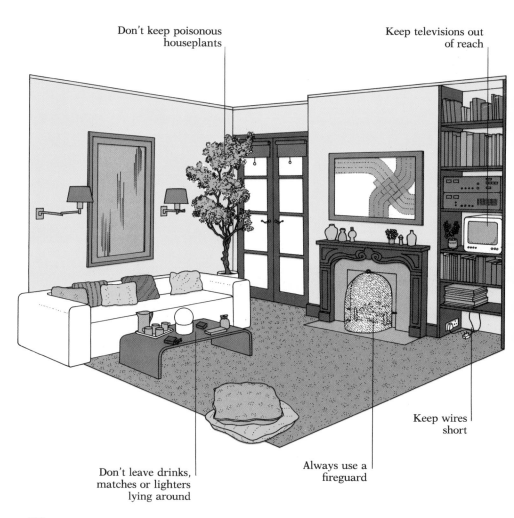

Don't keep poisonous houseplants

Keep televisions out of reach

Keep wires short

Don't leave drinks, matches or lighters lying around

Always use a fireguard

The bedroom

□ Put bars and safety locks on all windows and don't leave furniture near them.
□ All furniture should have rounded corners; if they don't, put on special plastic safety corners.
□ Store toys and games at a low level so your child doesn't have to stretch or climb up to get at them.
□ Don't leave toys lying around on the floor.
□ Don't put an electrical fire anywhere near your child's bed at night because he could throw off his blanket or quilt and cause a fire.
□ If the bedroom's upstairs leave a safety gate at the top of the stairs.
□ Buy non-flammable nightclothes.
□ Wall-mounted lights are safer because they have no cords trailing on the floor.
□ Never leave your baby alone when the cot side is down.
□ Never leave your baby alone on the changing table, even for a second.

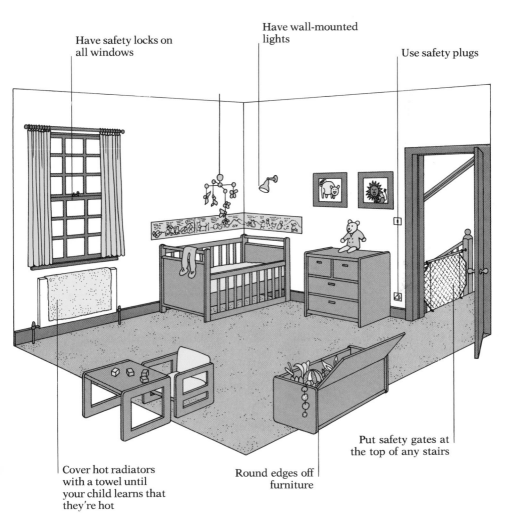

Have safety locks on all windows

Have wall-mounted lights

Use safety plugs

Cover hot radiators with a towel until your child learns that they're hot

Round edges off furniture

Put safety gates at the top of any stairs

Halls, stairs and passageways

☐ Fit a safety gate to the top and bottom of the stairs.
☐ Never leave anything lying on or near the stairs. Make sure that doors, hallways and stairs are well lit.
☐ Electric switches should be in convenient places.
☐ Bannisters should be secure and only have narrow gaps.
☐ Don't have open-plan staircases – your child could easily fall between the stairs or off to one side.
☐ Stair carpets should be fitted well so that they don't slip. Any tears or holes should be patched immediately with heavy-duty tape.

The yard

☐ Have childproof locks on all gates.
☐ Fence off a swimming pool or pond.
☐ Never leave a wading pool with water in it; empty it and either deflate it or store it upside down.
☐ Fit any rainwater collecting devices with a lid. Your child can drown in as little as two inches (5 cm) of water.
☐ Remove all poisonous plants.
☐ Pull up all mushrooms or toadstools as soon as they appear.
☐ Bury any animal excreta before your child has the chance to play with it or eat it.
☐ Store all gardening tools in a locked shed.

POISONOUS PLANTS
▲ *Causes skin irritation*
■ *Causes mouth- and throat-lining irritation*
● *Causes stomach and intestinal irritation*
◆ *Causes poisoning of the system*

Poison oak

Houseplants	
Caladium	
Castor Bean	● ◆
Dieffenbachia	▲ ■
Elephant's ear	▲ ■
Mistletoe	● ◆ ■
Philodendron	▲ ■
Poinsettia	▲

Ivy	●
Laurel	◆
Oleander	◆
Rhododendron	◆
Wisteria	●
Yew	●

Jack-in-the-Pulpit	■ ●
Mayapple	◆
Moonseed	◆
Poison Ivy	▲
Poison Oak	▲
Rosary Pea	◆
Snakeroot	● ◆
Yellow Jessamine	◆

Poinsettia

Rhododendron

Ornamental	
Bleeding Heart	▲ ■ ◆
Daphne	▲ ■ ●

Forest Growth	
Baneberry	● ◆
Bittersweet	● ◆
Bloodroot	● ◆
Deadly Amanita	◆
Fly Agaric Mushroom	◆

Flower Garden	
Autumn Crocus	◆
Belladonna Lily	● ◆
Christmas Rose	▲ ●
Daffodil	●
Foxglove	▲
Hyacinth	◆
Hydrangea	● ◆
Iris	◆
Larkspur	◆
Lily of the Valley	◆ ◆

☐ When mowing the lawn keep your toddler well away.

☐ Never tinker with your car when your child is playing outside.

☐ Your clothesline should be strung above your child's reach.

☐ Lock away all pesticides, plant sprays and car cleaners.

☐ Never leave lengths of rope lying about.

☐ Fence off your trash cans so your child can't rummage about inside them.

☐ Make regular checks on the safety of any swings, slides or Jungle Jims in your garden.

ROAD SAFETY
It's never too early to teach your child the safety code for crossing the road. Whenever you want to cross the street always go to a pedestrian crossing. Stop by the curb, hold your child's reins or hand, look in both directions for traffic and listen. If traffic is coming, let it pass. Look in both directions again and when nothing is coming walk across; don't run. Continue to look and listen as you cross. Keep up a running commentary on what you're doing and why. Make sure your child understands why you're looking.

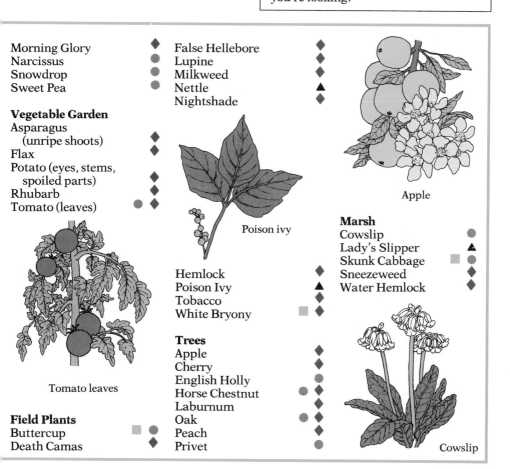

Morning Glory
Narcissus
Snowdrop
Sweet Pea

Vegetable Garden
Asparagus
  (unripe shoots)
Flax
Potato (eyes, stems,
  spoiled parts)
Rhubarb
Tomato (leaves)

Tomato leaves

Field Plants
Buttercup
Death Camas

False Hellebore
Lupine
Milkweed
Nettle
Nightshade

Poison ivy

Hemlock
Poison Ivy
Tobacco
White Bryony

Trees
Apple
Cherry
English Holly
Horse Chestnut
Laburnum
Oak
Peach
Privet

Apple

Marsh
Cowslip
Lady's Slipper
Skunk Cabbage
Sneezeweed
Water Hemlock

Cowslip

301

EMERGENCY FIRST AID

A basic knowledge of first aid is always useful; the ability to act quickly and efficiently could save your child's life in an extreme situation.

Choking

The best thing to do with a small baby is to hold him by his feet so that he's hanging upside down, and then pat his back between the shoulder blades to dislodge the foreign body from his windpipe. With an older child, hold him firmly around the waist and tip him forward over your arm until his head is at about the level of your knee. Then go through the same procedure as described for a baby, sharply hitting his back between the shoulder blades until he coughs up the object. Your child may only cough the object into his mouth. To prevent reinhalation, hold his head and chin steady with your left hand and hook the object out with the forefinger of your right hand. Be very careful not to push whatever's in his mouth back down his throat. If you're still concerned about your child, seek medical aid immediately.

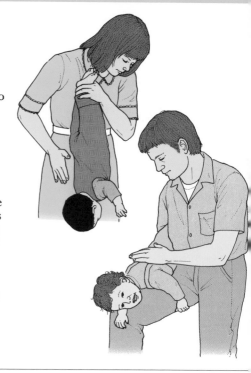

Heavy bleeding

1 Take any piece of clean cloth and press the edges of the wound together until the blood clots and stops.

2 If there's a bone protruding, or if there's something in the wound like glass, press round rather than on it.

3 Lay your child on the ground and raise the affected limb above the level of his body. Cutting down on the amount of blood that gets to the limb and speeding the flow of blood to the vital organs (brain, heart, kidneys) will counter the risk of shock. Contact your doctor as soon as possible because the wound will probably need stitching.

4 If your child is bleeding from a place that is difficult to compress, like the groin, lay him down and flatten the blood vessel that is bleeding by pressing your fist or the heel of your hand against the underlying bone.

Unconsciousness

1 First check that your child is still breathing and that you can feel his pulse. The best place to feel his pulse is the carotid artery, located a short way under the jaw in line with the tip of the ear lobe.

2 Having done this, put your child into the recovery position. Turn him on to his stomach and bend one of his arms up to support the upper body. Bend his knee up to support the lower body and turn his head to one side. Dial for an ambulance immediately. If your child isn't breathing you must give him mouth-to-mouth resuscitation.

Mouth-to-mouth resuscitation

1 Tuck your child's head back so that the air passages are open, and check that nothing is blocking his throat.

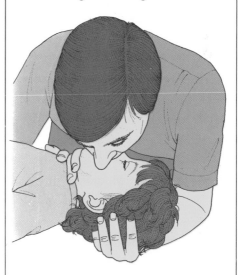

2 Put your mouth over his nose *and* his mouth and breathe gently into his lungs at a rate of 20 breaths per minute. Check his breathing after four inflations. Continue doing this until breathing starts again, then place him in the recovery position. If your baby is unconscious, follow the same procedure but breathe into the lungs at a rate of 24 breaths per minute. Dial for medical assistance as soon as possible or take your child straight to a hospital.

Electric shock

Switch off the power source immediately. If you cannot locate the power source *don't* touch your child; you could get a shock yourself. Find something which does not conduct electricity, such as a piece of wood or plastic tubing, and use it to push your child away from the wire or socket. Make sure that you and whatever you use are both dry before you do this. If his breathing has stopped send for medical help, then give mouth-to-mouth resuscitation.

Sometimes an electric shock can cause medical shock, with low blood pressure, thready pulse, pale face, clammy skin, sweating, dizziness and rapid breathing. If this is the case take your child immediately to the nearest hospital emergency room. If it's only a frightening shock, reassure your child and then lie with him until he has settled down.

Burns

1 Since fire rises, your child will only make matters worse if he runs around in a panic. If he's on fire, put him on the ground as quickly as possible.

2 Unless you have water near at hand to throw over the flames, you'll have to smother them by covering the child in a blanket, towel or coat. Don't use synthetic fabrics as these will melt when they're in contact with the heat.

3 If nothing else is available, lie on the child yourself to smother the flames, but make sure you lie flat or you will create a tunnel that could cause the flames to fan up and set you on fire too. Have your child examined by a doctor as soon as possible.

Drowning

If possible, send someone for help. Remove your child from the water, lay him on his back, and give mouth-to-mouth resuscitation, *even* if you think your child is dead. Continue doing this until medical assistance arrives.

Poisoning

If you even suspect that your child has swallowed a poison, contact your local hospital or poison center immediately. Your child may have severe stomach pains and will probably vomit. Hold him in such a way that there's no risk of his inhaling and choking on any vomit. *Never* attempt to induce vomiting in your child – you could cause more harm if what he's swallowed is corrosive. Corrosive substances include caustic soda, weed killers, paraffin, disinfectant, bleach and other ammonia-based household cleaners. Look for signs of burning around his mouth – if you see them, he's probably swallowed one of these substances. Give him water or milk to cool the burning.

If your child is unconscious, place him in the recovery position; if he has stopped breathing, give him mouth-to-mouth resuscitation, taking care not to burn your own mouth.

Broken bones

Don't move your child, especially if you suspect that he may have injured his back or neck. Make him as comfortable as possible and steady the affected limb. Call for medical assistance immediately.

FIRST AID KIT

1 A packet of absorbent cotton wool
2 Sterile gauze squares in various sizes
3 A box of adhesive dressings in various sizes
4 A roll of 2 in. (5 cm) gauze bandage
5 2 or 3 crêpe bandages
6 A roll of 1 in. (2.5 cm) adhesive tape
7 A sterilized eye pad with bandages
8 Triangular bandage made of a stiff material
9 Safety pins
10 Blunt-ended tweezers
11 Blunt-ended scissors
12 Soluble baby aspirin
13 Milk of magnesia for indigestion
14 Sun screen with the highest protection factor
15 Junior paracetamol elixir
16 Calamine lotion
17 A bottle of surgical spirit for cleaning wounds
18 Insect-repellant spray
19 A simple antiseptic cream, such as a 2% cetrimide cream

305

17 Home medicine

Any parent is going to be distressed when his or her child becomes ill. The difficulty can lie in not being able to identify what's wrong with the child and in not being able to tell how serious the ailment really is. All children get ill at some stage, but, thanks to modern medicine, few illnesses now pose the threat they once did. Doctors are on hand to identify the ailment and prescribe treatment. Your job as the parent is to provide the essential nursing and comfort.

WHEN TO CALL YOUR DOCTOR   0–3

You must start off believing that most doctors take your concern seriously. Along with many other doctors, I quickly learned that one person whose opinion can't be dismissed is the mother's. A mother usually knows instinctively if her child is well or not. And if any sensible mother feels strongly enough that her child is unwell, then a doctor ignores this at his or her peril. One indication of illness in a child is unusual behavior – not eating as usual, being rather quiet or not as boisterous as usual. Only a person who is close to the child can pick up these early warning signs. So your guideline should be, when in doubt, consult your doctor. This is particularly true if any of the following warning signs is noted:

Temperature
● If the temperature rises above 100°F (38°C), and there are apparent signs of illness.
● If the temperature rises above 103°F (39.4°C), even if there are no apparent signs of illness.
● When a fever, having been high, drops and then rises again.
● When the temperature is accompanied by infantile convulsions (see p. 318).
● When your child has a stiff neck and a headache as well as a fever.
● When your child has had a temperature of more than 100°F (38°C), for three days.
● Your baby's face, hands and feet seem normal, but his skin feels cold and he is drowsy, unusually quiet and limp (possibly hypothermia).

Wounds
● When your child has had any kind of serious accident or burn.
● When your child has lost consciousness, no matter how briefly.
● When the wound is deep or has caused serious loss of blood.
● When your child has been bitten by an animal, a human or a snake.
● When acid gets into your child's eye.
● When the eye has actually been pierced by an object.

Pain and discomfort
● When your child feels sick and dizzy and complains of headaches.
● When your child complains of blurred vision, especially after being hit on the head.
● When your child has severe pains at regular intervals.
● When your child has a pain in the right side of his stomach and feels sick.

Breathing
● If your child's breathing becomes labored and his ribs are being drawn sharply inward with each breath.

307

Loss of appetite

- If your child's normally a good eater.
- If your baby's under six months.

Vomiting

- If the vomiting is violent, prolonged or excessive.
- If your baby is very young – it may cause rapid dehydration.

Diarrhoea

- If your baby's very young – it could cause dehydration.
- If it's accompanied by abdominal pain, temperature or obvious signs of illness.

What to tell your doctor

Once you've decided to call your doctor, he or she will probably ask you the following questions. It's important to give accurate answers.

☐ "What is the baby's temperature and were there any fluctuations in it – if so, what were the readings?"
☐ "Was the onset of the fever quick or slow?"
☐ "Is the child's throat red? Does it have any white spots?"
☐ "Are the neck glands swollen?"
☐ "Are there any additional symptoms like vomiting or diarrhoea?"

USING A THERMOMETER   0–3

Your child's temperature will probably fluctuate between 97.5°F and 99.5°F (36°C and 37.5°C). It will be at its lowest at night when your child is asleep and highest in the afternoon; it will also be high if your child has been running around.

Although you'll probably be able to tell if your child is feverish just by looking at him, there may be occasions when you have to take his temperature. Don't, however, rely on the thermometer reading as an accurate reflection of your baby's health. Children can be ill with no fever, or well with a high temperature.

You must not take your child's temperature by mouth until you're absolutely sure that he can be trusted not to bite down and break the glass. This is usually not until he's about six or seven years old, but the age does vary.

Types of thermometer available

The two types of thermometer available at present are the mercury style and the heat-sensitive style. Until your child is about five, use the stubby-ended rectal thermometer. Make sure you buy one with the shortest reading time – some take only 30 seconds. It's also possible to buy special baby thermometers which give readings down to 77°F (25°C). This is good to have in the house because babies lose heat more rapidly than adults and can have a lower temperature when ill.

The other style of thermometer is the strip or disc of heat-sensitive material which you press flush to the forehead. In 15 seconds either the color changes, an F (Fever) or an N (normal) appears, or the actual temperature registers. This method isn't as accurate as a mercury thermometer, but it does give a quick and easy indication of whether or not your child has a temperature.

Reading a mercury thermometer

Rotate the thermometer between your first finger and thumb until you can see the mercury column clearly. This is not as easy as it sounds because you will see a thin line when the column is viewed from the side and a thick line when it's viewed straight on. It is the thick line you should observe. On the front of the thermometer you will see a scale with a small arrow at 98.6°F (36.9°C). This is the average, normal body temperature.

Before taking your baby's temperature always check to make sure the column of mercury is down below the beginning of the scale. Having taken your child's temperature for the required amount of time, remove the thermometer, wipe it, and read it. Wash it with soap and cold water before storing.

TAKING A TEMPERATURE READING
By thermometer
Rotate the thermometer until you see a thick strip of mercury. Read the temperature off the mercury column.

Normal temperature

By heat strip
Follow the manufacturer's instructions. The strip generally lights up according to the temperature registered.

Normal temperature

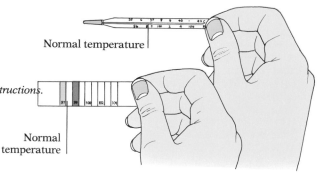

Taking your child's temperature

Taking your child's temperature rectally is the most efficient way, although you may need some help to do it initially. If you're in doubt, ask your doctor to show you how. Two methods of taking temperature rectally are shown below; use the one you're most confident with.

As your child gets older it's possible to take his temperature by placing the thermometer underneath his arm, in his armpit. This method can be used with younger children if you really don't want to use the rectal method.

RECTAL METHOD

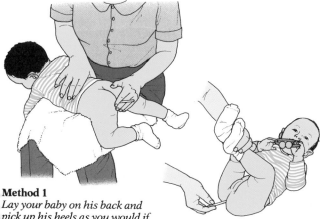

Method 1
Lay your baby on his back and pick up his heels as you would if you were changing his diaper. Having first lubricated the tip of the thermometer with a little baby cream or vaseline, push it gently no more than one inch (2.5 cm) into the rectum. Leave it for at least two minutes.

Method 2
Lay your baby across your lap

with one hand pressing down on the baby's back to prevent him from moving. Gently insert the thermometer, lubricated as before, but this time slip it between your first and second finger and gently keep it in place by resting your palm on the baby's buttocks. Don't grip the thermometer too firmly.

ARMPIT METHOD

Put the bulb of the thermometer in the center of your child's armpit and bring the arm back to the side of his body to secure it. Hold it in this position for two minutes.

GIVING MEDICINE 0–1

Most baby medicines are prepared as syrups which have to be taken with a spoon or dropper. With a newborn baby, make sure that any implements used have been sterilized in a sterilizing solution. Your baby may start to cry when he takes the medicine, but don't worry – it's far more important that he swallow it and keep it down. When a child is ill, the importance of taking medicine outweighs every other consideration. This is one situation where blackmail is justifiable. When necessary, use the most powerful reward you can think of to get your baby to accept the medicine.

USING A DROPPER

Cradle your baby in the crook of your arm so that his head is slightly upright – never have him lying flat because this makes swallowing difficult. Fill the dropper with the specified amount of medicine. Place the dropper in the corner of your baby's mouth and gently compress the nipple.

USING A SPOON

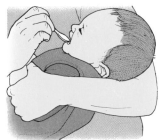

Sterilize the spoon. Sit with your baby on your lap and gently open your baby's mouth by pulling down his chin. Place the tip of the spoon on his lower lip, raise the angle of the spoon and gently let the medicine run into his mouth at the right speed for comfortable swallowing.

USING YOUR FINGER

If both the dropper and the spoon prove ineffective, try dipping a carefully-washed little finger into your baby's medicine and letting him suck it off. It's more important that your baby take the medicine than that he take it in an orthodox way.

ADMINISTERING DROPS

 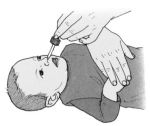 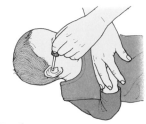

Eye drops
Pull down his lower lid and let the drops fall between his eye and the eyelid. Get someone to hold the baby still.

Nose drops
Lay your baby on a flat surface and angle his head backward. Gently drop the liquid into each nostril.

Ear drops
Lay your child on his side before administering the drops in the usual way.

GIVING MEDICINE   1–3

Medicines for older children usually come in tablets which are swallowed, or in liquids, which are taken off a spoon. Ear and nose drops are administered in the same way for babies and adults. If your child is making a great deal of fuss about having drops, you *must* stay calm. Get your partner to help you hold the child firmly while you administer the drops.

As your child gets older, try not to be too insistent that he take medicine, since this will only make him more obstinate in his refusal. It usually helps to show your child that you are willing to take some yourself. If he really doesn't like the taste, try diluting it with his favorite drink.

Giving tablets

If the doctor prescribes tablets for your child, make them more palatable by crushing them between two spoons and then mixing them with a spoonful of honey, jam or ice cream. Whatever the medicine, make sure to follow your doc-

tor's instructions precisely, giving the medicine at the required times. This is important because some medicines have to stay at a certain level in the blood, and the level will drop if the interval between doses is too long.

Put the tablets between two spoons, as shown, and press down on them. Mix the tablets with honey, jam or thick yogurt and give this to your child.

NURSING YOUR CHILD   0–3

All mothers are called on to act as nurse, since all children fall ill at one time or another. Mothers make excellent nurses because they put the health and comfort of their children before almost anything else. Many children become "momish" when they are ill and want to be with their mothers all the time. Very often it's not just the mother's company they require but the mother's physical contact. Ill babies need a lot more nursing, cuddling and affection than usual. If you're still breast-feeding, you'll probably find that your baby wants more "comfort sucks." Make sure that these are given.

Should he go to bed?

Unless your doctor advises otherwise, trust your own common sense and your child's natural inclinations. If he wants to stay up, he should be allowed to do so, even if he has a temperature. But do make

sure he gets plenty to drink so he doesn't become dehydrated. Also make sure he rests when he feels tired, and that his room temperature is a fairly constant 72°F (22°C).

One of the most potent medicines is the sight and sound of you and the reassurance they bring, so keep your sick child as close to you as possible. Let him rest on a couch, sofa or chair in whatever room you happen to be in – including your bedroom. This way, your child will be able to see, talk to, and be entertained by anyone who comes into the house, rather than be cut off from the rest of the family in his bedroom. When he's tired, however, it's time to put him to bed. But don't just leave him alone. Visit him at regular intervals (about every half an hour), and find the time to stay and play a game, read a book, or do a puzzle. If you have other children, encourage them to do the same thing.

When he's on the road to recovery, make sure he's kept busy enough that he can distinguish between night and day. If he hasn't been watching television, let him watch it before he goes to sleep. Then read him a story to calm and quiet him, as you would usually do.

Feeding your sick child

There are no longer any hard and fast rules about the sorts of food you should give a sick child; unless directed by your doctor, you can feed him whatever he wants. It's time for you to relax most of the rules, dietary and otherwise. Let him eat and drink what he wants, and as much as he wants. You'll probably find that he prefers to be fed little but often. If he loses interest in food, never force him to eat. For two or three days, food really isn't important, but liquids are. If your child has a temperature, and especially if he's vomiting, make sure he drinks plenty of liquids (at least two pints a day). The most nutritious liquids are milk and fresh fruit juices. If your child isn't keen on milk, serve it in a milk shake, a flavored drink, custard, ice cream, or yogurt. Fresh fruit juices, with all their vitamins and minerals, are excellent, so indulge your child in his favorites. There is nothing especially nutritious about the fizzy glucose drinks that are recommended.

Your child may eat little while he's ill, but he'll quickly make it up as his appetite increases. The return of his appetite is an invariable sign that your child is on his way to recovery. At this point, feel free to spoil him with his favorite foods and those that have been previously limited to treats. He'll be anxious to make up for all the lost meals, and any weight loss will be made up quickly.

Treating your child's temperature

The first thing to do is make sure your baby is not wearing too many clothes. Remove a few layers if he is. Also make sure that he's not covered by more than a few blankets, and that there's a good supply of fresh air in the room (by leaving a window open slightly).

A good method of reducing your child's temperature if it's above 103°F (39.4°C) is by tepid sponging. This means exactly what it says: wiping your child's skin down with lukewarm water. Check your child's temperature every ten minutes when you are doing this and stop when the temperature falls below 102°F (38.5°C). There's no risk of chilling him if you stop as soon as this temperature is reached.

Cover a waterproof sheet with a towel and lay your child on it. Fill a basin with lukewarm water. Dip a sponge or a soft flannel into the tepid water and gently rub it all over your child's skin – first the face and then the trunk and the limbs. Tepid water allows the blood vessels to stay dilated. When it evaporates from the surface of the skin, it absorbs heat from the blood and has a cooling effect. Don't think you will bring down the temperature faster by using cold water. You may, in fact, cause the temperature to rise, since cold water causes the blood vessels of the skin to contract, and the blood cannot lose heat efficiently. The faster the rate of evaporation, the greater the cooling effect, so if you have a fan, use it on your child – it may help to bring his temperature down.

After tepid sponging, make sure your child's skin is dry. Do not dress him in pajamas but cover him lightly with a cotton sheet. If his temperature rises again, repeat the tepid sponging.

Keeping your child isolated?

We now know that there's no point in practising the old-fashioned rule of isolating a child with an infectious disease from the rest of the family. This practice, which involved sterilizing all utensils and cleaning his laundry in a separate wash is now considered pointless, since most infections are caught and passed on within 48 hours, during which time the symptoms are very often unclear. Chances are that by the time your child develops a fever, the other members of the family will have been exposed to the bacterium or virus anyway, and will be carrying it themselves.

Keeping your sick child amused

When your child is ill, relax all rules. Let him play whatever games he wants to, even if you've previously forbidden them. If he wants to paint, put a polythene sheet across the bed. Be flexible about tidiness – the bedroom is bound to get messy, but don't make a fuss about it.

Your child could easily get bored lying in bed, especially if he's not well enough to play by himself. If you can, move a television into his room – it will provide him with ready stimulation and make him feel special, which will do a lot to keep his spirits up. Leave him a remote control device, or be near at hand so you can switch channels for him. Whatever else you do, give him your company. Sit on the side of his bed, cut pictures out of magazines for him, help him with his coloring book, play games, sing songs, chat, read a story – just be there. You're the best cure there is. As your child's nurse, you're in a unique position to please your patient, and you should devote yourself completely to this task.

COMFORT AND RECUPERATION TIPS

● Give your child treats. For a sore throat give ice cream; for queaziness give mashed potato.

● Cool cotton sheets are soothing to a feverish child. Change the bed regularly.

● When your child is vomiting, stay with him, and cover his forehead with the palm of your hand. Give him something like a mint or a chocolate to suck afterward to take away the bad taste.

● Put a table next to his bed for his toys, books, fruit juice or water.

● Make an "invalid's work table" by cutting a semi-circle out of an inverted cardboard box and placing it over your child's lap. Or put a sanded wooden plank over two chairs, on either side of the bed.

● Buy some new toys for your child. Don't give them to him all at once, but one at a time.

● If your child isn't feeling too ill, wrap the toys up before you give them to him. Ask him to guess what's in the packages by feeling them, then let him have the fun of tearing off the paper.

If your child has to go to hospital

It's likely that your child will have to go into hospital at some point, although most hospitals try to avoid admitting children under the age of four because the effect is so unsettling, both to the child and to the parents. If, however, your child has to go, the following advice may make the situation less traumatic.

☐ Don't lie to your child about what will happen. Explain why he's got to go, but tell him you'll see him most of the time he's there.

☐ Go with your child to the hospital. Well-run wards allow the parent to undress the child. They sometimes even provide beds for parents so they can stay with the child for the length of his stay. Try to get your child admitted to such a hospital.

☐ Make sure you pack your child's comforter if he has one, as well as some of his favorite toys and games. This is very important. The worst aspect of going into hospital is the change in routine – being taken away from all that's familiar, and the people he loves and trusts the most.

☐ Expect your child to behave slightly out of character when he comes out of the hospital. The stay may affect his sleeping habits as well as his bowel and bladder control. Take account of this; your child will gradually return to normal.

☐ If you know your child is going into the hospital, introduce him to the idea of it during play. Buy a toy stethoscope and practice being a doctor on your child's teddy bear or dolls. Get your child to handle your "instruments" and play at being doctor.

☐ Explain what hospitals are all about – how people go there to get better (explain that even animals have hospitals, too). Make hospitals seem as natural to your child as fire stations or supermarkets.

☐ Include books on hospitals or doctors in your child's "library." The more he reads and sees about hospitals the less frightening the experience will be.

MEDICAL INDEX

Asthma

Asthma is allergic reaction that affects the lining of the air passages. This lining is very sensitive – it responds to the allergen not only with wheezing, but with an increased susceptibility to infection. The lining of the air passages goes into spasm and secretes large amounts of mucus. This makes it difficult for your child to breathe, so that his face becomes pale and his lips turn blue. The allergen that causes this to happen will be something your child has inhaled, such as dust, pollen, feathers or fungal spores. As mentioned on page 316, many small babies wheeze if they have an attack of bronchitis or bronchiolitis (inflammation of the smaller tubes). This wheezing should not be confused with asthma. They are not the same. Wheezing is not caused by an allergy and will stop when the child grows bigger and his bronchial tubes expand. This condition is not allergic in origin.

What to do
If attacks of asthma persist, ask your doctor to refer you to a specialist. As your child gets older, the doctor will probably expose him to various allergens to determine whether he is hypersensitive to any specific substance. If a substance is isolated, you can then do everything possible to avoid it. If your child is sensitive to feathers and house dust, for instance (both of these are very common causes of allergy), you can get rid of all bedding which contains feathers, down or hair, and you can keep furnishings, carpets and curtains in your child's room free from dust. The key to this allergy is a small mite (the house dust mite) which lives in house dust. There are nearly always more mites in damp houses than in dry ones, so you must keep your home as dry as you can.

Emotional factors also sometimes play a role in asthma. While asthmatic children tend to be very bright and intelligent, they also tend to be very sensitive. They need a lot of care and attention. If your pediatrician suggests that emotional factors are playing an important part in your child's asthma, it's up to you and your family to see what you can do about improving the atmosphere in the home and minimizing the stress in your child's life.

It's very important that you and the rest of the family keep asthma in perspective. Many parents of asthmatic children are so over-anxious and over-protective, the whole household revolves around the asthmatic child. This is an unwise way to behave, since your child may use his attacks as a way of manipulating you.

The treatment of asthma is complicated, so be sure to get very clear instructions from the pediatrician on what to do under certain circumstances. Make sure you know what to do if an asthma attack comes on suddenly, out of the blue.

Bites

The chances of your child being bitten by a domestic animal, like a dog, or by another child are relatively high; the chances of your child being bitten by a snake depend of course on where you live.

What to do
The treatment given for a cat, dog or other mammal bite depends on the depth of the wound and on whether or not your child's tetanus inoculation is up to date. If the bite is superficial, clean the wound and bandage it if necessary. If the wound is serious, however, or on your child's face, then you *must* see your doctor. He will need to know the date of your child's last tetanus shot and, if necessary, give him a booster. Bites from other children usually need only be cleaned and bandaged, but if you're worried, don't hesitate to contact your doctor.

If your child is bitten by a snake, get him to a hospital or poison center immediately. Don't let him walk or sit – lay him flat on the seat of your car. If possible, identify the snake. If you are in an area where poisonous snakes are prevalent, seek advice as to whether you should keep emergency serum on hand.

Blisters

Blisters are formed as a protection to the body where it has been chaffed, burned or rubbed.

What to do
A blister should be left alone. Never prick it; leave it intact as long as you can. If a blister is in an exposed area, simply cover it with a small gauze pad kept in place with tape. The blister will subside of its own accord and the skin will become dry and fairly hard. It will change its color to a rather dark pink and it will gradually fall off. Don't do *anything* to disturb this natural process.

Bronchitis and pneumonia

Bronchitis is frequently caused by complications in the aftermath of infectious childhood diseases (see p. 331) like measles and whooping cough. What happens is that the infecting organism enters the lungs and weakens their defences. The bronchial tubes become inflamed and produce a lot of mucus. The lungs begin to function less efficiently. The mucus, which can't be expelled, becomes infected. The initial signs of bronchitis or pneumonia are an increased breathing rate; difficult breathing, and a rather bluish color around the mouth. When mucus begins to pool in a small air passage, the deeper part of the lung below this blockage becomes sealed off. The mucus may collect to the extent that it renders a small section of the lung completely solid; this area then has pneumonia. If a larger air passage becomes blocked off, the area with pneumonia can be quite extensive.

What to do
If you notice any of the symptoms, contact your doctor immediately. While waiting for your doctor, do the following: keep the air moist by boiling a kettle in the room. Never leave your child alone in a room with boiling water, however – stay with him, and try to make him feel comfortable and secure. Support your baby's back by leaning him on two or three pillows – breathing will be easier in this upright position. Whatever you do, don't panic! Stay calm.

After examining your child, your doctor will probably prescribe antibiotics, which you should administer according to instruction.

Burns

It is almost inevitable that your child will burn himself on a radiator or hot tap at some stage, despite your efforts to stop him.

What to do
Leave a minor burn alone and never burst a blister. Don't apply anything to it. The best treatment is to cover the burn with a piece of clean gauze (a freshly laundered cotton handkerchief will do). Ask your doctor's advice if you are worried.

If your child has been severely burned he must be taken to the nearest hospital emergency room for proper treatment.

Catarrh and runny nose

Neither persistent yellow catarrh (catarrh which continues for more than five or six days), nor a runny nose are normal. Both of these signs indicate that your child may be suffering from chronic sinusitis or a chronic infection of the nose and throat. Both need consultation with your doctor and fairly rigorous treatment with antibiotics. If this doesn't work, ask your doctor to refer your child to an ear, nose and throat specialist.

What to do
As the ear, nose, throat and lungs are connected by a very small set of tubes,

anatomically speaking, an infection in any one place can very quickly creep along the tubes to infect another. Chronic tonsillitis, for instance, will lead to chronic infections of the middle ear unless it's treated. Any of these chronic infections can cause irreparable damage to your child's health, so see your doctor if symptoms continue for more than a week.

Chickenpox

This is a relatively mild infection which children invariably catch, since it's one of the most contagious of all childhood diseases (see p. 330). Your child will be contagious from 24 hours before the spots appear to the time that they scab over. The chickenpox virus is a close relative of the one that causes shingles (herpes zoster), so adults, particularly older ones, can catch shingles from a child with chickenpox.

Chickenpox often starts with a temperature of 100°–102°F (38°–39°C). In very small children, however, there is hardly any rise in temperature; the rash may be the first sign. This will appear in waves over three or four days and will be extremely itchy. At first the spots are like dark red pimples, but within a couple of hours they will have developed a small blister on top which resembles a drop of water. This will eventually scab over and drop off. The rash usually starts on the trunk and then spreads to the face, the scalp, the arms and the legs. In the worst cases, it can also appear inside the mouth, nose, ears, vagina and anus.

What to do
The most important thing to do is to stop your child from scratching the spots. If you don't, the scabs may come off and the resulting wound may become infected and leave a scar. The best treatment for this is calamine lotion, applied at regular intervals. Keep your child's nails short to minimize the risk of infection. If he finds the itchiness is so intense that he can't get to sleep, ask your doctor for a sedative. If your child is still wearing diapers, leave them off as much as possible.

Colds

A cold is caused by a virus which we cannot treat in a complete or comprehensive way. There is no known antibiotic to which the virus is sensitive, so it cannot be killed. This means it has to be overcome by the body's own defence mechanisms, which will take from 10 to 14 days, regardless of what we do.

The common cold virus infects and inflames the membranes of the nasal passages and throat. This produces the well known symptoms of sore throat and runny nose. Quite often the viral infection weakens the body and allows a secondary bacterial infection; at this point, what began as a clear nasal discharge becomes yellow and pussy. The tonsils and adenoids may become swollen and so may the glands in the neck. Tonsillitis usually requires antibiotic treatment, so consult your doctor (see p. 327). Colds are common in young children, and five or six colds a year is quite common. Babies under six months are less likely to catch colds because of the antibodies they receive from their mothers, especially if they're breast-fed.

What to do
A cold can cause quite a lot of distress in a young baby, because it may block the nose and prevent breathing during feeding. Don't let your child suffer in this way; consult your doctor as soon as possible. You will probably be given nose drops to use before each feeding, and these will keep the nasal passages clear long enough for the baby to nurse. Never use nose drops for more than a few days at a time unless your doctor prescribes it.

Because the nose, sinuses and upper air passages in an infant are all connected by very short tubes, an infection in one part can quickly spread to another. For this reason a cold in a child may rapidly become sinusitis, bronchitis, tonsillitis, and sometimes otitis media (infection of the middle ear). If your child complains of a sore throat or earache (see p. 320), consult your doctor immediately because specific antibiotic therapy will almost certainly be needed.

Older children seem to feel the tiresome symptoms of a cold less than adults. They rarely feel under the weather and seem to suffer it quite cheerfully, so there is no reason to use patented drugs and medicines in the way one might for an adult.

Cold sore/Herpes simplex

Cold sores have nothing to do with a cold other than the fact that it's the high temperature accompanying the cold which activates the virus in the skin. The herpes simplex virus lives permanently in the nerve roots buried in the skin. The virus is dormant most of the time, but if the body is heated up for any reason – a cold or any other viral infection, sunlight, or ovulation in the middle of the menstrual month – the viruses are "tickled" back into action. The first well-known symptom is an itching in the skin, followed by a tenderness and soreness in the skin, and a swelling which later turns into blisters. The blisters take about 24 to 36 hours to develop and ten to 14 days to clear up.

What to do
If you notice the herpes blisters coming up, take your child to your doctor immediately, Idoxuridine solutions are available which, if painted on to the affected area early enough, can contain or minimize the attack of herpes.

The herpes virus is passed on by direct contact. Most children who get cold sores – usually around the lips, nose, cheeks and chin – get them through adults who kiss them. If one parent has cold sores, it's quite normal for others in the family to catch the virus from him; if your child gets it, it's equally probable that he'll infect others as well.

Conjunctivitis

Conjunctivitis is an inflammation of the conjuntiva, the outer covering of the eye. It makes the eye look red, and it can feel itchy or sore.

What to do
If your child develops "a red eye," examine it first to see if there's a foreign body trapped underneath the lid – if there is, remove it. If there doesn't seem to be anything in the eye, but it remains sore and waters a great deal, keep the eye closed by covering it with a small pad of cotton wool that is held in place by two pieces of tape placed crosswise across the eye. Conjunctivitis may need specific antibiotic treatment, so take your child to your doctor.

Convulsions

We don't always know the cause for fits or convulsions, but in most children between the ages of one and three, they are caused by a rise in body temperature. Young children's brains are more easily affected by this than adults; the irritation stimulates the nerves controlling the muscles which in turn react by contracting violently. A child who is having a fit will become unconscious and twitch uncontrollably. His eyes will roll up and he may froth slightly at the mouth. His breathing will be heavy and his teeth will be firmly clamped; he may also become incontinent. When the convulsion is over, your child will fall asleep – directly, or after briefly coming to.

What to do
Never leave your child alone. Although you desperately want to call help you must stay by your child in case he is sick and inhales his vomit. This is a real hazard, so place him on his stomach with his head to one side. Loosen his clothing and remove any furniture that's near him in case he kicks against it and hurts himself. Don't try to restrain him. Don't try to place anything in his mouth. Contrary to popular belief, convulsionists rarely bite or swallow their tongues and you can do more damage by trying to prise open his jaws. Once the fit's over or he's fallen asleep call the doctor at once.

If your child has a fit of this sort you should try to prevent high fevers occurring in the future. Use tepid sponging (see p. 312), and remove extra clothing or blankets when he gets hot. Ask your doctor about the latest anti-convulsant drugs which your child might benefit from.

Coughing

Coughing is the body's natural reflex to irritation of the throat, the very back of the nose and the membranous lining of the air passages. It usually accompanies an infection of the upper airways, the throat or the sinuses. The purpose of the cough is to remove excess mucus or phlegm which has come up into the back of the throat from the lungs or the nose and sinuses. By coughing the phlegm is loosened, brought up into mouth and then swallowed. Any germs existing in it are then killed by the acid in the stomach. (A common cause of coughing at night is mucus dripping from the nose and sinuses into the back of the throat.)

What to do
A cough which is merely a response to irritation and not to the presence of excess mucus is called an unproductive cough because it doesn't cough out any phlegm. A cough which *does* get rid of the mucus is called a productive cough.

An unproductive cough serves no useful purpose and can be extremely irritating to a small child; it can even prevent sleep. It is important to differentiate between a dry, unproductive cough and a wet, productive one which produces phlegm because the treatments are entirely different.

Cough suppressant medicines are used to suppress unproductive coughs and expectorant medicines are used to help a productive cough get rid of phlegm. You should keep a bottle of cough suppressant medicine, prescribed by your doctor, in the house in case your child develops an unproductive cough.

You can ease the irritation of a night time cough by turning your child on to his side or his front, or by propping him on pillows (if he's over a year old). Never let the coughing get so severe that a pro-

longed bout of it causes your child to vomit; always consult your doctor before this happens.

A productive cough, however, should *never* be suppressed because it is serving a useful purpose. It is helping to overcome infection by clearing mucus from the air passages. A productive cough that lasts for more than 48 hours should be treated by a doctor.

Croup

Croup quite often accompanies a cold and usually only occurs in children between the ages of one and five. The name is given to the sound of air being inhaled through a constricted windpipe, past inflamed vocal cords. Your child may go to bed feeling quite well but then wake with a very tight chest and have great difficulty breathing in; exhaling will be easier.

What to do
If you notice this kind of breathing you should call your doctor immediately. On occasion the breathing can be so laboured that there's a risk of suffocation. If this is the case take your child straight to a hospital. Otherwise, stay with your child until the doctor arrives. Difficulty with breathing can be very frightening and your presence will reassure him. To make breathing easier, prop up your child in an upright position with pillows, and make sure that he is comfortable. If he's very alarmed take him on your lap, hold him firmly and try to get him to breathe with you. Listening to you breathing in and out will take his mind off his own fear – if he's relaxed his breathing will be easier. Make sure the air in your child's bedroom isn't too warm as this can dry and irritate the already inflamed air passages. Open the window and let some cool air blow in. Since humid air is soothing to the passages, take him into the bathroom with the doors and windows shut, and the hot water running in the shower. Sit him on your lap and read him a story, while the steam fills the room. When your child is in his own room boil a kettle, but never leave

it unattended. When you see your doctor, ask him for advice about treating croup, so you know how to deal with it in the future.

Cuts and grazes

Examine any wound to see if it is deep and bleeding profusely. If it is, see your doctor.

What to do
Clean the area with a diluted antiseptic solution (cetrimide 1% is a good one, and it's available at all chemists). If you don't have any, dissolve one teaspoon of salt in a glass of water and use it as a cleansing solution.

Earache

Earache is a common ailment in babies and young children. You can understand why if you know something about the structure of the ear. Think of the ear as two sections separated by a membrane, the ear drum. The first section – the auditory canal – is a passage leading from the opening of the ear to the ear drum. The second section, behind the ear drum, is called the middle ear. Inflammation of the outer ear is called otitis externa; inflammation of the middle ear is called otitis media. The Eustacian tubes, which are rather short and wide in small children, link the middle ear to the back of the throat. Their purpose is to equalize pressure in the ears, but they are often the source of ear problems in small children.

Otitis media is the most common ear ailment. Because babies spend most of their time lying down, it is easy for bacteria to travel from the nose and throat straight to the middle ear. This inflames the mucus membrane of the Eustachian tubes, causing them to become blocked. The bacteria are then trapped in the middle ear, where they multiply.

Obviously, no small child can tell you that his ear hurts, but if he has inexplicable fever, vomiting, diarrhoea and loss of appetite, and certainly if he pulls at his ear, you would be right to suspect that his ears are troubling him.

What to do
If you suspect your child has earache, call your doctor immediately. If the cause is otitis media, he will prescribe antibiotics and possibly nose drops. The antibiotics will combat the bacteria, and the nose drops will keep the Eustachian tubes from getting blocked up, and risking further infection. Never, ever put anything into your baby's ears, or apply hot compresses to the outside of the ear. Leave the treatment to your doctor. If the earache is caused by a boil, or something else in the outer ear, don't treat it yourself. Call your doctor!

Eczema

Infantile eczema often goes hand in hand with asthma, and the two are quite commonly seen together. Eczema produces a fairly generalized rash on the face, behind the knees and on the inner side of the arms and wrists. The rash is usually itchy, dry, red and scaly; in its worst state, it can ooze quite profusely. Eczema waxes and wanes; it can be brought on by a cold, a sleepless night, or an upset stomach.

Like asthma, infantile eczema is nearly always hereditary and associated with an allergy. Asthma and other allergic conditions often run through the family, so if one is allergic to penicillin, others may have asthma, eczema or hay fever.

What to do
The best treatments for infantile eczema are prescribed by pediatric dermatologists. Ask your doctor to refer your baby to a specialist so he can get the most modern treatment. An experienced dermatologist will also know when to introduce a new treatment when other medications have stopped working.

The treatment of infantile eczema is rather promising: many children improve around the age of two, and many more recover by the age of seven. Usually it will disappear by the teens, although the child always retains the possibility of developing eczema again in later life – particularly if he experiences a severe mental or physical trauma.

For the everyday care of a baby with eczema of the skin, do the following: Avoid over-bathing – soap and water are dehydrating, and cotton wool soaked with baby lotion will do just as well. Pay close attention to cleanliness, particularly around the diaper area and face. Avoid wool next to the skin – it can be irritating and make the eczema worse. Rub in the soft, mild creams and ointments that your doctor recommends. Use them exactly as prescribed.

Epilepsy

After febrile convulsions, the next most common cause of fits in children is epilepsy. Epilepsy can take two forms: petit mal and grand mal.

With petit mal your child suddenly "blanks out" for a few minutes and looks very pale and vacant. He won't fall down or become incontinent but he'll be completely unaware of his surroundings. When he snaps out of the fit he'll carry on as normal, as if nothing had happened. Contact your doctor if this ever happens.

A child suffering from grand mal exhibits exactly the same symptoms as one suffering from febrile convulsions.

What to do
Deal with either form of epilepsy in exactly the same way, then seek immediate medical advice. Your doctor will probably order a electroencephalogram (EEG) to confirm epilepsy. Studies have shown that it's psychologically inadvisable to treat children suffering from epilepsy as "epileptic." Treat your child as normal, but take certain precautions. Leave the bathroom door open in case of an attack while he's in the bath and keep a close eye on him when he's swimming or sailing.

Fingers caught in door

Until your baby learns how doors work, there's always the risk that his fingers will get caught.

What to do
If the skin is badly broken and there is serious bleeding, take your child to the nearest hospital emergency ward immediately. If the finger is bleeding profusely, place your thumb and forefinger on either side of the crushed finger just beyond the palm of the hand, at the joint where the finger starts. This will stop the blood from getting to the end of the finger, and prevent it from hemorrhaging. Don't use any other form of first aid. Don't try to put your child's hand in any particularly position; let him take up the position of maximum comfort. Don't give your child any painkillers.

If your child's pain and the swelling fingers do not subside within 24 hours, put the arm in a sling to keep the hand upright, making sure that your child moves his elbow several times an hour so it doesn't stiffen. Consult your doctor.

German measles (rubella)

This is a viral disease, like measles, but it isn't as serious or contagious (see p. 330). The initial symptoms are a mild cold with a runny nose, a sore throat, and a temperature of 100°F (38°C). The rash usually appears two days after your child starts to feel unwell. The spots start behind the ears and on the forehead before moving down the body. They're pale and flat, and not as close together as in measles. They only last for a few days. The glands on the back of your child's neck will almost always swell up and remain swollen after the rash has gone.

What to do
It's important to ask your doctor for an accurate diagnosis, not just for your child – he'll need an inoculation at puberty – but for any pregnant women with whom he has been in contact. The infection is so mild that there's nothing specific to do, other than keep your child comfortable and amused. You should, however, keep him indoors until the rash has been gone for a few days.

Gluten sensitivity

Gluten sensitivity is an allergic response to the protein contained in most cereals and grains. Unwittingly, therefore, you feed your baby with an allergen each time you give him a bowl of cereal or a slice of bread (either brown or white).

A child with gluten sensitivity initially shows a "failure to thrive." This means that he will often be sleepy and lacking in energy. He will also gain weight more slowly than usual. He will alternate between loose stools and stools of a fatty consistency which sometimes remain floating in the bowl when you try to flush them away. The allergic reaction in the lining of the bowels prevents both proper digestion and proper absorption of fatty substances. Your child may have frequent bouts of diarrhoea and be irritable much of the time. If the condition goes undiagnosed in girls, it can lead to a delay in the onset of menstruation. In its very ad-

vanced stage, gluten sensitivity, or coeliac disease, produced quite abnormal body configuration. The body and limbs will have little fat on them and the ankles may swell. The abdomen will become distended, the muscles of the legs and arms wasted, and the tongue smooth. Oddly enough, these children also tend to have long eyelashes.

Luckily, gluten sensitivity is not very common. The fact that it is caused by something as common as cereal or bread should not make you unnecessarily wary or over-anxious about your child's diet.

What to do
Once a diagnosis has been made your child has to be given a gluten-free diet, which means that wheat, rye, barley and oats will have to be excluded. A doctor or nutritionist will recommend a proper diet which your child will have to remain on for life. Once the gluten-free diet takes affect – usually in two days – you'll notice a marked improvement in the mood of your child. His appetite will improve, and he will begin to gain weight. Within a few weeks, you'll notice a change in the appearance and regularity of his stools. After being on a gluten-free diet for six months to a year, your child should be within the normal range for weight. His height will take about two years to recover.

Hives (see Urticaria)

Infectious fevers (see p. 330)

Measles

This is a highly infectious disease; it can also lead to serious complications, such as pneumonia and meningitis (see p. 331). Your child is most likely to catch the disease between the ages of one and six; it takes its most serious form under the age of three.

It generally takes one to 12 days for the symptoms to appear after your child has been infected. The first symptoms are similar to those of a normal cold – runny nose, a hoarse cough and a fever. For the first two days the temperature will be 100°–102°F (38°–39°C). It may fall briefly before rising as high as 104°F (40°C). The rash usually appears at this stage, starting off as small, scarlet-colored, slightly raised spots. These eventually merge into irregular areas of a ruddy-brown color. The rash generally starts on the throat and behind the ears, then spreads to the face and the body. Your baby's eyes may become red and sore.

What to do
Call your doctor, who will confirm that your child has measles if he finds small red spots, each with a white center, inside your child's mouth (these are known as Koplik's spots). While your child has fever, follow the general instructions for coping with high temperatures (see p. 312). Bathe his sore eyes with cotton wool soaked in lukewarm water, and dim the lights if that makes him more comfortable. He probably won't be very hungry when he's feverish, but make sure he takes adequate amounts of liquid by providing him with small but frequent drinks. If he still has a high temperature four days after the rash appears, call your doctor again. Also call him if he becomes semi-conscious or if symptoms include an earache, labored breathing, or a phlegmy cough.

Between the ages of one and two your child can be inoculated against measles (see p. 329). If he's exposed to measles before he's been inoculated, your doctor may give him gamma globulin which will either prevent the disease or reduce its severity.

Mumps

This disease is uncommon in children under five (see p. 330). When the infection does occur, however, you may first notice that your child seems under the weather. A more specific symptom will be the swelling of the glands in front of, and under the ear, on one side of your child's face. This will be accompanied by fever, during which your child may become delerious. The other side of your child's face will swell up some days later, after his temperature has fallen, and then risen sharply again. His neck will be stiff and his throat will be sore. He will complain of a very dry mouth.

What to do
Call your doctor. Although there's no specific treatment, you can do a lot to make your child comfortable. Reduce his temperature, with your doctor's approval, by tepid sponging and baby paracetamol. If your child finds it difficult to chew, feed him liquid foods; and always give him plenty to drink.

Nettle rash (see Urticaria)

Nose bleeds

Hemorrhaging from the nose is most often caused by damage to a patch of small blood vessels lying very near the surface of the skin, just inside the nostrils. This is uaually caused by nose picking or injury during rough play.

What to do
This small patch of blood vessels can bleed quite a lot, but try not to panic. Calmly hold your child's head *down*. Never hold it upright or tip it back because blood which is swallowed can irritate the stomach and cause vomiting. It will only increase the blood pressure in the head and create a tendency for the nose to bleed again.

Apply gentle pressure with your thumb and first finger on either side of the nose until bleeding has stopped. This will usually happen in two or three minutes. If nose bleeds occur quite frequently, take your child to the doctor, who may refer him to a specialist for cauterization of the delicate areas inside the nose.

Penis caught in a zipper

This unfortunate accident happened to my son, William, when he was about six years old.

What to do
Never, ever try to move the zipper yourself, either up or down, as this will only increase the injury and cause your child excruciating pain. Take your child as fast as you can to the nearest hospital emergency room. On your way to the hospital, gently place a cold water or ice compress over the zipper, unless your child objects to it. Comfort him during the ride with a single dose of paracetamol elixir.

When you get to hospital, a local anaesthetic will be injected into your child's penis. This looks more painful than it feels – so distract your child while the doctor is doing this by talking or reading to him, and concentrating his attention on you. When the penis is thoroughly numb the zipper will be undone. There will no doubt be quite a lot of bruising and swelling on your child's penis, according to the severity of the pinching. William's penis remained rather frighteningly swollen for about five days and he found it painful to urinate for about 48 hours. There was no particular treatment which we were advised to use on the torn skin. If you're extremely concerned, ask your doctor. There is no harm in applying a thin smear of 0.5% cetrimide cream, say three times a day. Let your child do it if he can. You don't have to cover over the area of broken skin.

Rashes

Most rashes are caused internally. In young children they are a classic symptom of some of the more common infectious fevers (see p. 330).

What to do
Rashes usually involve damage to the small blood vessels in the skin and there is very little you can do to correct this. You can relieve the symptoms of itching and burning, however, by applying a cooling lotion, like calamine. If the rash is infected, or if there are tiny blisters in the rash, seek medical advice immediately. It's better not to use anti-sting or anti-burn sprays on a rash because they often contain powerful local anaesthetics that can produce allergies in the skin.

Roseola infantum

This disease is often confused with German measles (see p. 330). Your child will suddenly get a very high temperature of 102°–104°F (39°–40°C), without any other symptoms. As soon as his temperature returns to normal he'll develop a rash of pale red spots.

What to do
Contact your doctor for an accurate diagnosis. No specific treatment is needed, other than keeping the fever down (see p. 312).

Scarlet fever

This is an extreme throat infection caused by a strain of streptococcus bacillus. It can occur at any age (see p. 330). The first signs are a sore throat and a fever. The tonsils become swollen and inflamed and your child may have headaches and vomit. About three days later a rash of tiny spots may appear around his neck and in his armpits; this will then spread over his whole body. The tongue's surface may become red and swollen, and if the infection goes untreated the skin may start to peel from the fingertips, the palms and the soles of the feet.

What to do
Contact your doctor for an accurate diagnosis. He'll probably give your child antibiotics or sulphonamides to minimize the severity of the illness. This is about all you can do, except to watch out for signs of earache. Should earache develop, contact your doctor again.

Splinters

All splinters, except large ones or those which are deep and cause your child discomfort, should be left alone. If your child isn't bothered, you shouldn't be either. Many small splinters are expelled by growing skin anyway and simply emerge on the surface and get rubbed off.

What to do
If a splinter becomes infected, break the skin of the pussy area with a sterile needle. The pus will drain away and the splinter should become free of its own accord. If you attempt to remove a splinter or open up an infected one, do the following: calm your child as much as you can. Never say that it will be painless; it won't and your child won't trust you again. Sterilize the needle either by boiling it in hot water for five minutes or, better still, waving the tip of the needle through a flame five or six times. Get the help of another adult who can hold the affected area steady despite the tears and protests of your child. When the needle is cold, gradually break the skin at the most superficial part of the splinter. Use a pair of eyebrow tweezers to pull the end out once it is freed, then bathe the area with a solution made from a glassful of water and a teaspoonful of salt. Finally, put a little antiseptic cream on the area, and leave it open to the air.

Sprains
Because their need for activity is so much stronger than their powers of coordination, children can sprain their hands and ankles quite easily. In a sprain a ligament is quite often torn, and this causes swelling. Your child won't want to put pressure on the joint, and will find it painful to move.

What to do
The best treatment for a sprain is rest; all strain on the sprained part should be avoided. If you feel you must do something, however, apply poultices. Dissolve magnesium sulphate, bicarbonate of soda or even salt in a glass of water until some of the powder remains in the bottom of the glass. Make a poultice with this supersaturated solution by wringing out a pad

of gauze or linen in the solution and bandaging it fairly firmly to the bruised area. Apply this poultice every one or two hours unless your child finds it more comfortable to have you bind the affected joint with a crêpe bandage.

Sticky eye
A sticky eye is fairly common in the first day or so after your baby is born and it is nearly always due to blood or amniotic fluid getting into the baby's eye during birth.

What to do
There's always the possibility that the sticky eye is caused by a bacterial infection, so consult your doctor in case antibiotics are needed. Usually all that's needed, however, is careful cleansing with a cotton wool swab soaked in sterile water. When you wash the eye, draw the swab from the inside corner near the nose to the outer corner and then throw it away. Use a separate swab for each eye. When you lay your baby down to sleep, make sure he isn't placed on his side with the sticky eye close to the mattress because the unaffected eye might become contaminated with pus when your baby turns over.

Stings
It's almost inevitable that your child will be stung by a bee or wasp at some stage, and that he'll be very upset when it happens.

What to do
Don't try to squeeze a sting. This may spread the irritating chemical on the end of the sting deeper into the skin. Instead, remove the sting with a pair of tweezers. Don't use sting preparations that contain anti-histamines; they may cause an allergy of the skin and are better avoided. One of the best household remedies to relieve the pain is a piece of cotton wool or gauze which has been soaked in a solution of bicarbonate of soda, and held in place over the sting with a piece of tape.

Should your child be stung inside the mouth, call your doctor immediately. While you are waiting, get your child to rinse his mouth out with a bicarbonate of soda solution. If you can't reach your doctor, and the inside of your child's mouth is swelling, give him a piece of ice, an ice pop or ice cream to suck. Find an adult to accompany you and your child to the hospital. If necessary, lie your child down in the back seat of the car and take him to the hospital alone.

Styes

A stye is an infection in the hair follicles of the lower eyelashes. It looks like a small boil on the eyelid – a red swelling with a central area of pus.

What to do
Eyes are very precious. Never take chances, and consult your doctor if you're at all worried. Don't use any of the patent medicines available from drug stores, since they may make specific antibiotics less effective should they be prescribed by your doctor. If the eyelash is loose and your child is cooperative, release the pus inside the stye by pulling the hair out. It won't be painful because the infection will already have dislodged the hair from its follicle. Another thing you can do is bathe the stye with cotton wool dipped in a salt solution made by adding one teaspoon of salt to a glassful of lukewarm water.

Squints

Your newborn baby may squint until the age of eight or ten weeks, by which time he'll have learned to use his two eyes together (stereoscopically).

What to do
There's nothing wrong with this kind of early squinting but if it persists after three months, ask your doctor for the name of an eye specialist. Early treatment is important, otherwise the imbalance of the eye muscles – which probably caused a squint – may remain uncorrected.

Sunburn

Most children's skin is very sensitive to sunlight. Be careful about exposing their skin to the sun too quickly, especially on vacations when they haven't had much sunshine at home.

What to do
Preventing sunburn is a lot easier than treating it. Keep all but the weathered parts of your baby's body (such as the lower arms and legs) covered up when you first go into strong sunshine. Protect the exposed parts of the skin with an ultra-violet sun-screen cream. Use the one with the highest protection level and apply it every two or three hours and after your child has been in the water.

Always cover your baby's head with a hat and introduce him to the sunshine gradually. Don't expose his body to the sun for more than five to ten minutes on the first day and then increase the length of exposure by no more than five or ten minutes on successive days. If the sun is extremely strong, it's better to keep your child indoors.

If by chance your baby does get sun-burned, calamine lotion will cool him down, and paracetamol elixir will do a lot to relieve the soreness in the skin and bring his temperature down. If your baby is restless and ill, take his temperature; if it goes up, he may be developing heat stroke, so call a doctor.

Thread worms

This is the most common type of infecting worm. These thin, ¼ in (6 mm) long white worms live in the rectum. The females crawl through the anus to lay their eggs on the surrounding skin. This produces the classic symptoms of itching, especially at night. When your child scratches his bottom he may pick up some of the eggs under his fingernails. If he then puts his hand in his mouth, the eggs will be in-gested again.

What to do

If you notice your child scratching his bottom, especially at night, save your child's stools and examine them for thread-like worms. If you find them, consult your doctor immediately. He will prescribe a single-dose treatment which will eradicate not just the worms, but the eggs as well. Because worm infection spreads easily to other members of the family, everyone should be given the anti-worm treatment, and repeat it after two weeks. Keep your child's nails short, and make sure he washes his hands after going to the bathroom.

Tonsillitis

The job of the tonsils is to trap infections as they enter the body through the mouth, and localize them in the throat. For this reason tonsillitis is usually part of a throat infection. The tonsils send warning signals to the rest of the body when an infection is beginning so the body can alert all its defences. The adenoids serve exactly the same function, but at the back of the nose instead of in the throat. Tonsils are most important to a child up to the age of ten. Their defence system has to be very strong during these early years, when they are most likely to meet infection. If your child has tonsillitis he will complain of a very sore throat. His tonsils will look red and swollen, and may have white patches on them.

What to do

Have a doctor check your child; he'll probably prescribe antibiotics to combat the infection. To make your child's throat feel better, give him as much ice cream and cold liquid as he wants.

It used to be fashionable to remove tonsils and adenoids, despite their usefulness. Nowadays, ear, nose and throat surgeons feel that before tonsillectomy can be considered, the child must experience severe and recurrent attacks of tonsillitis, possibly associated with ear infections and deafness. Even with these symptoms, children rarely have their tonsils removed under the age of four. The most serious side effect of tonsillitis is infection of the middle ear leading to chronic deafness. If your child has recurrent attacks of tonsillitis, always be on the lookout for deafness and refer your child to a specialist.

Toxocara

This roundworm is found in cats and dogs. Its eggs are passed on in their feces, so your child is taking a risk when he plays on ground where animals have defecated. If he puts his dirty hands into his mouth, he can ingest the eggs, which will burrow through the intestinal wall and travel through the bloodstream to the lungs. They are then coughed up, swallowed and continue to develop in the intestines. There are usually no symptoms, though if your child has more than one worm he may have abdominal pain and suffer from a loss of appetite.

What to do

Prevention is better than cure. Don't allow pets into your child's play area at home and take care when you go to public parks. If your child is diagnosed as having toxocara he will be prescribed a medicine to get rid of it. Follow your doctor's instructions carefully.

Urticaria

Urticaria is the general term used for an allergic skin reaction. It's also known as nettle rash or hives. Children tend to lose their susceptibility to hives as they grow older. It's very easy to diagnose because it's the only skin rash which will disappear completely within a few minutes.

The rash, which is very itchy, often looks like a bad nettle sting; it can also form large red patches with uneven edges. It may result in swelling of the eyes, lips and tongue. If the latter occurs, get in touch with your doctor immediately. Aspirin, according to some reports, is one of the most common causes of hives in children, accompanied by a swelling of the face, eyelids and mouth.

What to do
Relieve the itchiness by cooling it with applications of calamine lotion. There is no need for any specific treatment unless the attacks are persistent. If they are, ask your doctor to refer you to a child dermatologist, who will investigate your child's rash and try to find a cause.

There is a particular form of urticaria called papular urticaria which is caused by flea bites, usually from the fleas on the family cat. I remember well the case of a child who used to appear in our clinic once a month the day after she had visited her grandmother. It was the grandmother's cat, we discovered, who had the fleas. The cure for this kind of urticaria is to get rid of the fleas on the cat – not the cat!

Whooping cough (Pertussis)

This is one of the most dangerous diseases, especially if your child is under a year old (see p. 330). As with most childhood diseases, whooping cough starts off with a runny nose, a cough and a slight temperature. This period can last for up to two weeks, followed by periods of severe paroxysmal coughing when your child will have difficulty drawing breath. This is when the characteristic "whoop" occurs.

What to do
Call in your doctor immediately. He will prescribe antibiotics which, if administered early enough, prove effective in stopping chest infections. He'll also show you how to tap your child's chest to loosen the phlegm that is pooling there. When your child starts on a coughing bout, hold him firmly and try to calm him down. If he's tense he'll find it even more difficult to catch his breath. Prop him in a half-sitting position to make breathing easier between fits. Eating may provoke vomiting. Try giving small amounts of easily-eaten food (mashed if necessary), and try giving them immediately after a coughing fit.

IMMUNIZATION   0–3

The aim of immunization is to protect both individuals and communities from outbreaks of infectious diseases. When the rate of immunization is high, the rate of infection in that community is invariably low. Every parent has a dual responsibility to his own children, and to others in the community, and should take steps to have all their children properly immunized. It's worth it! Immunization has proven to be one of the most successful forms of preventive medicine ever practised. Some people think that because a certain disease has been eradicated from their community there's no need to immunize their children. But it's only through continuing immunization programs that the community remains safe from recurring epidemics like whooping cough or diphtheria.

Immunization works by preparing the body to repel infection. The body is not prepared the first time it comes into contact with a bacterium or virus; it has to be exposed to the infection once in order to "recognize" it. Through exposure, we produce antibodies and antitoxins to kill off the specific bacterium and neutralize its poisons. Most of us have to have an infection once before our defences are marshalled. Immunization does this for us. Through injections, drops taken by mouth, or scratches on the skin, small numbers of weakened germs are introduced into the body in sufficient quantity to stimulate the production of antibodies and antitoxins.

Most immunization programs start at four months, but arrangements vary in different countries. Ask your doctor for a schedule for your child. Keep a record of the dates and kinds of shots your baby has had. It will be useful if you change doctors or need the information for school records or travel abroad.

It is quite common for a small red bump to develop on or around the spot where the shot is given. If, in addition, your baby becomes irritable, contracts a fever, develops a high pitched scream, or has convulsions, get in touch with your doctor.

Whooping cough vaccination has been the subject of controversy for the past five or ten years – ever since doctors discovered an association between immunization and inflammation of the brain (encephalitis). The latest medical research and opinion is that the number of recorded cases is so small, it's still better for your baby and for the community to endure the very low risk involved in taking whooping cough vaccination. There are some babies, however, who should be placed in a special category and not immunized against whooping cough: these are babies who have had a convulsion or who have a relative who suffers from fits.

Make an appointment to discuss your child's continued immunization program before he starts nursery school. This is the time to consider immunizing your child against measles, and giving him boosters of shots he took as an infant.

IMMUNIZATION CHART

Disease	Time	Reaction	Protection
Diphtheria, pertussis, tetanus	*Injections at 3, 5–6 and 9–11 months; repeat at 5 years*	*Child may become feverish; the site of the injection may be sore*	*Diphtheria and tetanus have to be repeated*
Polio	*Oral vaccine at 3, 5–6 and 9–11 months; repeat at 5 years*	*None*	*Has to be repeated*
Measles	*Injection at 14 or 15 months*	*Child may become feverish and have slight rash*	*Not known how long protection lasts*
German measles	*Injection for girls between 10 and 14 years*	*Child may complain of sore joints*	*Not known how long protection lasts*
Tuberculosis	*Injection at 13 years*	*The site of the injection may be sore and stiff*	*Lifelong*

INFECTIOUS FEVERS

Disease	Incubation period	Symptoms
Measles (see p.322)	10–12 days	Runny nose, cough, inflamed eyes, fever, vomiting, diarrhoea, white (Koplik's) spots, rash behind the ears, then on the face, then on the body
German meales (see p.322)	17–18 days	Slight temperature, enlarged glands at the back of the neck, rash behind the ears, then on the forehead and the rest of the body
Roseola (see p.324)	7–14 days	A high temperature with slight cold symptoms; a pink rash when temperature goes down
Chicken pox (see p.317)	14–16 days	Dark red, irritating groups of spots which emerge every three or four days
Whooping cough (see p.328)	5–14 days	Slight temperature, runny nose, slight cough then a convulsive cough followed by whooping breath
Mumps (see p.323)	17–21 days	Swelling and soreness of the glands at the sides of the face and in front of the ears; painful swallowing, and dry mouth
Scarlet fever (see p.324)	2–5 days	Lack of appetite, fever, vomiting, swollen glands, tiny red spots

Treatment	Complications	Immunity	Prevention
No specific treatment other than baby aspirin to reduce the fever. If secondary infection of the ears or lungs occurs, antibiotics will be necessary	*Earache, pneumonia, encephalitis*	*Lifelong*	*Inoculation between 12 and 24 months*
No specific treatment	*None to your child but fetal damage could occur in a pregnant woman*	*Lifelong*	*Inoculation for girls between the ages of 10 and 14*
No specific treatment	*Possibly infantile convulsions*	*Usually lifelong*	
Relieve itching with calamine lotion. Treat infected spots with prescribed cream	*Rare*	*Lifelong*	*None*
Antibiotics must be given early to be effective; fresh air. Possibly raise your child's head in bed to make breathing easier	*Very rare nowadays although there's the possibility of bronchitis or pneumonia*	*Lifelong*	*Inoculation between 3–6 months*
Plenty to drink, soft food if chewing is painful	*Meningitis, inflammation of the testicles*	*Lifelong*	*None*
Penicillin with rest in bed as long as fever lasts	*Rare*	*Lifelong*	*None*

18 Personal records

During your baby's first year the date of every milestone—every inoculation, each new tooth, and so on—will seem permanently etched on your mind. As the years pass, however, and second or third children join your first, you'll find that you forget not only the trivial facts, like when your baby first rolled over on her back, but also important information, like the dates of inoculations. For this reason we've included a set of charts which will help you keep track of the events affecting you all.

Baby's name_____
Born_____19____
At_____

Baby's name_____
Born_____19____
At_____

FAMILY MEDICAL HISTORY

	Birth date	Illnesses
Father	_____	_____
		_____
Mother	_____	_____
		_____

Family allergies and chronic conditions
_____
_____

BIRTH RECORD
Baby's name_____
Time of birth_____
Date of birth_____
Duration of pregnancy_____
Mother's health during pregnancy:
    Illness_____
    Medication_____
    Problems_____

Delivery:
    Type_____
    Monitoring_____
    Drugs_____
    Problems_____
    Consultant_____
    Hospital_____
    Length of stay_____

Height_____ Weight_____
Blood type_____
Type of feeding:
Breast_____ Bottle_____

BIRTH RECORD
Baby's name_____
Time of birth_____
Date of birth_____
Duration of pregnancy_____
Mother's health during pregnancy:
    Illness_____
    Medication_____
    Problems_____

Delivery:
    Type_____
    Monitoring_____
    Drugs_____
    Problems_____
    Consultant_____
    Hospital_____
    Length of stay_____

Height_____ Weight_____
Blood type_____
Type of feeding:
Breast_____ Bottle_____

ILLNESS, INJURY and ALLERGY RECORD

Illness	Duration	Date

Injuries		Date

Allergies _____

ILLNESS, INJURY and ALLERGY RECORD

Illness	Duration	Date

Injuries		Date

Allergies _____

IMMUNIZATION RECORD

Immunization	Baby 1 Date/Age	Baby 2 Date/Age
Diphtheria pertussis, tetanus		
Diphtheria, tetantus booster		
Polio		
Polio booster		
Measles		
German measles		

DEVELOPMENT RECORD

	Baby 1	Baby 2
Holds head up for a few seconds		
Smiles		
Laughs		
Sleeps through night		
Rolls over		
Sits unsupported		
Crawls/Shuffles		
Waddles about		
Walks		
First tooth		
Starts solids		
Is weaned		
Feeds 'self		
First words		
Points to parts of the body		
Makes simple statements		
Pedals tricycle		
Stays dry throughout nap		
Can do up buttons		
Draws a circle		
Gains bladder control		
Gains bowel control		
Starts playschool/ nursery school		
First visit to the dentist		

TELEPHONE NUMBERS

Doctor/Pediatrician	
Ambulance	
Health visitor	
Local hospital	
Poison center	
Dentist	

HEIGHT AND WEIGHT CHARTS

As in every other aspect of development, your child will grow and put on weight at his or her own rate. While it's interesting to plot your child's development and compare it to the average, you should never become obsessive or anxious about it.

The graphs on the left-hand column on the following pages plot the typical growth patterns of children of high, low and medium birth weight. The graphs on the right-hand columns are for your use.

To record your baby's weight, first weigh your baby. Then go along the bottom axis until you find his or her age. Cast your eyes up the vertical axis until you reach your baby's weight. Mark the point at which the two axes meet. For height use length and age as the axes.

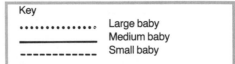

Key

.... Large baby
——————— Medium baby
– – – – – – – Small baby

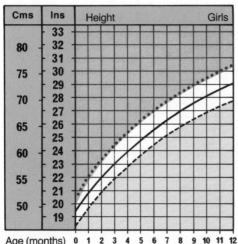

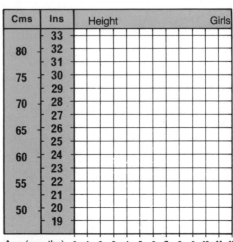

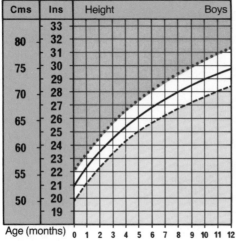

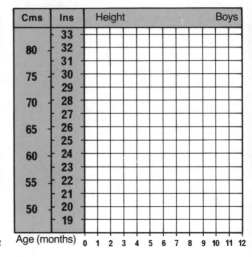

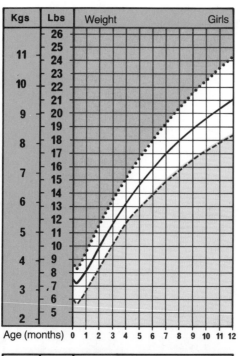

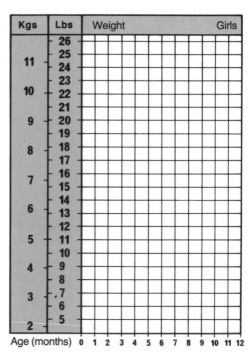

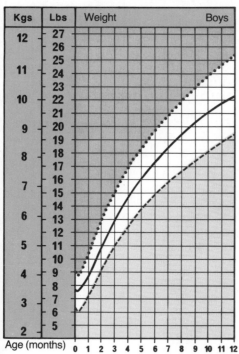

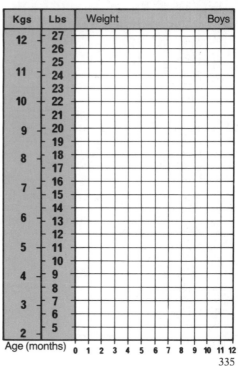

HEIGHT AND WEIGHT CHARTS 1–3

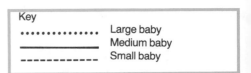

Key
.... Large baby
———————— Medium baby
– – – – – – – – – Small baby

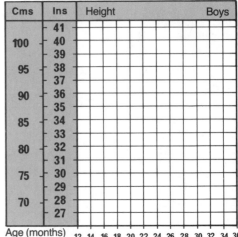

Cms	Ins	Height	Girls

Age (months) 12 14 16 18 20 22 24 26 28 30 32 34 36

Cms	Ins	Height	Girls

Age (months) 12 14 16 18 20 22 24 26 28 30 32 34 36

Cms	Ins	Height	Boys

Age (months) 12 14 16 18 20 22 24 26 28 30 32 34 36

Cms	Ins	Height	Boys

Age (months) 12 14 16 18 20 22 24 26 28 30 32 34 36

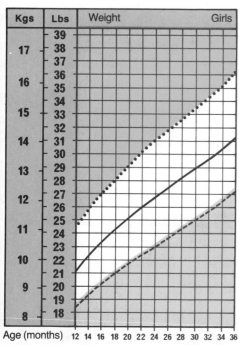

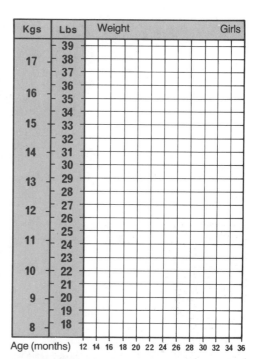

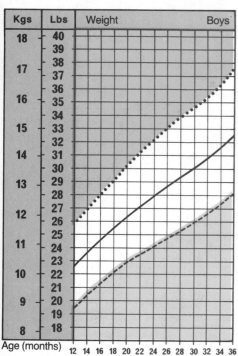

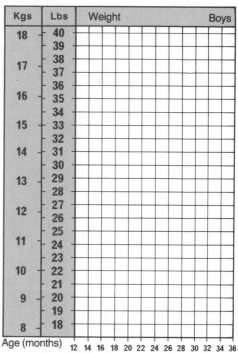

Age (months)

Index

Acknowledgements

Dorling Kindersley would like to thank the following for their help in the preparation of this book: Debbie Lee and Sandra Schneider for design help; Vision International, Gary Marsh, Kuo Kang Chen, Coral Mula, Les Greenyer, Nick Oxtoby, O'Connor Dowse and Peter Searle for their art and photograph services; Wendy Hawley and Jacob, Linda Cole and Ben, Mike Staniford and Polly, Janet Abbott and Stephen for being models for reference shots; Babyboots, Mothercare, YHA Services, DBNMA and La Cicogna for kindly lending us equipment and, finally, all the parents who gave us their personal tips on baby care.

Photography
Anthea Sieveking

Photographic Services
Adrian Ensor
Negs

Illustration
Edwina Keene

Additional Illustrators
Jim Robins
Lindsay Blow
Richard Lewis